BLUE
LEGALITIES

Duke University Press   Durham and London   2020

BLUE LEGALITIES

The Life & Laws of the Sea

IRUS BRAVERMAN AND
ELIZABETH R. JOHNSON, EDS.

Library of Congress Cataloging-in-Publication Data
Names: Braverman, Irus, [date] editor. | Johnson, Elizabeth R,
[date] editor.
Title: Blue legalities : the life and laws of the sea / Irus Braverman and
Elizabeth R. Johnson, eds.
Description: Durham : Duke University Press, 2020. | Includes
bibliographical references and index.
Identifiers: LCCN 2019013466 (print) | LCCN 2019980792 (ebook)
ISBN 9781478005926 (hardcover)
ISBN 9781478006541 (paperback)
ISBN 9781478007289 (ebook)
Subjects: LCSH: Law of the sea. | Economic zones (Law of the sea) |
Global environmental change.
Classification: LCC KZA1145 .B58 2020 (print) | LCC KZA1145
(ebook) | DDC 341.4/5—dc23
LC record available at https://lccn.loc.gov/2019013466
LC ebook record available at https://lccn.loc.gov/2019980792

COVER ART: Oceanographic Museum of Monaco, 2013. Courtesy of
The Ocean Agency / XL Catlin Seaview Survey.

IB: For my mentor, colleague,
and friend Guyora Binder

ERJ: For my parents, Joyce and Dan,
whose love of the ocean proved infectious

Contents

Introduction

BLUE LEGALITIES

Governing More-Than-Human Oceans

ELIZABETH R. JOHNSON AND IRUS BRAVERMAN

Law and the Sea: Toward Turbulent Legalities

The surface of the sea has long been viewed as a blank space. As Carl Schmitt famously quipped in 1950, "On the waves, there is nothing but waves" (2003, 43). In the popular imaginary, the oceans continue to be seen as a place outside conventional politics. Futurists and libertarian technophiles envision the sea surface as a frontier upon which new forms of governance and ways of life might flourish. In their depths, the oceans have long been—and largely remain—impenetrable to our bodies and senses. Remotely operated vehicles, like the US National Oceanic and Atmospheric Administration's (NOAA) *Deep Discoverer*, return images of what appears to be a different world altogether. As Stefan Helmreich writes, the oceans are "haunted by the figure of the alien" (2009, xi).

Despite (or precisely because of) this haunting, attempts to demystify the oceans are increasingly underway. David Attenborough's famous *Blue Earth* series has introduced millions to the seas and their other-worldly inhabitants, insisting audiences view the oceans not as a world away, but as part of a deeply interconnected, and increasingly fragile, ecological system. Accordingly, the oceans now appear as a bellwether of a coming ecological catastrophe that will affect terrestrial and marine environments alike. With growing regularity, the mainstream media features dramatic images of bleached coral reefs, floating islands of garbage, persistent red tides, and endangered fauna. Frequent stories expose the public to grim statistics on declining fisheries, increasing ocean acidification, and the ubiquitous spread of plastics. As the Australian culture and politics magazine *The Monthly* recently declared, we seem to be witnessing the "end of the oceans" (Bradley 2018, 1).

But just as evidence mounts that marine ecologies are facing collapse, the ocean is also becoming a new frontier for resource extraction and economic expansion. In fact, growing the "blue economy" has become a central component of national and regional strategies in coastal states around the world. Such strategies incorporate an increasing number of conventional and renewable resources, deep-sea mineral mining (Katherine G. Sammler and Susan Reid, this volume), biopharmaceutical production (Helmreich 2009), wind and wave energy (Stefan Helmreich, this volume), dredging sand to create land for real estate and state expansion (Jennifer L. Gaynor, this volume), and the cultivation of algae biofuels (Amy Braun, this volume). Across these diverse sectors, ocean environments appear not as a limit to continued expansion, but as a promising site of endless, and highly profitable, economic production (Patil et al. 2016).

Blue Legalities appears amid this move toward a blue economy. It joins a wave of scholarship in the social sciences and humanities that responds to, and corresponds with, these transformations, newly heralded under the banners of blue humanities (Gillis 2013; Mentz 2009) and critical ocean studies (DeLoughrey 2017; Ingersoll 2016). Drawing on environmental humanities and new materialisms, this novel scholarship grapples with the tensions that surround the more-than-human ocean. This work includes Philip E. Steinberg's and Kimberley Peters's extensive writing on marine geographies (Steinberg 2001, 2011; Steinberg and Peters 2015), Stefan Helmreich's *Alien Ocean* (2009), the edited volume *Thinking with Water* (Chen, MacLeod, and Neimanis 2013), Zoe Todd's writing on fish and Indigeneity (2014), Elizabeth DeLoughrey's work on postcolonial literature and the oceans (2007, 2015), Stacy Alaimo's *Exposed* (2016), Karin Amimoto Ingersoll's *Waves of Knowing* (2016), and Irus Braverman's *Coral Whisperers* (2018). Collectively, this scholarship draws attention to the spaces, histories, and lives of the sea. More critically, however, it interrogates what we think we know—and what we don't know—about oceans, challenging strongly held assumptions about our earthly planet and ourselves. It is an ethical and politically engaged literature that demands we rethink our patterns of life on, and with, the seas.

Blue Legalities is inspired by this emerging literature about oceans and their inhabitants, often referred to as the "blue turn." But as compelling as this blue turn has been, we argue here that it has yet to substantively and creatively take up questions of ocean law and governance. Warming temperatures, increased pollution, sea-level rise, ocean acidification, bioharvesting, and deep-sea and sand mining have been raising concerns about long-established assumptions in both national and international law. The rapid technological and ecological changes that have taken place over the past few decades are prompting serious reconsiderations of how the seas are governed, suggesting an urgent need for more critical attention to the laws of the sea, in their broadest and most pluralistic iterations. *Blue Legalities* offers such an intensified analysis. Specifically, the interdisciplinary contributors of this volume contemplate different ways in which our political frameworks and legal infrastructures have been made, contested, and remade in the oceans.

This goes to highlight one of the primary motivations for this volume: unblackboxing law. Just as science renders its procedures and technical work invisible and neutral, so, too, do legal rules and procedures—such as those related to sovereignty, authority, territory, and jurisdiction—make invisible certain ideological assumptions and obscure the labor undertaken for their construction. And just as the understanding of science should not be the domain of scientists alone and should involve a critical stance toward these practices, the study of law, too, should not be confined to lawyers and legal scholars. Accordingly, the contributors to this volume consider law from different academic backgrounds, including geography, anthropology, law, political science, history, gender studies, English, and environmental studies. We collectively draw upon these transdisciplinary trajectories to think critically about ocean law, thus contesting the hegemony of legal experts in this regard.

There is already a steady body of scholarship about ocean law. However, this scholarship has mostly been confined to a positivistic analysis of state laws and international treatises that pertain to the sea. Indeed, much has been written about ocean law with a capital *L*—namely, the formal statutes, regulations, case law, and international treaties that govern the seas and their inhabitants (see, e.g., Bishara 2017; Craig 2012; Harrison 2011; Nyman 2013; Ranganathan 2016; Scheiber and Paik 2013; Stephens and VanderZwaag 2014; Tanaka 2008). In most of it, the oceans and their inhabitants appear to be passive to the legal infrastructures imposed upon them. While we recognize that formal laws and administrative bodies are important and prevalent and should not be ignored as such, we are not concerned only with law's official and binding articulations. Instead, we follow in the wake of other legal scholars who have been pursuing questions around the constitution of legalities in terrestrial contexts to argue that the law permeates our understandings of space and matter. We then apply this argument beyond the terrestrial environments to engage with the vexing problems associated with the ocean's watery worlds.

By turning toward the relationship between governance and the life of ecological networks, this volume joins a growing literature on more-than-human legalities. Drawing in particular on Anna Grear's work on law and the Anthropocene (2015), Andreas Philippopoulos-Mihalopoulos's writing on nonhuman materialities (2016a, 2016b), Irus Braverman's explorations of nonhuman legalities (2015; 2016; 2018b), and Alain Pottage's explorations of materiality in the biosciences (2012; Pottage and Marris 2012), this volume focuses attention on the microscale questions concerning ocean law and its biopolitical enframings. Rather than start with an assumption of law as a prediscursive entity, we follow Pottage's lead to consider the seas themselves and, interconnected to that exploration, to also study various laws as socio-scientific, heterogeneous, and material phenomena. Like much of the literature on the blue turn in the social sciences and humanities, this body of legal scholarship, too, has been influenced by science and technology studies and new materialisms. Contributors to this volume apply these rich insights to consider the ordinary and extraordinary projects of governing oceans.

The volume's chapters are grounded in a careful empirical analysis that spans historical time periods and geographic locations. The contributors emphasize the extent to which soft standards, temporal imaginaries, and scientific guidelines govern various aspects of ocean life as well as how they prescribe and regulate the everyday practices of scientists, managers, and other actors who operate in and impact this space. Whereas traditionally not perceived as legal actors per se, following the practices of these various experts in fact reveals an entire new world of varied and plural laws. At the same time, we also consider the connections as well as the frictions that emerge where systems of governance interact with complex geophysical, ecological, economic, and technological processes. Such a broader and more relational understanding of legalities makes space for critical inquiries. Some of the central questions that emerge from this more relational understanding include: How are existing systems of governance adjusting to the abrupt and radical changes that threaten the health of the oceans? And how might thinking with the seas and their inhabitants engender opportunities for the contestation and transformation of ocean governance?

This volume's interdisciplinary contributors present varied responses to these questions. Neither univocal nor singular, these responses demonstrate that blue legalities are not of one ocean, nor of one law; instead, they are made up of the multiple and messy registers through which we engage the seas. Such legalities of the seas evince what Stephanie Lavau has referred to in the context of fresh water governance as a "multiple reality" that hangs together in "untidy entanglement[s]" (2013, 428). We emphasize the vast and unusual challenges associated with regulating this multiple and fluid reality as it manifests in the spaces, matters, and lives of the sea.

Alongside their messiness and multiplicity, oceans are also dynamic and unstable. Steinberg and Peters write that the seas are a "space of churning" (2015,

258). Amid "processes of 'arranging,' 'gathering,' 'mixture,' and 'turbulence,'" the oceans exist in a near constant state of re-formation (256). This volume brings the churn of this reality to light by showing how, from the turbulence of thinking with ocean legalities, possibilities for more plural relations between time, place, and law may emerge. Accordingly, this introduction explores four central themes: the vast legalities between knowledge and ignorance, temporal governance in the Anthropocene, a sea of lines and laws, and governing with more-than-human sea creatures.

The Vast Legalities between Knowledge and Ignorance

Emergent from our examinations of both ocean Law and its laws—namely, of the macro, as well as the micro, scales of law—is the enhanced reliance of these forms of governance on scientists and scientific discourse. The relationship between knowledge, imagination, and ignorance finds a fruitful substrate in the sea. Long held in the deep, matter and fantasies resurface in legal and scientific accounts of maritime spaces. This collection carefully unravels the coproduction of ocean matter, scientific knowledge, and legislative classifications and enframings.

The oceans have historically been characterized by inaccessibility and in-determinacy. For centuries, much of this space was mostly unknown. Cartographers of the fifteenth and sixteenth centuries made up for the absence of knowledge by filling the seemingly blank spaces with fantastical monsters and mermen. Today, ignorance remains central to the seas' legalities. In the legal literature, the opacity of the oceans is most often understood to incapacitate managers of marine resources or conservationists who seek to curb pollution and battle other perils (Charles 1998; De Wolff 2017). According to many scholars, scientists, and policy makers, the proper government of ocean resources requires the management, and even the excision, of ignorance (see, e.g., Pauly 2013). This, precisely, is how the scientists in Jessica Lehman's chapter, "The Technopolitics of Ocean Sensing," approach the acquisition of marine data. Imagining the sea as a "borderless space" and as the object of a global science that could "benefit all of humanity," these scientists have released thousands of robotic devices into both national and international waters. Meant to facilitate better governance through obtaining more complete data, autonomous underwater robots like Argo floats collect "real-time" readings on temperature, salinity, and movement of the planetary ocean.

These attempts to eradicate ignorance are undergirded by the assumption that knowledge production takes place outside and before the law. Indeed, scientific knowledge is typically considered as preceding the law and as providing the foundation for legal inscription. But, of course, scientific and legal practices are deeply entangled. This volume's contributions show how attempts to manage, harness, and govern oceans also shape ontological and epistemological claims—what Sheila Jasanoff refers to as the "co-production" of scientific knowledge practices and law. She writes that "the law is now an inescapable feature of the conditioning environment that produces socially embedded . . . science" (2008, 762). How we come to know the oceans and their inhabitants as objects of study thus neither precedes nor merely services the law. Rather, scientists produce knowledge through legal systems and via governmental frameworks. At the same time, techno-physical and scientific practices also shape regulatory and administrative systems. As Lehman shows, the widespread use of autonomous robots both contests and reshapes legal infrastructures. Specifically, their use imposes a universal regulation of the seas, thereby challenging the longstanding sovereign control of nation-states over their territorial waters.

Alongside the efforts to acquire ever greater repositories of knowledge that would eliminate the unknown, blue legalities are also shaped by what Robert Proctor and Londa Schiebinger call "agnotology": the production of ignorance (2008). In paying attention to the ways that scientific and legal frameworks are imbricated, this volume's contributors highlight how not only determinacies, but also indeterminacies, are coproduced and even exacerbated to make ocean spaces more manageable. In other words, the *un*productive and *counter*productive aspects of knowledge are made to matter for ocean governance. In some cases, knowledge of the complexities of geophysical and ecological processes in the ocean is ignored, overwritten, or willfully avoided to better administer the seas.

Stefan Helmreich makes just that point in his contribution to this volume, which focuses on the controversy surrounding the attempted building of a seawall around an Irish golf course owned by US president Donald Trump. While his permit proposal references scientific data that links sea-level rise to climate change, Trump himself has actively, and notoriously, denied this connection. According to Helmreich, Trump's simultaneous deployment and disavowal of climate science illuminates how "science and law are rhetorically coproduced at one moment and torn asunder at another." In this instance of sovereign claims to space and power, "dissimulation and misdirection" reign.

We find evidence of the important role of ignorance in Holly Jean Buck's chapter as well, where it is precisely the lack of attention to ocean acidification in climate legislation that has enabled the rise of the scientific imaginary of a geoengineered planet. Finally, in Jessica Lehman's account, it is ignorance of the law, rather than ignorance of the sea, that enables the use of autonomous robots and facilitates scientific research. As Astrida Neimanis argues in her chapter in the context of buried toxic contaminants, the "full knowability" of the sea will always elude us. One of the challenges for blue legalities is figuring out how to insist on accountability and justice in the absence of complete knowledge.

Beyond blurring the boundaries between knowledge and ignorance, the mysterious and seemingly alien nature of the seas also troubles distinctions between matter and fantasy. As Stacy Alaimo writes: "Terrestrial humans have often found it more convenient to imagine that the seas are imaginary than to undertake the scientific, cultural, and political work necessary to trace substantial interconnections between human discourses, human practices, and marine habitats" (2012, 179). Understanding ocean imaginaries is therefore an important undertaking.

In her chapter, "The Sea Wolf and the Sovereign," Stephanie Jones examines how such maritime imaginaries—their symbols, metaphors, and fantasies— have shaped the history and spatial politics of the sea. Taking inspiration from Jacques Derrida's writing on the animal, Jones looks to the figure of the sea wolf, demonstrating how her appearance in the literature configures sovereign power, with its paradigms of legality and illegality. In particular, Jones connects the sea wolf's liminal form of life to human stories about piracy on the high seas. As she argues, such stories have in fact legitimized the sovereign state's foundational relationship to violence.

Knowledge and fantasy blur also in contemporary attempts to legitimize future visions of sovereignty. Elizabeth R. Johnson's chapter, "The Hydra and the Leviathan," shows, accordingly, how the US military channels scientific research to create a future geopolitical sea space that is favorable to US interests. Like the researchers in Lehman's chapter, in this chapter, too, military strategists and the scientist they fund endeavor to know more about what lies beneath the sea surface. But unlike the operators of the Argo floats who use robotic devices to expand scientific knowledge, the military strategists here use these devices to enhance military capacity. These efforts are justified on the back of a geographical imaginary (Gregory 1994) composed of militarized histories, imagined threats, and speculative futures. Dangers that allegedly lurk beneath the oceans' depths haunt this production of cutting-edge weaponry, which gains traction through a combination of advanced material technology and detailed security risk calculations.

Interrogating the interconnections between knowledge, fantasy, and ignorance as well as between fabulous and mundane political practices helps us understand how power is made operative through techno-scientific engagements with the seas. Just as importantly, it also provides a path for challenging intractable—and often deeply unjust—configurations of sovereignty.

Temporal Governance in the Anthropocene

While the US military has been advocating for a less risky sea, many scientists claim that it is human activities that have put the oceans at risk in the first place. In 2004, geologist Will Steffen coined the term "the Great Acceleration" to highlight how human activities, predominantly the global economic system, became the prime drivers of change on earth. The twenty-four graphs he charted to express the acceleration in human activity since the industrial revolution (see, e.g., Steffen et al. 2015) were foundational for the formalization of the Anthropocene concept. According to these graphs, the oceans have been ameliorating climate change, as well as other effects of human activity. Indeed, the International Union for Conservation of Nature (IUCN) established that more than 93 percent of heat captured by greenhouse gases has been absorbed by the oceans since the 1970s. If the oceans were not absorbing this heat, the average global temperatures on land would be far higher—around 122°F—instead of the current average of 59°F (Schlanger 2017).

In performing this ameliorating function, ocean ecologies have become not only an early casualty of the Anthropocene, but also a bellwether of what the future has in store for the rest of the earth. Estimating sea-level rise, scientists predict that the oceans will encroach upon human settlements, flood coastal cities, and shrink continents. Postcolonial scholar Elizabeth DeLoughrey writes in this regard: "If there is any agreement about climate change, it is that our planetary future is becoming more oceanic. . . . Sea level rise is perhaps our greatest sign of planetary change, connecting the activity of the earth's poles with the rest of the terrestrial world, producing a new sense of planetary scale and interconnectedness through the rising of a world ocean" (2015, 353). In his recent book, *The Water Will Come: Rising Seas, Sinking Cities, and the Remaking of the Civilized World*, journalist Jeff Goodell offers, similarly, that "despite international efforts and tireless research, there is no permanent solution—no barriers to erect or walls to build—that will protect us in the end from the drowning of the world as we know it" (2017, back cover).

Catastrophe comes in other forms as well. We are already witnessing the dramatic effects of plastic waste on marine ecosystems as media images of whales, turtles, and albatross with stomachs full of plastics appear with ever greater frequency. In addition to sea-level rise and pollution, scientists worry about what they identify as the "triple threat" to marine ecologies: ocean acidification, ocean warming, and deoxygenation (Rogers and Laffoley 2013). Ocean acidification in particular is often referred to as climate change's "evil twin" (Holly Jean Buck, this volume). Absorbing elevated amounts of carbon dioxide from the atmosphere, the changing chemistry of the ocean is resulting in a decrease in the rates of calcification by reef organisms and thus in an increase in the dissolution of the reef sediments that form reef structures. Reef disappearance in turn causes an accelerated loss of fish habitat and growing coastal erosion (Bakke 2017, 53–54). Oceanographer Sylvia Earle put it this way: "Now we know: If the ocean is in trouble, so are we. It is time to take care of the ocean as if our lives depend on it, because they do" (2014).

Yet despite the inevitable futures of collapsed fisheries and dead reef-building corals, international climate and biodiversity treaties have largely ignored the scientific evidence on ocean acidification. As Holly Jean Buck shows in this volume, the complexity and relative invisibility of ocean acidification have made this process seem peripheral to the massive anthropogenic changes in the oceans. Moreover, imaginaries of heightened planetary management have boosted scientific investments in geoengineering techniques, thus strengthening narratives that figure climate futures as technologically controllable. These efforts resonate with the "Good Anthropocene" approach adopted by the Breakthrough Institute and other Silicon Valley optimists, in which humans figure as the technologically endowed producers of a well-worked planet (Asafu-Adjaye et al. 2015).

Consistent with the "Good Anthropocene" approach, novel developments in biomedicine and the rise of the blue economy have infused new value to the seas and their inhabitants. Rather than seeing them as a grim casualty of human history, advocates of the blue economy have indeed come to view the oceans as a resource for sustainable technological and biotechnological enhancement (European Commission 2012; Helmreich 2007; Johnson 2016). In her chapter, "Got Algae?," Amy Braun shows how, as land resources dwindle, industrial and venture capitalists harness sea life and matter for food, energy, carbon sequestration, and genetic resources. Utilizing practices of enclosure and privatization—including aquaculture, deep-sea mining, seaweed and algae harvesting, and marine bioprospecting—these entrepreneurs portray oceans as utopian spaces of limitless, yet sustainable, development.

Whether we are hurtling toward catastrophe or toward a technologically endowed utopia, the future that figures in both the Anthropocene and the blue economy literatures follows the modern understanding of time as a linear, secular, and unidimensional passing from past to future. In contrast to these universal accounts of time, many of this volume's chapters reveal the rich polychronic natures of the oceans. In Susan Reid's contribution, for example, the deep, slow time of the seas' geologic and evolutionary pasts calls into question basic assumptions of temporal progression. Specifically, Reid argues that by encouraging a "mine first, observe and legislate later" approach, UNCLOS's instrumental view of the oceans has enabled deep-sea mining operations. Countering such approaches, she relates to the sea as a "cogenerative, transitional realm, thrumming with material agency and life." Reid thus not only imagines more sensitive and durative parameters of livability, but also shows how we might shift the foundations upon which policies and actions are based. In her words: "At a time when planetary environmental systems are in stress and decline, there is a vital place for new imaginaries with which we might all navigate and transition."

Considering multiple temporal registers that move beyond the linear is crucial for crafting the oceans' new imaginaries. Michel Serres's scholarship on nonlinear topologies is instructive in this context. In an interview with Bruno Latour, Serres compared time to a handkerchief: laid flat, the distances between one point and another can be measured. Crumpled in one's pocket, however, "two distant points suddenly are close, even superimposed" (Serres and Latour 1995, 61). His most evocative passage on nonlinear time references the movement of water: "Beneath the Mirabeau Bridge flows the Seine . . . [But] all the water that passes beneath the Mirabeau Bridge will not necessarily flow out into the English Channel; many little trickles turn back toward Charenton or upstream" (58). For Serres, what we often consider history is not necessarily in the past. Patterns and norms laid down in time can, much like water, circulate in eddies and whirlpools or flow back upstream. As the recent political climate demonstrates, blind faith in temporal and social progress is often erroneous—and dangerous.

Christina Sharpe's *In the Wake* (2016) highlights how such temporal currents are lived in the present. Specifically, Sharpe uses the multiple meanings of the term *wake* to consider how past violence continues to resurface in the lives of African Americans today and how persistent forms of trauma and terror followed slave boats sailing across the Atlantic. The past that concerns Sharpe, in which some lives are designated as ungrievable by law and made unlivable in practice, is in fact never past. Similar to Serres's understanding, in this context, too, the past "reappears, always, to rupture the present" (Sharpe 2016, 9). In the wake, "the semiotics of the slave ship continue: from the forced movements of the enslaved to the forced movements of the migrant and the refugee, to the regulation of Black people in North American streets and neighborhoods, to those ongoing crossings of and drownings in the Mediterranean Sea, to the brutal colonial reimaginings of the slave ship and the ark; to the reappearances of the slave ship in everyday life in the form of the prison, the camp, and the school" (21).

Immigration and asylum policies and legal regimes also formalize and solidify traumatic ocean routes. Following boats that carry migrants across the

Mediterranean and elsewhere, one finds dehumanizing legislation being forged in Europe, in the United States, and in Australia. In their wake, death tolls mount while the lives of survivors are displaced, suspended, and often made unlivable through detention and poverty (Lyons 2018). The connections between ocean and terrestrial policies are clearly visible in the use of offshore detention facilities, such as Australia's Christmas and Nauru Island camps. There, asylum seekers await justice with little recourse to human rights laws (Coddington 2018; Mountz and Loyd 2014; Welch 2014; Zeweri 2017).

Other violent pasts and toxic legacies also threaten to reemerge in the ocean. In Astrida Neimanis's chapter, "Held in Suspense," the potential rupture of past into present haunts contemporary politics around the Baltic Sea. Following World War II, hundreds of thousands of tons of unused chemical warfare agents were dumped into the Gotland Deep. While contemporary legal regimes prohibit such dumping, at the time, this form of waste management was considered a safe and viable solution to the problem of disposing of unused munitions. The sea was viewed as a limitless repository, a blue hole into which unwanted terrestrial things could simply be made to disappear.

But the past has in fact not passed. What was dumped then is now resurfacing. Uncertainties around the severity and timing of the chemicals' reemergence, Neimanis finds, incapacitate legal resources so that matter and law are simultaneously "held in suspense." The problem is not a technical one, she emphasizes; it does not rest in the inability of science or the law to address the waste of the Gotland Deep. It is, rather, one of response-ability (Haraway 2008). The turbulence of ocean histories and materialities thus forces a response to the violence of past, and present, displacements. Recognizing the complexity of our potentially catastrophic ecological futures requires, in Neimanis's words, "that we must find ways to call ourselves to account, to enact an ethics of curiosity and care, to do politics even if we know they are always incomplete." For Neimanis, even such incomplete attempts to alter the ecologically and politically degrading status quo are crucial if we are to work toward social and ecological justice.

A Sea of Lines and Laws

Alongside the temporal distinctions, other turbulent boundaries—such as those between land and sea, water and ice, and atmospheres and waves— threaten to upend the "static and binary divisions that so often characterize legal rhetoric" (Philip E. Steinberg, Berit Kristoffersen, and Kristen L. Shake, this volume). While international law attempts to account for the unique characteristics of the oceans, their fluid properties and countless indeterminacies have resulted in claims that oceans "resist inscription" (Boucquey et al. 2016, 8). Still, myriad inscriptions—scientific, legal, and cultural—proliferate and overlap across ocean space, establishing, undoing, and redoing its boundaries.

The 1982 UN Convention on the Law of the Seas (UNCLOS) is undoubtedly the most comprehensive contemporary inscription of ocean sovereignty, jurisdiction, and use. UNCLOS is a monumental treaty with 320 articles divided into 17 parts that establish normative concepts, such as the 12-mile territorial sea, the 200-mile Exclusive Economic Zone (EEZ), the high seas, and the seabed and ocean floor beyond national jurisdiction (or "the Area"). Mapping the ocean into these multiple zones and jurisdictions, UNCLOS sketches the political geography of today's oceans and sets up the normative framework that governs it. While it attempts to hold open legal space for oceanic indeterminacies, it simultaneously creates and fixes inscriptions across the seas.

UNCLOS's jurisdictional powers lie in its acknowledgment and ratification by territorial nation-states. In this sense, it is both reified and constrained by the legal and political powers that have created it. Under UNCLOS's jurisdictional matrix, national sovereignty typically diminishes with increasing distance from land. While the nearshore territorial sea confers full national sovereignty over both the ocean's surface and water column and the ocean bed, the EEZ delineates a hybrid bundle of spatial rights and responsibilities farther offshore (Katherine G. Sammler, this volume). In that 200-mile-wide ribbon, coastal states maintain sovereign rights to pelagic and sessile resources while surface waters are international (UNCLOS, Articles 58 and 87). Yet farther offshore, beyond the EEZ, the ocean surface and the water column are referred to as the "high seas." Here, freedom reigns as "No State may validly purport to subject any part of the high seas to its sovereignty" (UNCLOS, Article 89). Meanwhile, any national claims on the seabed beyond the EEZ (i.e., in "the Area") have been categorically invalidated by UNCLOS in an effort to protect it as a "common heritage of mankind" (UNCLOS, Article 136). British geographer Stephen Graham describes this way of governing as the "classical, modern formulation of Euclidean territorial units jostling for space on contiguous maps" (2004, 20).

Further attempting to reinforce UNCLOS's role as protectorate of life, the UN is currently negotiating a new regulatory platform for the deep sea, with special emphasis on marine biodiversity and the expansion of marine-protected areas beyond national jurisdiction (Payne 2017). Issues of conservation in the deep seabed have provoked a crisis in national sovereignty, invoking questions about how to transform a space previously characterized by freedom, with relatively limited regulation, into a space with enhanced protections for sea life and matter.

Notably, the Euclidian demarcation of space was integral to the history of ocean governance well before the establishment of the UN and the ratification of UNCLOS. The tremendous investment by early Western administrations in inscribing the seas is detailed in Zsofia Korosy's chapter, "Whales and the Colonization of the Pacific Ocean." There, she shows how eighteenth-century cartographic techniques demarcated spaces of sovereign legal authority in the seas. Such eighteenth-century renderings of ocean space enabled colonial expansion on land as well. By "allowing both seen and unseen spaces to be conceived as congruent wholes within defined boundaries," Korosy writes, cartographic representations of both sea and land legitimized colonial fantasies about sovereignty over terrestrial areas scarcely known. The violence that followed—perpetrated against ocean-dwelling whales and land-dwelling humans alike—catalyzed new ways of viewing the land as a repository of resources to be extracted, used, and abused with legal authority.

The methods of demarcation and geographical reasoning developed in the eighteenth century are just as central to ocean governance today. In their chapter, "Edges and Flows," Philip E. Steinberg, Berit Kristoffersen, and Kristen L. Shake examine the mapping of Norway's icy northern waters. They describe how locating the ice's edge has become a practice of translating what is fluid and indeterminate into fixed and knowable borders. As Steinberg and his co-authors show, legal reasoning intensifies and reifies cartographic inscriptions by insisting on "stable definitions and fixed distinctions." The project of ocean inscription thus creates, in their words, "a world of lines and laws." By defining the boundary between fluid and solid states, cartographers and legislators have effectively erased the physical indeterminacy of ice from the map, making the Arctic more governable for resource extraction. Just as Korosy's eighteenth-century cartographers produced lines and laws to facilitate the extraction of fuel in the form of whale blubber, the Norwegian government has been remapping its border zone in order to expand oil extraction in the Arctic.

Such practices in lines and laws reveal a mounting tension in ocean governance: on the one hand, the seas are configured as a global common; on the other hand, they are perceived as providing a repository of globally profitable commodities. This tension has long underpinned the establishment and negotiation of marine space and its corresponding legalities (Snyder and St. Martin 2015). Few modern concepts have been as influential in stoking this tension—and for the development of law, political science, economics, or environmental studies in this context—as Garrett Hardin's "Tragedy of the Commons" (1968). Hardin's vision of a depleted commons has dominated legal discussions about how to govern public spaces and has frequently been deployed in the context of marine resources (mainly fisheries) and marine pollution (Ranganathan 2016). Global contributions to ocean waste and to the spread of microplastics are often considered perfect examples of Hardin's tragedy. But as legal scholar Surabhi Ranganathan notes, conservation efforts that vilified common resource management in the seas have ended up sparking legislation that dispossessed both Indigenous and settler communities from critical resources. In other words, Hardin's concept inadvertently set the stage not for more sustainable management, but for more efficient extraction (Ranganathan 2016; see also Locher 2018; St. Martin 2009).

The tension between resource protection and exploitation underpins many of the legal frameworks for ocean governance. The establishment and expansion of the juridical continental shelf and the EEZ have been viewed as emblematic of this tension. In 1945, former US president Harry Truman tripled the resource claims of the United States, thereby starting the race for sovereign expansion (DeLoughrey 2015, 355). This was one of the first assertions of exclusive jurisdiction beyond the traditional territorial seas. The post-1946 rezoning of the ocean constituted "the most dramatic change to global mapping since the post–World War II era of decolonization" (355). It is no wonder, then, that the postwar ocean zones have been viewed as the ultimate symbol of the twentieth-century neocolonial scramble.

The development of technologies that enabled the exploitation of minerals in the seabed in the 1960s intensified that scramble. Most notable was the newfound ability to mine manganese nodules at depths of over three thousand meters (Harrison 2013, 37). The rise of seabed mining in the twentieth century radically reshaped the ocean: rather than being merely a "navigational surface or fishing commons," the seabed became a constellation of "places for fixed capital investment" (Ranganathan 2019). The efforts to capitalize on minerals and fossil fuels beneath the seabed have been so rapid that they have triggered a legal revolution (Harrison 2013, 37). Ongoing technological advances allow developed countries to excavate the seabed, resulting in what developing countries have often referred to as neocolonial ocean grabs (Pinkerton and Davis 2015; see also Ranganathan 2019). In light of these transformations, it is difficult to view the demarcations established by UNCLOS, and promoted through other cartographic efforts, as fixed and stable. Instead, the oceans have become the latest Wild West—a frontier playground for exertions of national sovereignty and power that extend logics of land into sea.

Beyond this scramble for existing territorial anchors to extend their reach through legislation, nation-states are now also extending the land itself into the ocean, with significant legal implications. Jennifer L. Gaynor's chapter in this volume shows, accordingly, how increasing state capture and contestations over resource extraction in Southeast Asia have driven island and coastal states to engage in massive terraforming projects. These projects of sand redistribution stretch and transform legal distinctions between land and sea, and international court tribunals are called upon to adjudicate which landforms count as territory, with entitlements over adjacent waters, and which are merely rocks and sand.

Clearly, then, there is much at stake when inscribing boundaries and binaries onto the sea and decisively distinguishing land from water. By historicizing and problematizing legal borders, this volume contributes to the telling of myriad ocean stories with the aim of furthering protective policies. Along these lines, Katherine G. Sammler's chapter, "Kauri and the Whale," studies the controversies over New Zealand's Foreshore and Seabed Act of 2004, which has enabled the extraction of seabed minerals. This legislation has generated much friction between two clashing worldviews: one embracing a Western land/sea binary, the other based in Indigenous Māori traditions that assign holistic customary rights extending from mountains to sea. According to Sammler, Indigenous ontologies provide alternative ways of governing that challenge the essentialism of national sovereignty and that can better accommodate the fluidity of oceans. Instead of seeing the oceans as a fixed Euclidean space within which power is exercised, this worldview ushers in a "wet ontology" that allows for mobility within and between novel jurisdictions (Steinberg and Peters 2015). Such a wet ontology would arguably diversify and expand the potential for "postcapitalist waterworlds," supporting efforts to decolonize the seas (DeLoughrey 2015, 359; see also St. Martin 2009).

Governing with More-Than-Human Sea Creatures

Among the public, calls for the conservation of ocean resources and the rethinking of marine governance are often channeled through considerations of marine life. Orcas, humpbacks, octopuses, and pelagic sea angels are merely a few of the ocean's charismatic creatures who have captured the human imagination. In spite of their charisma, however, the ocean's nonhuman lives have often been neglected by legal scholars and policy makers alike. When considered, they tend to be the passive subjects of conservation management or fisheries regulations, made to live (and die) under legal infrastructures that were typically crafted for the management of terrestrial species. But the inhabitants of ocean space also shape and resist regulatory enframings, thereby sketching and stretching our understandings of laws in unexpected ways.

The vast differences between land and sea animals have been fruitful for scientific and philosophical inquiries. In *Other Minds: The Octopus, the Sea, and the Deep Origins of Consciousness* (2016), Peter Godfrey-Smith examines the evolutionary divergence of humans and octopuses. His work is driven by a curiosity about the startling intelligence of cephalopods—a class of marine mollusks that includes the squids, cuttlefishes, and octopuses—and their development within bodies so unlike our own. In the book, he attunes readers to the unique attributes of these creatures, highlighting communicative capacities and evolutionary histories that are so different from those of vertebrates, yet are undeniable "accomplishments" of life. Cephalopods have long been considered so morphologically and behaviorally divergent from creatures of the terrestrial world that some have even offered that they must hail from another one altogether. In *Octopus: Physiology and Behavior of an Advanced Invertebrate*, Martin Wells contended along these lines that "the octopus is an alien" (1978, 8). In the decades that followed, scientists commenting on the evolutionary oddity of cephalopods have frequently invoked his claim. Most recently, a widely debated article on life's "cosmic origins" dwells on the unique qualities of the octopus's genome as evidence of "unearthly" beginnings (Steele et al. 2018, 12).

We find more of the same fascination with the unearthly in the ways that scientists write about extremophiles. The ubiquitous tardigrade offers a vivid example. This microscopic invertebrate's ability to suspend life by pausing metabolism in unfavorable environments has challenged conventional understandings about the boundary between life and death. Similarly, the tube worms and ghost crabs who live in hydrothermal vents thousands of meters deep and produce energy through chemosynthesis seem entirely unworldly. It is no wonder, then, that even the marine biologists on NOAA's recent *Okeanos Explorer* expedition referred to the unknown creatures they observed on the abyssal plain as "unidentified swimming organisms."

Thinking with marine animals takes us beyond questions of extending existing legal infrastructures into the depths of debates about just ethical frameworks and more expansive conditions of care. A wealth of literature is currently emerging that examines how thinking with animal life might reconfigure our ethical comportment, engendering what Donna Haraway refers to as a stronger sense of "response-ability" (2008). In thinking with animals, Haraway and her interlocutors envision a post-Cartesian world in which subjectivity is neither individual nor autonomous, but rather situated across a shared, multispecies planet.

Queer theorists have also turned to the oceans and their organisms as a resource for thinking beyond and outside the traditional coordinates of being human as heteronormative and gender conforming. Eva Hayward, for example, has shown how thinking with cup corals and starfish incites us to reconfigure the "meat and meaning" of the body. For Hayward, speaking, writing, and singing of starfish generates an "inter-somaticity" and "a kind of nearness that invokes a voluptuary of trans-speciation, and imagines a co/passionate kind of presence" (2008, 80). Learning with sea organisms, she argues, we might create new "ethics of mattering" (Hayward 2012, 185).

Confronting wet ontologies and epistemologies also reveals that human animals have never been dry—that we are in fact those alien creatures that we see as other. Along these lines, Stacy Alaimo's work considers how thinking and engaging radically different life-forms forces us to think beyond our human exceptionalist tendencies and to recognize that "like our hermaphroditic, aquatic-evolutionary ancestor, we dwell within and as part of a dynamic, intra-active, emergent, material world that demands new forms of ethical thought and practice" (Alaimo 2011, 283). According to Alaimo, thinking with sea creatures may engender unexpected affinities (283; see also Harvell 2016).

Astrid Schrader emphasizes such affinities in her contribution to this collection. Looking at the rhythmic lives of marine microbes, she asserts, we are "haunted" by past generations: the rhythms of dead cyanobacteria colonies govern the metabolism of living populations. Thinking with these populations challenges how we understand the divides between living and dead, between individuals and populations, and among species. For Schrader, haunted microbes reconfigure questions of justice and law, shifting the central discussion from the relation between norms and "forms of life" toward a politics of temporally entangled modes of existences. Drawing on Derridean legal scholar Drucilla Cornell, Schrader thus develops what she calls a "marine microbiopolitics," which works to unseat the primacy of the autonomous liberal humanist subject. Such an unseating of the liberal subject not only undermines the position of the autonomous human in the law; it also shifts the role of science in relation to biopolitics, turning it into a resource for rethinking conceptions of justice.

Accounts of law will inevitably shift when we move away from our anthropocentric bias to more carefully consider less-like-us lives and matter. In her chapter, "*Clupea liberum*," for example, Alison Rieser showcases the largely unknown historical role of the Atlantic herring in the development of the modern state. She argues, in particular, that the herring was central to formative seventeenth-century debates over the Freedom of the Seas principle. This fish's seemingly intentional arrivals and disappearances were part of the oceanic imaginaries of the polities of the North Sea basin, where novel legal institutions were competing to regulate rapidly changing economies and shore up national interests (see also Rieser 2017). With their particular habits and biological properties, the Atlantic herring thus performed an active role in producing the Freedom of the Seas doctrine, which in turn shaped modern legal regimes that pertain to the seas writ large. Clearly, thinking with marine organisms can challenge our assumptions about the relationship between life and law.

While the herring were central to the constitution of major principles of Western legalities, many other forms of ocean life have been much less visible to the law. Reef-building corals are a good example of the initial blindness, later turned into an ill-fit, between law and various marine forms of life. This ill-fit has become evident from the recent attempts to know and classify marine species for laws that deal with endangered species protection (Braverman 2018a). Trying to determine whether or not they are endangered, legal administrators and conservation managers have debated what is the relevant unit for counting a coral individual: is it the polyp, the colony, or the genotype? As it turns out, each division carries significant problems. The coral scientists and managers soon realized that modern Western laws about endangerment were enacted with tigers, lions, and bears in mind—and not with invertebrates such as corals. Braverman describes, accordingly, how "legal administrators, equipped with words and paper, stretch, bend, and lengthen legal norms to fit the particularities and peculiarities of coral life—thereby breathing life into corals. Their imperative is to make the coral visible to the law, and they have been using the legal and scientific language of endangerment for this purpose" (Braverman 2018a, 183).

Corals have also challenged the definitions of harm and death, which are central to nature protection laws. For example, the term "take" is a core tenet of the US Endangered Species Act of 1973 and intended to prevent any harm to listed species by physical injury. But rather than harming the coral animal, the breaking off (or "fragging") of corals in fact creates new life and is therefore utilized by coral nurseries for restoration purposes (Braverman 2018a, 164). It is no wonder, then, that the plan to list two Caribbean Acropora coral species as endangered triggered a wave of protests among coral scientists and managers alike, much to the bafflement of government administrators, who assumed that these experts would be thrilled with the proposed legal up-list and its enhanced protection (165).

If corals have become the focus of protection through their legal designation as threatened and endangered, Braverman's contribution to this collection reveals those attempts to manage the ocean that focus on legal acts of killing. In particular, she examines the historical and contemporary use of robotic machinery in attempts to "control" the crown-of-thorns starfish outbreaks that have been damaging the Great Barrier Reef. These robotics "make die" as part of a biopolitical gaze that extends beyond human and nonhuman life to consider machinic ways of seeing and killing. As robots displace humans in marine life management, we find that ways of knowing and governing life are increasingly embedded within technological prosthetics. These prostheses, which have been providing important access to the deep sea, have also become apparatuses of governance that in turn shape this space.

Yet dealing with the major threats to ocean creatures may be beyond the capacity of advanced technologies as well as the scope of national and international laws. Since existing laws are typically restricted to the national scale, conservation managers and policy makers are concerned that they might not be adequate for resolving the global problems of our era. For these and other reasons, legal scholars have argued that "climate change challenges the capacity of law," referring to it as a "super wicked problem" (Weaver and Kysar 2017, 296). Will more plural, dynamic, and planetary legalities be better equipped at protecting existing ecosystems and forms of ocean life from their projected decline?

Final Notes on Turbulences

Like climate change, the governance of the ocean is a wicked problem. But while altering ocean management is absolutely crucial, especially in the face of the growing ecological crises in the Anthropocene, we must at the same time acknowledge that it requires a radical rethinking: both of our existing assumptions and of our existing institutions and regulatory apparatuses. After all, ocean governance is not a managerial or technical problem to be solved through the acquisition of more and better knowledge or through an expansion of existing legal regimes. The unique material and symbolic dynamics of the sea and its inhabitants thus force us to de- and uncenter our systems of governance and our modes of regulation. Put differently, recognizing the fluidity of land and sea requires a reconsideration of the existing institutions, temporal frameworks, and categories with which we engage the oceans, illuminating our responsibilities toward these spaces and to what lies and lives within them.

Existing on the edge of law and haunted by the figure of the alien, the seas have been central to the construction of terrestrial institutions and modes of governance. Reversing the continental gaze into the sea, ocean imaginaries may creep onshore, inspiring openings for flows, transformations, and relationalities. Such wet ontologies and their accompanying wet creatures and structures have already manifested in wet coalitions, resistances, and emancipations on, in, and near the sea (Katherine G. Sammler, this volume; Hadjimichael n.d.; Steinberg and Peters 2015). Specifically, thinking with sea organisms such as the Atlantic herring, whales, crown-of-thorn starfish, green algae, and bioluminescent *Pyrocystis fusiformis,* as well as with such sea phenomena as ice, waves, buoys, remotely operated vehicles, humanoid robots, and forgotten chemical weapons, invites the crafting of alternative regulatory frameworks that contest the existing linear inscriptions of the sea. In some of these physical and temporal sites, political struggle may lead to more just and ecologically sustainable practices of knowing—to a mode of governing with care. *Blue Legalities* therefore not only points to the myriad ways in which legal structures are adrift at sea but, more importantly, it also hints at the vast opportunities for other legalities—and ways of knowing, understanding, and relating to the world—to emerge.

Acknowledgments

We would like to thank the contributors of this volume for their helpful comments on the introduction. We are also grateful to the Baldy Center for Law & Social Policy for the generous workshop grant that made this book possible.

References

Alaimo, Stacy. 2011. "New Materialisms, Old Humanisms, or, Following the Submersible." *Nordic Journal of Feminist and Gender Research* 19 (4): 280–84.

Alaimo, Stacy. 2012. "Dispersing Disaster: The Deepwater Horizon, Ocean Conservation, and the Immateriality of Aliens." In *American Environments: Climate-Cultures-Catastrophe,* edited by Christof Mauch and Sylvia Mayer, 177–92. Heidelberg: Universitätsverlag.

Alaimo, Stacy. 2016. *Exposed: Environmental Politics and Pleasures in Posthuman Times.* Minneapolis: University of Minnesota Press.

Asafu-Adjaye, John, Linus Blomqvist, Stewart Brand, Barry Brook, Ruth De-Fries, Erle Ellis, Christopher Foreman, et al. 2015. *An Eco-Modernist Manifesto.* April. https://static1.squarespace.com/static/5515d9f9e4b04d5c3198b7bb/t/552d37bbe4b07a7dd69fcdbb/1429026747046/An+Ecomodernist+Manifesto.pdf.

Bakke, Monika. 2017. "Art and Metabolic Force in Deep Time Environments." *Environmental Philosophy* 14 (1): 41–59.

Bishara, Fahad Ahmed. 2017. *A Sea of Debt: Law and Economic Life in the Western Indian Ocean, 1780–1950.* Cambridge: Cambridge University Press.

Boucquey, Noelle, Luke Fairbanks, Kevin St. Martin, Lisa Campbell, and Bonnie McCay. 2016. "The Ontological Politics of Marine Spatial Planning." *Geoforum* 75 (October): 1–11.

Bradley, James. 2018. "The End of the Oceans." *The Monthly,* August. https://www.themonthly.com.au/issue/2018/august/1533045600/james-bradley/end-oceans.

Braverman, Irus. 2015. "More-Than-Human Legalities." In *The Wiley Handbook of Law and Society,* edited by Patricia Ewick and Austin Sarat, 307–21. London: Wiley.

Braverman, Irus, ed. 2016. *Animals, Biopolitics, Law: Lively Legalities.* London: Routledge.

Braverman, Irus. 2018a. *Coral Whisperers: Scientists on the Brink.* Oakland: University of California Press.

Braverman, Irus. 2018b. "Law's Underdog: A Call for Nonhuman Legalities." *Annual Review of Law and Social Science* 14: 127–44.

Charles, Anthony T. 1998. "Living with Uncertainty in Fisheries: Analytical Methods, Management Priorities and the Canadian Groundfishery Experience." *Fisheries Research* 37 (1): 37–50.

Chen, Cecilia, Janine MacLeod, and Astrida Neimanis, eds. 2013. *Thinking with Water*. Montreal: McGill-Queen's University Press.

Coddington, Kate. 2018. "Settler Colonial Territorial Imaginaries: Maritime Mobilities and the 'Tow-Backs' of Asylum Seekers." In *Territory beyond Terra*, edited by Kimberley Peters, Philip Steinberg, and Elaine Stratford, 185–202. London: Rowman & Littlefield.

Craig, Robin Kundis. 2012. *Comparative Ocean Governance Place-Based Protections in an Era of Climate Change*. Cheltenham, UK: Edward Elgar.

DeLoughrey, Elizabeth. 2007. *Routes and Roots: Navigating Caribbean and Pacific Island Literatures*. Honolulu: University of Hawai'i Press.

DeLoughrey, Elizabeth. 2015. "Ordinary Futures: Interspecies Worldings in the Anthropocene." In *Global Ecologies and the Environmental Humanities: Postcolonial Approaches*, edited by Elizabeth DeLoughrey, Jill Didur, and Anthony Carrigan, 352–72. New York: Routledge.

DeLoughrey, Elizabeth. 2017. "Submarine Futures of the Anthropocene." *Comparative Literature Journal* (special issue) 69 (1): 32–44.

De Wolff, Kim. 2017. "Plastic Naturecultures: Multispecies Ethnography and the Dangers of Separating Living from Nonliving Bodies." *Body and Society* 23 (3): 23–47.

Earle, Sylvia A. 2014. "'Mission Blue' Warning: The Ocean Is Not Too Big to Fail." *Daily Beast*, August 15. https://www.thedailybeast.com/mission-blue-warning-the-ocean-is-not-too-big-to-fail.

European Commission. 2012. "Blue Growth Opportunities for Marine and Maritime Sustainable Growth." Communication from the Commission to the European Parliament, the Council, the European Economic and Social Committee, and the Committee of the Regions. September 13. https://ec.europa.eu/maritimeaffairs/sites/maritimeaffairs/files/docs/body/com_2012_494_en.pdf.

Gillis, John. 2013. "The Blue Humanities: In Studying the Sea, We Are Returning to Our Beginnings." *Humanities* 34 (3). https://www.neh.gov/humanities/2013/mayjune/feature/the-blue-humanities.

Godfrey-Smith, Peter. 2016. *Other Minds: The Octopus, the Sea, and the Deep Origins of Consciousness*. New York: Farrar, Straus and Giroux.

Goodell, Jeff. 2017. *The Water Will Come: Rising Seas, Sinking Cities, and the Remaking of the Civilized World*. New York: Little, Brown and Company.

Graham, Stephen. 2004. "Vertical Geopolitics: Baghdad and After." *Antipode* 36 (1): 12–23.

Grear, Anna. 2015. "Deconstructing Anthropos: A Critical Legal Reflection on 'Anthropocentric' Law and Anthropocene 'Humanity.'" *Law and Critique* 26 (3): 225–49.

Gregory, Derek. 1994. *Geographical Imaginations*. London: Wiley-Blackwell.

Hadjimichael, Maria. n.d. "The Right to the Sea." Editor's note on the reclaimthesea.org website, The Right to the Sea: Coming Together Demanding Environmental and

Social Justice with a Global Movement to Reclaim Our Oceans and Coastlines. Accessed August 15, 2018. http://reclaimthesea.org.

Haraway, Donna. 2008. *When Species Meet*. Minneapolis: University of Minnesota Press.

Hardin, Garrett. 1968. "The Tragedy of the Commons." *Science* 162 (3859): 1243–48.

Harrison, James. 2011. *Making the Law of the Sea: A Study in the Development of International Law*. Cambridge: Cambridge University Press.

Harvell, Drew. 2016. *A Sea of Glass: Searching for the Blaschkas' Fragile Legacy in an Ocean at Risk*. Oakland: University of California Press.

Hayward, Eva. 2008. "More Lessons from a Starfish: Prefixial Flesh and Transspeciated Selves." *WSQ: Women's Studies Quarterly* 36 (3): 64–85.

Hayward, Eva. 2012. "Sensational Jellyfish: Aquarium Affects and the Matter of Immersion." *Differences* 23 (3): 161–96.

Helmreich, Stefan. 2007. "Blue-Green Capital, Biotechnological Circulation and an Oceanic Imaginary: A Critique of Biopolitical Economy." *BioSocieties* 2 (3): 287–302.

Helmreich, Stefan. 2009. *Alien Ocean: Anthropological Voyages in Microbial Seas*. Berkeley: University of California Press.

Ingersoll, Karin Amimoto. 2016. *Waves of Knowing: A Seascape Epistemology*. Durham, NC: Duke University Press.

Jasanoff, Sheila. 2008. "Making Order: Law and Science in Action." In *Handbook of Science and Technology Studies*, 3rd ed., edited by Edward J. Hackett, Olga Amsterdamska, Michael Lynch, and Judy Wajcman, 761–86. Cambridge, MA: MIT Press.

Johnson, Elizabeth R. 2016. "Governing Jellyfish: Eco-Security and Planetary 'Life' in the Anthropocene." In *Animals, Biopolitics, Law: Lively Legalities,* edited by Irus Braverman, 59–78. London: Routledge.

Lavau, Stephanie. 2013. "Going with the Flow: Sustainable Water Management as Ontological Cleaving." *Environment and Planning D: Society and Space* 31 (3): 416–33.

Lazarus, Richard J. 2009. "Super Wicked Problems and Climate Change: Restraining the Present to Liberate the Future." *Cornell Law Review* 94: 1153–33.

Locher, Fabien. 2018. "Historicizing Elinor Ostrom: Urban Politics, International Development and Expertise in the U.S. Context (1970–1990)." *Theoretical Inquiries in Law* 19 (2): 533–58.

Lord, Austin. 2019. "Turbulence." *Society and Space Online*. March 17. http://societyandspace.org/2019/03/17/turbulence/.

Lyons, Kate. 2018. "Revealed: Asylum Seekers' 20-Year Wait for Home Office Ruling." *The Guardian*, August 17. https://www.theguardian.com/uk-news/2018/aug/17/revealed-asylum-seekers-20-year-wait-for-home-office-ruling?CMP=share_btn_tw.

Mentz, Steven. 2009. "Toward a Blue Cultural Studies: The Sea, Maritime Culture, and Early Modern English Literature." *Literature Compass* 6 (5): 997–1013.

Mountz, Alison, and Jenna Loyd. 2014. "Transnational Productions of Remoteness: Building Onshore and Offshore Carceral Regimes across Borders." *Geographica Helvetica* 69: 389–98.

Nyman, Elizabeth. 2013. "Oceans of Conflict? Determining Potential Areas of Maritime Disputes." *SAIS Review of International Affairs* 33 (2): 5–14.

Patil, P. G., J. Virdin, S. M. Diez, J. Roberts, and A. Singh. 2016. *Toward a Blue Economy: A Promise for Sustainable Growth in the Caribbean: An Overview.* Washington, DC: World Bank.

Pauly, Daniel. 2013. "Beyond Duplicity and Ignorance in Global Fisheries." In *Ecological Dimensions for Sustainable Socio Economic Development*, edited by Alejandro Yáñez-Arancibia, Raymundo Dávalos-Sotelo, John W. Day, and Enrique Reyes. WIT Transactions on State-of-the-Art in Science and Engineering, vol. 64, 519–36. Southampton, UK: WIT Press.

Payne, Cymie. 2017. "Biodiversity in High Seas Areas: An Integrated Legal Approach." *Insights* 21 (9). https://www.asil.org/insights/volume/21/issue/9/biodiversity-high-seas-areas-integrated-legal-approach.

Philippopoulos-Mihalopoulos, Andreas. 2016a. "Flesh of the Law: Material Metaphors." *Journal of Law and Society* 43 (1): 45–65.

Philippopoulos-Mihalopoulos, Andreas. 2016b. "Lively Agency: Life and Law in the Anthropocene." In *Animals, Biopolitics, Law: Lively Legalities,* edited by Irus Braverman, 139–210. London: Routledge.

Philippopoulos-Mihalopoulos, Andreas. 2018. "And for Law: Why Space Cannot Be Understood without Law." *Law, Culture and the Humanities* (first published online, March 23).

Pinkerton, Evelyn, and Reade Davis. 2015. "Neoliberalism and the Politics of Enclosure in North American Small-Scale Fisheries." *Marine Policy* 61 (November): 303–12.

Pottage, Alain. 2012. "The Materiality of What?" *Journal of Law and Society* 39 (1): 167–83.

Pottage, Alain, and Claire Marris. 2012. "The Cut That Makes a Part." *BioSocieties* 7 (2): 103–14.

Proctor, Robert N., and Londa Schiebinger. 2008. *Agnotology: The Making and Unmaking of Ignorance.* Stanford, CA: Stanford University Press.

Ranganathan, Surabhi. 2016. "Global Commons." *European Journal of International Law* 27 (3): 693–717.

Ranganathan, Surabhi. 2019. "Ocean Floor Grab: International Law and the Making of an Extractive Imaginary." *European Journal of International Law* 30 (2): 573–600.

Rieser, Alison. 2017. "The Herring Enlightenment: Adam Smith and the reform of British fishing subsidies, 1783–1799." *International Journal of Maritime History* 29 (3): 600–619.

Rogers, Alex, and Dan Laffoley. 2013. "Introduction: The Global State of the Ocean; Interactions between Stresses, Impacts and Some Potential Solutions." Synthesis Papers from the International Programme on the State of the Ocean 2011 and 2012 Workshops. *Marine Pollution Bulletin* 74 (2): 491–94.

Scheiber, Harry N., and Jin-Hyun Paik, eds. 2013. *Regions, Institutions, and Law of the Sea: Studies in Ocean Governance.* Leiden: Nijhoff.

Schlanger, Zoë. 2017. "If Oceans Stopped Absorbing Heat from Climate Change, Life on Land Would Average 122°F." *Quartz*, November 29. https://qz.com/1141633/if-oceans-stopped-absorbing-heat-from-climate-change-life-on-land-would-average-122f.

Schmitt, Carl. (1950) 2003. *The Nomos of the Earth in the International Law of the Jus Publicum Europaeum.* New York: Telos.

Serres, Michel, and Bruno Latour. 1995. *Conversations on Science, Culture, and Time: Michel Serres with Bruno Latour*. Ann Arbor: University of Michigan Press.

Sharpe, Christina. 2016. *In the Wake: On Blackness and Being*. Durham, NC: Duke University Press.

Snyder, Robert, and Kevin St. Martin. 2015. "A Fishery for the Future: The Midcoast Fishermen's Association and the Work of Economic Being-in-Common." In *Making Other Worlds Possible: Performing Diverse Economies*, edited by Gerda Roelvink, Kevin St. Martin, and J. K. Gibson-Graham. Minneapolis: University of Minnesota Press.

St. Martin, Kevin. 2009. "Toward a Cartography of the Commons: Constituting the Political and Economic Possibilities of Place." *Professional Geographer* 61 (4): 493–507.

Steele, Edward J., Shirwan Al-Mufti, Kenneth A. Augustyn, Rohana Chandrajith, John P. Coghlan, S. G. Coulson, Sudipto Ghosh, Mark Gillman, Reginald M. Gorczynski, Brig Klyce, et al. 2018. "Cause of Cambrian Explosion—Terrestrial or Cosmic?" *Progress in Biophysics and Molecular Biology* 136 (August): 3–23.

Steffen, Will, Wendy Broadgate, Linda Deutsch, Owen Gaffney, and Cornelia Ludwig. 2015. "The Trajectory of the Anthropocene: The Great Acceleration." *Anthropocene Review* 2 (March): 81–98.

Steinberg, Philip E. 2001. *The Social Construction of the Ocean*. Cambridge: Cambridge University Press.

Steinberg, Philip E. 2011. "Free Sea." In *Sovereignty, Spatiality, and Carl Schmitt: Geographies of the Nomos*, edited by Stephen Legg, 268–75. London: Routledge.

Steinberg, Philip E., and Kimberley Peters. 2015. "Wet Ontologies, Fluid Spaces: Giving Depth to Volume through Oceanic Thinking." *Environment and Planning D: Society and Space* 33 (2): 247–64.

Stephens, Tim, and David L. VanderZwaag, eds. 2014. *Polar Oceans Governance in an Era of Environmental Change*. Cheltenham, UK: Edward Elgar.

Tanaka, Yoshifumi. 2008. *A Dual Approach to Ocean Governance: The Cases of Zonal and Integrated Management in International Law of the Sea*. Farnham, UK: Ashgate.

Todd, Zoe. 2014. "Fish Pluralities: Human-Animal Relations and Sites of Engagement in Paulatuuq, Arctic Canada." *Etudes/Inuit/Studies* 38 (1–2): 217–38.

UNCLOS (United Nations Convention on the Law of the Sea). 1833 UNTS 3; 21 ILM 1261 (1982), https://www.un.org/Depts/los/convention_agreements/convention_overview _convention.htm.

Weaver, R. Henry, and Douglas A. Kysar. 2017. "Courting Disaster: Climate Change and the Adjudication of Catastrophe." *Notre Dame Law Review* 93 (1): 295–356.

Welch, Michael. 2014. "Economic Man and Diffused Sovereignty: A Critique of Australia's Asylum Regime." *Crime, Law, and Social Change* 61 (1): 81–107.

Wells, M. J. 1978. *Octopus: Physiology and Behavior of an Advanced Invertebrate*. London: Springer.

Zeweri, Helena. 2017. "Encounters on the Shore: Geographies of Violence in Australia's Contemporary Border Regime." *Rejoinder* 2 (Spring). http://irw.rutgers.edu/rejoinder -webjournal/borders-bodies-homes/294-encounters-on-the-shore-geographies-of -violence-in-australia-s-contemporary-border-regime.

1. SOLWARA 1 AND THE SESSILE ONES

SUSAN REID

The Bismarck Sea laps sluggishly but steadily at the hull of Nautilus Minerals's Deep-Sea Mining (DSM) production vessel. Suspended thousands of meters above the company's seabed quarry, the vessel's single rigid riser pipe descends to the seabed, disappearing in the darkness. In the twilight, dysphotic zone, around a thousand meters below sea level, photosynthesis ends, but the ocean's relationship with light endures. Masses of deep-sea creatures ascend nightly to feed on light-life at the surface; those at the bottom graze creaturely falls and rains of detritus from above. Beyond these photic connections, chemosynthesis mediates life at these depths. As it descends further, the riser pipe enters a world rich with microbial organisms and lively ecological communities of tube worms, gastropods, bivalves, and myriad others and their briny relations. Water temperature, darkness, pressure, sonic signals and organic, chemical, and mineral elements, co-constitute conditions of livability with creaturely and other lives. In the midnight of the aphotic depths, around fifteen hundred meters, the production vessel's riser pipe finally reaches its mining tenement at the crests of the black, sulphidic sediment-covered SuSu knolls. The toponymy of these volcanic peaks derives from the Pidgin-English word for women's breasts, which speaks volumes about the hypermasculinized enterprise and disembodied imaginaries with which the mining industry operates. One of the SuSus, named Suzette, holds 2.47 million metric tons of copper-gold deposit (Yeats et al. 2014, 1) and is the target for Nautilus Minerals' Solwara 1 DSM operation. Suzette does not yet know it, but she, and the chemosynthetic communities supported by her hydro-thermal vents, are about to be legally cleaved, crushed, stripped of sediment, and terraformed.

The above account is speculative; the extraction machines are not yet running, the pumps and lights not yet switched on. But DSM production is imminent for the SuSu knolls. Though relatively small in scale, and within Papua New Guinea's (PNG) Continental Shelf and Exclusive Economic Zone (EEZ) jurisdictions, Solwara 1 is viewed as a physical test run for operationalizing DSM in the international seabed jurisdiction known as the Area. Across these jurisdictions mining activities are governed by the framework of the United Nations Convention on the Law of the Sea (UNCLOS 1982). This chapter examines the foundational imaginaries underpinning both the resource industry driving DSM and the international law that makes it possible. It highlights the ecologies being risked by both DSM resource frontiers and UNCLOS's development imperatives. As the chapter progresses, conceptual openings unfold for the emergence of more relational and ecologically sensitive counter imaginaries.

Solwara 1 marks the commercial beginning of DSM's removal of vast tracts of the planet's deep ocean seafloor. Opponents are concerned about the ecological damage that will result from excavating mineral deposits laid down over thousands of years around hydrothermal vents; or removing mineral-rich nodules scattered over the abyssal plains, which also formed over millennia. These are sites of extraordinary, and yet little known, ecological communities. DSM will also affect marine life in the water column and impact coastal island fishing communities. In their "Deep Sea Mining Briefing Paper," the Deep Sea Conservation Coalition reports that, at the 2017 United Nations Ocean Conference, more than thirty-five civil society organizations raised concern and called for DSM to cease (Deep Sea Conservation Coalition 2017, 5). Such opposition competes with consumer complicities amplifying demand for the minerals constituting the stuff of our contemporary lives.

As the human population increases so too does demand for such things as laptops, plumbing pipes, paints, cars, renewable technologies, and the raw materials from which they are made (Batker and Schmidt 2015, 12). For example, so great is the demand that over the next couple of decades the world's copper consumption will exceed all the copper ever mined to date (US Geological Survey, cited in Spicer 2013). Having depleted most of the easy-to-extract terrestrial mineral supplies, miners are turning to the ocean for more commercially profitable, high-grade copper, manganese, cobalt, and rare earth elements found in polymetallic nodules, polymetallic massive sulphide deposits, and seafloor massive sulphide (SMS) deposits (ISA 2012), such as those at Solwara 1.

Solwara's excavation on Suzette's hydrothermal vent sites will be relatively modest compared with enormous terrestrial mines. Nevertheless, Nautilus Minerals (Nautilus) anticipates removing an estimated 1.3 million tons of mineralized material from the seafloor per year (Nautilus Minerals, Inc. 2016, 24). This is resource-speak, nature as account. Quantified in the service of capitalism's demands the seabed becomes, in Jason Moore's apt figuration, "cheap nature" (2016). In the context of capitalism's commodity productions, the seabed becomes a supplier of cheap raw materials. Its natural elements and relations are considered ethically inferior to the profit needs of corporations and consumerist demands. Neither does the value attributed to these mineral elements fully account for the biological losses and environmental consequences of their extraction.

While resource extraction profits are private, environmental losses are public and planetary. Resource corporations lobby governments for legislation to secure title over their quarries and mitigate capital risk. Simultaneously, they pass on the risks of environmental harms to human and nonhuman communities. With a wink to corporate extractivists, UNCLOS provides the legal framework for DSM to thrive. Its conservation provisions gesture to environmental concerns but are notably weak and difficult to enforce. UNCLOS imports the precautionary principle supported by the Rio Declaration (1992) and the 1992 Convention on Biological Diversity (CBD), placing the burden of proof on corporations whose activities may pose a threat or cause irreversible harm. Such proof is difficult to verify in DSM's self-regulating environment: miners establish the environmental baselines against which their enterprises are measured; monitor their own progress against these baselines; and report on any changes. Operating several kilometers below the surface also makes it difficult for independent oversight or audit, and neither the International Seabed Authority (ISA) nor PNG or any small island nations have resources to deploy site-specific monitoring teams.

In the juridical imaginary, the ocean is valued as mineral stockpile, oil reserve, fish tank and food pantry, cabinet of potential pharmaceuticals, and endless supplier of materials in the service of the human project. It is an imaginary underpinned by cornerstone neoliberal values: cheap nature converted for capitalism's gain. Through its discursive practices, UNCLOS opens the seabed for business. Too bad for bivalves, tube worms, and other sessile residents and their relations. Law's foundations reveal the tenacity of Cartesian binarist conceptions that prioritize narrow economic concerns over lively, planetary natures. In this view, nature is subordinated and instrumentalized or, as Val Plumwood has written, "we lose track of it" (2002, 99).

SMS deposits form at hydrothermal vents when magma-heated mineral solutions, hot enough to melt lead, discharge into cool deep water and precipitate. Building over time, they form mineral-rich chimneys that can rise 45 meters over the seabed (SPC 2013, 11). Mining corporations are interested in the potential yields of individual chimneys, which can average around 276 tons of massive sulphides per year (Koslow 2007, 17). Beyond their mineral yield value, vents are habitats for extraordinary communities of extremophiles, such as chemosynthetic dependent organisms that use hydrogen sulphide as energy. These are the least understood ecosystems on the planet (Earle 2016; Van Dover et al. 2011). Chemosynthetic extremophiles form the basis of a vent food web that supports such organisms as mollusks, gastropods, tube-dwelling worms, sea anemones, and crustaceans (Judd 2016, 9; Van Dover et al. 2011, 2). Larval stages of these drift the currents to colonize vent and fall sites where they find islands of nutrition and hard substrate on which to attach. Excessive hunting by whalers and fisheries has decreased the number of large falls that make it to the seafloor. DSM would further diminish substrate options by destroying vent sites and removing seabed nodules. Drifting the widening distances between fewer sites would amplify life cycle vulnerabilities for colonizing organisms.

Governments and miners do not have adequate benchmarks to determine the extent of likely damage from DSM across complex ecologies and their intra-actions with material temporalities. Biological communities vary from sediment-dwellers to free-floaters or swimmers. Some transition seasonally and others inhabit different zones at different physical stages of their life cycles. Ecologies also interact with temporal variations ranging from deep, ancient, and slow-moving benthic and abyssal waters through to the faster moving currents and turnovers of pelagic layers. Decades long in duration, the 24/7 DSM exploitations soon to be licensed by UNCLOS will intra-act with these complexities.

With limited knowledge of the ocean's chemosynthetic and sunless worlds, it is impossible to accurately gauge DSM's impacts over diverse temporal scales. Communities found on, and around, manganese nodules are most vulnerable. In the slow time of the abyssal ocean, manganese nodules grow just millimeters every million years (Colazingari 2008, 118). Delicate nodule life-forms need the extremely slow growing nodules as hard substrate for living. In the sedimentary surrounds, worms and bacteria equally need this slow time of the deep. DSM will remove large tracts of the abyssal plain, suctioning up these phenomenally slow-growing nodules beyond any chance of foreseeable recovery.

Chances of recovery are better for naturally ephemeral vent ecologies that already exist in volatile environments characterized by frequent eruptions and chimney collapse. However, the cycles of rupture and recolonization to which vent ecologies are accustomed will be dwarfed by 24/7 mining operations. Nautilus acknowledges that the direct impacts to vent and other seafloor habitats will be severe (Nautilus Minerals Nuigini Ltd. 2008, 25), as does the ISA (Van Dover et al. 2011). Mining is a violence of immediacy to which creaturely communities can barely adapt in time, if at all. It also creates long-range harms that gradually unfold over time—a process captured by Rob Nixon's notion of "slow violence" (2011). It is hard to apprehend or bear witness to the consequences of mining over decadal and greater time spans, as this takes resources, people, money, expertise. The environmental harms of mining are, in the words of Nixon, "image weak," their temporal distances making them impossible to see (2011).

Environmental harms are compounded by poorly developed regulatory frameworks and insufficient knowledge of ecologies, material temporalities, and their interactions. Lack of such knowledge has not delayed the ISA from already granting twenty-nine exploration licenses to corporations and their sponsoring states, covering over a million square kilometers of the international seabed area in the Pacific, Atlantic, and Indian oceans. In the case of PNG's continental shelf jurisdiction, the government's 1992 Mining Act and the Environment Act of 2000 are not considered robust and lack sufficient protections for deep ocean ecologies (Blue Ocean Law and PANG 2016; Hunter and Taylor 2013). Despite the paucity of ecological information and poorly developed regulatory management and protections, the government of PNG and Nautilus are soon to commence mining the continental shelf beneath PNG's EEZ. In what seems a radical reversal of the precautionary principle, the ISA and miners view the lack of scientific knowledge of deep-sea life as no reason to delay progress of the DSM frontier. It is as if capitalism's resource ecology was in need of more preservation than living ecologies.

Seabed Frontiers in the Making

Despite decades of resource extractions, the promissory economic and social gains to nations such as PNG are scant. DSM also troubles those who recall community and ecological devastations and violences inflicted by terrestrial mining. The global and historic pattern of such events signals intent. As one flank of the extractivist strategy routinely disassembles natures and communities, the other hastens make-do collaborations between ill-equipped governments and international resource corporations. Anna Tsing describes how such resource frontiers are created when "the small and the great collaborate in a climate of chaos and violence" and forests, rivers, and seas are wrested "from previous livelihoods and ecologies to turn them into wild resources, available for the industries of the world" (2003, 5100).

Generations of PNG's communities continue to experience the chaos and violence of resource frontiers, including the island province of Bougainville, one of the most beautiful islands in the equatorial West Pacific. Panguna mine, operated by Bougainville Copper (now Rio Tinto), devastated the island's human and other communities through the 1970s and 1980s. The superlatives are justified. Donger doors are left squeaking in the wind as mining companies walk away from costly reparations, as Rio Tinto did in Bougainville. Governments and human and other communities are all left vulnerable when mining companies walk away leaving costly environmental damages, excavated mountainsides looted of ore, forests destroyed, and poisoned rivers flowing into the sea.

Solwara 1 is located in the Bismarck Sea, north of Bougainville, where it inaugurates the commercial appropriation of the deep seabed as a new resource frontier. As with terrestrial resource frontiers described by Tsing, DSM draws parallels with gold rush times, "shaped to the model of other wild times and places," a techno-frontier realizable because of industrial technology and "always open and expanding" (2003, 5101). The temporal, not yet mapped nature of terrestrial resource frontiers now extend seaward (Tsing 2003). Technoscientific deep-sea machinery mobilize across the largely unmapped, unsettled, yet territorialized seafloor. Ephemerality also attaches to frontier processes at the bottom of the sea where miners will move from spent tenement to next tenement, following the mineral commodity flows wherever the resources and fluid physicality of the deep sea allow. Resource frontiers are facilitated by difficult to enforce and less than rigorous environmental regulations (Blue Ocean Law and PANG 2016). Legislative frameworks loosely governing the DSM industry are, in the case of PNG's national law, still in development and fail to address the particular nature of DSM (Blue Ocean Law and PANG 2016). In the case of the ISA's international seabed jurisdiction, exploration licenses are granted in a self-regulating environment with the mining code still in draft. In contrast to the environmental violences and inchoate environmental protections attending the DSM resource frontier, the financial, contractual, and research strategies of mining corporations are meticulous.

Imaginaries at Sea

In this chapter's opening sequence, the deep ocean emerges as a cogenerative, transitional realm thrumming with material agency and life. This diverges from the Western imaginaries circulating beneath law, and influencing neoliberal capitalist expansions, where nature is represented as passive and instrumentalized. Such imaginaries seep into the seabed provisions of Parts V and VI of UNCLOS: the ocean is abstracted and flattened, and life-forms with no immediate commercial value are blindsided and discursively partitioned. They also guide Part XI and the ISA's mandate to exploit seabed minerals in conflict with conservation provisions, such as Article 145, and those throughout Part XII.

Examination of the ideological foundations of legal imaginaries is therefore critical if, as Klaus Bosselmann observes, the gap between the "promise of environmental protection and ecological realities [is] to be bridged" (Bosselmann 2010, 2425). Astrida Neimanis, Cecilia Åsberg, and Suzi Hayes rightly state that how we understand nature and the environment has "implications for laws, policies and individual actions" and "imaginaries are thus crucial to environmental governance" (Neimanis, Åsberg, and Hayes 2015, 482). In this sense, interrogating the Enlightenment imaginaries still influencing ocean law, and the DSM corporations it privileges, elicits insights to the relational and representational limitations at the heart of UNCLOS's conservation failures.

Foregrounding the lively, physical ecologies and relationalities of the deep sea is just one strategy against the reductive imaginaries driving resource frontier expansions. Developing knowledges and imaginaries for the unseen and unrepresented relational subjects of the deep calls for rigorous imagination. Canonic feminist conceptual tools for building relational, situated, and embodied knowledges facilitate development of such knowledges and imaginaries. With this approach, I draw on the ocean itself as a knowledge provider: sieving oceanographic text to imaginatively draw out sticky salt water solutions and relations, to feel and comb through slimy sediment, and to push through open gills, down ridges, across basins, athwart currents and time. Attending to the ocean's watery, material phenomenologies challenges Cartesian essentialisms by bringing visibility to the connections and coconstitutions across ocean bodies, creaturely and otherwise. New imaginaries emerge through situating attention in the transitional nature of ocean habitats, the diverse and temporally varying living conditions, vulnerabilities, and relationalities. De-partitioning the legal ocean amplifies the thick relations that intra-act in more-than-human watery worlds. Stacy Alaimo's "transcorporeality" provides an important figuration for thinking through the ethical implications of materialities that transition across porous, salt-watery bodies and ocean ecologies (2010, 2014). Such material flows result from, and disrupt, the enactments and discursive partitionings of law. Interpolating more-than-human considerations, transcorporeal material flows, and temporalities into the discursive practices of law and economics also debunks imaginaries that fictionalize humans as somehow separate from nature. I propose building relational ocean knowledge and imaginaries by thinking of law and capitalism's resource frontiers as ecological elements. This approach builds on Lorraine Code's "ecological thinking" methodology, which expands knowledge constituencies and interrogates conditions, influences, and vested interests of sedimented and exclusionary knowledge claims (2006). Just as the intra-actions of time, chemical elements, individual marine creatures, and ocean currents influence the habitability of ocean environments, so too the enactments of law and the activities of resource corporations influence particular conditions of habitability.

Bringing law, ecologies, and other ocean lives and relations onto the same plane of consideration generates flash points for law's radically violent, habitat-changing practices to be named and contested. Insisting on recognizing the missing living real of ocean inhabitants in negotiations for DSM expansions would entail imaginatively discerning their indescribable, mysterious, temporal, and vulnerable qualities and coconstituencies: Where legal imaginaries partition lives, draw out the relations across bodies, materials, and zones and interpolate the vibrant existence of these into legal text. Where there is backgrounding or voiding, raise into clear view the liveliness that disputes its erasure. Where there is a propensity to see other lives as frozen in time, explore and find stories across life stages, taking the longer considered view over time against claims of urgency. As a counter to tropes of vastness and nature's endless resilience, imagine and speak of habitability, conditions of vulnerability, livability, and the intimate exchanges that make these possible.

What emerges through this chapter is a sense of how the filaments of an ocean justice approach need to navigate expanding resource frontiers and human populations, climate change, ocean ecological decline, and our shared needs for habitability differently conditioned. In these early days for ocean justice, I propose thinking with the ocean's midnight aphotic depths, invoking it to bubble up through a juridical imaginary that would deny its lively worlds and our relations with them. Throughout this chapter, I work imaginatively and iteratively to unfold insights from marine sciences, interrogate corporate representations of DSM resource frontiers, and challenge development imperatives that would hasten ecological ruins. As Nautilus will likely be the first to get mining machinery off the barges and down to the seabed, I interrogate its

Solwara 1 operation in terms of how DSM corporations represent ocean nature and mediate their deep-ocean relations. Later, the chapter interrogates certain provisions of UNCLOS for a sense of how the law operates discursively in the service of resource corporations.

Solwara 1 and the DSM Resource Frontier

Nautilus's website promotes Solwara 1 as pioneering, masterly, economically beneficial, and ultimately necessary for the ongoing supply of raw materials essential to global manufacturing. Environmental tropes familiar to terrestrial mining are relied on: the mining area is small against the scale of the vast oceanic seabed; ocean nature is resilient, species return, places recover. For Pacific island nations with limited natural resources, the ocean is promised as "a cornucopia of goods and services" (Baker and Beaudoin 2013, 43); DSM is good for communities and will significantly increase small island nations' GDP (Spicer 2013).

With the impossibility of a firsthand view, knowledge of Solwara 1 operations relies in part on Nautilus's representations. Demonstration videos available on the company's website depict DSM on, and in, a natureless sea. The production vessel is stationed on a still surface. "State-of-the-art" remotely operated vehicles (ROV) are lowered into the ocean: auxiliary cutter, bulk cutter, and a collecting machine. On a flood-lit seafloor, machines maneuver back and forth on caterpillar tracks as they cut, scrape, and crush the seabed into a big pile of mineralized material. In this disembodied, industrialized ocean a few small specks of matter are visible but no fish or plumes of disturbed material. The machines are alone.

A sense of urgency accompanies the promotional literature: an imperative to realize the DSM future, its bold progress is not to be impeded. DSM's technological future is material and yet, as Rob Nixon observes in his example of the environmentally risky offshore oil industry, "the unwise risks are immaterial" (2011, 269). Potential environmental violences and unmanageable disasters are unseen in accounting ledgers and noticeably kept from view on Nautilus's website. Neither is there evidence that the company makes comparable investments in promoting pioneering, state-of-the-art emergency and clean-up technologies.

Joystick Mining

DSM machinery embodies the intensely material nature of the deep ocean and its creaturely forms. Resembling knobbly, hard-shelled crustaceans that have evolved to survive harsh benthic conditions, Nautilus's "pioneering" deep-seabed machinery gleams with Bauhausian biomimicry. It is a reminder of just how much humans have learned from other animals in terms of function-fit design and adaption to environmental and material challenges. DSM machinery is just as at home on the seabed as the ghost crabs it will obliterate. The remote ingenuity of ROVs excises from memory and sensitivity the creaturely inspiration of our design borrowings as well as the natural habitats in which we interfere. Through the disembodiment of our capitalist enterprises, and in the quest to sate material pleasures, we have generated the cyborg, to use Donna Haraway's figuration; it is our prosthetic limb reaching to grab at the seabed: "The machine is us, our processes, an aspect of our embodiment" (1991, 180).

In another Nautilus promotional video, a group of men in high-visibility work gear operate ROVs from their consoles—joystick mining. Stefan Helmreich (2009) refigures Haraway's cyborg as a "submarine cyborg" that mediates worlds, bridging the differences between interior and exterior, water and air. The submarine cyborg "makes explicit the physical character of information translations necessary to maintain the integrity of self-regulating entities" (Helmreich 2009, 214–15). While it mediates the world in the name of science, its information yields chart future quarries for corporate exploitation. The DSM cyborg follows, landing heavily on the seabed, armored to prevail against the deep ocean's physical challenges. This variation of the submarine cyborg is incurious about its situatedness and seeks not so much to mediate worlds, but, rather, to deploy different worlds against one another.

Juridical Seabed Imaginaries

UNCLOS also mediates worlds through its discursive representations of the ocean and as arbiter of which marine life-forms count. It facilitates the development of the seabed resource frontier and, through structural and discursive elements, detaches from the impacts of its own operation. UNCLOS's juridical scaffolding is achieved by territorializing ocean space. But these are zones of an imaginary vulnerable to disruption by the living ocean world. In the territorialized, essentialist version, the ocean functions as a voluminous fluid space hosting living and nonliving resources, water, and basin geologies. This contrasts with the living, dynamic ocean, which is cogenerative with, and through, creaturely lives and material temporalities. Delineations of the juridical ocean's territorial zones defract and disassemble in the ripple and chop of watery life transitions. Across the water column, law's vertical carves separate the territorial sea, EEZ, and high seas. However, these boundaries become more ambiguous as rising sea levels and melting ice edges unsettle baseline certainties.

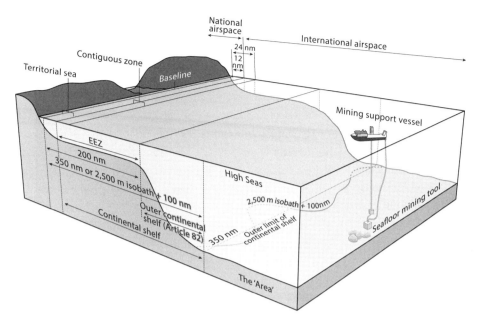

FIGURE 1.1. International maritime jurisdictions. Cartographer: Chris Orten. Credit: International Seabed Authority (ISA).

As land transitions to seafloor, living creatures with tails, tentacles, or flagella migrate, jettison, and float their lives, indifferent but vulnerable to activities condoned by UNCLOS's enactments of territory. Law's horizontal carves separate the seabed beneath the territorial sea, the seabed of the continental margin and the deep-ocean seabed beyond national jurisdiction, known as the Area (see figure 1.1). Under the regime of the Area, over 40 percent of the planet's surface is appropriated by international law for potential mining activities.

Presiding over this international resource frontier is the ISA—seabed real estate broker and environmental sheriff.

Although the ISA has already issued several exploration licenses, full-scale mining production on the international seabed is a few years away. DSM on continental shelf jurisdictions is here: in late 2017 Japan commenced hydrothermal mineral mining at sixteen hundred meters, and Solwara 1 is expected to commence commercial production in 2019–20, providing Nautilus Minerals secures the necessary financing. UNCLOS Part VI is the continental shelf regime that provides states with exclusive sovereign rights to explore and exploit the natural resources of their continental shelf—an area extending two hundred miles outward from the baseline from which the territorial sea is measured (UNCLOS, Article 76). Through complex geophysical assessments and calculations that determine outer extended continental shelf areas, some nations also enjoy extended jurisdiction out to a maximum of 350 nautical miles. Royalties will be payable to the ISA, in relation to mining production in these extended regions, because such activity encroaches into the Area, which is deemed as common heritage of mankind.

A state's legal right to a continental shelf is based on the principle of natural prolongation established in the *North Sea Continental Shelf Cases* (North Sea Continental Shelf 1969) and adopted in UNCLOS Article 76(1) as "the natural prolongation of its land territory." Through this principle, the law rerenders the continental shelf as a terrestrial extension, despite it lying under thousands of meters of water. Complex, intra-active ocean elements and relations are effectively redacted in a governance framework based on law of the land. UNCLOS Article 77 then establishes what a coastal state can do with the continental shelf and seabed within its jurisdiction.

The Seabed and the Sessile One

Close reading of Article 77 demonstrates how the discursive partitions and reductivisms of law render ocean nature as a territory fit for mining. In the first instance, Article 77(4) defines natural resources as being "mineral and other non-living resources of the seabed and subsoil together with living organisms belonging to sedentary species." Like the indiscriminate haul of a purse-seine fisher, UNCLOS vanishes diverse, lively organisms, bundling them with minerals and other elements in the catchall category of "natural resources." Article 77(4) defines living natural resources as "living organisms belonging to sedentary species, that is to say, organisms which, at the harvestable stage, either are immobile on or under the seabed or are unable to move except in constant physical contact with the seabed or the subsoil." If a marine creature's status is sedentary, UNCLOS deems it "harvestable," a euphemistic term likening commercial sedentary fisheries to gathering garden fruit. Legal scholars note that the inclusion of living resources, such as sedentary species, came late in the development of the continental shelf regime (Rothwell et al. 2015, 183). The regime developed as a response to the offshore resource frontier that emerged in the 1940s and to pressure from coastal nations and mining industrialists seeking to secure exclusive rights to the hydrocarbon resources on their continental shelf. Conservation of living organisms is, therefore, not a strong feature of a regime based on resource exploitation. Although a broad duty to conserve living organisms is generally provided in Part XII and, more specifically, by Articles 192 and 193, the provisions are ambiguous in relation to creatures residing in the continental shelf area and even more so in relation to the extended continental shelf area. Under Parts V and VI of UNCLOS, a coastal state has the right to explore and exploit nonliving resources and living creatures of their seabed. Part V, the EEZ regime, includes conservation objectives but expressly excludes sedentary fisheries from such consideration (UNCLOS, Article 68). As Donald Rothwell and Tim Stephens note, if they so wish, "coastal states may exploit [sedentary fisheries] to extinction" (2010). In relation to Article 77, conservation of living creatures is not even a distinct option. Read narrowly, Article 77(1) expressly states that a coastal state's sovereign rights over their continental margin are limited to exploration and exploitation of natural resources. In other words, the range of legal actions available excludes conservation. With luck, but no guarantee of effect, this would be balanced by the general environmental protection obligations of Article 192 and via conservation obligations arising from the CBD and other international environmental law instruments.

While UNCLOS's seabed conservation options are unclear, Article 77 goes on to discursively construct a legal setting in which the livability conditions for living organisms is subordinated and disappeared in the interests of mining extraction. One way it achieves this is to apply a veil of ambiguity to the sedentary species impacted by Article 77(4), many of which have life cycles complicated by different bodily forms and stages of mobility and attachment. Beyond such traits as free-swimming or sedentary, UNCLOS is unclear on the distinction between the living resources of the seabed and the EEZ's water column. The sessile ones of UNCLOS Part VI and the creatures swimming freely through the watery EEZ of Part V may be the same marine entity at different life stages. It is too bad for creatures in their sedentary stage that they do not spend more time as larvae in the EEZ, where they might at least have Article 56(1) and some human self-interest conserving their numbers. As it is, they do not enjoy protection under the continental shelf regime. Having conservation measures available for some creatures but not all, based on where they inhabit and their commercial value, is one way that UNCLOS partitions lives. Another way is through the partitioning of the life stages of creaturely lives. For the purposes of ensuring regional cooperation in managing and conserving commercially valuable fish species, UNCLOS acknowledges that some species found in the EEZ have different life stages across national jurisdictions. For example, UNCLOS Articles 66 and 67 apply respectively to anadromous species, such as salmon, and catadromous species, such as eels. As well, there is an acknowledgment in Article 77(4) that creatures transition at different stages; this is qualified, however, by the word "harvestable." The provision refers not to a creature's own life stages, but to the stage at which it becomes useful to humans—when it becomes *harvestable*.

The sessile ones referred to in Article 77(4) have different experiences and needs over different life stages, and not all of the stages find them fixed or sedentary. Bivalves, for example, spend a portion of their lives dispersed as larvae, floating the briny transport of midocean currents or drifting along-axis currents at the seafloor (Baker et al. 2010). Some may settle nearby; others will drift afar to perhaps colonize new islands of vent deposits, such as at the SuSu Knolls. Once the bivalve larva finds mineral, spent flesh, or bone substrate to settle, it transitions into a sedentary filter feeder, deriving nutrient from the ocean waters. Lively relationships are then developed as much with the water column as with its seabed scaffold.

The difficulty of accommodating different life-forms and stages into Article 77(4) can be attributed principally to the subordination of conservation needs to powerful development interests. Under UNCLOS's discursivities, when the bivalve attaches to the seafloor it becomes both harvestable for the purposes of sessile fisheries and rendered invisible for the purposes of mining's removal of the seabed. As a discursive seabed fixture, the bivalve is redacted along with complex imbrications of other creaturely lives and relations. Refiguring the bivalve in this way also brackets out the creature's previous larval self and severs its relationship with the water column. Beyond its discursivity, UNCLOS physically and ecologically interacts with the ocean by licensing destruction of biotic life, hollowing habitats, and instituting only partial ecological protections. In the absence of express conservation obligations, the seabed is prepared for mining.

Countering the Accounts: Life Stages, Livability, and Vulnerability

Among the strategies for countering UNCLOS's instrumentalized representations and flattened accounts of nonhuman nature is the insistent assertion and interpolation of lively ocean worlds into novel and more just legal discursivities. Simultaneously reading scientific texts and discerning material relationalities, livability conditions, and vulnerabilities within the legal operation of UNCLOS indeed allows alternative imaginaries to stream through the gaps left by law's renderings, calling out its distortions and limitations. Such ruptures may create conceptual openings for recognizing and developing more-than-human responsibilities.

Against the law's ocean, myriad lives emerge daily to squirm, wriggle, pump, and glide from seabed to surface, entraining sediment particles as they rise. It is the largest migration of animals on the planet. Searching for food and avoiding predators, they rise in the shelter of night to the moonlit surface, coming through very real physical boundaries, such as the thermocline and halocline. Dawn signals a necessary dive and sink back to the safety of darkness. Seasonal rains of detritus and fall arrivals reconstitute the seabed with pulses of nutrition. Seeping through the seabed and cracked rocks, cold seawater from the water column travels several kilometers below to mix with the chemicals and minerals of magmatic fluids. Mineralized, slightly acidic solution, heated to around four hundred degrees, returns to the seafloor, crosses the seabed divide, and discharges up into the water column. In this way the seabed is always dissolving, reconstituting, and co-elemental with the water column, as ocean. Imagining the seabed in this way, through its relationalities and sensitive to the interactions of creaturely life, water, lithics, and dynamics, troubles legal abstractions and cultivates both intimately relational and more expansive planetary imaginaries. This is thinking ecologically, reconfiguring, rethinking relationships all the way down (Code 2006).

Creatures move through the salt-watery dimensions of ocean and transition at different life stages, which may manifest as eggs, juveniles, larval, adulthood, and older age. Life-forms, including humans, all transition and, as we do, the experiences of vulnerability and conditions of livability change depending on which life stage we are at and such factors as material resources. Martha Fineman takes up the condition of vulnerability in the context of legal subjecthood to conceptualize an enduring aspect of the human condition (Fineman 2008, 8; also see Fineman and Grear 2013). As Anna Grear (2015) notes, while Fineman's theory developed within the context of human rights, it can be repurposed to include the enduring vulnerabilities of other planetary lives, including, I suggest, oceanic ones. Situating vulnerability into ocean realms requires paying attention to the transitioning life stages of creatures and the physical, material, and social conditions needed for livability. For example, seabed sediment is nurturing ooze for eggs and larvae but also provides a condition of livability for free-swimming adults. Against the development imperatives of UNCLOS, how might an ecologically tilted imaginary guide ocean legalities and generative practices that respect and respond to conditions for livability?

Thinking through the lens of vulnerability has relational potential across human and other worlds. Imagining different conditions of livability in deep ocean also suggests turning down the human register a little in order to discern ocean differences with sensitivity. Absence of sunlight, or the dense pressure caused by cubic kilometers of moving seawater, are often seen as conditions against which deep-sea creatures have had to adapt. Through a different lens, those same elements also enable life as conditions of livability. Pressure functions like a great muscle around each organism, providing containment of organs, holding bodies together. Moving up through the water column to escape mining plumes is no option for slow-growing, slow-moving deep-sea creatures whose only escape is sideward across the ocean floor and bottom layer of seawater. Darkness, too, enables life in the benthos. Rather than a state that creatures have had to adapt to, creaturely existence depends on darkness to provide camouflage from predators, keep temperatures cool, and to provide the conditions for bioluminescent communication between creatures. Alaimo's description of life at this depth as a "violet black ecology" unmoors heliocentric models of human sovereignty by situating creaturely livability in a vast aphotic realm (Alaimo 2014, 235).

Under the 24/7 regime of DSM, the lights will not be switched off for years, and in this process organisms vulnerable to light may be damaged; others, dependent on their violet black habitat, will migrate away (Bashir et al. 2012; Nautilus Minerals Nuigini Ltd. 2008). How might these operations interfere with the daily cycles of the sea? How might the diurnal migrators (small creatures, zooplanktons), who move from depths to the surface, experience the churned plume of chemical and mineral particles? How might the sparse detritus rain that makes it all the way from the surface to the floor interact with the plume material? What new blend of chemicals, minerals, and toxic potentials will constitute the seabed surface once the mining machines depart? How might the sessile ones filter the fine balance of organic, chemical, and mineral nutrients they need? How might the continuous engine sounds of the ROVs interfere with the sonic frequencies sea creatures use to communicate and navigate? Chemosynthetic organisms are elementally sensitive to chemical environments and traces at depth, finding new substrates through chemical signals. How might DSM interrupt this chemical communication as they drift the currents seeking new vent substrates to colonize?

Bearing Witness

Unable to dwell in the deep ocean or witness its habitats, relations, and intra-actions firsthand makes us significantly reliant on marine scientific accounts. Creating alternative ocean imaginaries, therefore, requires reading such accounts deeply and imagining with "epistemic humility," as Code suggests (2006, 207). In the interests of ocean justice, building knowledge and new imaginaries requires informed speculation in the interstitial spaces of science and law. Lively transitional materialities, creatures, and relations coalescing as ocean nature are poorly represented in development-focused environmental reports and governance instruments. Bringing them into visibility may require stretching epistemic texts beyond taxonomic and scientifically framed enquiries or binary representations. Bearing witness to what's missing might be a matter of reading these accounts closely to discern vested interests and unasked questions. Which elements in legislation or policy keep the living ocean beyond view, and what are the operative ideas underwriting "patterns of legitimacy and credibility and their opposites" (Code 2006, 29)? In the self-regulating environment of DSM, bearing witness might also be to discern absences in the facts or methodologies of environmental impact assessments. Different, situated sea-truthings may emerge through iterative processes that take seriously yet challenge the representations and accounts of legislators, miners, scientists, and consumers.

Conclusion: Taking Time

We humans are intimately in a soak with the more-than-human ocean world. At a time when planetary environmental systems are in stress and decline, there is a vital place for imaginaries with which we might all navigate and transition. Thinking and imagining relationally and ecologically cultivates more sensitive interactions with ocean ecologies. We might also situate more prudently the intensity of our demand for material stuff in the context of creaturely livability and vulnerability. How might law transition toward alternative governance approaches that enable and sustain conditions of ocean habitability? There is a compelling place in law to better recognize the different registers of temporality. Legal apparatuses must be put in place that acknowledge life stages and associated vulnerabilities of creatures on the same plane as the commercial claims of corporations. Time also soaks through a measured precautionary approach. Rather than a mine first, observe and legislate later approach, wisdom suggests taking the longer view or, as Rachel Carson encouraged, waiting "an extra season or two" (cited in Code 2006).

Thinking ecologically with the deep ocean and its long, slow-time relationalities requires, as Code (2006) noted, placing time into our observations and responses. Astrida Neimanis and Rachel Loen Walker conceptualize such a watery slow time, inflected with generative, transcorporeal materiality, as "thick time" (2014). At benthic and abyssal depths, ocean waters transition in such thick time, very slowly but generatively. It is in the long-range time of this high-pressured old ocean that vent ecologies and delicate nodule life-forms grow. Reliant on their sedimentary surrounds, worms and bacteria equally need this slow time of the deep to exist. Thinking with the seafloor calls for meditations on slow formation transitions at the edge of stillness: thinking with the sessile ones.

References

Alaimo, Stacy. 2010. *Bodily Natures: Science, Environment and the Material Self.* Indianapolis: Indiana University Press.

Alaimo, Stacy. 2014. "Violet-Black." In *Prismatic Ecology: Ecotheory beyond Green,* edited by Jeffrey Jerome Cohen, 233–51. Minneapolis: University of Minnesota Press.

Baker, Elaine, and Yannick Beaudoin, eds. 2013. "Deep Sea Minerals, vol. 2: Deep Sea Minerals and the Green Economy." Report. December. Nouméa, New Caledonia: Secretariat of the Pacific Community.

Baker, Maria C., Eva Z. Ramirez-Llodra, Paul A. Tyler, Christopher R. German, Antje Boetius, Erik E. Cordes, Nicole Dubilier, Charles R. Fisher, Lisa A. Levin, Anna Metaxas, et al. 2010. "Biogeography, Ecology, and Vulnerability of Chemosynthetic Ecosystems in the Deep Sea." In *Life in the World's Oceans,* edited by Alasdair D. McIntyre, 161–82. London: Blackwell.

Bashir, Musa, Sung-hee Kim, Evangelia Kiosidou, Hugh Wolgamot, and Wei Zhang. 2012. "A Concept for Seabed Rare Earth Mining in the Eastern South Pacific." LRET Collegium 2012 Series. https://www.southampton.ac.uk/assets/imported/transforms/content-block/UsefulDownloads_Download/7C8750BCBBB64FBAAF2A13C4B8A7D1FD/LRET%20Collegium%202012%20Volume%201.pdf.

Batker, David, and Rowan Schmidt. 2015. "Environmental and Social Benchmarking Analysis of Nautilus Minerals Inc. Solwara 1 Project." Report. May. Nautilus Document Reference SL01-NMN-XEE-RPT-0180–001. Tacoma, WA: Earth Economics. http://www.nautilusminerals.com/irm/content/pdf/eartheconomics-reports/earth-economics-may-2015.pdf.

Blue Ocean Law and the Pacific Network on Globalisation (PANG). 2016. "Resource Roulette: How Deep Sea Mining and Inadequate Regulatory Frameworks Imperil the Pacific and Its Peoples." Report. June. Guam: Blue Ocean Law, PC. http://nabf219anw2q7dgn1rt14bu4.wpengine.netdna-cdn.com/files/2016/06/Resource_Roulette-1.pdf.

Bosselmann, Klaus. 2010. "Losing the Forest for the Trees: Environmental Reductionism in the Law." *Sustainability* 2 (8): 2424–48.

CBD (Convention on Biological Diversity). 1992. 1760 UNTS 69. Adopted June 5. New York: United Nations. https://www.cbd.int/doc/legal/cbd-en.pdf.

Code, Lorraine. 2006. *Ecological Thinking: The Politics of Epistemic Location.* New York: Oxford University Press.

Colazingari, Marco. 2008. *Marine Natural Resources and Technological Development: An Economic Analysis of the Wealth from the Oceans.* New York: Routledge.

Deep Sea Conservation Coalition. 2017. "Deep-Sea Mining Briefing Paper." July 31. http://www.savethehighseas.org/resources/publications/deep-sea-mining-briefing-paper.

Earle, Sylvia. 2016. "Deep Sea Mining: An Invisible Land Grab." *Mission Blue* blog post, July 20. https://www.mission-blue.org/2016/07/deep-sea-mining-an-invisible-land-grab.

Fineman, Martha Albertson. 2008. "The Vulnerable Subject: Anchoring Equality in the Human Condition." *Yale Journal of Law and Feminism* 20 (1).

Fineman, Martha, and Anna Grear, eds. 2013. *Vulnerability: Reflections on a New Ethical Foundation for Law and Politics.* Farnham, Surrey, UK: Ashgate.

Grear, Anna. 2015. "Towards New Legal Foundations? In Search of Renewing Foundations." In *Thought, Law, Rights and Action in the Age of Environmental Crisis*, edited by
Anna Grear and Evadne Grant, 283–313. Cheltenham, UK: Edward Elgar.

Haraway, Donna. 1991. "A Cyborg Manifesto: Science, Technology, and Socialist-
Feminism in the Late Twentieth Century." In *Simians, Cyborgs, and Women: The
Reinvention of Nature*, 149–81. New York: Routledge.

Helmreich, Stefan. 2009. *Alien Ocean, Anthropological Voyages in Microbial Seas*. Berkeley: University of California Press.

Hunter, Tina, and Madeline Taylor. 2013. "Deep Sea Bed Mining in the South Pacific."
Background paper. Queensland, Australia: Centre for International Minerals and
Energy Law, University of Queensland.

Independent State of Papua New Guinea. Mining Act. No. 20 of 1992.

Independent State of Papua New Guinea. Environment Act. No. 64 of 2000.

ISA (International Seabed Authority). 2012. "Environmental Management Needs for
Exploration and Exploitation of Deep Sea Minerals." Report of a workshop held by the
International Seabed Authority in collaboration with the Government of Fiji and the
SOPAC Division of the Secretariat of the Pacific Community in Nadi, Fiji, Novem-
ber 29 to December 2, 2011. ISA Technical Study No 10. Kingston, Jamaica: Interna-
tional Seabed Authority.

Judd, Simon. 2016. "Deep Sea Mining PNG's Sensitive Marine Ecosystems." *Mining
Monitor*, March. http://www.mpi.org.au/2016/04/deep-sea-mining-pngs-sensitive
-marine-ecosystems.

Koslow, Tony. 2007. *The Silent Deep: The Discovery, Ecology and Conservation of the Deep
Sea*. Chicago: University of Chicago Press.

Moore, Jason W. 2016. "The Rise of Cheap Nature." In *Anthropocene or Capitalocene? Nature,
History, and the Crisis of Capitalism*, edited by Jason W. Moore, 78–115. London: PM Press.

Nautilus Minerals Inc. 2016. Annual Information Form for the Fiscal Year Ended December 31, 2015. http://www.nautilusminerals.com/IRM/PDF/1735/AnnualInformationF
ormforfiscalyearendedDecember312015.

Nautilus Minerals Nuigini Ltd. 2008. "Environmental Impact Statement, Solwara 1 Project," vol. A: Main Report. September http://www.nautilusminerals.com/irm/content
/pdf/environment-reports/Environmental%20Impact%20Statement%20-%20
Main%20Report.pdf.

Neimanis, Astrida, Cecilia Åsberg, and Suzi Hayes. 2015. "Post-humanist Imaginaries."
In *Research Handbook on Climate Governance*, edited by Karin Bäckstrand and Eva
Lövbrand, 480–90. Cheltenham, UK: Edward Elgar.

Neimanis, Astrida, and Rachel Loen Walker. 2014. "Weathering: Climate Change and
the 'Thick Time' of Transcorporeality." *Hypatia* 29 (3): 558–75.

Nixon, Rob. 2011. *Slow Violence and the Environmentalism of the Poor*. Cambridge, MA:
Harvard University Press.

North Sea Continental Shelf Cases: *Federal Republic of Germany v. Denmark; Federal
Republic of Germany v. Netherlands*. February 20, 1969. ICJ Reports 3, 22.

Plumwood, Val. 2002. *Environmental Culture: The Ecological Crisis of Reason*. London:
Routledge.

Rio Declaration on Environment and Development. 1992. (Rio Declaration) (Annex 2). Report of the UN Conference on Environment and Development, Rio de Janeiro, June 3–14. UN Doc. A/CONF.151/26, vol. 1. Reproduced in *International Legal Materials* 31, no 4 (1992): 874–80.

Rothwell, Donald, Oude Elferink, Karen Scott, and Tim Stephens, eds. 2015. *The Oxford Handbook of the Law of the Sea*. Oxford: Oxford University Press.

Rothwell, Donald R., and Tim Stephens. 2010. *The International Law of the Sea*. Oxford: Hart.

SPC. 2013. "Deep Sea Minerals: Sea-Floor Massive Sulphides: A Physical, Biological, Environmental, and Technical Review (Vol. 1A)." Edited by Elaine Baker and Yannick Beaudoin. Secretariat of the Pacific Community (SPC). http://dsm.gsd.spc.int/public /files/meetings/TrainingWorkshop4/UNEP_vol1A.pdf.

Spicer, Wylie. 2013. "Legalising Seabed Access: Deep Sea Mining: Out of Our Depth." October 18, 2013. http://www.deepseaminingoutofourdepth.org/legalising-seabed -access/.

Tsing, Anna L. 2003. "Natural Resources and Capitalist Frontiers." *Economic and Political Weekly* 38 (48): 5100–5106.

UNCLOS (United Nations Convention on the Law of the Sea). 1982. UN Doc A/ Conf.162/122. December 12.

Van Dover, C. L., C. R. Smith, J. Ardron, S. Arnaud, Y. Beaudoin, J. Bezaury, G. Boland, D. Billett, M. Carr, G. Cherkashov, et al. 2011. *Environmental Management of Deep-Sea Chemosynthetic Ecosystems: Justification of and Considerations for a Spatially-Based Approach*. ISA Technical Study No. 9. Kingston, Jamaica: International Seabed Authority.

Yeats, Christopher J., Joanna M. Parr, Raymond A. Binns, J. Bruce Gemmell, and Steven D. Scott. 2014. "The SuSu Knolls Hydrothermal Field, Eastern Manus Basin, Papua New Guinea: An Active Submarine High-Sulfidation Copper-Gold System." *Economic Geology* 109 (8): 2207–26. http://econgeol.geoscienceworld.org/content/109 /8/2207.full.

2. HELD IN SUSPENSE

Mustard Gas Legalities in the Gotland Deep

ASTRIDA NEIMANIS

Mustard Gas, at Sea

Chemical weapons are direct descendants of the expansion of industrial chemistry in the nineteenth century followed by the amplification and rise of chemical engineering, capitalist economies, and modern warfare in the twentieth. Sulphur mustard, more commonly known as mustard gas, is one agent among many birthed through the complex tangles of the military industrial complex. First weaponized by German chemist Fritz Haber during World War I (also known as the "chemists' war"), mustard gas had killed or seriously injured more than a million people by war's end.[1] The chemical horrors of World War I were in part what stayed the widespread use of weaponized chemical agents when world war erupted for a second time in the late 1930s (Ndiyae 2007, 45). Yet, despite this show of restraint, the problem of chemical weapons lingered: following World War II, governments were left with the problem of what to do with stockpiled chemical munitions.

Water's impetus to dissolve other matters into its planetary bosom is part of a larger aqueous imaginary, whereby water serves the purpose of washing away human sins. As the Greek myth of the River Lethe reminds us, drinking from Lethe's waters enabled one to forget earthly life and all it had gathered (MacLeod 2013, 48). These powers of erasure and dissolution are connected to an imaginary of the ocean as unfathomable. As represented in monsters and other uncanny creatures at the outer corners of early maps, "here be dragons" signaled a void beyond knowledge. In this imaginary, which persists in various guises (Alaimo 2012; Helmreich 2009), the sea is not only a universal solvent, but also pure alterity (Mentz 2009). Those matters swallowed up by the

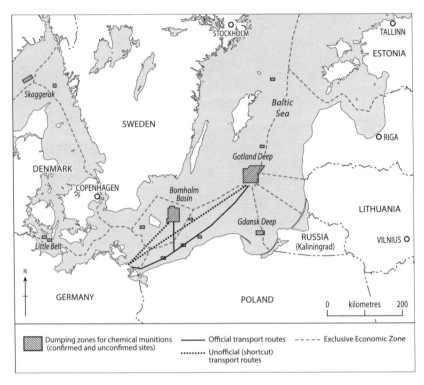

FIGURE 2.1. Map of dumping zones for chemical munitions in the Baltic Sea. Cartographer: Chris Orten. Reprinted with permission of Chemical Munition Search and Assessment (CHEMSEA) EU Baltic Sea Region (BSR) Project No. 69.

sea become part of its unknowable abyss—not only forgotten, but rendered unintelligible.

It should come as no surprise, then, that in a toxic materialization of this imaginary, several hundreds of thousands of tons of those chemical souvenirs of twentieth-century wars came to rest at the bottom of our planetary seas. Under a contemporary international legal regime—including the 1997 Chemical Weapons Convention that regulates the development, production, stockpiling, use, and destruction of chemical weapons, the 1972 London Convention and its 1996 Protocol on the dumping of waste at sea, as well as the more generalized United Nations Convention on the Law of the Sea (1982)—such relinquishing of hazardous waste to the oceanic abyss would be clearly prohibited; we will return to examine some of the specific provisions of these legal instruments below. Following World War II, however, such dumping was not only legal, but considered "a safe and sound technique for the disposal of hazardous waste" (Lott 2015, 61), and "the best and most practical solution" for disposing of unused munitions (Missiaen and Henriet 2002, 2).

Our contemporary reevaluation of the harms of dumping hazardous waste in the sea notwithstanding, it is worth noting that this midcentury surmisal is not entirely baseless. After all, not only did our aqueous imaginary posit oceans as beyond knowability (and thus somehow beyond a capacity to be harmed by us), but water's (somewhat erroneous) reputation as a "universal solvent" is also a fact of its chemistry. H_2O has a unique ability to dissolve both acids and bases, and, under the dilutional influence of massive amounts of ocean water, toxicants can undergo rapid hydrolysis. An abyssal imaginary is thus shored up by a kind of chemical "forgetting," too. This admission is neither to condone sea dumping as a good decision nor, certainly, to suggest that our current legal prohibitions are misguided. It is rather to serve as a reminder that the ocean is a special kind of dumping ground, where its layered, specific materialities determine the afterlives of relinquished human detritus.

Nor are all sea dumps equivalent, neither historically nor materially. While post–World War II caches of chemical weapons are scattered across the watery globe from the North Atlantic to the South Pacific, the meaning of each site is determined by local conditions: depth, water temperature, currents, local marine ecologies, and ongoing human interactions with those waters, to name but a few. Moreover, decision-making about these dumps implicates geopolitics, technologies, and territorial zones. This chapter is particularly interested in the European chemical weapons stocks that have come to lie on the floor of the Baltic Sea, in a basin known as the Gotland Deep. This basin carves out a ditch several hundred meters deep in the middle of the Baltic, roughly equidistant to the terrestrial nations of Sweden, Latvia, Lithuania, Poland, and Russia's enclave of Kaliningrad, and in close proximity to Germany and Denmark (see figure 2.1). Sweden's Gotland Island—famous for the Battle of Visby eight centuries ago—looms to the northwest, reminding us that war is nothing new to these waters, while the heavy commercial and recreational traffic of the present-day Baltic add multiple layers of anthropogenic incursion and dependence. In addition, while at some dumping sites near Denmark and Norway entire munitions-laden ships were scuttled whole, dumping in the Gotland Deep was more dispersed—not only in and around this basin, but also sprinkled overboard en route to their destined burial grounds from various points of terrestrial departure. As a result, accurate records of the number and location of sites or of total quantities dumped do not exist. Estimates nonetheless suggest that from two thousand to ten thousand tons of chemical munitions were sunk in and around this location, the majority containing mustard gas.

Three quarters of a century later, these chemical munitions are surfacing: in fishers' nets (causing injury and death to those making the haul), disguised as amber and washed up on the Baltic's white sandy beaches, in transnational research initiatives that reveal changed biomarkers for cod and mussels that swim in the regions of the dumpsites, in scattered spectacular news stories, and perhaps even (as suggested by inconclusive pathology reports by Swedish biologists) on the faces of a few dead seals, inadvertently caught in fishing gear and potentially exposed to the weaponized gases (Moreaus et al. 2016).

Indeed, while a marine abyss can hold all kinds of secrets, this does not mean that the ocean could fully fulfil its role as solvent for this toxic legacy; such powers were sadly overestimated. As cultural theorist Janine MacLeod (2013) points out, the myth of the River Lethe, noted above, is sometimes accompanied by the story of Mnemosyne—the river of memory. Just as readily as the ocean swallows up all we divest ourselves of, the sea is also understood as a repository of deep pasts—a well of remembrance. Against the slow dissolve of the Big Blue, then, these infrequent surfacings of chemical weapons (on fleshy bodies, in scientific research, and, imaginatively, via chapters such as this) ignite a different oceanic feeling: one of spectacular, if semisubmerged, violence now explosively reanimated. Pressing against a forgotten and unintelligible past is a clear-and-present danger.

Without a doubt, the actuality of chemical weapons littering the seabeds of this relatively shallow, heavily trafficked sea—a major source of food, commerce, and recreation for the sixteen million people who live along these densely populated shores—is disconcerting. In this chapter, however, rather than choose between the sea of slow dissolution and the spectacular upswell of its chemical reactivations, I want to dwell in the liminal suspension suggested by the presence of these weapons caches in the Gotland Deep. Drawing on various conceptual frames offered by environmental humanities scholars Stacy Alaimo, Peter van Wyck, and Michelle Murphy, I first explore some of the ways this state of suspension is both the driver and the result of tangled materialities that converge and emerge at these dump sites. I then examine how apparatuses of law and regulation also are part of these same currents of suspension. As we will see, although we might imagine the law as primarily concerned with fixity, the ocean legalities of the Gotland Deep illuminate how suspension's refusal to ever fully arrive also frames the legal regimes that might address these caches.

It is important to note that in drawing attention to a kind of suspension of legality itself in the Gotland Deep, my aim is not to criticize the incapacity of legal regimes to contain the ineffability of these weapons dumps. Instead, I wonder how this seeming inefficacy might be an invitation to rethink how ocean legalities could better live with suspension in the Anthropocene. In spite of important criticisms we might lodge against the discourse of the Anthropocene and its naming event (see, e.g., Crist 2013; Neimanis 2017; Todd 2015), the inclusion of this word in our twenty-first-century lexicon signals both a material inscription upon our planet as well as an epistemological watershed. It is an Anthropocene imaginary, after all, that in Kathryn Yusoff's words is "radically reorganizing" how we imagine time and our human relation to it (2017). Our current era is one where linear tales of cause and effect must give way to epistemologies of entanglement, latency, and a necessary suspension of certainty. While we may, more than ever, require both science and legal regimes of accountability, we are simultaneously confronted by situations where more facts do not necessarily mean more knowledge and where proliferating legal instruments struggle to capture the uncanny temporalities and tangles of the issues requiring redress. In this context, might dwelling in suspension also be an opportunity to consider what other legalities, politics, and accountabilities we might require in order to rise to this challenge?

Suspension as Precaution

In her article "States of Suspension: Trans-corporeality at Sea," feminist and queer environmental humanities scholar Stacy Alaimo begins by reminding us (via *Merriam-Webster*) of the various definitions of suspension: "To debar temporarily, especially from a Privilege; To hold in an undetermined or undecided state awaiting further information; To keep from falling or sinking by some invisible support as buoyancy; To keep fixed or lost (as in wonder or contemplation)" (Alaimo 2012, 476). Indeed, the concept of suspension can do important work. For example, as Alaimo notes, if we recognize limits to our human mastery over the more-than-human world "as a suspension of humanist presumptions," this might clear the way for "an epistemological–ethical moment that debars us from humanist privilege; we might be kept 'fixed or lost as in wonder or contemplation.'" Suspension, in Alaimo's parsing, might be "a pause in action," akin to the precautionary principle—the juridical and policy-oriented idea that codifies the more colloquial notion of "better safe than sorry." Given the unknowability that inhabits any ocean ontology, we may be well advised to pay more attention to what this precautionary principle—in both its legal and more commonsensical applications—might teach us as we learn to wait "an extra season or two" before making decisions whose consequences cannot be known in advance (Susan Reid, this volume, quoting Rachel Carson). In this sense, suspension can instill care and curiosity. Suspension can allow for assessment, judiciousness, and the opportunity to direct our actions more thoughtfully.

In pausing in the conceptual territory of suspension, Alaimo opens up important space—a more "capacious" kind of epistemology, as she calls it elsewhere (see Alaimo 2008)—for an appreciation of the filigree lineaments of connection that bind us in relations at once exceedingly fragile, delicate, and vulnerable to rearrangement yet also difficult to fully sever: we are bound to one another in our transcorporeality (to use Alaimo's key term for the transit of matters between bodies), in one way or another, for better or for worse.

Yet, if suspension really is akin to the "precautionary principle," as Alaimo suggests, this might also imply an eventual resolution: if we just wait long enough, information will come, the mists will clear, *we will know what to do*. As Alaimo puts it, we will be prudent; we will "await 'further information.'" Alaimo stresses that suspension here is not a state of inaction; rather, it holds the heavy labors required to stay our society's eager anthropocentric hand. To paraphrase Susan Reid (this volume), time soaks through the precautionary principle; in legal terms, it extends and torques the moment of decision and responsibility. But while the logic of precaution might be beyond reproach, this gesture of patience opens up a key question for further contemplation: is there nonetheless a risk that suspension might also suggest an eventual knowability and an epistemology of patience?[2] In other words, while suspension as prudence is a welcome invitation, we might look more closely at how the spaces and times of suspension, thus interpreted, might be inadequate to some of the tangled environmental challenges we currently face.

In the Gotland Deep, for example, where chemical weapons are currently *both* dissolving *and* resurfacing, patience may not be the orientation we require. If we look closely at the matters entangled within these weapons caches, what emerges is a nonlinear sense of time and a shifting idea of place. This benthic habitat resists a positivist mapping. The chemical agents themselves, as well as the bodies and milieus with which they intra-act, engender a murky site of environmental, social, political—and legal—inquiry, one without clear boundaries.[3]

Entangled Conditions of Suspension:
The Poison, the Sea, and the War

To make this point, we could begin with the matter of mustard gas itself. Sulphur mustard is a blistering agent, also known as a vesicant. Mustard gas is also classified as persistent, insofar as its relatively low level of volatility means it does not evaporate or disperse quickly. While its biomagnification through the food chain is not as dramatic as the case of persistent organic pollutants (POPs), it pervades the bodies it comes into contact with in ways often incalculable and/or unknown. For those bodies that come into contact with this potentially lethal toxin, its "insidious" qualities (Hoenig 2007, 1) complicate the time and place of contamination: symptoms only appear hours after exposure, but chronic effects can persist unpredictably for decades. Bodies require time as well as large investments of care. "Cause of death," in such cases, can resist a straight answer.

To complicate matters further, when set adrift into the elemental world of the nonhuman sea, the solidity of our knowledge of mustard gas measurement and effect begins to dissolve. Chemistry tells us that sulphur mustard is about twice as persistent in seawater, and thus slower to dissipate there, and that the corrosion rate of the steel canisters that contain the mustard gas is about 0.1 mm per year in seawater. But the Baltic is a special kind of sea. The exchange of water through its straits is quite limited, and this results in a rather brackish soup, five times less saline than most open ocean waters (Leppäranta and Myrberg 2009, 1) and not uniformly so. As salinity slips, so too do the metrics for measuring the rate of mustard gas dissolution; rates of leakage "cannot be estimated given present knowledge" (Beldowski et al. 2016, 86). Corrosion is also a multispecies affair, as the dissolution of the canisters is aided by the labors of hungry microbes. Yet, in the anoxic depths of the Baltic, there is very little bacterial activity (Carstensen et al. 2014). Moreover, in part thanks to a permanent halocline, and the topography of the seafloor itself, the water is also much colder in the Gotland Deep than elsewhere in this otherwise shallow sea (Wieczorek 2012, 4). As a result of these cold temperatures, the sulphur mustard can become encapsulated within a shell of itself. In time, it might solidify completely. Scientific estimates of the time frame of contamination risk from mustard gas range from none at all or already passed to several hundreds of years into the future. Causal claims themselves are subject here to ongoing dissolution. These chemical agents are thus suspended between a hastening of hydrolysis enacted by the sea and a torpor, or resistance to move on, solidified by the anoxic cold waters. In these murky depths, neither calculability nor containability of toxic threat ever quite arrives.

Entangled within these toxic materialities is also the time and place of the militarization of the sea. On one view, we might attempt to relegate the problem of chemical weapons to a militarized past from which we have moved on. We might narrate our push to atone for our folly, first with the Chemical Weapons Convention and other legal instruments (we will return to these below), then with transnational research and cooperation, culminating in private sector development of "off-the-shelf technology" to clean up these benthic messes, once and for all. In this version, "the war" and the militarization of the Gotland Deep are somehow contained in the time and space of the dumping itself.

Yet, the island of Gotland, adjacent to the basin, and its surrounding waters have been militarized for centuries. Even though, when asked, inhabitants of the island seem to know little about any kind of sunken chemical weapons, they live with war all around them, all the time (Neimanis, Neimanis, and Åsberg 2017). Island backroads are lined with ancient Viking runes, and the local museum animates stories of conquest and invasion going back to the beginning of the past millennium. In the public library hangs a massive tapestry commemorating the 1361 Battle of Visby. And, despite its tiny size, the Baltic seabed is home to literally thousands of shipwrecks—many of them souvenirs of wars past. In a more contemporary mode, a drive to the East Coast from the capital of Visby produces a chance encounter with a makeshift outdoor art gallery, where whimsical sculptures are built from old bomb casings and other military relics, likely washed up on Gotland's shores (Neimanis, Neimanis, and Åsberg 2017). And in late 2015 the Swedish government announced that due to increased geopolitical tensions between Western Europe and Russia, the island would be remilitarized and troops restationed there.

Can we be certain, then, that "the chemists' war" is in the past, when militarization worlds a tentacular existence? War infuses these benthic and littoral spaces, stretching the time of mustard gas back to gather earlier articulations of these tensions—but also pushes them forward, leaking into the future. War is not an event with a clear beginning and end, but a process. In the Gotland Deep, war is both sunken in a benthic trench of the past and also reanimated by the chemical burn on the snout of a seal. The militarization of bodies, places, and matters similarly seeps through space and time, keeping the question of war unresolved and in suspense.

Environmental Threat and Chemical Regimes of Living-in-Suspense

The matters of mustard gas, the sea, and the war bring to mind cultural theorist Peter van Wyck's analysis of environmental threat versus "risk." For van Wyck, threat is distinct from risk for two reasons. The first pertains to the noncalculability of threat. Drawing on the work of Francois Ewald, van Wyck avers that risk "is but a neologism of the insurance industry" (2003, 84). Risk assumes that whatever event we are speaking of "can be made part of an actuarial calculation" (86). We might also add, risk can be litigated and legislated, according to legalities of culpability where we can reasonably "get the story straight." However, the environmental risks with which we now grapple elude this calculability—which is why van Wyck instead calls them threats. Threat, as van Wyck underlines, is "nonlocalizable and noncalculable." Unlike risk, threat is "a lively and creative force" (xxi). Threat is always already at work, swimming among those ineffable dragons of the oceanic dissolve, never fully knowable or calculable.

Van Wyck's evaluation of threat thus holds the tension of suspension: present but incalculable, dormant but also animated, gone but still very much here. In other words, the resistance of threat to calculability (what we might call a certain and discrete knowability) is not the same as saying that threat does not exist; it is just that, in van Wyck's words, threat exists "above and below thresholds": below in the sense of operating "at and below the level of biology," but above in its "transnational" and "transgenerational" character, where effects by definition leak beyond the scope of what can be reasonably calculated (86).

Threat thus seems an apt way to describe chemical weapons in the Gotland Deep. For example, while biologists cannot detect much damage at the level of generic health effects of other marine organisms around the chemical dumpsites, they nonetheless record higher stress responses at organ, tissue, cellular and subcellular levels of cod and blue mussels (CHEMSEA 2013, 52)—in other words, "below the level of biology." Moreover, these dumps—unsettled by deep ocean currents, or brought to the surface in a fisher's net, or on a seal's whiskers—clearly traverse thresholds in space. Their threat is also transgenerational: while arsenic concentrations, shifts in microbial speciation, and chronic toxicity to vertebrates and invertebrates in the Gotland Deep cannot be modeled confidently, changes are already anticipated in the toxic threat of these corroding canisters. Threat already stretches incalculably, into the past and the future, where toxic dangers entangle with submerged but resurfacing militarisms. Scientists, for instance, admit the remote possibility of "terrorist recovery and reweaponisation of chemical agents" (Greenberg, Sexton, and Vearrier 2016) that lie beneath. In short, potential futures in the Gotland Deep, while undetermined and incalculable, will not arrive entirely unanticipated.

Moreover, the case of mustard gas in the Gotland Deep shows us that murky "threat" does not become more calculable "risk" simply by virtue of greater quantity, particularity, or specificity of data. When compared to many other chemical weapons dumps in the planet's seas, the Gotland Deep is a well-researched site. Thanks to extensive transnational research efforts, particularly in the previous decade, the scientific literature on Baltic Sea dumping is relatively robust. Despite incomplete records from the time of the dumpings, we still know that we are dealing with *this* chemical agent, intra-acting with *these* metal canisters, in *this* sea, at *these* depths, in *these* times. Yet—and this is the key point—this information does not render the situation calculable. Instead what we face is a continuously diffracting phenomenon, whereby variables multiply. Each new piece of information introduces more possibilities, but not necessarily more certainty. While CHEMSEA, the EU-financed Chemical Munitions Search and Assessment project, and similar research initiatives call for "further studies . . . especially for time trends" related to chemical contamination (2013, 82), they also admit the inconclusiveness of the models they are grappling with. A 2008 briefing paper by the European Parliament suggests that, "although much effort has been devoted to attempt to determine corrosion rates, the results have been ambiguous" (European Union 2008, 3), while environmental impacts of toxicity are variously described as "complex" (3) and "ambiguous" (4). This same report notes that "estimating an overall cost for the recovery and remediation of all dumped munitions in the Baltic Sea is problematic" (9). Or, as the CHEMSEA report states, chemical agents "represent scattered point sources of pollution of unknown magnitude and difficult to control. . . . The amount of available data does not enable predictions on the development of the situation" (2013, 82). Scientists call for more research, but in this epistemology of chemical threat in the watery deep, more data does not necessarily mean more knowledge.

To further elaborate this tension, we could turn to what feminist historian Michelle Murphy has called "chemical regimes of the living." In Murphy's exposition, this concept pertains primarily to the ubiquity of synthetic chemicals saturating everyday life. In such a regime, argues Murphy, "molecular relations extend outside of the organic realm and create interconnections with landscapes, production, and consumption, requiring us to tie the history of technoscience with political economy" (2008, 697). Similar to van Wyck's assessment of environmental threat that is nonlocalizable and noncalculable, Murphy's chemical regimes of the living describe distributed phenomena and thus are fundamentally uncontained. While greater awareness of our embeddedness in such regimes is relatively recent, Murphy reminds us that these entanglements are the slow accumulation of around two hundred years of industrial production. Elsewhere, Murphy explicitly describes the temporal dimension of these regimes as latency, or lag. "In temporal terms," Murphy writes, "latency names the wait for the effects of the past to arrive in the present. . . . It names how the past becomes reactivated. Through latency, the future is already altered" (2013, 106).

The idea of "chemical regimes of the living" thus provides a complementary way of understanding sulphur mustard dumpsites, and the war that they index, not as bounded in space and time, but as tangled infrastructures that make and are made by other bodies, times, places, and structures. They accumulate slowly, their reach is extensive and (again, unlike environmental risk) difficult to calculate. By drawing on Murphy's concept of chemical infrastructures, we discover that militarization is not compartmentalized from capitalism, science, recreation, or communication. Militarization participates in writing and rewriting our environments, including those at the bottom of the sea.

Although life at the bottom of this anoxic sea is relatively sedate, the lineaments of myriad activities (increased gas pipeline building, seabed mining, cable burying, drilling, scuba diving, and underwater research itself) extend to stir up an uncertain future that will also continue to activate chemical afterlives. These souvenirs of war thus condition and are conditioned by how these multiple disturbances might unfold. And, as the Baltic Sea suffocates from industrial pollution and agricultural runoff, it is no small irony that Fritz Haber, the German chemist credited for weaponizing sulphur mustard, went on to win a Nobel prize for his work on industrial chemical fertilizers in 1919. This is to say: if our concern is for the environmental well-being of these waters, our work today might not be to assess which is the greater threat to the Baltic—leaking chemical munitions or ongoing agricultural fertilizer runoff?—but rather to examine the ways in which these phenomenon are part of the same chemical regimes of the living, which are ineluctably wrapped up in regimes of war.

We could say, riffing on Murphy's own terminology: what we discover in the Gotland Deep are not just chemical regimes of the living, but also chemical regimes of living in suspense. My question, therefore, remains: how do we inhabit the productive space of suspension that Alaimo opens up when it is not temporary—something that, too, will pass—but rather fundamental, epistemological, and even ontological?[4] And to follow from that: what kind of conceptual but also legal or regulatory frameworks might accommodate such suspension?

Suspended Legalities

Generally, we humans don't like being held in suspense; our relationship to chemical weapons is no different. Thus, after the chemical horrors of the first World War, and the massive stockpiling (but restrained use) of chemical weapons in the second, world powers embarked upon the creation of legal frameworks that might limit future deployment.

The 1945 Potsdam Conference's plans for the demilitarization of Germany included the dividing up of its chemical weapons stores in order to destroy them—sometimes burned or buried in situ, but far more commonly dumped at sea. The most significant step taken toward the prevention of further chemical warfare, however, came with the Convention on the Prohibition of the Development, Production, Stockpiling, and Use of Chemical Weapons and on Their Destruction—also known as the Chemical Weapons Convention, or CWC, which entered into force in April 1997. The CWC's main aim is to eliminate, worldwide, an entire category of weapons of mass destruction and to prevent future rearmament. As its title suggests, the CWC is also concerned with the means of destruction of existing stockpiles. Indeed, perhaps affected by chemical memories slowly surfacing from Mnemosyne's waters, the CWC now explicitly bans any marine disposal of chemical warfare agents.

At the same time, these benthic wartime souvenirs are out of time with the legal regimes that want to call us to account. Primarily concerned with weapons produced after 1945, the CWC cannot do much to account for weapons already littering the seabed. Weapons produced before 1925 count simply as "toxic waste" demanding no responsibility for destruction, except as determined by national legislation, and perhaps more significantly, this waste is no longer subject to international oversight and monitoring. The same applies to weapons produced between 1925 and 1945 that the Technical Secretariat of the CWC has deemed "unusable"; no provisions enforce any kind of responsibility of removal. Ambiguity swims through many other paragraphs. For example, declarations of sea-dumping of weapons prior to 1985 is "optional" for states parties, and the CWC places no responsibility on the recovering or abandoning party of chemical weapons recovered from the sea at any time at all. Essentially, the CWC is silent on the destruction of sea-dumped weapons recovered after 1984 and similarly silent in regard to the remediation of weapons dumped at sea prior to 1972. In other words, in these silent shadows, the legal obligations of both those who manufactured and dumped the weapons, as well as those in whose waters they lie, remains suspended.

The issue of dumped weaponized chemicals, however, is not one of disarmament alone, but also one of environmental protection. When, in the latter half of the twentieth century, environmental concerns became part of new international legal frameworks, environmental protection for marine habitats was included. The most pertinent legal instruments for promoting and protecting ocean environments are the Convention on the Prevention of Marine Pollution by Dumping of Wastes and Other Matter, also known as the London Convention of 1972, and its follow-up (less permissive, more prohibitionist), the 1996 London Protocol. These are fleshed out with a number of more circumscribed instruments—the number and diversity of which index the complexity and tangled nature of this question.[5] In the specific case of the Baltic, marine environmental protection is also under the purview of the

1992 Convention on the Protection of the Marine Environment of the Baltic Sea Area, as administered by its governing body, the Helsinki Committee, or HELCOM. While these various regimes would certainly have prohibited the dumping of chemical weapons in the Gotland Deep, and while these legal tools have helped dramatically reduce dumpings since the mid-1980s, again, the weapons that rest in the Gotland Deep are out of time with these regimes. While these dumps work to mix and torque pasts, presents, and futures, legal accountability will not look back.

To disarmament and environmental pollution legislation we could also add the law of the sea. The 1982 United Nations Convention on the Law of the Sea (UNCLOS) informs these other frameworks and provides the context through which they should be read. It includes provisions for the protection and preservation of the marine environment, for example, and mandates that Baltic states cooperate in eliminating pollution and preventing or minimizing damage. Attending to pollution, such as that caused by the dumping of mustard gas seventy years ago in the Baltic Sea, however, would also be subject to conditions of technical and financial feasibility and safety. As we discover in HELCOM reports, the dominant opinion is that removal is *neither* entirely cost-effective *nor* safe. That is to say, UNCLOS provides a context to read these weapons caches as best left just where they are.[6]

And, even as these different regimes inform one another, they do not necessarily behave symbiotically. A briefing report from the EU Parliament points out, for example, that states disagree as to whether dumped munitions should be handled primarily within the environmental context or within the context of disarmament (European Union 2008, 6). Some in fact oppose the leading role taken by the Organisation for the Prohibition of Chemical Weapons (OPCW) in this matter (6). Indeed, the intersection of law of the sea, environmental law, and disarmament law makes for a "complicated combination" (Lott 2015, 60). One might hope that such a multipronged apparatus for addressing the problem would increase its chances of efficacy; many hands on deck, so to speak, might ensure that the job gets done. But just as more pieces of information about the chemical weapons dumps do not necessarily lead to more knowledge, with these ocean legalities it might be the case that the increasing fissures introduced through various regimes mean that accountability can orchestrate a stealthy getaway. For example, while the London Protocol's ban on dumping at sea is incorporated into the CWC (Part IV(A) of the Verification Annex), some of the relevant states parties to it (Russia, the US, and Finland, for example) are not parties to the 1996 London Protocol (Lott 2015, 62). The issue drifts away, eludes capture.

Moreover, if responsibility for these sites is in part a function of marine territories, we find that the Gotland Deep site is situated, again, at the intersection of possibilities: the dump is located where the Exclusive Economic Zones (EEZ) of five different Baltic countries converge (see figure 2.1, where country territorial zones are indexed by the pale dotted line). Even if legal accountability were placed on those states which now harbor these toxic souvenirs, their existence is suspended between territorial regimes. While state parties may be quick to assert how far their lands extend beneath the water when such industrial issues as drilling, prospecting, and mining are at stake (see Susan Reid, this volume; Philip E. Steinberg, Berit Kristoffersen, and Kristen L. Shake, this volume), forgetting is more common when it is an issue of expensive, and potentially dangerous, remediation. In other words, jurisdiction is similarly held in suspense.

One of Murphy's key points about chemical regimes of the living is that their toxic effects are "purposively posited as existing outside the accountability of corporations, and in the context of neoliberal governments, outside the scope of regulation" (Murphy 2008, 697). She argues that even as technoscience renders these regimes legible in ways they might not have been in the past, in our contemporary chemical regimes these effects are "nonetheless irrelevant to corporate accountability" (698). To this, we could reasonably add the question of legal accountability. Like the dispersed suspension of the phenomenon itself, "the costs, in lives and dollars of externalized molecular relations are distributed into proximate, peripheral, or even distant landscapes" (698). Responsibility is suspended, and even forgotten. For Murphy, this indicts an evasion of accountability for the uncontainable effects of chemical infrastructures.

We could extend Murphy's indictments to our brief survey of legal regimes that might respond to chemical weapons in the Gotland Deep: too little, too late, too timid, too ambiguous, too ineffectual. The weapons still lie in suspense, and it seems there is little pressure, from a legal standpoint, to do much about that. The important point, though, is not that the legal framework for addressing the ecological risks of these weapons caches is simply inadequate—as though *if only* we had said this or *if only* we had legislated that or drawn the borders of territorial waters *here* or included this clause *there*, we would establish the legal regime that would make it all right. Suspension does not allow us this comfort. If these regimes represent the legal response, we might instead pause a little longer to ask, in utmost seriousness: what kind of response is this? That is: might these ocean legalities, always missing their mark, appropriately reflect the fundamental suspension of the weapons caches themselves?

Perhaps the point is this: while legal regimes have appropriately been called out on their ineffectualness in the face of anthropogenic harms to nonhuman waters, should our focus be a critique of legal regimes because they refuse to apportion justice clearly, once and for all, as anchored to contained times, matters, and places—when the objects of their attention refuse this logic themselves? Instead of seeking a justice of calculation and containment, we may need to seek different legal logics.

Seeking Accountability in Anthropocene Seas

How can ocean legalities help us *remember* these chemical legacies when oceans—in their very materiality—insist that we also, in certain ways, forget? That is, how might ocean legalities nonetheless attend to this event's uncanny persistence in time, its refusal to be fully known, its uncontainable and incalculable presence in benthic space? While Murphy rightly critiques the ways in which chemical regimes of the living allow for the evasion of (state, corporate) accountability, how might legal or other regimes of accountability still hold onto the suspended materialities of these oceanic military archives without reducing their ineffability to an easily apportioned cause or blame?

This question might be put otherwise: how do we account for ourselves and our actions when that self, and the bodies and environments it effects, refuse full knowability, certainty, and boundedness in time and space? We might return, then, at the close of this chapter, to Alaimo's evocation of suspension and how it also intersects with the ethics and politics of transcorporeality that she elaborates more fully elsewhere (Alaimo 2010). As Alaimo explains, because of the transits of matters that travel across and through our own human bodies in a way that connects them to myriad other bodies in a transcorporeal ontology, "the material self cannot be disentangled from networks that are simultaneously economic, political, cultural, scientific, and substantial." On this "ever-changing landscape of continuous interplay, intra-action, emergence," she continues, a once "ostensibly bounded human subject" now finds herself "swirling in a landscape of uncertainty" (Alaimo 2010, 21).

Extending Alaimo's analysis, we could add that once ostensibly bounded environmental questions are similarly now swirling in tangles that stretch forward and backward, tentacularly reaching into and out of myriad worlds. So, while Alaimo might suggest that suspension is linked to an epistemology of patience in ways we find inadequate to phenomena like chemical weapons in the Gotland Deep, in the context of transcorporeality, she also suggests that the end of waiting might never arrive. It is in this state of suspension that we must find ways to call ourselves to account, to enact an ethics of curiosity and care, to do politics even if we know they are always incomplete.

This might in fact be *the* challenge of the Anthropocene. Despite the critiques we may have of a geological naming event that again puts the Anthropos at the center, the advent of the Anthropocene (at least in our cultural imaginaries, if not securely as a geological epoch) announces that such complexity is here to stay. No longer can we retreat to easy demarcations of nature and culture, just as we can no longer easily compartmentalize the damage in which we have participated and in light of which we hope we can make someone accountable or call someone to fix—by law or other regulatory means. In other words, even as we insist upon accountability, we must also make decisions that eschew certainty and predetermined, knowable courses of action. We must somehow cultivate an ethics and politics of suspension.

This is a serious provocation; this is still our work to do—as environmental, legal, political, and cultural scholars, but also as human beings affecting and being affected by these tangled ocean legalities.

Acknowledgments

Thank you to Susan Reid for research assistance. This chapter is part of a larger research project whose lead investigators are Astrida Neimanis (University of Sydney) and Cecilia Åsberg (Linköping University), with key inputs from Aleksija Neimanis (National Veterinary Institute, Sweden), Britt-Marie Bäcklin and Charlotta Moraeus (Environmental Research and Monitoring Department, Swedish Museum of Natural History), and Anders Östin (Swedish Defense Research Agency). Research for this project has been supported by The Seed Box: A MISTRA-FORMAS Environmental Humanities Collaboratory, the Australian Academy of Humanities, the University of Sydney Faculty of Arts and Social Sciences Research Grants, and the University of Sydney School of Historical and Philosophical Inquiry Incubator Grants.

Notes

1 Only a small number of those exposed to mustard gas died immediately, but over a million humans suffered its battlefield effects. Indeed, a key point about mustard gas is the lag of its symptoms and its persistence in both environments and living bodies: its effects are damaging and debilitating but not immediately lethal. Humans involved in the development and production of mustard gas also suffered chronic illness; to this add the persistent chemical violence endured by nonhuman species and the environment in the manufacture and deployment of chemical weapons (Ndiyae 2007).

2 In that article, Alaimo goes on to develop an understanding of blue-green environmentalisms as productive sites of suspension with "no solid ground, no foundation, no safe place to stand" (2012, 490). I return to how suspension can also be connected to this lack of certainty at the close of this chapter.

3 See also Philip E. Steinberg, Berit Kristoffersen, and Kristen L. Shake (this volume) for an argument of how the materiality of the sea—namely, in its frozen and melting forms—creates boundary trouble.

4 See Astrid Schrader (this volume) for a different account of the strange temporal ontologies of the sea, which she pushes for us to understand (following Derrida) as "hauntologies."

5 For example: the 1972 Oslo Convention on Dumping Waste at Sea, the 1974 Paris Convention on Land-Based Sources of Marine Pollution, the 1991 Convention on Environmental Impact Assessment in a Transboundary Context (Espoo), the Convention of the Protection of the Marine Environment of the North-East Atlantic (OSPAR), and the Convention for the Prevention of Pollution from Ships (MARPOL).

6 HELCOM (and most other authorities) advise that sea-dumped munitions are best left "in place and undisturbed" (Greenberg, Sexton, and Vearrier 2016, 90); the US Army Technical Center for Explosives Safety even suggests that, if recovered, "returning munitions to the sea is advised unless the munitions can be safely secured" (89).

References

Alaimo, Stacy. 2008. "Trans-corporeal Feminisms and the Ethical Space of Nature." In *Material Feminisms*, edited by Stacy Alaimo and Susan Hekman, 237–64. Bloomington: Indiana University Press.

Alaimo, Stacy. 2010. *Bodily Natures: Science, Environment, and the Material Self*. Minneapolis: University of Minnesota Press.

Alaimo, Stacy. 2012. "States of Suspension: Trans-corporeality at Sea." *Interdisciplinary Studies in Literature and Environment* 19 (3): 476–93.

Beldowski, Jacek, Zygmunt Klusek, Marta Szubska, Raisa Turja, Anna I. Bulczak, Daniel Rak, Matthias Brenner, et al. 2016. "Chemical Munitions Search and Assessment: An Evaluation of the Dumped Munitions Problem in the Baltic Sea." *Deep-Sea Research II* 128: 85–95.

Carstensen, Jacob, Jesper H. Andersen, Bo G. Gustafsson, and Daniel J. Conley. 2014. "Deoxygenation of the Baltic Sea during the Last Century." *PNAS* 111 (15): 5628–33.

CHEMSEA Consortium. 2013. "CHEMSEA Findings: Results from the CHEMSEA Project—Chemical Munitions Search and Assessment." http://underwatermunitions.org/pdf/CHEMSEA_Findings_24.01.pdf https://www.researchgate.net/publication/324149647_CHEMSEA_Findings_-_Results_from_the_CHEMSEA_project_chemical_munitions_search_and_assessment.

Crist, Eileen. 2013. "On the Poverty of our Nomenclature." *Environmental Humanities* 3: 129–47.

European Union. 2008. "An Introduction to the Political and Technical Challenges Posed by Sea-Dumped Chemical and Conventional Weapons: The Case of the Baltic Sea." Briefing paper, December 22. Brussels: Directorate General External Policies of the Union.

Greenberg, M. I., K. J. Sexton, and D. Vearrier. 2016. "Sea-Dumped Chemical Weapons: Environmental Risk, Occupational Hazard." *Clinical Toxicology* 54 (2): 79–91.

Helmreich, Stefan. 2009. *Alien Ocean: Anthropological Voyages in Microbial Seas.* Cambridge, MA: MIT Press.

Hoenig, Stephen. 2007. *Compendium of Chemical Warfare Agents.* Berlin: Springer.

Leppäranta, Matti, and Myrberg, Kai. 2009. *Physical Oceanography of the Baltic Sea.* Berlin: Springer.

Lott, Alexander. 2015. "Pollution of the Marine Environment by Dumping: Legal Framework Applicable to Dumped Chemical Weapons and Nuclear Waste in the Arctic Ocean." *Nordic Environmental Law Journal* 1: 57–69.

MacLeod, Janine. 2013. "Water and the Material Imagination: Reading the Sea of Memory against the Flows of Capital." In *Thinking of Water*, edited by Cecilia Chen, Janine MacLeod, and Astrida Neimanis, 40–60. Montreal: McGill-Queens University Press.

Mentz, Steve. 2009. "Toward a Blue Cultural Studies: The Sea, Maritime Culture, and Early Modern English Literature." *Literature Compass* 6/5: 997–1013.

Missiaen, Tine, and Jean-Pierre Henriet, eds. 2002. "Chemical Munition Dump Sites in Coastal Environments." Brussels: Federal Office for Scientific, Technical, and Cultural Affairs (OSTC), Federal Ministry of Social Affairs, Public Health and the Environment.

Moreaus, Charlotta, Britt-Marie Bäcklin, Aleksija Neimanis, and Anders Östin. 2016. "Nya sårskador hos säl—koppling till kemiska stridsmedel?" In *HAVET 2015/2016: Om miljötillståndet i svenska havsområden*, 113–15. Gothenberg, Sweden: Havsmiljöinstitutet.

Murphy, Michelle. 2008. "Chemical Regimes of the Living." *Environmental History* 13 (4): 695–703.

Murphy, Michelle. 2013. "Chemical Infrastructures of the St Clair River." *Toxicants, Health and Regulation since 1945*, edited by Soraya Boudia and Nathalie Jas, 103–15. London: Pickering & Chatto.

Ndiyae, Pap. 2007. *Nylon and Bombs: DuPont and the March of Modern America.* Baltimore: Johns Hopkins University Press.

Neimanis, Astrida. 2017. *Bodies of Water: Posthuman Feminist Phenomenology.* London: Bloomsbury.

Neimanis, Astrida, Aleksija Neimanis, and Cecilia Åsberg. 2017. "Fathoming Chemical Weapons in the Gotland Deep." *Cultural Geographies*, July (online first).

Todd, Zoe. 2015. "Indigenizing the Anthropocene." In *Art in the Anthropocene: Encounters among Aesthetics, Politics, Environment and Epistemology*, edited by Heather Davis and Etienne Turpin, 241–54. Ann Arbor, MI: Open Humanities Press.

Van Wyck, Peter. 2003. *Signs of Danger: Waste, Trauma, and Nuclear Threat.* Minneapolis: University of Minnesota Press.

Wieczorek, Gunda. 2012. "Spatiotemporal Scales of the Deep Circulation in the Eastern Gotland Basin/Baltic Sea." *Marine Science Reports* No. 88. Warnemünde: Leibniz-Institut für Ostseeforschung.

Yusoff, Kathryn. 2017. "Epochal Aesthetics: Affectual Infrastructures of the Anthropocene." *Accumulation*, March 29. http://www.e-flux.com/architecture//121847/epochal-aesthetics-affectual-infrastructures-of-the-anthropocene.

3. KAURI AND THE WHALE

Oceanic Matter and Meaning in New Zealand

KATHERINE G. SAMMLER

Geopolitically, demarcating the borders of ocean jurisdictions granted under the 1982 United Nations Convention on the Law of the Sea (UNCLOS) has stabilized many international disputes over ocean resources and boundaries. Offshore jurisdictions conceived by UNCLOS are delineated as distances from coastal baselines, marking a fixed land/sea line of reference. Yet Aotearoa New Zealand has struggled with translating and implementing UNCLOS, as many in the country question the very division of territory and property along a land/sea binary. New Zealand legislation written to determine rights and responsibilities offshore has sparked fierce debates and protests, demonstrating not only the ambiguity within the multiple understandings of ocean space written into UNCLOS, but also that this treaty is categorically incompatible with other ways of knowing and practicing ocean spaces. Specifically, the coastline bisection and subsequent nationalization of submerged lands is in direct conflict with Indigenous Māori cosmologies and tribal land rights that interpret landscapes and seascapes as an interrelated whole. Environmental politics stemming from this worldview call into question dominant Western and colonial epistemology and ontology and inform radically new frameworks for deriving sovereignty and practicing environmental management.

Interpreting and implementing the jurisdictions drawn up in UNCLOS have been an experiment in offshore governance through conflicting performances of territory and sovereignty in the ocean. Grappling with the ocean's materiality and dynamism, as a chaotic and flowing field, enacting the territorial logic of baselines has created social and political divisions in New Zealand leading to the ongoing controversies surrounding the division of offshore space and management. Focusing on disputed uses of offshore spaces necessarily confronts the inherent ambiguity of the social and political process of partitioning watery space (Baldacchino 2010). The geophysical, hydrological, and biological materiality and mobility of oceans partially influence the logic of UNCLOS and national enactments of the international treaty, even as attempts are made to legislate around these intrinsic ocean features. Regulators must contend with the agency of the living and nonliving natures as they enact static borders among mobile bodies. Ships on the surface, whales, and human bodies, whether on deck or partially submerged, engender relational social and legal meanings, which have been enrolled in multiple and conflicting territorializations of the ocean. Categorical distinctions between landscapes and seascapes, static and mobile structures and bodies, human and nonhuman actors, have resulted in a complex matrix of offshore rights and responsibilities (Sammler 2016).

Enacting these ontological and ethical divisions counters the UNCLOS declaration, which states in its preamble that "the problems of ocean space are closely interrelated and need to be considered as a whole." This contradiction, and its subsequent partitioning effects, is particularly significant in Aotearoa New Zealand, where "unlike western models of property, Māori relationship to the land is ontological, so that one's sovereignty is formed out of a genealogical relationship to the land, sea, and to nonhuman species" (DeLoughrey 2015, 356). This chapter follows calls to attend to multiple geopolitical, biopolitical, and ontological dimensions toward a rigorous oceanic studies (Blum 2010; Helmreich 2009; Lehman 2013; Steinberg and Peters 2015), applying an onto-epistemological framework to incorporate how discursive practices are causally related to material phenomena. In doing so, it makes explicit how the practices of knowing and being are entangled, to include an "understanding of the roles of human *and* nonhuman, material *and* discursive, and natural *and* cultural factors in scientific and other social-material practices" (Barad 2007, 26; emphasis in original). This chapter thinks beyond how ocean life and non-life are imagined toward how they are practically enrolled in various ways to enact borders, perform territories, produce political spaces, and make claims of sovereignty (see also Povinelli 2016). This includes careful examination of the shifting legal arguments made to justify emergent ocean uses, as well as how the material engagement of the ocean can be used to resist extractive industry, allowing alternative legalities to emerge.

The following discussion begins by investigating the complexities and controversies that emerge from the oceans of New Zealand, beginning with the kinship of the kauri and the whale, emphasizing the ontological differences between Western categorizations and Māori cosmologies. The implementation of land and sea divisions via baselines has led to political unrest in Aotearoa

New Zealand and the rise of an independent Māori parliamentary party. Struggles over offshore Indigenous property rights have been taking place among proposed development of seabed mineral projects. This chapter considers baselines as a political technology (Elden 2010). This means reading the baseline as a calculative apparatus that enacts cuts to refashion lively ocean worlds into divisible spaces and objects in direct opposition to Māori tribal holdings that span mountains to sea. Legislation nationalizing the foreshore and seabed, along with projects seeking to mine offshore, have created rifts in New Zealand society at the center of ongoing protests. Some protestors have taken their actions offshore. These protestors are meeting with challenges to their right to protest on and in the sea. While the freedom of navigation is enshrined in the UNCLOS treaty, particular ships—nuclear vessels, whaling boats, and activist flotillas—have encountered restrictions, demonstrating the difficulties and ambiguities of emergent offshore governance. Looking to specific moments, as the New Zealand government continues to produce legislation to (re)shape an ocean governance apparatus, this chapter will demonstrate how these events ground politics within material and lived oceans.

This research partially draws on four months spent in New Zealand in the austral winter of 2014, hosted by the University of Auckland. The in-country data collection included roughly thirty interviews with government employees from such institutions as the New Zealand Environmental Protection Authority, New Zealand Petroleum and Minerals, and the Ministry of Māori Development, as well as leading national scientists and academics; participation in conferences, workshops, and debates; and visits to archives, museums, black-sand beaches, fern forests, and kauri stands.

Kauri Rāua Ko Parāoa (Kauri and the Sperm Whale)

Ina rā o nehe	In times long past
Te ūnga o Parāoa ki uta	A sperm whale came ashore
Te kī nāna ki a Kauri	And spoke thus to the kauri
E Kau! Hoake tāua	Kauri! Come with me
Ki tai te tio nā te mauru.	to the sea which is fresh and cool.
Kāo! I tā Kauri	No! Said the kauri
Ngākauria koe te taitai	you may like the sea
Engari au te tū iho nei	but I prefer to stand here
Ōkū wae ki rō onetapu.	with my feet in the soil.
Heoi e tā Parāoa	All right said the whale
Tēnā ia, whakawhitia ngā kiri.	then let us agree to exchange our skins.

Nā reira ia	So that is why
Te kiri rākau kauri	the bark of the kauri
I rauangi, i kī nā i te hinū.	is thin and full of resinous oil.

—WALL TEXT, Te Ao Tūroa (Māori Natural History Gallery), visited August 17, 2014

While dominant understandings of a land-sea binary were codified by international law, Māori cosmologies and mythologies do not share this Western ontology nor necessarily divide natures—materially, practically, or politically—as demonstrated by tribal governance of areas that regard customary rights from mountains to sea. As Garth Harmsworth and Shaun Awatere explain, a fundamental tenet of Māori belief, *whakapapa*, engenders "connection, lineage, or genealogy between humans and ecosystems and all flora and fauna" (2013, 275). This includes a relationship with environments as a whole, a network of connections, as defined by *ki uta ki tai*, "a whole-of-landscape approach, understanding and managing interconnected resources and ecosystems from the mountains to the sea" (Harmworth and Awatere 2013, 275). Whakapapa situates both human and more-than-human bodies and materials within a smooth framework of kinship, entanglement, correspondence, exchange, and dispersed agency. One account, central to Northern Māori mythology, offers some insight into the smooth exchange of materials, bodies, and narratives between the *hydro* and *geo* spheres by the shared origin account of kauri and whale.

Indigenous to New Zealand, kauri (*Agathis australis*) are towering trees reaching upward to fifty meters (see figures 3.1 and 3.2). Northern Māori oral traditions present kauri to be the father of the sperm whale. Due to their incredible size, both are esteemed as *rangatira* (chiefs). Beyond their immensity, they are comparable in their smooth, yet textured, greyish-brown exterior, both bark and skin enclosing valuable oils, where, "kauri gum is like the ambergris found in the intestines of the sperm whale" (Tāmaki Paenga Hira [Auckland War Memorial Museum], visited August 17, 2014). Due to its combustibility, Māori long used kauri resin for cooking and lighting, similar to how spermaceti, the oil of the sperm whale (*Physeter macrocephalus*), was used in early Western industrial nations. Colonizing Europeans harvested and sold kauri timber, known for its resistance to seawater and sturdy, straight-grained lumber for masts and spars. Used for various wares domestically and abroad, this tree, like the whale, was exploited to near collapse in the nineteenth century.

Other Māori narratives also bridge land and sea, employing human and more-than-human entities that openly exceed or exchange categories. The two main islands that constitute Aotearoa New Zealand are not presumed to be static land within a moving sea but, rather, as moving amid the ocean as canoe

FIGURES 3.1–3.2. The 800-year-old McKinney Kauri, with close-up of marker, Parry Kauri Park, Warkworth, New Zealand. Photos by author, July 6, 2014.

and fish. Epeli Hau'ofa offers some broader Pacific context when he writes, "Continental men, namely Europeans . . . introduced the view of 'islands in a far sea' . . . tiny, isolated dots in a vast ocean. . . . Our ancestors, who had lived in the Pacific for over two thousand years, viewed their world as 'a sea of islands' rather than as 'islands in the sea'" (1994, 153; see also DeLoughrey 2015). This continental gaze forms the dominant hegemonic view of oceans as seen from land, drawing lines of division between land and sea, between kauri and whale. Categorical binary divisions as an apparatus of settler colonial governance of difference and markets are defined by Elizabeth Povinelli (2016) as geontology. Povinelli's understanding of geontopower ensures the enclosure of life (*bios*) from nonlife (*geos, meteoros*) as a "way of sorting the world [that] makes sense only from the disciplinary logic of geology, a disciplinary perspective that relies on natural types and species logics" (Povinelli 2016, 11). Applied to ocean spaces and resources, divisions are employed to categorically enclose land (*geos*) from sea (*hydros*), human (*anthropos*) from animal (*zoe*), and surface seas (*pelago*) from deep ocean (*abbyso*) and seafloor (*bathy*). As Māori traditions instead draw lines of connection, instituting cuts between land/sea, human/ nonhuman, creating discrete, bounded entities, goes against Māori whakapapa. The legislative implementation of these cuts in the form of baselines and off- shore resource appropriation by the New Zealand national government led to widespread protest. Resulting political actions demonstrate the divergent on- tologies, worlds at odds, "the world in which the dependent oppositions . . . are sensible and dramatic and the world in which these enclosures are no longer, or have never been, relevant, sensible, or practical" (Povinelli 2016, 16).

Developing Divisions

In a contemporary context, borders of nation-states and the spatial category of sovereign territory are often imagined as predominantly fixed. Politically con- structed boundaries can be concealed as wholly technical, or even scientific, affairs, as if a coastline were an essential and stable object. Yet current events are reminders of how national boundaries are produced and in flux, demonstrated by the dredging up of islands in the South China Sea for their associated liquid territories and the shifting of sands across the Singapore Strait, as discussed in Jennifer L. Gaynor's chapter in this volume, or the disappearing territory, par- ticularly of Pacific Island nations, due to sea-level rise.

Intrinsic to defining ocean boundaries are baselines, the technical division between land and sea. Defined as "the low-water line along the coast as marked on large-scale charts officially recognized by the coastal State" (UNCLOS, Article 5), the baseline is a mechanism by which dynamic and shifting coastlines are transmogrified into static political borders. Baselines are geopolitically significant because not only do they provide the foundation for measuring maritime jurisdictions, but they also delimit the outermost extent of a nation's territorial land (Bateman and Schofield 2008). They are therefore a significant part of the discursive means by which the totality of the ocean is disassembled from an interrelated whole and reconfigured as disparate parts.

Following Stuart Elden's (2010) notion of territory as a political technology, made up by techniques to calculate, evaluate, and control both land and sea, the highly technical knowledge employed to delineate offshore territories can be examined alongside the political negotiations involved in making claims on these spaces. Baselines are one apparatus within the political technology for ocean territorialization, an act of measurement that "enacts agential cuts that produce determinate boundaries and properties of 'entities'" (Barad 2007, 148). While represented as natural, approximations of the coastline, baselines create meaning through social-material practices of boundary making; they enact cuts that fashion land and sea spaces into discrete entities. They are the foundational technical and political apparatus used by UNCLOS to partition the ocean. To consider the political technologies used to bound offshore territories, the materiality and mobility of ocean spaces and beings must be addressed. Yet, the national government in New Zealand has struggled to legislate around these issues, and, in response, the partitioning of land and sea through the implementation of baselines and nationalization of the seabed has provoked passionate demonstrations. Controversies persist as seabed mining projects seek to commodify ocean minerals.

Drawing a Line, Creating a Rift

The Foreshore and Seabed Act (2004) claimed all submerged lands and associated resources as property of the Crown, subsuming them under national authority. This became the central focus for political actions over clashing worldviews, one that embraces a Western land/sea binary inherent in ocean jurisdictional boundaries and another based in Māori cosmologies contending that sovereignty extends from mountains to sea. Interpreted as trampling Māori customary title to offshore spaces, the volatile debates stemming from these diverging ideologies triggered vigorous protests, or *hikoi*, in the capital city of Wellington. The rift inherent in this legislation "went off like an atomic bomb in the New Zealand political landscape. . . . These events fractured New Zealand society" (interview, September 4, 2014).[1] The dispute initiated a UN

Special Rapporteur report on human rights and fundamental freedoms of Indigenous people (United Nations Commission on Human Rights 2006) and instigated the formation of an independent Māori parliamentary party. The Foreshore and Seabed Act was finally replaced in 2011 by the Marine and Coastal Area (Takutai Moana) Act. This legislation notwithstanding, an incredible amount of contention and confusion continues over the status of ocean spaces and resources.

In implementing parts of the Marine and Coastal Area Act, the Ministry of Māori Affairs (now renamed the Ministry for Māori Development) required *iwi* (Māori tribes) to submit applications to have their customary marine title over marine and coastal areas recognized. Submissions required that Māori prove continued exclusive occupation since the Treaty of Waitangi was signed with the British in 1840. Many iwi refused to participate in proving property rights over places they had never relinquished. Other New Zealanders have been worried they will lose access to the ocean if iwi rights are recognized. A government employee explained, "You gotta sort of tilt your head to the left and squint to get your head around [this act]; whilst no one owns it [the coastal waters], there are a set of rights underneath. First of all, starting from the top, is that the non-ownership applies to the physical stuff, the water column you can do all sorts of things in the water column, fishing and navigation and all that stuff remains. So, all New Zealanders' rights to navigate, recreate, fish, are codified in here" (interview, September 4, 2014). Resource rights and issues of access, in the water and on the seabed, are still being determined as iwi applications, due back in 2017, are still being sorted.

Beyond the foreshore, the New Zealand government has contended with questions surrounding ocean resources and access within its expansive offshore jurisdictions. In practice, ocean space allows multiple uses to be stacked on top of one another, opening it up to a complex matrix of rights and responsibilities in both the horizontal and vertical dimensions. As the seafloor is being looked to as the next frontier for large-scale resource extraction, New Zealand has been surveying its offshore riches. The island nation has been one of the first to develop seabed mining legislation and regulatory bodies. This experimental industry aims to cut away chunks of the seabed or dredge up loose materials from the seafloor, crush them, and pump them up to a surface support ship. While there has yet to be a large-scale commercial seabed mining project operating in New Zealand or elsewhere, coalition movements aligning along Indigenous and environmental issues have arisen around the ecological damages of these nascent excavation practices. Some have taken their protests to sea, blocking survey and extractive vessels with boats and even bodies. Some protestors exchange their skins for survival suits to submerge themselves into the sea, employing thick buoyant neoprene, designed for ocean immersion, enclosing a body's trunk and limbs to resist lethally hypothermic seawater. These bodies in the sea have posed new challenges to the government regarding policing within ocean territory, specifically in the arguably ambiguous jurisdictions called the exclusive economic zones (EEZS). Within this watery, dynamic field, the mobility of bodies is guaranteed by UNCLOS, as one of its fundamental tenets to maintain global flows is freedom of navigation. However, as discussed below, some nations want to choose whose bodies, and which ships, are allowed within their EEZS.

Ocean Materiality

The complexities that ocean materiality brings to offshore delimitation and governance are key factors in unpacking the logic of UNCLOS. The mobility of water bodies, ship bodies, and animal bodies within, across, and through fixed jurisdictions forced the creation of new spatial logics to control ocean resources. Oceanic studies in the social sciences and humanities have raised critiques about the ocean being theorized as a frictionless space for globalization, as merely a metaphor for fluidity, mobility, and contingency (Bélanger 2014; Blum 2010, 2013; Helmreich 2011; Lambert, Martins, and Ogborn 2006; Steinberg 1999). Yet determined materialist approaches have embraced oceans as water, waves, flows, and energies, addressing the more-than-human physical characteristics that exert powerful agency. Some scholars include the biological as important components to engage the oceanic, addressed through human-coast or human-ship experiences (Brown and Humberstone 2016; Lehman 2012; Peters 2012) or more-than-human sea animal studies (Helmreich 2009; Johnson 2016). In this volume, Astrida Neimanis describes the ocean is a chemical solvent suspending toxic materiality, an impermanent benthic depository of chemical weapons. In Philip E. Steinberg, Berit Kristoffersen, and Kristen L. Shake's chapter, the sea ice confounds legal objectification by transcending the abstractions of earth-system disciplines. More than just a conduit between atmo-, bio-, geo-, and hydro-spheres, the ice edge is always slipping between systems as its dynamically changes states—solid, liquid, gas—failing to collapse to the dimensionality of a bounded line. As with the ice, the political and legal regimes created to manage oceans only partially and sporadically confront ocean materiality.

After years of deliberations, the UNCLOS treaty produced a jurisdictional matrix representing a horizontal gradient of diminishing sovereignty with

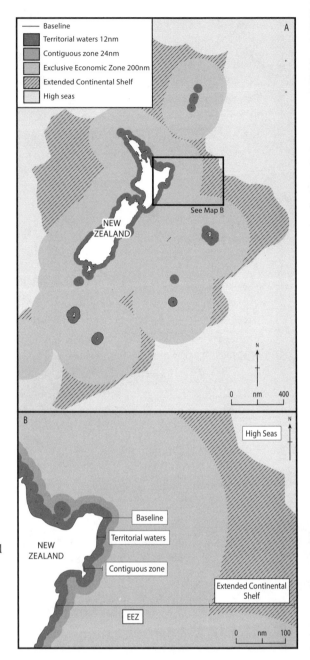

FIGURE 3.3. UNCLOS jurisdictions:
territorial waters (12 nm), full territorial
sovereignty; contiguous zone (24 nm),
customs enforcement; exclusive
economic zone (200 nm), sovereignty
over resources but not control of
navigation. Image by author.
Data source: United Nations, 2016.

increasing distance from land (Sammler 2016); where full national territorial sovereignty is granted nearshore, a different bundle of spatial rights and responsibilities is granted further offshore (see figure 3.3). Offshore space is largely designated as EEZs, a sort of hybrid jurisdiction where coastal states are granted sovereign rights over resources but not outright sovereignty over the space itself (Jacques and Smith 2003). Predominantly the objects of state sovereignty are resources "for the purpose of exploring and exploiting, conserving and managing ... whether living or non-living" (UNCLOS, Article 56), not the space containing them, enabling extraction without the full territorial responsibility. At the same time that offshore resources are secure, all other states maintain the right to peacefully navigate unrestricted through all nations' EEZs (UNCLOS, Articles 58 and 87), posing a conundrum for states reluctant to abandon the idea of full territorial sovereignty. As will be demonstrated below, the temptation to fully territorialize the EEZ, to establish the same sovereign control as on land, has proven difficult for many countries—New Zealand for example—to resist.

Ambiguity and Overterritorialization

The attempted balance of state's rights within EEZs has prompted assorted incidents. Despite guaranteed navigational rights, ships have indeed been stopped, deterred, or taken to international court when passing through another nation's EEZ jurisdiction. A routine function of states, to regulate borders, restrict access, and manage crossings, makes governments reluctant to relinquish offshore territorial sovereignty. Examples include various notifications or restrictions within an EEZ, such as the EU banning single-hulled heavy grade oil tankers from accessing their ports and France unilaterally demanding the interception of ships releasing ballast water out to ninety miles from shore. In fact, the International Maritime Organization (IMO) can be petitioned to designate Particularly Sensitive Sea Areas (PSSAs) and change shipping routes to create areas to be avoided for the protection of "ecological, socio-economic, or scientific attributes" (International Maritime Organization 2005). Some coastal states have petitioned to designate almost their entire EEZ as a PSSA (Caron and Scheiber 2014). Jon Van Dyke discusses this trend as a new norm of customary international law "that allows coastal states to regulate navigation through their EEZ based on the nature of the ship and its cargo" (2005, 121).

While the EEZ is designated as high seas for navigational purposes, open to all states and common to all (UNCLOS, Articles 58 and 87), ambiguities emerge in managing the conflicting rights and responsibilities of a coastal state and navigating state. Despite UNCLOS expressly proclaiming that ocean spaces "need to be considered as a whole" (UNCLOS, Preamble), the jurisdictions it prescribes nationally compartmentalize resource management. Yet, at the same time, coastal states have limited recourse under this treaty to address transnational environmental fallout from ship pollution and the transportation of hazardous materials, hazards exacerbated by the ocean's ability to mix, dissolve, and circulate pollutants, in contradiction to the intended fixity of borders, as if the discrete political units act as physical barriers. In the case of navigation, the political boundaries must be permeable. By this logic, ship activities are regulated by the IMO, not UNCLOS, releasing them from governance within the domain of territorial sovereignty. The slow creep of mining and hydrocarbon development farther and farther offshore is only one of many anxieties inherent in the proliferation of ocean uses. The history of whaling and nuclear testing in the Pacific also gives rise to specific apprehensions in the region (Vltchek 2013).

A Nuclear Past

The devastating nuclear testing history in the Pacific motivated the New Zealand Parliament to pass the Nuclear Free Zone, Disarmament, and Arms Control Act in 1987. This law bans nuclear-powered or nuclear-armed vessels from using ports or navigating New Zealand's internal waters and territorial seas as well as the airspace above New Zealand's territory. This legislation caused friction with other nations, especially the United States, which terminated its security commitments to New Zealand, agreed upon in the 1951 Australia, New Zealand, United States Security Treaty (ANZUS). As it is the policy of the United States to neither confirm nor deny the existence of nuclear weapons on its warships, this legislation effectively banned all American Navy ships. The first US Navy ship to enter New Zealand's territorial waters after creation of the nuclear-free zone wasn't until 2016, almost three decades later. While not publicly confirmed as a non-nuclear propelled or armed ship, New Zealand's prime minister restated the country's nuclear-free policy to soothe any public concerns elicited by the USS Sampson's visit.

In 2000, New Zealand's Green Party attempted to pass the Nuclear Free Zone Extension Bill, amending the original legislation to include the EEZ. Their justification was that, "under the Law of the Sea, ships have some rights of navigation through this zone; yet if those ships carry a cargo which could contaminate marine resources for centuries, this creates a conflict with the purpose of the EEZ. This bill resolves that conflict, for NZ, in favour of environmental protection" (Green Party of Aotearoa New Zealand 2000). This amendment lost in Parliament in 2002, but it would have prohibited nuclear-propelled ships and ships carrying radioactive fuel or waste from transiting their 4-million-square-kilometer EEZ and demonstrates that interpretations of navigation within this jurisdiction are multiple. Despite UNCLOS's definition of fixed and distinct boundaries, the EEZ is a hybrid space being performed by various actors, and the product of ongoing political negotiation.

Whalers Not Welcome

More recently, New Zealand has expressed its view that Japanese whaling vessels are not welcome to transit their EEZ. In 2014, when a whaling vessel did enter, the Japanese ambassador was called to the capital for a rebuke by New Zealand's foreign minister, Murray McCully. He conveyed, "the deep disappointment of the New Zealand Government that Japanese whalers had been insensitive to the views of New Zealanders by entering New Zealand's EEZ" (McCully 2014). While at the same time admitting that the "Government has no legal means of excluding any vessel . . . [and] while the Japanese vessel has a right to pass through our EEZ, it is disappointing a request not to do so was ignored" (McCully 2014). The regulation of whaling vessels is a stand-in for the desire to regulate whale bodies—or the capture, slaughter, and transport of them—aligning with the justification of environmental protection in the declaration of a nuclear-free zone.

While New Zealand tests its ability to exclude ships from transiting its EEZ, operationalizing gaps and ambiguities created by this jurisdiction, this is certainly not the only coastal nation to confront such uncertainties. Struggles over extraterritorial spaces are taking place through the rifts opening within the land/sea binary that is used for delimiting territorial sovereignty, revealing entanglements that undergird negotiating oceanic space as a medium of multiple materialities, mobilities, and meanings. While theoretical understandings of territory and sovereignty recognize that these categories are never stable (Elden 2013), oceans make a prodigious space for examining emerging ruptures in relationships between states, space, and power. Uncertainty surrounding how much control states have in their offshore jurisdictions is culminating in frictions both between nations and within them. This ambiguity of governance raises not only questions regarding responsibilities concerning conservation and environmental degradation, but also conflicts over each coastal nation's infringements on the rights of other states and nonstate actors. New Zealand's implementation of ocean governance legislation has incurred intense debates from the start. The enactment of baselines and subsequent national appropriation of all submerged lands prompted Indigenous Māori groups to mobilize against the ontological and legal division of land and sea.

Mobilities and Flows

Sovereignty is defined within the EEZ as pertaining to extraction, exploration, and conservation. However, while the sovereignty over resources is explicit, the space itself is considered international commons, where all states benefit from the "freedoms of navigation and overflight, freedom to lay submarine cables and pipelines" (UNCLOS), same as on the high seas. Nevertheless, these freedoms must be "exercised with 'due regard' to the right of the coastal state to exploit the resources of the EEZ and the responsibilities of the coastal state to protect the marine environment" (Van Dyke 2005, 108). This delicate balance between state's rights promulgates tensions that have largely been playing out between foreign-flagged vessels and coastal states. However, conflicts are emerging in New Zealand over the government's ability to regulate its own citizens within their EEZ. Clashes between protesters near offshore extractive infrastructures have confused the policing of bodies and vessels at sea, forcing renewed scrutiny over inclusive and exclusive uses of this space.

Stephen Graham has called on scholars of geopolitics to move beyond the "classical, modern formulation of Euclidean territorial units jostling for space on contiguous maps" (2004, 20). As Steinberg and Kimberley Peters highlight, the ocean is not a fixed Euclidean space within which power is exercised, but a turbulent material volume of Lagrangian flows with multiple and nonlinear temporalities. Such materiality gives rise to what they refer to as a "wet ontology" that can assist in better understanding how "power is simultaneously projected on, through, in, and about space" (Steinberg and Peters 2015, 261). This theoretical trajectory offers considerable potential for examining heterogeneous political spatial arrangements and territorial configurations that are not produced or maintained by conventional means, falling outside dominant practices based on the imaginary of discrete borders delimiting an internally sovereign area (Agnew 2013). A wet ontology refocuses mobility as a part of territory and territoriality, and allows for an analysis of mobility within and through novel jurisdictions, such as the EEZ. This theoretical vantage is helpful in analyzing the proposed exploitation of precious sediments that flow from land, downstream and into the foreshore.

From Mountains to Seabed Mining

The New Zealand government has been working to initiate institutions and regulations for the seabed mining industry. The experimental nature of seabed mineral extraction, as well as the increasing distance and depth of offshore hydrocarbon drilling, have motivated multiple concerned groups to organize protest campaigns against such development on environmental and jurisdictional grounds. Kiwis Against Seabed Mining (KASM) formed in 2004 in reaction to a proposal to extract ironsand off the coast of Taranaki Bight on the North Island, also home to the world's rarest, and critically endangered species, Maui's dolphin (interview, August 5, 2014). Local iwi also organized, with one of the focal points directing attention to the origins of the coastal iron-rich sand flowing from sacred Mt. Taranaki (see figures 3.4–3.7). The black sands of Taranaki's beach and seabed are made of titanomagnetite containing high concentrations of iron ore. These sands originate from the flanks of the volcanic mountain, eroded by streams and rivers into the sea, representing a direct material exchange from mountains to sea, a connection that illustrates a Māori understanding of whakapapa.

Operating new mining technologies at unfamiliar depths is full of uncertainty and potential hazards. Regulation addressing environmental management in the EEZ was undertaken in 2012 by New Zealand's Exclusive Economic Zone and Continental Shelf (Environmental Effects) Act. The opacity and indeterminacy of the ocean as a medium, shrouding the seafloor beneath, dominates the imaginaries and practices of mining operations. As one government scientist put it, "At least with fisheries being surface, you can sort of see what's going on. If you are three thousand meters down or four thousand meters down with manganese nodules, then it's so much harder to actually measure what's happening, period. And that's a major problem for governance as well as natural science" (interview, July 29, 2014). While the ironsand mining proposed off Taranaki is relatively shallow compared to deep manganese nodule extraction, the environmental impacts are concerning. Demonstrators walked, biked, and surfed five hundred miles along the Taranaki coast to raise awareness about the proposed project. These actions were considered successful in raising awareness, as 4,850 submissions were sent to the Environmental Protection Authority (EPA) regarding the mining permit, with only a handful supporting the project (Baxter 2018). The permit was denied consent by the EPA in 2014, citing concerns over environmental impacts and uncertainty regarding economic benefits to the nation (Sammler 2016). However, the mining company, Trans-Tasman Resources, resubmitted its application and was

FIGURES 3.4–3.7. Black ironsands wash down from Mt. Taranaki and into the sea. Their dark color and magnetic properties signify the coveted ore within. Indigenous and environmental groups voice opposition to a proposed mining project off their shores. Clockwise from top left: Mt. Taranaki; black sands of Taranaki Beach; iron within the sands align with magnetic field; protest sign in the Taranaki region. Images by author.

granted a permit in August 2017, prompting several groups to submit appeals. The approval was then overturned by the High Court in August, 2018, ruling that the "adaptive management" approach violates the precautionary principles built into the EEZ act. The decision has been sent back to the EPA for consideration of the implications.

Bodies at Sea: Emerging and Submerging Oceanic Activism

In reaction to increasing offshore exploitation, environmental activists have taken their protests to sea. Boats and kayaks have been used to physically interfere with, and voice political opposition to, extractive industries and ecological destruction. Protests on the water, by what some have dubbed kayaktivists, have been taking place in many locations around the world over the past several years. In Japan, Russia, and the United States they have blocked ships conducting seafloor resource surveys or towing offshore drilling equipment. For example, in 2015 demonstrators took to the Puget Sound in Washington state and the Willamette River in Oregon to block Shell's drilling platform from sailing for the Arctic. In Okinawa, hundreds rallied in 2014, many in kayaks and canoes, in support of Japanese sovereignty against the US military base on the island and the new construction underway to relocate the base on an environmentally sensitive bay. While these actions took place within territorial or internal waters, the trajectory for extractive projects farther offshore is provoking opponents to follow.

New Zealand protesters have also taken to the sea in reaction to deepwater oil drilling. Some bring signs and banners to sea to voice opposition, while others have used their boats to block ships associated with developing these resources. In 2013, a group called Oil Free Seas sailed a flotilla more than a hundred nautical miles offshore to block the Texas-based company Anadarko from drilling for oil in the Deepwater Taranaki Basin. In reaction to such protests, in 2014 the government amended the Crown Minerals Act to create protective exclusion zones around exploration and extraction vessels as well as artificial structures within New Zealand's EEZ. These noninterference zones authorize the New Zealand Defence Force to arrest and detain boat protesters, who then face steep fines and even incarceration (New Zealand Parliament 2014). Within the EEZ, the New Zealand Ministry of Business, Innovation and Employment (MBIE) admits that there are "no clear enforcement powers" to restrict a ship's freedom of navigation, as territorial sovereignty ends at twelve nautical miles (MBIE 2013, 2). UNCLOS does offer a provision for coastal states to construct artificial islands, installations, and structures, which allows for a safety zone up to five hundred meters (these zones are intended to protect extractive industry and energy-generation platforms within settled jurisdictions, unlike the artificial islands being built by China to bolster its territorial claims, as in the Spratly case discussed by Gaynor in this volume). The state may take appropriate measures to ensure the safety both of navigation and of any structure (Article 60). While this allows for some type of regulation of vessels entering a static exclusion zone, there is still ambiguity about whether it is legal to enforce such zones for mobile vessels. These gaps in jurisprudence have created legal battles and overturned court decisions all the way up to the Supreme Court of New Zealand.

In 2011, a skipper was arrested as part of a protest with the iwi of Te Whānau ā Apanui for interfering with a Petrobras vessel conducting under-sea oil exploration surveys in the EEZ. He and several other protesters entered the water in survival suits to block the vessel's path. Because the vessel was not a fixed structure, and because the skipper's body was not considered a "vessel," the application of law was unclear. However, the Supreme Court of New Zealand ruled to uphold his arrest for interfering with the ship's operation. In its ruling on *Teddy v. New Zealand Police* (2015), the court dismissed the police's justification that New Zealand ships are part of the territory and instead utilized the 1994 Maritime Transport Act, stating that it was amended to remove "any doubt about the extraterritorial effect," and concluding that "there are also now new offense and enforcement provisions in the Crown Minerals Act (1991) dealing with conduct interfering with structures or ships engaged in mining activity in the territorial sea, in the exclusive economic zone or above the continental shelf" (Supreme Court of New Zealand 2015, Article 11). Debates continue over whether it is a violation of UNCLOS to regulate navigation outside territorial waters, but the New Zealand government has so far upheld these amendments, attempting to fill legal gaps and quell uncertainty surrounding offshore resource extraction.

Conclusion

These examples highlight how the ocean's geophysical and biological materiality gets leveraged by different interest groups for geopolitical, national, Indigenous, and environmental motivations as well as "the epistemological impact of colonial ontologies" (Prescod-Weinstein 2017) on the New Zealand seascape. As governments and Indigenous and environmental groups struggle over the definition of rights and responsibilities within ocean spaces, there is potential for an intervention, to choose ontological cuts with greater care, "to take responsibility for the epistemological and ontological worlds we enact through the paths we walk and talk" (Sundberg 2014, 40) and boat and swim.

Māori and other Indigenous and transnationalist theorists and activists have long invoked multiplicities beyond the essentialism of land-sea binaries and invoked more-than-human ontologies in environmental governance and sovereignty struggles. One recent example in New Zealand, the Te Urewera Act of 2014, gave legal personhood to what was previously a national park, with "all the rights, powers, duties, and liabilities of a legal person" (16). The act poetically approaches Te Urewera with whakapapa as "ancient and enduring, a fortress of nature, alive with history . . . a place of spiritual value, with . . . an identity in and of itself, inspiring people to commit to its care" (8). Pita Sharples, a Māori academic (and the minister of Māori affairs when this legislation passed) recognizes that this onto-epistemological shift provides "a profound alternative to the human presumption of sovereignty over the natural world" (New Zealand Parliament 2014). Parliament has since granted personhood to the Whanganui River, recognizing it as "an indivisible and living whole, from the mountains to the sea, incorporating its tributaries and all of its physical and metaphysical elements" (Whanganui iwi and the Crown 2011, Subpart 1.2). Oddly enough, despite these shifts, these acts expressly maintain the mining rights of the Crown, as authorized under the Crown Minerals Act. Despite this reluctance to completely remove state mineral resource sovereignty, the legal espousal of Indigenous ontology sets a precedent that Māori legal scholar Jacinta Ruru (2014) highlights as "undoubtedly legally revolutionary . . . in Aotearoa New Zealand and on a world scale."

Within the ruptures in relationships between states, space, and power furnished by oceanic materiality and mobility, introducing more-than-human bio- and geophysical connections and sovereignties provides alternative frameworks to the state's writing of the sea. Exchanging colonial epistemologies for nonbinary counternarratives, which "challenge the (geontological) ground on which the state derives its sovereignty, including the state's claims to the strand, seabed, and creatures of the ocean" (DeLoughrey 2015, 367), generates new practices of resistance to extractive industries. Ambiguities within EEZs offer potential for expanded state control, but are also productive for legally and bodily challenging national resource claims. Reversing the continental gaze and preponderance of extending land metrics into the sea provides the potential for ocean imaginaries to creep onshore, creating openings for flows, transformations, and relationalities, building on Steinberg and Peters (2015) "wet ontologies" toward manifesting "wet" coalitions, resistances, and emancipations on, in, and near the sea (Hadjimichael n.d.).

Acknowledgments

This research was supported by the National Science Foundation (NSF) under Grant No. 1415047. Any opinions, findings, and conclusions or recommendations expressed in this material are those of the author and do not necessarily reflect the views of the NSF. Fieldwork also benefited from a fellowship from the Social Science Research Council.

Note

1   Generic titles, instead of full titles or names, are used for those interviewed in order to remove any identifying information. This choice was made given the extreme controversy surrounding the issue and the tightly knit community of people involved.

References

Agnew, John A. 2013. "Territory, Politics, Governance." *Territory, Politics, Governance* 1 (1): 1–4.

Baldacchino, Godfrey. 2010. *Island Enclaves: Offshoring Strategies, Creative Governance, and Subnational Island Jurisdictions.* Montreal: McGill-Queen's University Press.

Barad, Karen. 2007. *Meeting the Universe Halfway: Quantum Physics and the Entanglement of Matter and Meaning.* Durham, NC: Duke University Press.

Bateman, Sam, and Clive Schofield. 2008. "State Practice Regarding Straight Baselines in East Asia—Legal, Technical and Political Issues in a Changing Environment." Paper presented at the Fifth Conference of the IAG/IHO Advisory Board on the Law of the Sea (ABLOS) on Difficulties in Implementing Provisions of UNCLOS, Monaco, October 16–17.

Baxter, Cindy. 2018. "As We Head to the High Court, a Look Back at How We Got Here." Kiwis Against Seabed Mining website. https://kasm.org.nz/latest/as-we-head -to-the-high-court-a-look-back-at-how-we-got-here.

Bélanger, Pierre, ed. 2014. "Wet Matter." *Harvard Design Magazine* 39 (Fall/Winter).

Blum, Hester. 2010. "The Prospect of Oceanic Studies." *Proceedings of the Modern Language Association* 125 (3): 670–77.

Blum, Hester. 2013. "Introduction: Oceanic Studies." *Atlantic Studies* 10 (2): 151–55.

Brown, M. Mike, and Barbara Humberstone, eds. 2016. *Seascapes: Shaped by the Sea.* New York: Routledge.

Caron, David D., and Harry N. Scheiber, eds. 2014. *The Oceans in the Nuclear Age: Legacies and Risks.* Leiden: Brill Academic.

DeLoughrey, Elizabeth. 2015. "Ordinary Futures: Interspecies Worldings in the Anthropocene." In *Global Ecologies and the Environmental Humanities: Postcolonial Approaches,* edited by Elizabeth DeLoughrey, Jill Didur, and Anthony Carrigan, 352–72. New York: Routledge.

Elden, Stuart. 2013. *The Birth of Territory.* Chicago: University of Chicago Press.

Graham, Stephen. 2004. "Vertical Geopolitics: Baghdad and After." *Antipode* 36 (1): 12–23.

Green Party of Aotearoa New Zealand. 2000. New Zealand Nuclear Free Zone Extension Bill. http://www.converge.org.nz/pma/a230600.htm.

Hadjimichael, Maria. n.d. "The Right to the Sea." Editor's note on the Reclaim the Sea website. Accessed March 25, 2017. http://reclaimthesea.org/therighttothesea.

Harmsworth, Garth R., and Shaun Awatere. 2013. "Indigenous Māori Knowledge and Perspectives of Ecosystems." In *Ecosystem Services in New Zealand—Conditions and Trends*, edited by J. R. Dymond, 274–86. Lincoln, NZ: Manaaki Whenua Press.

Hauʻofa, Epeli. 1994. "Our Sea of Islands." *Contemporary Pacific* 6 (1): 148–61.

Helmreich, Stefan. 2009. *Alien Ocean: Anthropological Voyages in Microbial Seas*. Berkeley: University of California Press.

Helmreich, Stefan. 2011. "Nature/Culture/Seawater." *American Anthropologist* 113 (1): 132–44.

International Maritime Organization. 2005. "Particularly Sensitive Sea Areas." http://www.imo.org/en/OurWork/Environment/PSSAs.

Jacques, Peter J., and Zachary A. Smith. 2003. *Ocean Politics and Policy: A Reference Handbook*. Santa Barbara, CA: ABC-CLIO.

Johnson, Elizabeth R. 2016. "Governing Jellyfish: Eco-Security and Planetary 'Life' in the Anthropocene." In *Animals, Biopolitics, Law: Lively Legalities*, edited by Irus Braverman, 59–78. London: Routledge.

Lambert, David, Luciana Martins, and Miles Ogborn. 2006. "Currents, Visions and Voyages: Historical Geographies of the Sea." *Journal of Historical Geography* 32 (3): 479–93.

Lehman, Jessica S. 2013. "Relating to the Sea: Enlivening the Ocean as an Actor in Eastern Sri Lanka." *Environment and Planning D: Society and Space* 31 (3): 485–501.

McCully, Murray. 2014. "EEZ Entry 'Unhelpful.'" Ministry of Foreign Affairs press release. February 10. https://www.beehive.govt.nz/release/eez-entry-%E2%80%9Cunhelpful%C2%9D-mccully.

Ministry of Business, Innovation and Employment. 2013. "Regulatory Impact Statement: Protection of Offshore Petroleum and Mineral Activity from Unlawful Interference." April 19. https://treasury.govt.nz/publications/risa/regulatory-impact-statement-protection-offshore-petroleum-and-mineral-activity-unlawful-interference.

Museum of New Zealand [Te Papa Tongarewa]. 1998. "Kauri (*Agathis australis*)." Mountains to Sea Collection. Accessed March 25, 2017. https://collections.tepapa.govt.nz/topic/1016.

New Zealand Parliament. 2014. "*Tūhoe* Claims Settlement Bill, Te Urewera Bill—Third Readings." July 23. Hansard (Debates) vol. 700, 19463. https://www.parliament.nz/en/pb/hansard-debates/rhr/document/50HansD_20140726_00000128/t%C5%ABhoe-claims-settlement-bill-te-urewera-bill-third-readings.

Peters, Kimberley. 2012. "Manipulating Material Hydro-Worlds: Rethinking Human and More-Than-Human Relationality through Offshore Radio Piracy." *Environment and Planning A* 44 (5): 1241–54.

Povinelli, Elizabeth A. 2016. *Geontologies: A Requiem to Late Liberalism*. Durham, NC: Duke University Press.

Prescod-Weinstein, Chanda. 2017. "The Self-Construction of Black Women Physicists." Paper presented at the conference Critical Histories and Activist Futures: Decolonizing Science by Reconstructing Observers, Yale University, February 24–25.

https://medium.com/space-anthropology/decolonizing-science-by-reconstructing -observers-d62168fca19f.

Ruru, Jacinta. 2014. "Tūhoe-Crown Settlement—Te Urewera Act 2014." *Māori Law Review* (October). http://maorilawreview.co.nz/2014/10/tuhoe-crown-settlement-te -urewera-act-2014.

Sammler, Katherine G. 2016. "The Deep Pacific: Island Governance and Seabed Mineral Development." In *Island Geographies: Essays and Conversations*, edited by Elaine Stratford, 10–31. New York: Routledge.

Steinberg, Philip E. 1999. "Navigating to Multiple Horizons: Toward a Geography of Ocean-Space." *Professional Geographer* 51 (3): 366–75.

Steinberg, Philip E., and Kimberley Peters. 2015. "Wet Ontologies, Fluid Spaces: Giving Depth to Volume through Oceanic Thinking." *Environment and Planning D: Society and Space* 33 (2): 247–64.

Sundberg, Juanita. 2014. "Decolonizing Posthumanist Geographies." *Cultural Geographies* 21 (1): 33–47.

Supreme Court of New Zealand. 2015. *Teddy v. New Zealand Police*. February 17. NZSC 6. https://www.courtsofnz.govt.nz/cases/elvis-heremia-teddy-v-new-zealand-police-1 /@@images/fileDecision.

Treaty of Waitangi. 1840. http://www.tiritiowaitangi.govt.nz/treaty/translation.pdf.

UNCLOS (UN Convention on the Law of the Sea). 1982. Part VII: High Seas. http:// www.un.org/depts/los/convention_agreements/texts/unclos/part7.htm.

UN Commission on Human Rights. 2006. *Indigenous Issues: Human Rights and Indigenous Issues; Report of the Special Rapporteur on the Situation of Human Rights and Fundamental Freedoms of Indigenous People, Rodolfo Stavenhagen, Addendum*. January 17. http://www.refworld.org/docid/441182070.html.

Van Dyke, Jon M. 2005. "The Disappearing Right to Navigational Freedom in the Exclusive Economic Zone." *Marine Policy* 29 (2): 107–121.

Vltchek, Andre. 2013. *Oceania: Neocolonialism, Nukes and Bones*. Waikato, NZ: Atuanui Press.

Weizman, Eyal. 2002. "The Politics of Verticality." *Open Democracy*, April 23. https:// www.opendemocracy.net/ecology-politicsverticality/article_801.jsp.

Whanganui iwi and the Crown [Whanganui River Claims Settlement]. 2011. "Record of Understanding in Relation to Whanganui River Settlement." October 13. http://www.ngatangatatiaki.co.nz/wp-content/uploads/2015/04/DocumentLibrary _WhanganuiRiverROU.pdf.

4. EDGES AND FLOWS

Exploring Legal Materialities and Biophysical Politics of Sea Ice

PHILIP E. STEINBERG, BERIT KRISTOFFERSEN,

AND KRISTEN L. SHAKE

The ice edge is quite fascinating. We don't know where it is, and every time it pops up, there is debate. In that sense, it is somewhat similar to [Fisheries Minister] Per Sandberg.
—ERNA SOLBERG, prime minister of Norway, in 2015

In the quotation reproduced above, Norway's prime minister makes a some-what strained, if nonetheless humorous, analogy between two fair-weather friends of her center-right Conservative Party.[1] Per Sandberg is a leader of the Conservative Party's far-right coalition partner, the Progress Party, and is famous for courting controversy with provocative statements that tend to leave his establishment allies, like Prime Minister Solberg, wincing. For Solberg, Sandberg is a moving target, an unpredictable ally who can never be fully trusted. The ice edge, for Solberg and indeed for the Norwegian legal system as a whole, poses similar problems. For the past fifteen years the ice edge in the Barents Sea has played a central role in shaping the space of the Norwegian petrostate, yet it remains elusive: a dynamic line with a geophysical indeterminacy that perpetually evades and complicates attempts to use it for spatial planning.

In this chapter, we take up the challenge laid down by Prime Minister Solberg by engaging a growing body of literature on sea ice cover. We turn to the multiple properties of sea ice as we explore how this geophysical border zone upends the assumed static and binary divisions that so often characterize legal rhetoric. In doing so, we explore how the ice edge challenges not only divisions between geophysical spaces (e.g., land versus water, water versus ice) or between legal classifications (territory versus nonterritory), but also assumed divisions between packages of earth system processes and scalar categories. The ice edge, we argue, is not simply a geophysical boundary; it is also a zone of interaction and interchange that forms a vital link between physical, chemical, biological, and legal systems in the polar regions and beyond. We conclude, therefore, by asserting that a legal geography of the ice edge must account not only for sea ice's dynamism in both space and time and its ontological indeterminacy, but also for the way it draws connections among physical, chemical, and biological processes that scientific scholars all too often perceive as being in isolation.

Lively Ice

The edge of the continuous sea ice zone in the Arctic is, by definition, a zone of transition; in fact, the word *edge* belies the intricate morphological characteristics that constitute an area of vibrant physical, chemical, and biological interactions. Sea ice can never be defined as simply frozen seawater. Sea ice exists amid processes of freezing, melting, and other vectors of transformation and is thus always in a state of formation and dissolution. Furthermore, because sea ice occurs in various combinations with liquid seawater, fresh water, land, air, and other objects, its presence is always partial; its definition, always contestable. The transference of heat from one fluid medium to the other, in this case the cooling and heating of gaseous atmosphere and liquid ocean, is a mutually constitutive process that functions at a variety of temporal and spatial scales (Thomas and Dieckmann 2008). Therefore, even if one were to adopt a singular definition allowing for the demarcation of sea ice as a singular object, it still would be impossible to define a *zone* of sea ice, let alone that zone's *edge*. And even if one were able to define a linear sea ice edge, mapping it would be challenging because that edge is rarely (if ever) static, moving in response to wind and ocean currents from hourly to seasonal timescales, as well as longer-term trends in average seasonal positions associated with climate change (Steinberg and Kristoffersen 2017).[2]

Further complicating our understanding is that sea ice serves a range of functions. The same area of sea ice may be a hazard to a ship, a highway for a dog sled or snowmobile, and a refuge for a polar bear (Aporta 2011; ICC 2008; Krupnik et al. 2010). Sea ice may simultaneously be a barrier to movement, a surface across which movement is facilitated, and an element that, in its lateral drift, *is* movement (Peters 2015). Sea ice is also crucial for providing a diverse range of marine ecosystem services, and these are amplified in the marginal ice zone where sea ice intermixes with open water.

At the ice edge, physical and chemical processes combine to provide for the propagation and production of a menagerie of flora and fauna, from the micro to the macro. The physical formation of ice induces the replenishment of more nutrient-rich water from the depths to support biological production. Flow along the ice edge creates upwelling, the physical movement of deeper, more saline, nutrient-rich water up to the surface, displacing less nutrient-rich, fresher water (Barber et al. 2015). Far from being a unidimensional cover that closes the surface off from the atmosphere above, the ice edge is a site for inter-action among numerous species of algae and larger fauna, such as seabirds, fish, and marine mammals. Algal communities in particular are abundant at the ice edge, where they provide the base energy for the marine ecosystem (Codispoti et al. 2013; Hill et al. 2013; Matrai et al. 2013). During the spring season, it is the melting, decaying, and subsequent retreating of the ice edge in response to increased solar radiation that not only helps to stratify (stabilize) the water column for the propagation of marine plankton, but also releases large masses of under-ice algae (Arrigo and van Dijken 2015). Particularly notable is the capacity of sea ice to facilitate the propagation of light through the surface of solid ice and down to the water column below (Frey, Perovich, and Light 2011). Light availability is often a limiting factor in the ability of primary producers to propagate and thus forms the energetic foundation of the ecosystem (Arrigo et al. 2014).[3] But at the ice edge, as sea ice melts, its surface forms large melt ponds that from the air almost appear to be azure blue lagoons. These melt ponds play a crucial role in the onset of the spring bloom (Frey, Perovich, and Light 2011), even facilitating algal bloom under the sea ice itself (Arrigo et al. 2014). In this way, the ice serves as a medium through which energy from the atmosphere penetrates the surface. Plankton consume this energy and are then consumed by larger organisms, including humans. In short, the ice edge is a complex biogeochemical system, a site of lively interactions that transcend traditional notions of divisions between a system, its biota, and the processes that operate within this complex ecozone.

Amid this complexity, the transitional zone where ice meets water emerges as a powerful tool for rethinking the assumed geophysicalities that underpin the discourses of law, management, and planning that apply order to space. In her chapter in this volume, Jennifer L. Gaynor explores the dredged seabed as an ontologically provocative zone, as the intersection between the sea's liquid volumes and the shore's solid horizontalities forces us to rethink assumed materialities of both. In this chapter, we suggest much the same for sea ice, building on Philip E. Steinberg and Kimberley Peters's assertion that "the phenomenology of sea ice, as a particularly dynamic form of water, simultaneously destabilises conventional understandings of both geopolitics (as areal) and geophysics (as static), contributing to an ontological confusion that underpins much of the ongoing debate over the Arctic's future" (2015, 260). However, we go further, placing the "ontological confusion" of *what* ice is within a geographical confusion regarding *where* ice is, in an ever-moving zone of transition.

Drawing in particular on debates in Norway, where there has been active controversy over the legal status of sea ice and the location of its "edge," we argue that a legal geographic understanding of sea ice must necessarily be based on an appreciation of its multivalent forces. Paradoxically, however, we suggest that once the multiplicities of sea ice are taken into consideration it becomes increasingly difficult to designate sea ice as a legal object or to define its space through the identification of distinct edges. In his study of wave science, Stefan Helmreich (this volume) suggests a tension between attempts at defining laws *of* nature and applying law *to* nature. Our study of the Norwegian policy arena suggests a similar disjuncture between, on the one hand, the need to designate sea ice and its edge as an object and, on the other hand, the impossibility of doing so. However, this disjuncture also suggests opportunities for those seeking to design and apply legal knowledge in Norway's Barents Sea and beyond.

The Barents Sea as "Workable Arctic"

The Barents Sea is a 1.4 million km^2 section of the Arctic Ocean located south of Svalbard and north of the northernmost coastal boundary of Norway and Russia. The Barents, like many of the smaller seas in the Arctic, is located above a shallow shelf, where average depths measure just 230 meters. The marginal ice zone in this section of the Arctic has a key role in the mixing and formation of the waters that characterize this marine system; it is a region of atmospheric and hydrographic contrasts and transitions, with warmer, higher salinity water from the North Atlantic flowing and mixing with fresh melt waters from the Norwegian Coastal Current as well as fresh, colder waters from the Arctic, in a phenomenon known as the Polar Front. In the Barents, as disparate water masses collide, churn, cool, and become saltier, they contribute to one of the most essential geophysical mechanisms on earth: the overturning, or sinking, of water in the North Atlantic that drives the globe's ocean circulation (Anderson, Jones, and Rudels 1999; Martin and Cavalieri 1989; Oziel, Sirven, and Gascard 2015).

Over the past decade, sea ice cover in the Barents Sea has fallen more than in any other area in the Arctic, and the Barents is becoming the first virtually ice-free section of the Arctic Ocean during the summer and fall, though a significant amount of variability is evident in the northeastern section (Årthun et al. 2012; Oziel, Sirven, and Gascard 2015). While a fair amount of scientific uncertainty and debate remains regarding future projections (see Blanchard-Wrigglesworth et al. 2016; Serreze and Stroeve 2015), the general mechanisms behind ice decline are akin to the ice albedo feedback cycle (Barber et al. 2015): greater areas of open water invite an increased warming of the water, which reduces sea ice formation and may result in cascading impacts to the system's biota. Indeed, primary production of algae has been declining, and this is believed to reflect the area's changing hydrographic system (Arrigo and van Dijken 2015; Barber et al. 2015).

The Barents Sea's ecological significance is increasingly matched by its potential importance as a provider of oil and gas. Since the beginning of the twenty-first century, when Norway's oil and gas production hit its peak, the Barents has been identified as Norway's highest potential region for future development, where almost two-thirds of the undiscovered hydrocarbon deposits are expected to be located (Norwegian Petroleum Directorate 2018; see also Kristoffersen 2014). Indeed, Norway's oil and gas giant Statoil (2014) (now renamed Equinor) has designated the Barents as part of the "workable Arctic," which it distinguishes from the more challenging areas of the "stretch Arctic" and the "extreme Arctic." However, as Gavin Bridge (2011) details, making nature work for humanity requires processes of naming, categorizing, and ordering, and these efforts in turn reflect the economic, political, and cultural work of social institutions and discourses. Submerged within the simplified categories that result from these social institutions and discourses, though, is the considerable work performed by nature and its infinite processes. Sea ice, with its associated set of biogeochemically vibrant processes across a range of spatial and temporal scales, is now entrained in such a workable future for the Barents Sea, where Arctic nature is being rendered into economic or ecological assets (Bridge 2017).

Mapping the Ice Edge

Part of the work behind the incorporation of the Barents into a "workable Arctic" has involved identification of the ice edge, since Norway's Lofoten–Barents Sea Management Plan prohibits oil exploration in a number of environmentally sensitive zones, including "areas along the edge of the marginal ice zone and the polar front" (Ministry of Environment 2011, 137). And yet, this process, which would seem to involve drawing a line on a map at the point where ice extent meets open water, is anything but simple. As noted earlier, not only is ice dynamic in both space and time, but its edges lack the determinacy necessary for them to be used for zoning space. In addition, the solutions that one adopts for accommodating (or ignoring) ice's dynamism and its indeterminate edges reflect and shape perspectives on the relationship between ice and the atmospheric and biogeochemical (as well as human) processes with which its functionality is intertwined (Steinberg and Kristoffersen 2017). As the introductory quote from Prime Minister Solberg underscores, defining the ice edge every time it pops up in new policy documents and debates is highly contested and thus socially contingent. The complex and changing physical geography of Arctic sea ice thus creates a problem for establishing legal systems, as these processes are neither purely geophysical, biological, climatological, legal nor political.

Making the Arctic workable therefore occurs at specific moments, when certainties and simplifications are applied to complex biogeophysical processes, reducing them to bounded spaces that can then be used to sanction human activities (most notably, resource extraction). Such a moment occurred in January 2015, when the Norwegian government proposed an update to the Lofoten–Barents Sea Management Plan that would move the ice edge some seventy kilometers north of its previous location (which had been delineated in 2003) (figures 4.1 and 4.2). The government maintained its twelve-year-old methodology for measuring ice cover—drawing the line on the basis of a 30 percent or greater likelihood of 15 percent ice cover in the month of April—but use of an updated data set (1985–2014 instead of 1967–89) resulted in the ice-edge line's northern migration.[4] This precipitated a political outcry from environmentalists and opposition politicians, as well as their allies in the scientific community, in particular because the map was released on the same day that Norway opened fifty-four new oil exploration blocks to competitive bidding, including seven that included territory that lay north of the old ice edge limit but south of the new one. Prime Minister Solberg responded to her critics by noting that while the concurrence of the new location of the ice edge limit with the opening of a new round of exploration bids may have been fortuitous, it was due to forces that lay beyond her control: "We are not moving the ice edge," Solberg told the press. "It is actually nature that is currently moving the ice edge" (see TV 2 News Agency n.d.)

Although the new ice-edge map was produced by the Ministry of Climate and Environment, much of the data behind it was provided by the Norwegian Polar Institute (NPI), a directorate within the Ministry of Climate and Environment that is granted a high level of independence for scientific research, mapping, and environmental monitoring. While the NPI stood by its data, it warned against permitting drilling in over half of the new exploration blocks (NPI 2014a; see also Qvale and Andersen 2014). The NPI proposed that, instead

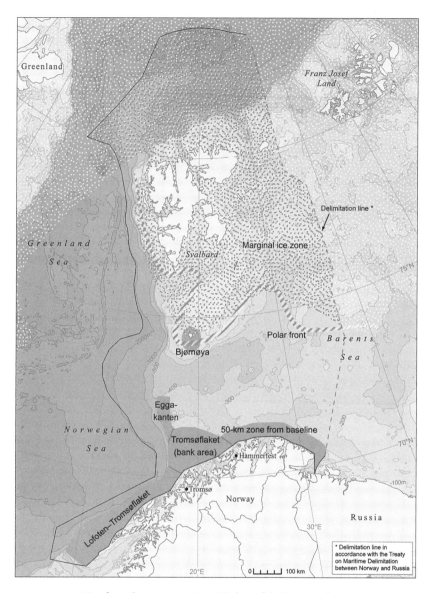

Greenland

Franz Josef
Land

Greenland
Sea

Delimitation line *

Svalbard

Marginal ice zone

75°N

Polar front

Barents
Sea

Bjørnøya

Egga-
kanten

300

Norwegian
Sea

50-km zone from baseline

Tromsøflaket
(bank area)

Hammerfest

70°N

Tromsø

Norway

Russia

-100m

Lofoten–Tromsøflaket

30°E

20°E

0 ⌊⌊⌊⌊⌊ 100 km

* Delimitation line in
accordance with the Treaty
on Maritime Delimitation
between Norway and Russia

FIGURE 4.1. Map from the 2010–2011 First Update of the Integrated Management Plan for the Marine Environment of the Barents Sea–Lofoten Area, indicating southern edge of marginal ice zone based on 1967–89 data (Ministry of Environment 2011, 23). Note that the eastern edge of the marginal ice zone's southern border is located close to the polar front. Map drawn by the Norwegian Polar Institute. Reprinted with permission of the Norwegian Ministry of Climate and Environment.

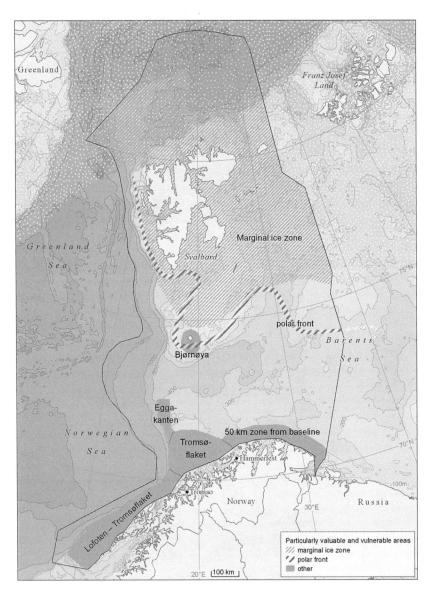

FIGURE 4.2. Map from the 2014–2015 Update of the Integrated Management Plan for the Barents Sea–Lofoten Area, indicating southern edge of the marginal ice zone based on 1985–2014 data (Ministry of Climate and Environment 2015, 25). Note that the eastern edge of the marginal ice zone's southern border is located much further from the polar front than it was in figure 4.1, indicating its northward migration. Map drawn by the Norwegian Polar Institute. Reprinted with permission of the Norwegian Ministry of Climate and Environment.

of using the thirty-year data set to define a series of fixed points of 30 percent likelihood that can be translated into a single line on a map, one should use the data set to identify monthly minimum and maximum sea ice extents for the thirty-year period. The area between the thirty-year minimum and thirty-year maximum lines would then be defined as a *zone*, indicating the area wherein, in a given month, there is a high enough likelihood of ice appearing that petroleum drilling and production should be banned according to the precautionary principle. As the Norwegian Polar Institute advised in a 2014 memorandum:

> A standalone monthly average limit for ice, which is used in the Management Plan, says nothing about the variation throughout the month, and thus has no information about where the ice edge / ice edge zone is within this period. Therefore, monthly maximum and minimum limits are more applicable, since they say something about where the boundary actually lies, along with the ice frequency and how it changes over time. (Norwegian Polar Institute 2014b)

The NPI therefore protested that twenty-nine of the fifty-four blocks were in areas that met the Management Plan's criteria for prohibition of petroleum activities for various parts of the year (Norwegian Polar Institute 2014a).[5]

As the phrase "ice edge / ice edge zone" in the NPI's memorandum suggests, part of the difference among the various parties reflects differences in terminology (see table 4.1). The scientific literature tends to distinguish between the marginal ice zone (MIZ) and the seasonal ice zone (SIZ) (e.g., National Snow and Ice Data Center n.d.). While the MIZ is the zone that at a given time is characterized by a mixture of ice extent and open water, the SIZ is the area of ocean across which the MIZ migrates over the course of a year. However, the SIZ term never appears in the Norwegian planning documents, leaving it unclear in documents like the Lofoten–Barents Sea Management Plan whether the MIZ refers to the standard definition or to the zone across which the MIZ annually migrates.[6] This confusion is replicated in references to the ice edge or the edge of the marginal ice zone. While the term *ice edge* generally is used as synonymous with the MIZ (i.e., the zone where at a given time there is a mixture of ice extent and open water) or perhaps its outer (water-facing) edge, at times it is used to indicate the southern (or northern) limit of the MIZ's annual migration (i.e., the southern or northern boundary of the SIZ). This latter meaning, for instance, is implied in the above quotation from Prime Minister Solberg, where the ice edge is identified as a singular object—a line—the location of which, but not its essence, can be shifted by external forces (in this case, nature).

TABLE 4.1. Three perspectives on the spatio-temporal variability of the ice edge / marginal ice zone in the Barents Sea.

Entity	Key objective	Planning solution
Ministry of Climate and Environment / Prime Minister	Construct stable planning tool	Median line: 30-year median of points with 30 percent April likelihood of ice extent
Norwegian Polar Institute / Environmentalists	Protect marine ecosystems	Protection zones based on monthly maximal lines: Using 30-year data, define zones based on maximal point of ice extent
Ministry of Petroleum and Energy / Oil industry	Avoid ice hazards while maximizing opportunity	Actual/observable standard: Continually adjust 50 km buffer zone around observed ice edge

Regardless of these differences in definition, the key point of contention between the Ministry of Climate and Environment and the NPI was not that one side understood ice as *dynamic* while the other conceptualized it as *static*. In fact, both sides acknowledged that the ice edge is an unstable object and that its movement cannot be controlled. However, the two sides drew different policy implications from this shared understanding. The NPI and its allies argued that the uncertainty and variability of the ice edge's movement patterns necessitated a precautionary approach, and the NPI therefore argued for the establishment of a large *zone of probability* to cover the range of areas where the formation of sea ice (and attendant ecological processes) were likely to occur. This would be operationalized by establishing the southern limit of the protected zone (i.e., the southern boundary of the SIZ) as the point of maximum ice extent at any point over the past thirty years, for any given month (Norwegian News Agency 2015; Norwegian Polar Institute 2014a, 2014b). By contrast, Prime Minister Solberg and the Ministry of Climate and Environment sought to smooth out variance in support of a static legal geography with determinate boundaries that could be used to make the Arctic workable. Although Prime Minister Solberg's "nature moved the ice edge" comment implicitly acknowledged that this line might need occasional adjustment due to nature's unpredictability, there was an underlying understanding that one could translate directly from the data to a line on a map to a planning zone, notwithstanding that the data was based on a series of aggregations and arbitrary assumptions about temporal variations and ice cover thresholds (Steinberg and Kristoffersen 2017).

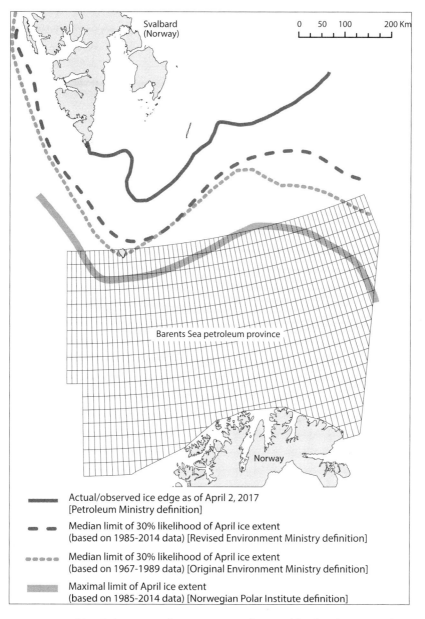

Svalbard
(Norway)

0   50   100   200 Km

Barents Sea petroleum province

Norway

━━━━ Actual/observed ice edge as of April 2, 2017
      [Petroleum Ministry definition]

━ ━   Median limit of 30% likelihood of April ice extent
      (based on 1985-2014 data) [Revised Environment Ministry definition]

••••• Median limit of 30% likelihood of April ice extent
      (based on 1967-1989 data) [Original Environment Ministry definition]

▬▬▬   Maximal limit of April ice extent
      (based on 1985-2014 data) [Norwegian Polar Institute definition]

FIGURE 4.3. Lines indicating northernmost point of permissible oil exploration in the
Barents Sea on April 2, 2017, under each of four ice-edge delimitations. Graphics courtesy
of Bjørn Hatteng/UiT. Sources: Norwegian Polar Institute, NASA, and NSIDC.

A third perspective has been adopted by the oil industry and its close ally, the Ministry of Petroleum and Energy, both of which favor a definition that prohibits exploratory drilling only in areas within fifty kilometers of the "actual/observed ice edge" (2013), defined by Minister of Petroleum and Energy Terje Søviknes as the "physical ice edge ... where there is ice at any given time" (Norwegian Broadcasting Agency 2017). On the one hand, this definition highlights the ice edge's variability; indeed it is so variable that the only relevant question is whether ice is present at a given moment. On the other hand, though, this definition is so attentive to variability that no attempt is made at data aggregation or prediction, hampering the potential for oversight or management. In practical terms, the Ministry of Petroleum and Industry's definition would allow drilling to occur in areas of the ocean that lie significantly north of the zone delimited by the Ministry of Climate and Environment's median calculation, especially in years of exceptional ice cover retreat (see figure 4.3).

Managing the Ice Edge

While these different methods for defining and mapping the ice edge reflect different perspectives on variability and probability, they also signal different perceptions of sea ice's intersection with the human and nonhuman ecologies and practices that characterize frigid oceanic waters, as these imply different perspectives on both time and space. For the Ministry of Petroleum and Energy, as noted above, "In areas closer than fifty kilometers to the actual/observed ice edge, exploration drilling in oil-bearing layers will not be allowed, in the period between December 15th and June 15th" (Ministry of Petroleum and Energy 2013). The oil industry's challenge, then, is not to determine the potential for whether sea ice will occur *in the future* (whether by means of a single probability, as proposed by the Ministry of Climate and Environment, or by means of a minimum-maximum zone, as proposed by the NPI), but to determine if sea ice is present *now*. As Petroleum and Energy Minister Søviknes elaborated when confronted with the idea of drilling in areas further north of the Ministry of Climate and Environment's ice edge, "It depends on what time you are up there. . . . In this area in the Barents Sea we can conduct exploration drilling in periods of the year which are not covered by ice" (Norwegian Broadcasting Agency 2017; see also Norwegian Petroleum Directorate 2017).

The Petroleum Ministry's approach to sea ice requires constant monitoring and rapid response to changes in ice conditions, and this is reflected in industry practice. In May 2014, when Statoil engaged in the far northern Hoop area, before being stopped by Greenpeace activists for several days, the company was, according to Exploration Director Irene Rummelhoff, well aware of "ice-issues" and was actively involved with "monitoring with information from the Meteorological Institute, planes and boats and satellites" (Qvale and Andersen 2014). Statoil boasts of its ability to quickly pack up exploratory equipment if ice conditions change: "We won't put ourselves in a situation where we operate with ice in the area," Rummelhoff continued.

These statements make clear that sea ice is seen by Statoil as a dangerous force that can disrupt drilling, much as maritime interests understand sea ice as a force than can disrupt shipping (Aporta 2011). When ice is understood solely as water that is frozen (i.e., as the opposite of a normative liquid state), it makes sense to abandon planning regimes that account for variability and trends. Instead, one simply must respond to the question of whether the watery environment in which one finds oneself at present is solidified enough to be classified as a danger. This concern suggests an imperative to invest in technologies for sensing and predicting the presence of ice and for rapidly removing infrastructure from environments where ice is forming, so as to avoid these dangers. Indeed, Norway prides itself on being an industry leader in these (and other) areas of offshore exploration and extraction (Ministry of Petroleum and Energy and Ministry of Fisheries and Trade 2017; Norwegian Academy of Technological Sciences 2005).

Missing from this perspective is that zones of possible (or temporary) ice cover may be of interest not simply because ice presence may pose a danger to drilling equipment, but also because the area around which ice forms and melts is associated with a rich ecosystem of primary production. If one takes this latter stance, the question of whether ice is present in any given year is largely irrelevant. Rather, what matters is that this is an area that (at least sometimes) is characterized by the ice-water interface. This is essentially the position of the Norwegian Polar Institute, and, as we have seen, it has led to a very different methodology for designating sea ice, defining its edge and regulating petroleum activity. For the NPI, the focus is less on identifying contemporary presence and more on demarcating a zone of probability. In short, Petroleum Ministry and NPI perspectives, in addition to revealing differing attitudes toward ice's variability in both time and space, also are rooted in different perspectives on why sea ice *matters* (and thus why its presence, or likelihood of presence, needs to be integrated into practice through legal regulation). The Petroleum Ministry's focus on contemporary presence stems from its understanding of ice as a dangerous object, whereas the NPI's focus on probability and variance stems from its understanding of the ice edge / ice edge zone as a crucial marine ecosystem.

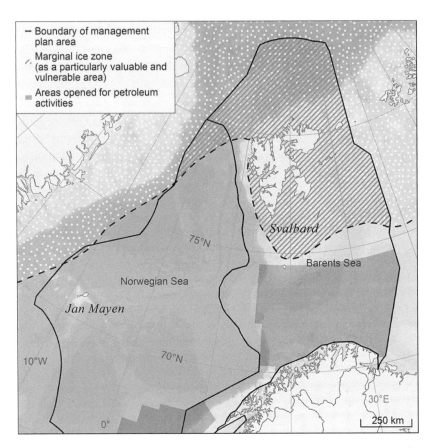

FIGURE 4.4. Map from the 2014–15 Update of the Integrated Management Plan for the Barents Sea–Lofoten Area, indicating southern edge of the marginal ice zone based on 1985–2014 data and the Barents Petroleum Province (Ministry of Climate and Environment 2015, 37). Map drawn by Norwegian Polar Institute. Reprinted with permission of Norwegian Ministry of Climate and Environment.

Set against these extremes, the Ministry of Climate and Environment's position charts a middle course, though it increasingly resembles that favored by the petroleum industry. The 2003 report that informed the 2006 Management Plan gives equal weight to the ice edge and the polar front as ocean features requiring protection. Indeed, the report highlights the polar front as "the most important oceanographic phenomenon that enhances biological production" (Olsen and Quillfeldt 2003, 55). While the polar front is roughly coterminous with the April ice edge (i.e., the southern edge of the SIZ), it dips south of this line in the eastern part of the region, thereby complicating efforts by the ministry to identify a single, determinate limit south of which petroleum activities are permitted. Thus, although the comprehensive map of protected areas in the proposed 2015 revision of the Management Plan (Ministry of Climate and Environment 2015) reproduces the map that appeared in the previous two Management Plans (Ministry of Environment 2006, 2011), albeit with a new ice-edge calculation based on more recent data (figure 4.2), another map in the 2015 revision, which indicates the Barents Sea Petroleum Province, fails to include the polar front. The reader is thus left with the impression that, thanks to the northern migration of the ice edge, the entire petroleum province is open for production (figure 4.4). This is also the message of a simplified map that was released to the public in January 2015 that reduces the seasonal ice zone to a single, determinate line (see Steinberg and Kristoffersen 2017). In effect, the message of these maps is that if, based on a thirty-year history, one can be at least 70 percent certain that a 15 percent sea ice concentration will not occur at a given point, then petroleum activities may be permitted.

Conclusion: Sea Ice Matters

To return to the quotation that began this chapter, while we agree with Prime Minister Solberg that sea ice is fascinating, it is not a singular entity that travels and propagates throughout the Arctic (here one season, gone the next). Although the binary division between sea ice and open water has provided the structure for state-sanctioned oil and gas exploration in the Barents (i.e., because sea ice is *there* we can drill *here*), the dynamism of the sea ice edge and its associated array of networked seasonal connections in time and space shatters any notion of sea ice as a perpetual aggregated entity. Sea ice is much more. It is simultaneously a zone of transition between opposing mediums, a change array for flow structure in the atmosphere and the ocean, a moving habitat, a site for the propagation of biological processes, and a jaggedly uneven line of retreat as larger order physical oceanographic and atmospheric forcings shift and alter its presence in this rapidly changing region.

In this chapter we have explored how, in a succession of reports, maps, management plans, and semiofficial statements, the Norwegian government has transformed the ice edge from a proxy for the shifting site of intense ocean-atmospheric energy exchange into a singular object to be used as a spatial planning tool—a part of what drilling proponents view as the workable Arctic. Reducing ice ecologies to a single line smooths over insecurities, gaps in scientific knowledge, and ecological risks involved in conducting economic activities above or below that line.

But the reduction of risk to a line does more than just create an abstraction that can be moved, as it was by Prime Minister Solberg in 2015. The reduction of risk to a line also means that it can be erased. This is effectively what occurred in April 2017, when the Ministry of Petroleum and Energy put another ninety-three blocks on the table and the Petroleum Directorate officially doubled its calculation of Norway's Barents Sea reserves by including new estimates north of the 2015 line. Minister Søviknes defended this recalculation by referencing the Ministry of Petroleum and Energy's "actual/observed" definition in which all Norwegian waters are available for exploration so long as ice is not actually present at the time of drilling. As he later explained to the press: "The entire ice edge debate has been messy because there are so many different definitions of the ice edge. In my view, we must relate to the facts, to where the ice actually is. The realities show that it is possible to open the northern Barents Sea for petroleum exploration" (Ytreberg 2017; see also Norwegian Broadcasting Agency 2017). Here, Søviknes suggests that the concept of an abstracted, predictable, and mappable ice edge is becoming less relevant for the spatial regulation of petroleum exploration and extraction: sea ice is being rescripted as neither an ecological zone nor an indicator of risk, but as an obstacle to be overcome through proper timing of drilling activities.[7]

We conclude by wondering whether the Norwegian story might have had a different ending if the process of ecologization and economization of the Barents Sea's materialities had played out differently (Bridge 2017). What if sea ice management were directed less toward protecting designated places of sea ice occurrence (whether based on a thirty-year trend or on current presence) and instead toward management of a zone where, amid probabilities of their occurrence, environmental and social processes were to be preserved? Such a shift would prioritize application of a precautionary approach within zones of probabilities. Research would focus on comprehension of the dynamic ecologies and biogeochemical processes within the seasonal ice zone rather than enhancement of remote sensing for classificatory purposes. New forms of mapping and legislating would be required for a politics of probability and processes. This proposed fusion of geography and law would require both disciplines to engage in introspection.

Geographic reasoning, exemplified by the map, tends toward the designation of fixed divisions, while legal reasoning also has a tendency to reify stable definitions and fixed distinctions. Acknowledgment of uncertainty, valorization of unknowable processes, recognition of complexity, and appreciation of dynamism all present challenges in a world of lines and laws. And yet there may be no alternative as we plan for a future of ecological survival, with or without sea ice.

Acknowledgments

Research for this chapter was made possible by support from the Leverhulme Trust–funded ICE LAW Project (IN-2015-033). We are grateful also to Dag Vongraven of the Norwegian Polar Institute for assistance with accessing and interpreting ice edge data.

Notes

Epigraph: Erna Solberg, prime minister of Norway, quoted in Landberg 2015.

1   All translations from Norwegian are by the authors.

2   As we discuss below, the difficulties of defining states and positions of sea ice are apparent in the way Norwegian regulations conflate and confuse such terms as *ice edge*, *marginal ice zone*, *edge of the marginal ice zone*, and *seasonal ice zone*. Here we follow the practice that prevails in the Norwegian media, referring to the "transitional zone between ice-free and ice-covered sea" (Ministry of Climate and Environment 2015, 25) as the ice edge, a feature that may range from a few hundred meters to several tens of kilometers (largely depending on wind conditions) and that may migrate hundreds of kilometers to the north and south over the course of a year.

3   Primary production refers to the photosynthetic transfer of energy into biomass, which then forms the basis for secondary transfer of energy into other, more complex living organisms.

4   In addition to updating the location of the ice edge, the data range increased from twenty-two to thirty years, the norm in climatological data modeling.

5   Similar concerns were raised by the Norwegian Environmental Agency (2014), a directorate that advises on climate and environmental policy.

6   For instance, while the text of the management plan (in the 2006, 2011, and 2015 versions) appears to refer to the MIZ using the standard scientific definition, the accompanying map identifies the entire area of annual migration—the SIZ—as the MIZ.

7   Even after the Ministry discounted the presence of ice as an environmental risk, other political actors highlighted other environmental threats. As a result, the number of blocks put out for bid ultimately was reduced from ninety-three to forty-nine, with thirty-eight of these located in the Barents Sea (Lorentzen 2018).

References

Anderson, Leif G., Peter E. Jones, and Bert Rudels. 1999. "Ventilation of the Arctic Ocean Estimated by a Plume Entrainment Model Constrained by CFCs." *Journal of Geophysical Research: Oceans* 104 (C6): 13423–29.

Aporta, Claudio. 2011. "Shifting Perspectives on Shifting Ice: Documenting and Representing Inuit Uses of Sea Ice." *Canadian Geographer* 55 (1): 6–19.

Arrigo, Kevin, and Gert L. van Dijken. 2015. "Continued Increases in Arctic Ocean Primary Production." *Progress in Oceanography* 136 (August): 60–70.

Arrigo, Kevin, Donald K. Perovich, Robert S. Pickart, Zachary W. Brown, Gert L. van Dijken, Kate E. Lowry, Matthew M. Mills, et al. 2014. "Phytoplankton Blooms beneath the Sea Ice in the Chukchi Sea." *Deep Sea Research Part II: Topical Studies in Oceanography* 105 (July): 1–16

Årthun, Marius, Tor Eldevik, Lars Smedsrud, Øystien Skagseth, and Randi Ingvaldsen. 2012. "Quantifying the Influence of Atlantic Heat on Barents Sea Ice Variability and Retreat." *Journal of Climate* 25 (13): 4736–43.

Barber, David G., Haakon Hop, Christopher J. Mundy, Brent Else, Igor A. Dmitrenko, Jean-Eric Tremblay, Jens K. Ehn, et al. 2015. "Selected Physical, Biological and Biogeochemical Implications of a Rapidly Changing Arctic Marginal Ice Zone." *Progress in Oceanography* 139 (December): 122–50.

Blanchard-Wrigglesworth, Edward, Antoine Barthélemy, Mattieu Chevallier, R. Cullather, Neven Fučkar, Francois Massonnet, Pamela Posey, et al. 2016. "Multi-Model Seasonal Forecast of Arctic Sea-Ice: Forecast Uncertainty at Pan-Arctic and Regional Scales." October. *Climate Dynamics* 1–12.

Bridge, Gavin. 2011. "Resource Geographies 1. Making Carbon Economies, Old and New." *Progress in Human Geography* 35 (6): 820–34.

Bridge, Gavin. 2017. "Economizing the Arctic: Polar Orientations." Framing paper for Anticipating Abundance: Economizing the Arctic workshop, Durham University, May 11–12.

Codispoti, Lou A., Vincent Kelly, Anne Thessen, Patricia A. Matrai, Steve Suttles, Victoria Hill, Mike Steele, and Bonnie Light. 2013. "Synthesis of Primary Production in the Arctic Ocean: III. Nitrate and Phosphate Based Estimates of Net Community Production." *Progress in Oceanography* 110 (March): 126–50.

Frey, Karen E., Donald K. Perovich, and Bonnie Light. 2011. "The Spatial Distribution of Solar Radiation under a Melting Arctic Sea Ice Cover." *Geophysical Research Letters* 38 (22): 1–6.

Hill, Victoria, Patricia A. Matrai, Elise Olson, Steve Suttles, Mike Steele, Lou A. Codispoti, and Richard C. Zimmerman. 2013. "Synthesis of Integrated Primary Production in the Arctic Ocean: II. *In situ* and Remotely Sensed Estimates." *Progress in Oceanography* 110 (March): 107–25.

ICC (Inuit Circumpolar Council). 2008. *The Sea Ice Is Our Highway: An Inuit Perspective on Transportation in the Arctic*. Ottawa: ICC-Canada.

Kristoffersen, Berit. 2014. "'Securing' Geography: Framings, Logics and Strategies in the Norwegian High North." In *Polar Geopolitics? Knowledges, Resources and Legal Regimes*, edited by Richard Powell and Klaus Dodds, 131–48. Cheltenham, UK: Edward Elgar.

Krupnik, Igor, Claudio Aporta, Shari Gearheard, Gita J. Laidler, and Lene K. Holm. 2010. *Siku: Knowing Our Ice: Documenting Inuit Sea Ice Knowledge and Use*. Berlin: Springer.

Landberg, Øystein K. 2015. "Erna Solberg tok en Obama" [Erna Solberg did as Obama]. *Aftenposten*, March 20. http://www.aftenposten.no/norge/politikk/Erna-Solberg-tok -en-Obama-46361b.html.

Lorentzen, Marius. 2018. "Tildeler nye lisenser i 24. konsesjonsrunde" [New licenses allotted in the 24th concession round]. *E24!*, June 18. https://e24.no/energi/terje -soeviknes/staten-er-klar-med-24-konsesjonsrunde-tilbyr-12-lisenser-til-11-oljeselskap /24373104.

Martin, Seelye, and Donald J. Cavalieri. 1989. "Contributions of the Siberian Shelf Polyn-yas to the Arctic Ocean Intermediate and Deep Water." *Journal of Geophysical Research: Oceans* 94 (C9): 12725–38.

Matrai, Pamela, Elise Olson, Steven Suttles, Victoria Hill, Lou A. Codispoti, Bonnie Light, and Michael Steele. 2013. "Synthesis of Primary Production in the Arctic Ocean: I. Surface Waters, 1954–2007." *Progress in Oceanography* 110 (March): 93–106.

Ministry of Climate and Environment (Norway). 2015. "Oppdatering av forvaltnings-splanen for Barentshavet og havområdene utenfor Lofoten med oppdatert beregning av iskanten" [An updating of the Management Plan for the Barents Sea and the ocean areas outside Lofoten with an updated estimate of the ice edge]. White paper no. 20. April 24. Oslo: Ministry of Climate and Environment. https://www.regjeringen.no/no/dokumenter/meld.-st.-20-2014-2015/id2408321.

Ministry of Environment (Norway). 2006. "Helhetlig forvaltning av det marine miljø i Barentshavet og havområdene utenfor Lofoten (forvaltningsplan)" [Management plan for the marine environment in the Barents Sea and the ocean zone outside Lofoten (the Management Plan)]. White paper no. 8. March 31. Oslo: Ministry of Environment. https://www.regjeringen.no/no/dokumenter/stmeld-nr-8-2005-2006-/id199809.

Ministry of Environment (Norway). 2011. "Oppdatering av forvaltningsplanen for det marine miljø i Barentshavet og havområdene utenfor Lofoten (forvaltningsplan)" [An updating of the Management Plan for the marine environment in the Barents Sea and the ocean areas outside Lofoten (the Management Plan)]. White paper no. 10. March 11. Oslo: Ministry of Environment. https://www.regjeringen.no/no/dokumenter/meld-st-10-2010-2011/id635591.

Ministry of Petroleum and Energy (Norway). 2013. "Nye muligheter for Nord-Norge, åpning av Barentshavet Sørøst for petroleumsvirksomhet" [New possibilities for northern Norway: The opening of the southeast Barents Sea for petroleum extraction]. White paper no. 10. June. Oslo: Ministry of Petroleum and Energy.

Ministry of Petroleum and Energy and Ministry of Fisheries and Trade. 2017. "Ny Vekst, Stolt Historie—Regjeringens Havstrategi" [New growth, proud history: The government's ocean strategy]. July 7. https://www.regjeringen.no/contentassets/1ed01965de3 249f689f1938ad3c0b672/nfd_havstrategi_webfil.pdf.

National Snow and Ice Data Center (United States). n.d. *Cryosphere Glossary*. Accessed October 18, 2018. https://nsidc.org/cryosphere/glossary.

Norwegian Academy of Technological Sciences. 2005. "Norwegian Petroleum Technol-ogy: A Success Story." Trondheim: Norwegian Academy of Technological Sciences. https://www.sintef.no/globalassets/upload/petroleumsforskning/dokumenter/forskningsboken_en.pdf.

Norwegian Broadcasting Agency. 2017. "The Debate." Debate with Minister of Petroleum and Energy Terje Søviknes. April 27. https://tv.nrk.no/serie/debatten/NNFA51042717/27-04-2017.

Norwegian Environmental Agency. 2014. "Forslag til utlysning i 23. Konsesjonsrunde, Miljødirektoratets vurdering av de foreslåtte blokkene" [Suggestions for the an-nouncement in the 23rd concession round, the Environmental Directorate's assess-ment of the suggested exploration blocks]. March 27. http://www.miljodirektoratet

.no/Documents/Nyhetsdokumenter/23konsesjonsrunde_miljodirektoratet
_uttalelse270314.pdf.

Norwegian News Agency. 2015. "Kraftige reaksjoner mot regjeringens iskant-avgjørelse"
[Strong reactions against the government's ice-edge decision]. *Dagbladet*, January 20.
https://www.dagbladet.no/nyheter/kraftige-reaksjoner-mot-regjeringens-iskant
-avgjorelse/60800310.

Norwegian Petroleum Directorate. 2017. "Doubling the Resource Estimate for the Barents Sea." April 25. http://www.npd.no/en/news/News/2017/Doubling-the-resource
-estimate-for-the-Barents-Sea.

Norwegian Petroleum Directorate. 2018. "Ressursrapport leting 2018" [Resource exploration report]. June 21. http://www.npd.no/no/Publikasjoner/Ressursrapporter/2018.

Norwegian Polar Institute. 2014a. "Høringsuttalelse—forslag til utlysning av blokker til
23. Konsesjonsrunde" [Written submission on the announcement of exploration blocks
in the 23rd concession round]. April 4. http://www.npolar.no/no/nyheter/2014/2014
-04-04-np-uttalelse-iskantsonen.html.

Norwegian Polar Institute. 2014b. "Iskant og iskantsone—fremstilling av iskantsonen
som sårbart areal" [Ice edge and ice edge zone—an account of the ice edge zone as
a vulnerable area]. April. http://www.npolar.no/npcms/export/sites/np/no/fakta
/iskant-ressurser/nedlastbart/iskant-og-iskantsone.pdf.

Olsen, Erik, and Cecilia von Quillfeldt. 2003. "Identifisering av særlig verdifulle områder i
Lofoten–Barentshavet" [The identification of particularly vulnerable areas in Lofoten–
Barentshavet]. May. www.npolar.no/npcms/export/sites/np/no/arktis/barentshavet
/forvaltningsplan/filer/yp.pdf.

Oziel, Laurent, Jerome Sirven, and Jean-Claude Gascard. 2015. "The Barents Sea Polar
Front and Water Masses Variability (1980–2011)." *Ocean Science Discussions* 12 (2):
449–92.

Peters, Kimberley. 2015. "Drifting: Towards Mobilities at Sea." *Transactions of the Institute
of British Geographers* 40 (2): 262–72.

Qvale, Peder, and Ina Andersen. 2014. "25 Prosent av all uoppdaget olje i verden kan
ligge bak iskanten" [25 percent of all undiscovered oil in the world may lie behind the
ice edge]. August 27. https://www.tu.no/artikler/25-prosent-av-all-uoppdaget-olje-i
-verden-kan-ligge-bak-iskanten/230453.

Serreze, Mark C., and Julienne Stroeve. 2015. "Arctic Sea Ice Trends, Variability and Implications for Seasonal Ice Forecasting." *Philosophical Transactions of the Royal Society A*
373 (2045): 1–16.

Statoil. 2014. "A Responsible Approach to Arctic Operations." Online feature story on
the EU Arctic Portal website. January 27. http://www.arcticinfo.eu/en/features/103-a
-responsible-approach-to-arctic-operations.

Steinberg, Philip, and Berit Kristoffersen. 2017. "'The Ice Edge Is Lost . . . Nature Moved
It': Mapping Ice as State Practice in the Norwegian and Canadian North." *Transactions
of the Institute of British Geographers*. 42 (4): 625–41.

Steinberg, Philip, and Kimberley Peters. 2015. "Wet Ontologies, Fluid Spaces: Giving
Depth to Volume through Oceanic Thinking." *Environment and Planning D: Society
and Space* 33 (2): 247–64.

Thomas, David N., and Gerhard S. Dieckmann, eds. 2008. *Sea Ice: An Introduction to Its Physics, Chemistry, Biology and Geology*. New York: John Wiley & Sons.

T V 2 News Agency. n.d. "Norsk klimaforsker: Det er mennesker som ødelegger isen i Arktis" [Norwegian climate scientist: There are people who destroy the ice in the Arctic]. Accessed April 10, 2019. https://www.tv2.no/v/989382/.

Ytreberg, Rune. 2017. "Vil bore lenger nord" [Will drill further north]. *Dagens Næringsliv* [Business Daily], May 9, 18. https://www.dn.no/avisen/DN%202017-05-09/18.

5. LIQUID TERRITORY, SHIFTING SANDS

Property, Sovereignty, and Space in Southeast Asia's
Tristate Maritime Boundary Zone

JENNIFER L. GAYNOR

Great Walls and Fledgling Islands: An Introduction

Building islands on a grand scale typically brings to mind China's filling in atolls to support its territorial claims or Dubai's offshore construction of fancifully shaped real estate. Yet these constitute only the most high-profile examples of large-scale land reclamation ventures around the world, many of them in Asia. This chapter, part of a larger project on contemporary land production, looks at how disputes in Southeast Asia set precedents for the 2016 ruling on China's claims in the South China Sea by the Permanent Court of Arbitration (PCA).

Located at the southwestern extremity of the South China Sea, the tristate maritime boundary zone is shared by Indonesia, Singapore, and Malaysia (see figure 5.1). This confluence of the South China Sea with the Singapore and Malacca Straits, well known as a global shipping superhighway, accounts for a third of global commerce and has the highest perennial incidence of piracy (Gaynor 2012). The waters of the tristate maritime boundary zone matter here for their place in a wider story of political economy and international legal approaches to conflicts over land reclamation. While most approaches to maritime issues stay immersed in the sea, island building reminds us that sometimes ocean matters reach beyond what is wet. More than a call to include the shore, which the sea constantly remakes, the point here is rather that people use land reclamation to produce dry ground in previously submerged areas, inventing islands and reinventing the coast. People, in this case, reshape maritime and coastal spaces, alter their significance, and transform the social relations they support.

China impressed the world with its bold island building in the South China Sea, which caused concern to its neighbors in ASEAN, the Association of

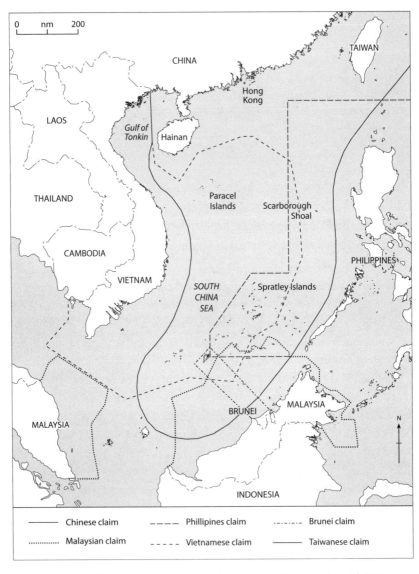

FIGURE 5.1. Southeast Asia claims map, emphasizing seas. Cartographer: Chris Orten, based on Voice of America 2012. Wikimedia Commons, public domain.

Southeast Asian Nations (Heydarian 2016). China's island building also caught the attention of top brass in the United States. At a speech in Canberra, Australia, in 2015, Admiral Harry Harris of the US Pacific Fleet said that "China is creating a great wall of sand with dredges and bulldozers" in the South China Sea, and he accused China "of undertaking an enormous and unprecedented artificial land creation operation" (Sanger and Gladstone 2015). Certainly, China's island building has raised political tensions, but is this artificial land creation unprecedented, or was Harris overstating the case? After all, also in the works are a "great wall of Lagos" and a "great wall of Jakarta," both of which use massive dredges to mobilize enormous amounts of sand (Lukacs 2014; Tarrant 2014). Promoted to protect coastlines threatened by sea-level rise and land subsidence, these "great walls," like islands made with the same technology, also simply create new land.

Below, the South China Sea legal decision serves as background and context for this chapter, in which I argue that instead of viewing specific projects as unprecedented, that distinction falls instead to the contemporary scale and pace of land reclamation carried out by the global dredging industry. The industrial magnitude of dredging and land reclamation—in effect, the industrial production of land—has opened new areas of legal and political contestation. Disputes in Southeast Asia's tristate boundary zone illustrate this. Yet, their outcomes also suggest paths forward, and paths to avoid, in subsequent legal claims and requests for arbitral clarification. In particular, these cases highlight the difficulty of halting dredging through environmental claims and underscore that clarification of sovereignty may not resolve questions about entitlements over maritime space. As will be seen below, the Philippines thus sought clarification about maritime entitlements and, hence, lowered the stakes on China's claims to sovereignty over particular features.

The South China Sea

Over the past several years, Beijing has turned seven reefs in the Spratlys into artificial islands to bolster its territorial claims within the "nine-dash line," an area covering much of the South China Sea. China had previously conducted reclamation activity in the Paracels. In the Spratly Islands, China's land reclamation gained dramatic momentum during 2015 and 2016: it occupied the islands it built, erected structures, paved runways, and installed military defenses (AMTI/CSIS 2017; Duong 2015; Poling 2016).

The Association of Southeast Asian Nations, as an organization, has walked a fine line on China's position and actions in the South China Sea. On the one hand, ASEAN has tried to push China to resolve territorial disputes and to intensify official consultations on a Code of Conduct. On the other hand, ASEAN has diplomatically refused to become an anti-China forum. China, for its part, has consistently stated that a Code of Conduct will not impinge upon the exercise of its sovereign claims in the South China Sea. Such statements and Beijing's continued reclamation activity seem to contradict what little progress has been made toward a Code of Conduct (Li 2014; McLaughlin 2014). Meanwhile, individual member states—most notably Vietnam, Indonesia, and the Philippines—have separately pursued a variety of measures independent of ASEAN, ranging from land reclamation of their own, military buildups, heightened patrols, and seizures of Chinese vessels to bilateral talks with China and international arbitration.

Rather than take legal measures to resolve conflicting territorial claims in the South China Sea, bilateral talks appeal to countries in the region for several reasons, including China's growing investments across Asia. Yet arbitration pursued by the Philippines recently had some success. China's contested claims to South China Sea features, and its island building on Mischief Reef, led the Philippines to turn to the PCA in The Hague to form a tribunal provided for under Annex VII of the United Nations Convention on the Law of the Sea (UNCLOS). The Philippines' decision to take this step, which produced the first major ruling on the South China Sea, follows the successes and failures of its ASEAN neighbors over the past fifteen years with claims related to land reclamation in other international legal venues.

Before having a look at those precedents below, the following overview clarifies the outcome of the case brought by the Philippines. On July 12, 2016, the arbitral tribunal at the PCA ruled, to the surprise of many observers, on the legal status of every feature in the Spratly Islands raised by the Philippines. Among its decisions, the tribunal invalidated Beijing's position on territorial claims within the "nine-dash line" based on ill-defined historical claims. The tribunal also found that of the seven Spratlys now occupied by China, two are reefs below water at high tide and thus generate no maritime entitlement, while four are described as "rocks" (as is Scarborough Shoal) and thus are entitled to only a 12–nautical mile sea. In other words, since these features are not legally islands, they do not generate an entitlement to an exclusive economic zone (EEZ), the 200–nautical mile area beyond and adjacent to a country's territorial sea, over which it exercises special rights of access and exploitation under international law. According to the arbitral tribunal, none of the Spratlys, including the largest natural features, are legally islands, for in the eyes of international law, they cannot sustain a stable human community or independent economic life. The judgment does not allocate any of the outcrops or islands to rival countries, but instead indicates only which maritime features are capable under international law of generating rights over surrounding seas (PCA 2016; Poling et al. 2016).

Beijing, not surprisingly, rejected the tribunal's ruling on the South China Sea case. Though the United States and its allies remained watchful for China to challenge the decision, the Chinese government has repeatedly said it would not recognize any such ruling (Muñoz 2016; Phillips, Holmes, and Bowcott 2016; Poling 2016). The day after the ruling was issued, Beijing demonstrated its disdain by landing a civilian aircraft on the new runway at Mischief Reef (Macias 2016). Nonetheless, the ruling makes clear that, thus far, China's island building has met with decidedly mixed results: Beijing's desire to extend its territorial baseline and EEZ seaward from these still-controversial footholds will not be condoned under international law.

The PCA ruling has emboldened ASEAN to move forward with diplomatic measures to resolve conflicting claims. Taking up a suggestion by Brunei, some ASEAN countries already employ a dual-track approach, working with China through the regional forum to maintain peace and stability in the South China Sea while, at the same time, trying to resolve matters through negotiation between the parties directly concerned (Xinhua News 2016). The revival of ties between Beijing and Vietnam, and their resulting joint communiqué on the South China Sea, exemplifies this approach (Nguyen Minh Quang 2017). Given that progress on negotiations over a Code of Conduct has stalled since the 2002 milestone, when China and ASEAN signed the Declaration on the Conduct of Parties in the South China Sea, skeptics can be forgiven for viewing the dual-track approach as simply a series of bilateral agreements. However, following the arbitral tribunal's 2016 ruling, ASEAN decided to go ahead with talks on the Code of Conduct in the South China Sea. In February 2017, ASEAN took up two contentious issues: the nonmilitarization of occupied features, and restraint in South China Sea activities, specifically those involving China. As current ASEAN chair, the Philippines leads these discussions. Yet, in negotiating the framework for the Code of Conduct, the Philippines has stated that it will not raise the issue of the arbitral tribunal's decision (Deogracias 2017; McLaughlin 2014).

In the wake of the tribunal's ruling, most coverage has overlooked the court's censure of the rampant destruction of marine life around reclamation sites. The judges held that the construction "had caused permanent and irreparable harm to the coral reef ecosystem." Beijing, by contrast, denies its island building has posed any danger to the region's natural habitat, going so far as to call it a model "green project" (Singh 2016). However, as work in international environmental history has shown, such greenwashing is not Beijing's exclusive preserve (Worster 1982). Like "improvements" made to degraded land, the politics of such claims also run deep. In early statements of political ecology, scholars called for approaches to land degradation that went beyond technical questions, to instead situate the analysis among environmental dynamics and social relations writ large (Blaikie and Brookfield 1987). Land reclamation sits in a similar, though changing, nexus.

The Industrial Production of Land

Analysis of China's island building in the South China Sea is dominated by strategic discourse. Alternatively, one could situate it analytically among other large-scale land reclamation projects pursued through the global dredging industry. Dredging and land reclamation have a long history in Asia. China's Grand Canal constitutes the largest civil engineering project prior to the industrial revolution. Parts of it date back to the fifth century, and by the thirteenth century, it linked five of China's river basins with more than two thousand kilometers of artificial waterways. In Japan, during the early Tokugawa period in the late sixteenth and first half of the seventeenth century, Edo (now Tokyo), was completely transformed by land reclamation, canals, and moats. While the ruling Tokugawa house went from being the strongest among domain leaders (*daimyo*) to heading the shogunate or military government (*bakufu*), it remade the local geography of Edo. Hibiya inlet was filled in to prevent merchant ships from entering the former naval port below the castle and, among many other artificial waterways, Dosanbori canal was dug to facilitate the delivery of rice and goods into the castle (Kuan 2013, 200). In mainland Southeast Asia, the Khmer Empire of the thirteenth century excavated many reservoirs and canals, some of which are still in use.

Dredging and reclamation on the scale we see in Southeast Asia today has its roots in a more recent history, however. Beginning in 1893, dredging in colonial Vietnam was carried out by private monopoly contractors who were paid to dig canals on ten-year agreements. In 1895, three steam-powered dredges set to work. A reorganization of the Department of Public Works in 1900 brought dredging further within the oversight of provincial councils eager to develop more territory and to expand revenues. This fiscal and administrative reorganization of the dredging process created a powerful new alliance of interests, linking provincial administrators, influential landowners, public works engineers, and the dredging enterprise. For the next thirty years, they accelerated the opening of new lands and profited from subsequent land concessions (Biggs 2010, 23–52).

The scale of contemporary dredging and land reclamation in Southeast Asia dwarfs these beginnings of their industrial manifestation on the mainland during the late colonial period. What remains similar, though, is the involvement of the state. Whether expanding existing coasts, or making new islands, land reclamation in Southeast Asia (including the South China Sea) falls into two categories: territorial expansion of states and real estate development. The overlap between these involves a coincidence of interests that appears to be no accident. In states with weak regulatory frameworks, skewed redistribution, and high inequality, the class interests of elites often do not look very different from those of their colonial counterparts in a previous generation. One can turn to the literatures on neoliberalism and the critique of development to discuss this at the theoretical level. However, in addition to the role of the state and elites, another point interests me here, namely, land production.

The capacity to produce land raises large questions that reach across disciplinary boundaries. Land has, of course, been treated in a variety of ways in economic theory. In neoclassical economics, land was a production factor of relatively little importance. More recent spatial analysis, including land use considerations and attention to environmental and resource problems, have stimulated new approaches to land in economic analysis. For instance, such fields as ecological economics incorporate biophysical analyses concerned with the interdependence and the coevolution of environmental, economic, and social systems (Hubacek and van den Bergh 2006, 18–22). Yet while their treatment of land is complex, recent approaches share with older ones a view of land as scarce and subject to competing uses.

Similarly, in landscape ecology, originating from an interaction between ecology, geography, and land use planning, a field that provides important spatial information to integrated modeling of social and natural science elements, land remains a given. It takes heterogeneous forms as "land cover," either altered through natural ecological systems or changed by human activities and land use (Hubacek and van den Bergh 2006, 22; Turner 1998). Yet, even in this view, land itself is not produced. The scale of land reclamation now possible changes that. Recent technological developments and the industry they support do not just signify incremental increases. Rather, the current scope and intensity of the global dredging industry make it a game changer for land reclamation.

Simply put, the scale at which land reclamation now takes place is nothing short of the industrial production of land. Giant dredges dislodge and suck sand up from the seabed to spew it out like so much liquid onto a particular shoal, until the floor of the sea rises above the high-water mark to become re-claimed land—a curious name, as though the sea had previously taken it.[1] This terraforming transforms the sand of the sea, desirable for qualities peculiar to its oceanic formation, into terra firma. Taking sand from the marine world and reconstituting it to create terrestrial places, land reclamation changes the shape of both land and sea and alters coastal ecologies. While sometimes undertaken to mitigate sea-level rise and land subsidence, and often bolstered by nationalist pride, this production of land serves expanding states and capital.

International Disputes

Such real estate development and state-sponsored territorial expansion both take place in Singapore, an island city-state and vibrant commercial hub with a growing population. Singapore no longer suffers the quandary of whether to enclose existing land and convert it to property, for it has effectively run out of land. Nearly the entire island consists of either urban areas or protected sanc-tuaries. Apart from these zones, large securitized tracts devoted to storing sand and gravel form exceptional spaces that effectively leverage the interior in order for the coast to grow (Comaroff 2014). Unlike other states that must compen-sate people for takings, or deal with the backlash of summary evictions and seizure, the state of Singapore, with the help of developers, instead opts to create new land through reclamation, from which they then reap rents and taxes.

Vessels that travel between the Indian Ocean and the South China Sea sail by Singapore through the densely trafficked tristate maritime boundary zone. Much of Singapore's economy revolves around this shipping, with its VLCCS (very large crude carriers) and ships with ever-deeper drafts requiring deeper ports. Hence, population and real estate account for only part of Singapore's expansion, which also manifests in facilities to service this economy, boosting Singapore's status as a hub of global commerce.

For over fifteen years, Malaysia has banned the export of river sand (for con-struction) and sea sand (for reclamation), since it discovered that materials for its own projects were being illegally diverted to Singapore. One might well ask why not obtain sand for land reclamation from deserts? However, even Dubai, so well-endowed with sand, cannot use it, since desert sand is too fine for both reclamation and construction. Malaysia's ban created a windfall for the black market in sand, little surprise, perhaps, given the region's long history of smug-gling. In 2008, according to the United Nations' Comtrade database, Singa-pore declared it imported 3 million tons of sand from Malaysia, yet Malaysia's figures show a staggering 133 million tons of sand reportedly exported to

Singapore, despite the ban. The murky billion-dollar illegal trade in sand feeds Singapore's insatiable demand, driving a huge web of corruption and theft in a country renowned for honest business practices and corporal punishment. Since Singapore's independence in 1965, its land area has grown from 581.5 to 710 square kilometers. By 2030 it plans to expand another 90 square kilometers, which would make it 30 percent larger than its original size, and about the same area as New York City. In short, Singapore imports more sand than anywhere else in the world (Milton 2010).

Singapore's demand for sand has had dramatic impacts in Malaysia, the Mekong delta, and across the water in Indonesia. Since dredging changes the course, flow, and sediment distribution of rivers, extensive dredging of the Mekong to extract sand bound for Singapore has caused the river to deposit sand unexpectedly in some places, yet has stripped away the river's banks at an alarming rate elsewhere (Bravard, Goichot, and Gaillot 2013; Forsyth and Bright 2016). So many companies have flocked to the sand dredging business in Vietnam that it is difficult for state agencies to keep track of them. The impact of dredging on the delta's hydro-ecology is the washing away of settlements and infrastructure, prompting one analyst to conclude, "Consequently, further engineering is necessary to fix the side effects of the unregulated exploitation of natural resources. Ironically, the engineering enterprises involved in this business do not only benefit from sand exploitation, but even create future work and business opportunities for themselves" (Benedikter 2014, 197–98). Such a cycle of dredging for sand, altering the hydro-ecology, accelerating abrasion, and creating a need to reengineer the shore has impacted both riparian and salt water environments.

For instance, in April 2002 Malaysia lodged a protest against Singapore's reclamation works around Pulau Tekong and Pulau Ubin, claiming they were causing transboundary environmental harm to Malaysia's territorial waters. After an unsuccessful meeting between the parties, Malaysia initiated proceedings in a bid to stop Singapore's reclamation around these islands. On September 5, 2003, Malaysia filed a request with the International Tribunal for the Law of the Sea (ITLOS) asking for provisional measures to stop the reclamation pending resolution of the case. ITLOS prescribed that the two states cooperate to establish a group of independent experts mandated to study the effects of Singapore's land reclamation and to propose measures to deal with adverse effects. The case raised their conflicting rights: Singapore's to reclaim part of its territorial sea for national needs, and Malaysia's to protect its maritime environment from harm. In the end, Singapore did not have to suspend its reclamation activities, and the case was ultimately resolved by a 2005 settlement agreement recommending that a "bite" be taken out of Pulau Tekong's southeastern

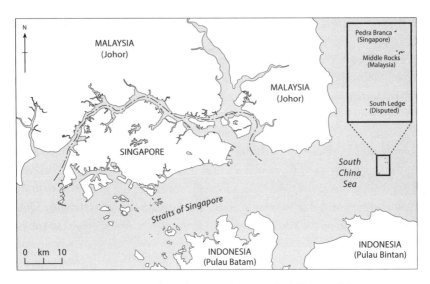

FIGURE 5.2. Tristate maritime boundary zone showing Pulau Tekong and the approximate locations of Pedra Branca, Middle Rocks, and South Ledge. Cartographer: Chris Orten. Reproduced with permission.

side, while a "nose" be added to its southern tip, to improve the flow of water and to ensure that the final reclaimed area of Pulau Tekong remains the same (Cheong, Koh, and Yee 2013; ITLOS 2003).

In 2003, Malaysia and Singapore requested that the International Court of Justice (ICJ) determine which of the two countries has sovereignty over Pedra Branca (Pulau Batu Puteh), Middle Rocks, and South Ledge, all located in close proximity to one another in the eastern part of the tristate maritime boundary zone (see figure 5.2). Each party's position was based on historical claims, partly reflected in their toponyms. For instance, Pulau Batu Puteh, literally "white rock island," is the Malay name for Pedra Branca, Portuguese for "white rock." This area has an intricate colonial history involving the Portuguese, the Dutch, and the English, with various treaties among imperial powers as well as between them and the rulers of Southeast Asian realms, mostly dating from the nineteenth century. Singapore's history after the dissolution of the Straits Settlement in 1946 is no less complex. It became a self-governing colony in 1958, merged with other former British colonies in 1963, joining the Federation of Malaya, and then, in 1965, left the Federation to become an independent and sovereign state.

The ICJ was not asked to rule about maritime entitlements in the case. It ruled only on the issue of sovereignty. Hence, it did not need to consider whether under international law Pedra Branca was "really" a "rock" or an "island." Since the court did not make decisions regarding maritime entitlements, its ruling could not settle the question of the maritime boundary. The 2008 ICJ judgment awarded Pedra Branca to Singapore, and the two clusters of granite 0.6 nautical miles to its south, known as Middle Rocks, to Malaysia. It also ruled that South Ledge, visible only at low tide, and hence incapable of generating a maritime entitlement, belongs to the state in whose territorial seas it lies.

In the wake of the court's decision granting Pedra Branca to Singapore, the Malaysian government told its people to stop calling it Pulau, dropping "island" from its name to imply that it was only a rock. The desired effect was to limit the extent of its maritime entitlement under Singaporean sovereignty. One wonders whether in the future Malaysians will once again be urged to call it *Pulau* Batu Puteh, since Malaysia recently reopened the Pedra Branca case. An appeal of the ICJ decision may be brought within ten years of the date of judgment, and within six months of the discovery of a new fact. Kuala Lumpur claims that new documents have been discovered in British archives backing its claim to Pedra Branca (Kyodo News Service 2017; Lim 2008).

Planned reclamation played an interesting role as a contributing factor in the ICJ's decision on this case. Plans to reclaim areas around Pedra Branca had been considered on various occasions during the 1970s by the Port of Singapore Authority. The court observed that while Singapore did not proceed with the reclamation and some of the documents were not public, the tender advertisement was public and attracted replies. Moreover, the proposed action, as advertised, went beyond the mere maintenance and operation of the lighthouse already in place, conduct supporting Singapore's case (ICJ 2008).

China may have expected similar factors to weigh in its favor and legitimize its more recent reclamation activities in the South China Sea. Yet, in the matter decided on July 12, 2016, the Philippines took an approach informed by this history of arbitration in the above cases. The Philippines neither made a case to stop reclamation on the grounds of environmental damage nor asked the arbitral tribunal to rule on the issue of sovereignty. Instead, it only requested clarification of the legal status of specific features in the South China Sea to determine whether and how much each engenders a maritime entitlement.

A number of issues remain unresolved in the tristate maritime boundary zone. The question of Pedra Branca's status concerns not only Malaysia, from whose Johor coast Pedra Branca lies a mere 7.7 nautical miles, but also matters to Indonesia, from which Pedra Branca is 7.6 nautical miles distant (Lim 2008). Following the ICJ ruling in 2008, the area between the cluster of Batu Puteh, Middle Rocks, and South Ledge and Indonesia's Bintan Island to

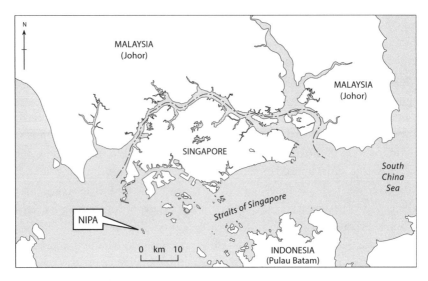

FIGURE 5.3. Tristate maritime boundary zone showing location of Pulau Nipa. Cartographer: Chris Orten. Reproduced with permission.

the south awaits further negotiation by Singapore and Malaysia. Malaysia has also not settled its territorial sea boundary with Indonesia in the eastern Singapore Strait, between Johor and the islands of Bintan and Batam, which became an issue after their marine enforcement agencies came face to face with each other. In addition, Singapore and Indonesia only ratified a treaty on their border in the eastern part of the zone, between Batam and Changi, in 2017 (Straits Times 2017). These pending boundary issues, and Malaysia's inability to halt Singapore's reclamation of Pulau Tekong with its environmental claim, provide the context for understanding, below, how Indonesia handled the dwindling size of Pulau Nipa (sometimes Nipah) in the western part of the tristate maritime boundary zone.

Pulau Nipa, or Nipa Island, is Indonesia's outermost island (*pulau terluar*) south of Singapore (see figure 5.3). In a country composed of over seventeen thousand islands, this small island came to the attention of President Megawati Sukarnoputri's administration in 2004 because it was disappearing. It seemed exceedingly likely that Singapore's extensive reclamation activity played a role, for as Singapore grew, Pulau Nipa shrank. Nipa's shrinking caused no small amount of consternation in Indonesia. Although it measured 60 hectares at low tide, at high tide it was reduced to a mere .62 hectares (National Geographic Indonesia 2013). The fear was not simply loss of land, but of two base point coordinates for the measurement of Indonesian territory. These points determined Indonesia's twelve–nautical mile territorial sea, as well as a further two miles of EEZ. Indonesian officials felt it was imperative to preserve Nipa, or the boundaries of state territory might shift. However, it was clear to Indonesia that bringing Singapore to court over the possible effects of its land reclamation might not turn out in its favor, given Malaysia's failure to stop Singapore's reclamation at Pulau Tekong.

Instead, an inspired public relations campaign was launched to save the island, foregrounding, in addition, the use of land reclamation. Starting in 2004, the government constructed a 3.5-meter-high retaining wall, and over the following two years a 5.2-meter-high, 4.3-kilometer-long embankment was constructed and reinforced with concrete tetrapods. This embankment encircles an area of nearly 43.5 hectares, divided into three zones, with a midsection of replanted mangroves. From 2006, Tentara Nasional Indonesia–Angkatan Laut (TNI-AL), Indonesia's navy (the region's largest), set up a post there and continues to build up the reclaimed land on Nipa.

On August 31, 2010, Indonesia and Singapore ratified a treaty on the delimitation of the territorial seas in the western Singapore Straits on the basis of the 1982 United Nations Convention on the Law of the Sea (UNCLOS), to which both countries are party. The territorial sea boundary agreed on in this treaty conformed with that in a treaty they signed in 1973, reaffirming the status quo. Amid the heightened tensions in the South China Sea, the government of Indonesia installed a plaque on Nipa, signed on June 2, 2012, by President Susilo Bambang Yudhoyono, which read: "Secure our forward posts for the sovereignty of the nation" (Budianto 2009; JPNN 2015; Nurdin 2015). Pulau Nipa went from being an outermost island (*pulau terluar*) to one most in front or the most forward island (*pulau terdepan*), a discursive shift that reflects the ongoing militarization of regional seas. Indeed, the treaty concluded between Indonesia and Singapore on the western tristate maritime boundary zone implicitly rested on more than just the impact of the public relations campaign over Pulau Nipa. The size of Indonesia's military, the largest in the region (including Australia), and Indonesia's contemporary emphasis on maritime issues, also probably played a role in diplomatic considerations.

Breaking New Ground: The Political Economy of International Law and Domestic Politics

The above cases show how states use, and sometimes circumvent, public international law fora to address disputes involving land reclamation that bear on territorial sovereignty and state control over resources. Yet the global dredging industry's partnerships with states also affect domestic politics. Treating domestic disputes separately from those between states may obscure the larger picture of political economy in which the industry forms public-private partnerships. Taking a view that encompasses both may help to reveal how such public-private partnerships impact the changing boundary between public and private international law.

Indonesia provides a good example of the tension between international relations and international law, on the one hand, and the internal politics of land reclamation, on the other. Recently, instead of criticizing Singapore for the effects of its land reclamation, Indonesia held it up as an exemplar of land reclamation success (CNN Indonesia 2016). This diplomatic flattery may reflect the recent wave of state-condoned reclamation activity in Indonesia and looks particularly curious given Indonesia's anti-*reklamasi*, or antireclamation, protests.

According to Susi Pudjiastuti, Indonesia's minister of maritime affairs, among thirty-seven places in Indonesia, seventeen have carried out reclamation projects and twenty locations are planning to do so. The minister met on April 10, 2016, for a public discussion to clarify what she called confusion over the process and to address concerns in Bali, which was the site the previous August of enormous coordinated, peaceful protests against plans for a mega-development in Benoa Bay. Bali's anti-*reklamasi* protest movement initially took its inspiration from the resistance of local coastal communities that depend on the sea for their well-being. The movement in Bali has benefited from its ability to garner an international audience. Whether in person or digitally—Indonesia has the second highest smartphone use in Asia—this large international presence has given Bali's protest movement not only a very broad audience, but also protection from potential mishandling by security forces or private militias. The country's high rate of smartphone use has also made possible broad information dissemination and fast mobilization, resulting in large, well-organized protests. Finally, Bali has also been able to mobilize an argument so far untapped by other anti-reclamation movements. Its unique Hindu-Balinese cultural and religious makeup (on which so much tourism income also depends) allows the anti-reclamation camp to claim that reclamation's despoiling would violate sacred space (Sinaga 2016). *Agama tirta*, literally the religion of holy waters, has been invoked to protect the sea.

At the Bali meeting, Minister Pudjiastuti explained that all plans must go through an environmental impact assessment and that, if the people reject the project, they can bring a class action suit (Sinaga 2016). Massive land reclamation plans are also slated for Jakarta Bay, where, similarly, local coastal fishing communities initially mounted protests. They and their supporters occupied one island under construction, and Lembaga Bantuan Hukum (LBH), Jakarta's Legal Aid Society, stepped in to offer assistance. Although the government put a stay on construction of the planned artificial islands, protestors and their supporters were disappointed to find that it was apparently a false moratorium. Given what they see as the apparent failure of government institutions, they have issued an "open subpoena" aimed at stopping construction of "G Island" in Jakarta Bay (LBH 2016a, 2016b).

Amid the growth of land reclamation projects across Indonesia, Singapore has embarked on a new project on Pulau Tekong. This time, it will employ Dutch engineering ingenuity to build dikes and polders. Although common in the Netherlands, this is a novel approach to land reclamation in Southeast Asia. By holding back the tides with seawalls and managing water outflow with pumping stations, Singapore will be able to reclaim land using less sand: keeping the land dry below sea level means it will not have to fill in as much solid volume (Dutch Water Sector 2016). This intended lowering of demand on regional sand supplies may, in addition, alleviate the project's potential impact on Singapore's relations with its neighbors.

Dutch engineering is also being put to work in the Jakarta Bay project. The Netherlands Ministry of Infrastructure and the Environment has publically announced how it and the Confederation of Netherlands Industry and Employers (VNO-NCW), through various cooperation agreements involving more than fifty companies, will employ a concept like the one proposed for Singapore's Pulau Tekong to create what some have called a "great wall of Jakarta." This enormous project aims to help the city of Jakarta mitigate its land subsidence problem, and the impact of rising sea levels (VNO-NCW 2016). On the ministry's website, an animated video with English subtitles explains the project, which is fascinating not only for what it proposes, but also for what it leaves out (Government of the Netherlands 2016). Elsewhere on the web, one can find images of the phantasmagoric digital mockups that depict this Jakarta Bay project, built in the shape of Indonesia's national symbol, the mythical bird Garuda, with its wings outstretched across the bay, protecting it, along with many very glitzy, highly developed islands. Such images appeared mostly on Indonesian news sites during 2016. However, in April 2014, this stunning urban planning rendering appeared in the Dutch newspaper *Het Financieele Dagblad* under the title "Nederland aast op waterwerken in baai van Jakarta." The title plays on two meanings of *aast*. It either reads "The Netherlands has its eye on waterworks in Jakarta Bay" or "The Netherlands preys on waterworks in Jakarta Bay" (Weissink 2014), a more sinister view that is underscored by the Dutch colonial past in Indonesia. Curiously, the digital renderings of dazzling islands, enclosed by a land mass in the shape of Garuda's outstretched wings, do not appear in the quaint, cheery video put out by the Netherlands Ministry of Infrastructure and the Environment. Indeed, in its explanation of the cooperative venture, no islands appear at all, though they were obviously planned and have already begun to take shape. Perhaps it was thought that justifications for the islands might appear secondarily, if building them could create a fait accompli, like Beijing's reclamation in the South China Sea.

Conclusion

Although island building in the South China Sea has received much attention, less prominent disputes within the tristate maritime boundary zone have set precedents that have affected maneuvers in the international legal arena. Those precedents helped to shape the Philippines' strategy in bringing its case for arbitration. In the ITLOS case decided in 2003, the environmental claims of one country were found to have only a limited impact on another's right to create reclaimed land in its sovereign waters. In the 2008 ruling of the ICJ, it turned out that the apparently straightforward request that the court rule on the sovereignty of specific features resolved neither the question of maritime entitlements nor that of maritime boundaries. Learning from these cases, the Philippines constructed an approach to arbitration on the South China Sea that did not pit an environmental claim against claims to sovereign space or request a determination of sovereignty. Instead, the Philippines sought answers from the PCA tribunal solely regarding maritime entitlements.

As for Indonesia, what happens in its sovereign maritime space concerns politics and business, in which the Dutch are also deeply involved. That no one has cried foul on this relation with the former colonial overlords is a measure less of a tendency to avoid possibly humiliating topics than of the stakes among local elites and between them and the potentially dispossessed. Both the requirement of state patronage to carry out such projects and the extent to which mass movements mobilize against them deserve further attention. As with the international cases, in the domestic sphere the support of sophisticated legal allies allows these movements to bring both moral suasion and arguments of law into an arena where they matter politically. This flexing of democratic muscles stands in sharp contrast to the way development proceeded under Suharto's authoritarian state.

While work on neoliberalism in the oceans tends to focus on what is wet—on fisheries, for instance (Mansfield 2004)—land reclamation represents the appropriation of space for particular interests. It transforms unclaimed fluid space into solid private or state space, arguably a relative form of accumulation by dispossession, even if the public has never been aware of what it possessed (Grydehøj 2015; Harvey 2003). However, in Indonesia, publics seem to be perfectly aware of what pending, in-process, and realized dispossession means. To disregard land reclamation when looking at the sea would be to miss important social and environmental changes taking place in the littoral and offshore that could be better analyzed in tandem. Hence, the wider project this work is part of ties together transformations in coastal and maritime space and in domestic and international arenas. That the global dredging industry responds, even if only indirectly, to the social and legal ramifications of its endeavors conducted with and through states invites scrutiny of more or less neopatrimonial states, their capture by corporate interests (Fukuoka 2015; Helman, Jones, and Kaufmann 2003; Kaufmann and Vicente 2011), and the citizens and interstitial denizens who resist and contest these cozy relations.

Note

1   Thanks to Philip E. Steinberg for bringing to my attention Joshua Comaroff's essay "Built on Sand: Singapore and the New State of Risk" (Comaroff 2014), which describes the liquidity of sand as a granular medium and as a commodity, as well as the liquidity of territorial boundaries altered by reclamation. It is good to know that the neologism *liquid territory*, coined in my earlier work and repurposed here, also worked for someone else.

References

AMTI (Asia Maritime Transparency Initiative)/CSIS (Center for Strategic and International Studies). 2017. "Update: China's Continuing Reclamation in the Paracels." AMTI/CSIS website, August 9. https://amti.csis.org/paracels-beijings-other-buildup.

ASEAN (Association of Southeast Asian Nations). 2002. "Declaration on the Conduct of Parties in the South China Sea." October 17. https://cil.nus.edu.sg/wp-content/uploads/2019/02/2002-Declaration-on-the-Conduct-of-Parties-in-the-South-China-Sea-1.pdf.

Benedikter, Simon. 2014. *The Vietnamese Hydrocracy and the Mekong Delta: Water Resources Development from State Socialism to Bureaucratic Capitalism.* Zurich: LIT.

Biggs, David. 2010. *Quagmire: Nation-Building and Nature in the Mekong Delta.* Seattle: University of Washington Press.

Blaikie, Piers, and Harold Brookfield, eds. 1987. *Land Degradation and Society.* London: Methuen.

Bravard, Jean-Paul, Marc Goichot, and Stéphane Gaillot. 2013. "Geography of Sand and Gravel Mining in the Lower Mekong River." *EchoGéo* 26 (October/December). http://echogeo.revues.org/13659.

Budianto, Lilian. 2009. "RI [Indonesia], Singapore Sign Maritime Boundary Agreement." *Jakarta Post*, March 11. http://www.thejakartapost.com/news/2009/03/11/ri-singapore -sign-maritime-boundary-agreement.html.

Cheong, Koon Hean, Tommy T. B. Koh, and Lionel Yee. 2013. *Malaysia and Singapore: The Land Reclamation Case; from Dispute to Settlement*. Singapore: Straits Times Press.

CNN Indonesia. 2016. "Berkaca dari Reklamasi di Singapura." April 15. http://www .cnnindonesia.com/nasional/20160415172432-20-124254/berkaca-dari-reklamasi-di -singapura.

Comaroff, Joshua. 2014. "Built on Sand: Singapore and the New State of Risk." In "Wet Matter." *Harvard Design Magazine* 39 (Fall/Winter). http://www.harvarddesignmagazine .org/issues/39/built-on-sand-singapore-and-the-new-state-of-risk.

Deogracias, Charmaine. 2017. "ASEAN Begins Talks on Code of Conduct in South China Sea amid Continued Tensions." February 6. http://news.abs-cbn.com/focus/02/06/17 /asean-begins-talks-on-code-of-conduct-in-south-china-sea-amid-continued-tensions.

Duong, Huy. 2015. "Massive Island-Building and International Law." AMTI/CSIS website, posted June 15. https://amti.csis.org/massive-island-building-and-international-law.

Dutch Water Sector. 2016. "Singapore to Adopt Dutch Polder Concept as New Land Reclamation Method at Pulau Tekong." Blog post, December 2. https://www .dutchwatersector.com/news-events/news/22419-singapore-to-adopt-dutch-polder -concept-as-new-land-reclamation-method-at-pulau.html.

Forsyth, Luc, and Gareth Bright. 2016. "Shifting Sands in the Mekong River." *The Diplomat*, January 27. http://thediplomat.com/2016/01/shifting-sands-in-the-mekong-river.

Fukuoka, Yuki. 2015. "Demystifying 'People Power': An Elite Interpretation of 'Democratization' in Southeast Asia." In *Routledge Handbook of Southeast Asian Democratization*, edited by William Case, 85–101. London: Routledge.

Gaynor, Jennifer L. 2012. "Piracy in the Offing: The Law of Lands and the Limits of Sovereignty at Sea." *Anthropological Quarterly* 85 (3): 817–58.

Government of the Netherlands. 2016. "Nederland Helpt Indonesië bij Havenontwikkeling en Kustversterking." https://www.rijksoverheid.nl/actueel/nieuws/2016/11/22 /nederland-helpt-indonesie-bij-havenontwikkeling-en-kustversterking.

Grydehøj, Adam. 2015. "Making Ground, Losing Space: Land Reclamation and Urban Public Space in Island Cities." *Urban Island Studies* 1: 96–117.

Harvey, David. 2003. *The New Imperialism*. New York: Oxford University Press.

Hellman, Joel S., Geraint Jones, and Daniel Kaufmann. 2003. "Seize the State, Seize the Day: State Capture and Influence in Transition Economies." *Journal of Comparative Economics* 31 (4): 751–73.

Heydarian, Richard Javad. 2016. "Sunnylands and America's Pivot to ASEAN." ASEAN/ CSIS website posting, January 12. https://amti.csis.org/sunnylands-and-americas-pivot -to-asean.

Hubacek, Klaus, and Jeroen C. J. M. van den Bergh. 2006. "Changing Concepts of 'Land' in Economic Theory: From Single to Multi-Disciplinary Approaches." *Ecological Economics* 56 (1): 5–27.

ICJ (International Court of Justice). 2008. "Sovereignty over Pedra Branca / Pulau Batu Puteh, Middle Rocks and South Ledge (*Malaysia v. Singapore*): Summary of the Judgment of 23 May 2008." May 23. https://www.kln.gov.my/pbp-icj/images/icj_judgment/14506.pdf.

ITLOS (International Tribunal for the Law of the Sea). 2003. "Case concerning Land Reclamation by Singapore in and around the Straits of Johor (*Malaysia v. Singapore*), Provisional Measures." October 8. https://www.itlos.org/fileadmin/itlos/documents/cases/case_no_12/Order.08.10.03.E.pdf.

JPNN. 2015. "Pulau Nipah, Wilayah Yang Langsung Berhadapan Dengan Singapura." January 31. http://www.jpnn.com/news/pulau-nipah-wilayah-yang-langsung-berhadapan-dengan-singapura.

Kaufmann, Daniel, and Pedro C. Vicente. 2011. "Legal Corruption." *Economics and Politics* 23 (1): 195–219.

Kuan, Seng. 2013. "Land as an Architectural Idea in Modern Japan." In *Architecturalized Asia: Mapping a Continent through History*, edited by Rujivacharakul, Vimalin, H. Hazel Hahn, Ken Tadashi Oshima, Peter Christensen, 189–204. Hong Kong: Hong Kong University Press.

Kyodo News Service. 2017. "Malaysia Reopens Pedra Branca Row with Singapore After a Decade." *South China Morning Post,* February 4. http://www.scmp.com/news/asia/southeast-asia/article/2068096/malaysia-reopens-pedra-branca-island-row-singapore-after.

LBH (Lembaga Bantuan Hukum). 2016a. "Pemerintah Harus Transparen Soal Moratorium Reklamasi Teluk Jakarta." May 5. http://www.bantuanhukum.or.id/web/pemerintah-harus-transparan-soal-reklamasi-teluk-jakarta.

LBH (Lembaga Bantuan Hukum). 2016b. "Somasi Terbuka Menolak Dilanjutkannya Reklamasi Teluk Jakarta." September 16. http://www.bantuanhukum.or.id/web/somasi-terbuka-menolak-dilanjutkannya-reklamasi-teluk-jakarta.

Li, Mingjiang. 2014. "Managing Security in the South China Sea: from doc to coc." *Kyoto Review of Southeast Asia* 15 (March). https://kyotoreview.org/issue-15/managing-security-in-the-south-china-sea-from-doc-to-coc.

Lim, Lydia. 2008. "Pedra Branca Ruling: Rough Seas or Calm Ahead?" *Straits Times,* May 31. Reposted in *Malaysia Today* http://www.malaysia-today.net/pedra-branca-ruling-rough-seas-or-calm-ahead.

Lukacs, Martin. 2014. "New, Privatized African City Heralds Climate Apartheid." *The Guardian,* January 21. http://www.theguardian.com/environment/true-north/2014/jan/21/new-privatized-african-city-heralds-climate-apartheid.

Macias, Amanda. 2016. "This Photo Says So Much about China's View of the South China Sea Ruling." *Business Insider*, July 24. https://www.businessinsider.com/photo-china-southern-airlines-mischief-reef-2016-7.

Mansfield, Becky. 2004. "Neoliberalism in the Oceans: 'Rationalization,' Property Rights, and the Commons Question." *Geoforum* 35 (3): 313–26.

McLaughlin, Tim. 2014. "South China Sea Again Dominates Summit Talks." *Myanmar Times*, August 10. http://www.mmtimes.com/index.php/national-news/11300-south-china-sea-again-dominates-asean-agenda.html.

Milton, Chris. 2010. "The Sand Smugglers." *Foreign Policy*, August 4. http://www.foreignpolicy.com/articles/2010/08/04/the_sand_smugglers.

Muñoz, Carlo. 2016. "U.S., Allies Watch for Challenge from China on Court Ruling over Sea Claims." *Washington Times*, July 12. https://www.washingtontimes.com/news /2016/jul/12/international-court-rules-against-china-territoria.

National Geographic Indonesia. 2013. "Kerasnya Nipa si Pulau Noktah Perbatasan RI." July 4. https://nationalgeographic.grid.id/read/13284249/kerasnya-nipa-si-pulau -noktah-perbatasan-ri.

Nguyen Minh Quang. 2017. "The Resurgence of China-Vietnam Ties." *The Diplomat*, January 25. http://thediplomat.com/2017/01/the-resurgence-of-china-vietnam-ties.

Nurdin, Ajang. 2015. "Pulau Nipa Terancam Tenggelam, Batas Indonesia Bakal Bergeser." *Liputan 6*, June 22. http://news.liputan6.com/read/2257248/pulau-nipa-terancam -tenggelam-batas-indonesia-bakal-bergeser.

Office of the Geographer, US Department of State, Bureau of Intelligence and Research. 1974. "Territorial Sea Boundary: Indonesia-Singapore." *Limits in the Seas*, no. 60, November 11. https://www.state.gov/documents/organization/61500.pdf.

PCA (Permanent Court of Arbitration). 2016. "The South China Sea Arbitration Award of 12 July 2016." Case No. 2013-19. https://pca-cpa.org/wp-content/uploads/ sites/175/2016/07/PH-CN-20160712-Award.pdf.

Phillips, Tom, Oliver Holmes, and Owen Bowcott. 2016. "Beijing Rejects Tribunal's Ruling in South China Sea Case." *The Guardian*, July 12. https://www.theguardian.com /world/2016/jul/12/philippines-wins-south-china-sea-case-against-china.

Poling, Gregory. 2016. "A Tumultuous 2016 in the South China Sea." AMTI/CSIS website, February 22. https://amti.csis.org/a-tumultuous-2016-in-the-south-china-sea.

Poling, Gregory, Michael Green, Murray Hiebert, Chris Johnson, Amy Searight, and Bonnie Glaser. 2016. "Judgment Day—The South China Sea Tribunal Issues Its Ruling." AMTI/CSIS website, July 11. https://amti.csis.org/arbitration-ruling-analysis.

Sanger, David E., and Rick Gladstone. 2015. "Piling Sand in a Disputed Sea, China Literally Gains Ground." *New York Times*, April 8. http://www.nytimes.com/2015/04/09/world /asia/new-images-show-china-literally-gaining-ground-in-south-china-sea.html?_r=0.

Sinaga, Eri Komar. 2016. "Menteri Susi Pudjiastuti Bicara Reklamasi Teluk Benoa di Bali." *Tribun News*, October 5. http://www.tribunnews.com/nasional/2016/10/05/menteri -susi-pudjiastuti-bicara-reklamasi-teluk-benoa-di-bali.

Singh, Abhijit. 2016. "A Looming Environmental Crisis in the South China Sea." AMTI/ CSIS website, August 12. https://amti.csis.org/looming-environmental-crisis-south -china-sea.

Straits Times. 2017. "Singapore, Indonesia Submit Third Sea Border Treaty to UN." September 27. https://www.straitstimes.com/asia/se-asia/singapore-indonesia-submit -third-sea-border-treaty-to-un.

Tarrant, Bill. 2014. "Sidebar: The Great Wall of Jakarta," *Daily Mail*, December 22. http://www.dailymail.co.uk/wires/reuters/article-2884494/SIDEBAR-The-Great -Wall-Jakarta.html?ITo=1490&ns_mchannel=rss&ns_campaign=1490.

Turner, Monica G. 1998. "Landscape Ecology." In *Ecology*, 77–122. New York: Oxford University Press.

VNO-NCW (Ministry of Infrastructure and the Environment and Confederation of Netherlands Industry and Employers). 2016. "The Netherlands to Assist Indonesia in Coastal Reinforcement and Port Development." Joint press release, November 23. https://www.government.nl/latest/news/2016/11/23/the-netherlands-to-assist -indonesia-in-coastal-reinforcement-and-port-development.

Voice of America News. 2012. "Challenging Beijing in the South China Sea." July 31. http://blogs.voanews.com/state-department-news/2012/07/31/challenging-beijing-in -the-south-china-sea/.

Weissink, Alexander. 2014. "Nederland aast op waterwerken in baai van Jakarta." *Financieele Dagblad*, April 2. https://fd.nl/search?q=Nederland+aast+op+waterwerken+in+ baai+van+Jakarta.

Worster, Donald. 1982. "World without Borders: The Internationalization of Environmental History." *Environmental Review* 6 (2): 8–16.

Xinhua News. 2016. "China Sticks to Dual-Track Approach to Solve South China Sea Issue: FM," July 24. http://www.china.org.cn/world/2016-07/24/content_38949917 .htm.

6. WAVE LAW

STEFAN HELMREICH

In his *Historia Anglorum: The History of the English People*, penned in the twelfth century, Henry, archdeacon of Huntingdon, included a homiletic narrative about the deeds of King Canute the Great, a monarch who in the early eleventh century ruled over Denmark, Norway, and England (see figure 6.1). Henry's chronicle elaborated upon a legend in which King Canute attempts to command the sea to cease its tides:

> At the height of his ascendancy, he ordered his chair to be placed on the sea-shore as the tide was coming in. Then he said to the rising tide, "You are subject to me, as the land on which I am sitting is mine, and no one has resisted my overlordship with impunity. I command you, therefore, not to rise on to my land, nor presume to wet the clothing or limbs of your master." But the sea came up as usual, and disrespectfully drenched the king's feet and shins. (Henry of Huntington [1133–1155] 1996, 367–69)

This story—sometimes known as "Canute and the Waves" (see Lord Raglan 1960)—has been employed by a range of commentators to describe the overreaching arrogance of ruling power, particularly when it comes to (under)estimating the forces of large-scale processes, both natural and social. Take as one reference the comments of Louisiana lawyer Stacy Head, who in 2005 slammed the New Orleans City Council's response to Hurricane Katrina—a call "to extend daylight-saving time just for Orleans Parish" (so people would have more time to work on repairing their houses)—comparing the council's actions to those of King Canute (Nolan 2009). The Canute story, used this way, points to the folly of seeking to control, in the realm of the political, energies that might rather belong to domains beyond the human or, if human (e.g., enduring social

FIGURE 6.1. Courtiers flattering King Canute's pride, telling him that ocean waves will roll back if he so commands them. Source: Getty Images. Reproduced with permission.

conventions, revolutionary forces), may be beyond full sovereign control. But, according to University of Cambridge professor of Anglo-Saxon, Norse, and Celtic Simon Keynes (see Westcott 2011), the story is ultimately and more importantly about Canute's wisdom, for Henry's tale concludes: "So, jumping back, the king cried, 'Let all the world know that the power of kings is empty and worthless, and there is no king worthy of the name save Him by whose will heaven, earth and sea obey eternal laws.'"

This tale, of course, is not only about wisdom, but also about a medieval king's recognition of God as the real master of the earthly realm. Canute's placement of his throne on the beach articulates a theory of human sovereign power that recognizes the limits of that power even as it draws that power's command from an appeal to a higher supernatural authority. Later retellings of the Canute story treat the waves as a symbol for forces of social transformation, for tides of immigration, and for human-induced climate change; in such adaptations, the point is also to draw attention to the inexorability of processes beyond full social or political capture.

But fast forward to the early twenty-first century and return to the physical, material forces of ocean waves. We live now in a world in which it *is* possible, to some extent, to control and command ocean waves: to build infrastructures that guard shorelines, to mold beaches that generate waves of stipulated measure and shape, and to engineer devices that harness wave energy. As historians of surfing and technology Peter Westwick and Peter Neushul have demonstrated in their book *The World in a Curl* (2013), the dimensions and profiles of waves around particular beaches and harbors have been created and destroyed many times, sculpted in response to changing coastal infrastructures and politics. And, as members of the IT University of Copenhagen's Alien Energy working group have shown, waves—in the form of wave energy—have been bundles of natural force that have been eagerly enrolled by corporate and national technological initiatives into possible energy markets and futures (Alien Energy 2017; Watts 2019; Watts and Winthereik 2017).[1] Relations among the natural, the energetic, and the political can now be imagined as synergetic, as wind waves become part of environmental infrastructures (Helmreich 2016), subject to the formatting force of political economic enterprise.

What new laws—laws not now viewed as divine edicts or as scientific descriptions of empirical regularities—do the waves of heaven, earth, and sea obey? Or, less fancifully put, what legal forms are in place to know, measure, and even control ocean waves?

Knowing Ocean Waves through Scientific and Legal Codes

What sorts of agencies have jurisdictional reach over knowledge about waves? For open ocean and near coastal waves, the International Convention for the Safety of Life at Sea, adopted by the UN's International Maritime Organization on November 1, 1974, and entered into force on May 25, 1980, charges national and international meteorological organizations with issuing, on a daily basis, "weather bulletins suitable for shipping, containing data of existing weather" (United Nations 1980, 412). Such data includes reports not only about phenomena above the ocean (wind, clouds), but also about phenomena *of* the ocean: "waves and ice" (United Nations 1980, 412).

Wave phenomena—just one slice of weather—become observational wave data when measured and monitored by such instruments as coastal and open-ocean floating buoys, satellites, ocean platforms (e.g., oil drilling platforms), and ships. That data usually includes information about wave height, wave period, and wave direction. Wave height turns out to be a less-than-straightforward measure, known not as the height of any individual wave, but rather as the statistical average of the highest third of waves in a wave field. Known as significant wave height, this measure is derived from processing a wave spectrum—that is, a wave field understood as a collection of various wavelengths. Dominant wave period is a similar statistical abstraction.[2] All of these measures of wave characteristics are the result of a long history of work in oceanography, fluid dynamics, meteorology, and coastal engineering. Significant wave height, for example, originates in the work of Scripps Oceanographer Walter Munk, who in the 1940s sought a way to calibrate scientific judgments of wave height to those folk judgments made by US marines who would be piloting amphibious craft into combat (von Storch and Hasselmann 2010, 5). The regnant scientific measure of wave height, then, was "co-produced" (Jasanoff 2004) along with and in response to a maritime, military, and operational demand. And the formalism of ocean wave energy spectra, which measures waves not as individuals, but as populations of varied wavelengths, became the source information for significant wave height when mathematicians and physicists entered wave science in force in the 1960s (Helmreich 2015; Irvine 2002; for more history of wave science, see also Cartwright 2010; Longuet-Higgins 2010; Tucker 2010). Wave height, derived from wave spectra, enfolds maritime, scientific, and mathematical operations, which then shape how waves can become objects of law.

What does wave data look like? The World Meteorological Organization (WMO) stipulates the format that such information should take. The WMO's *Manual on Codes* (World Meteorological Organization 2011) spells out technical regulations—described as "standard coding procedures"—to which weather reports and forecasts should conform. Instrumented observations of aspects of weather must therefore be filtered through a standardized syntax—this so that the WMO can route the data through its World Weather Watch program, a system of meteorological observation platforms, telecommunication networks, and computer programs that produce weather reports (World Meteorological Organization 2005, 2011). A wave observation, according to the manual, must follow the following convention:

> *WAVEOB* is the name of the code for reporting spectral wave data from a sea station, or from an aircraft or satellite platform

Essential to report in a WAVEOB file are

> Data for reporting identification (type, buoy identifier, date, time, location), indication of frequency or wave number, method of calculation, type of station, water depth, significant wave height and spectral peak period, or wave length, and optional wave parameters. (WMO 2011, A-129)

Scientifically and mathematically defined measurements and quantities made available by technologically tailored instruments, then, are here codified into standardized forms that can circulate into other technical domains, including those to do with legal regulation. Such forms emerge from the technical capacities of such instruments as buoys as well as mathematical models of wave action that have been crafted over decades to describe ocean waves (for an in-house history of the most popular wave measurement buoy, the Datawell Waverider, see Joosten 2013; see also Helmreich 2019). Previously created naming conventions and measures crafted by bureaucracies (date, time, location) join with complex scientific parameters (e.g., spectral peak period) to produce a wave record.[3] Sheila Jasanoff writes that "the law is now an inescapable feature of the conditioning environment that produces socially embedded . . . science" (2008, 762). The reverse is also true. For wave measurements germane to the purposes of the World Meteorological Organization, scientific frameworks have come to condition legal ones.[4]

Once wave data is codified, it may be accessed in various ways—by nation-states, corporations, citizens, and other interested parties. The story is more complicated than this, too, since many nation-states and other organizations have their own, additional systems of buoys and measures—so, in fact, the WMO regulations, while providing a common argot, do not fully determine how reporting is shaped in every instance. As Jennifer Gabrys writes in *Program Earth* (2016), the world's oceans are awash in sensors that have many masters and constituencies, looping into many systems of monitoring on the internet. Gabrys calls this the "becoming environmental of computation." What media scholars have called "media ecologies" (i.e., relations among media; see Postman 1970 for the Ur-articulation) have now become part of planetary ecologies. Indeed, the planet becomes known through media—seagoing, computational, satellite-generated, and more.[5]

But let me stay with the specifics of the WMO for a moment and its interdigitation with state and international organizations and their demands for wave reporting. In the United States, the National Weather Service stewards wave data. These days, that data can be retrieved online in graphical form, from which tabular graphs can also be accessed, listing wave heights in different regions. Such graphs are rendered into forms that can be read by humans (and not only processed by computers, which do not need things like graphs).

For European polities, wave data is stewarded by the European Center for Medium-Range Weather Forecasting (ECMWF), an intergovernmental organization that hosts the world's largest store of numerical weather prediction information.[6] This data, unlike that of the US Weather Service, is not immediately open to a wide public. The data is available to "national meteorological and hydrological services and research institutions from many of the [ECMWF]

Member and Co-operating States."[7] The countries that are members of the ECMWF may each have their own specific arrangement with the ECMWF and the data they seek from it. Commercial users can also make use of various wave-prediction products by paying licensing fees, the amounts of which will depend on whether they want to pay for medium range, extended range, or long-range wave models. For example, accessing an "Ocean Wave Model high resolution 10-day Forecast" can give a user such computed model data as a "2D wave spectra," defined—in terms really only decodable by people versed in wave and weather measurement—as "Wave variance spectrum archived as a field for each discretized frequency and directional bin (what is actually encoded is log10 of the variance spectrum)" (ECMWF 2016). An institution might also want something like "significant wave height of all waves with periods within the inclusive range from 10 to 12 seconds, where the significant wave height is defined as 4 times the square root of the integral over all directions and all frequencies between 1/12 and 1/10 Hz of the two-dimension wave spectrum" (ECMWF 2016). Such instrumented measures of wave phenomenology become, in other words, products to be purchased—and purchased under legal agreements about their use. So, we see here the coconstitution of wave science, wave law, and wave commerce.

The ECMWF owns the copyright on "all real-time meteorological information that results from the transformation or processing of data sets by the ECMWF forecasting system in the form of pictures, charts, text or data files, and has been prepared specifically to meet the operational requirements of an NMS" (ECMWF 2015). So, it is not just wave data that is here proprietary, but also the *models* within which such data sits and makes sense. The data and models are closely coupled; as Lisa Gitelman (2013) has put it, "'Raw data' is an oxymoron"—that is, data always comes with a model or a framework *within which it makes sense* (see Edwards 2010). And some of that sense-making, here, is about cents-making—about money.

Such standard measured and modeled waves also meet other legal regimes (on beyond the proprietary), ones that regulate human enterprise in domains affected by wave dynamics. So, take, for example, Australia's Standing Council on Transport and Infrastructure, which, in its setting of national requirements for the safety of commercial vessels, offers measures of what will count as "smooth waters" ("waters where the significant wave height does not exceed 0.5 metres from trough to crest for at least 90 per cent of the time") and what will pass as "partially smooth waters" ("waters where the significant wave height does not exceed 1.5 metres from trough to crest for at least 90 per cent of the time") (Standing Council on Transport and Infrastructure 2012, 8). The Australian legal standard for ship safety thus embeds wave measurements. Waves in the open ocean become technical objects (Rheinberger 1997), formatted according to the World Meteorological Organization, and, so shaped, become objects that might be known, in this Australian case, through the lens of a policy promulgated for vessel safety on the open seas, with legally imposed obligations and liabilities coupling to scientifically produced data (and see National Data Buoy Center 2009 for a document that offers ways of keeping data properly recorded and organized).[8] As Nadao Kohno of Japan's Office of Marine Prediction has observed, "Only windsea and two swell are regulated in ship reports. . . . If [the] wave height of [a] calculated wave component is lower than 0.2M, the component is neglected, following the [Manual on Codes]" (Kohno 2013, 2). What is interesting here is the way that a "wave" can be counted as technically—and therefore legally present *or not* depending on its height. There is nothing legally or scientifically out of the ordinary here, of course— classification is always social, is always about the pragmatics of use (Bowker and Star 2000)—but it does illustrate the power of regulation to make some aspects of waves relevant or not relevant to particular social projects. So, even if this is not an example of a successful King Canute–styled command of the sea resulting in a substantive change in the waters themselves, it is an example of how waves can indeed be brought within a grid of interested definition and governance. Waves are made to matter within frames of legal reference.

Protecting the Shore

The examples above are of waves as objects at sea, objects to be known through science and regulation. When waves arrive at shore, they become subject to a range of additional technical and legal frameworks. At a very basic level, they become processes that unfold within state (and international) jurisdictions. In the United States (and, indeed, in many other countries) waves may roll through federal territorial seas, the contiguous zone, the Exclusive Economic Zone, and above the outer continental shelf, all internationally recognized and defined (though, also, in many cases, still contested) zones of ocean territory. In countries where renewable wave energy—energy meant to be derived from wave action—is in play, commercial enterprises dedicated to extracting this power must grapple with such boundaries (Moran 2014).

Wave measurements also frame construction projects on the shore. Take, for example, the 2005 advisory on Hurricane Katrina recovery produced by the US Federal Emergency Management Agency (FEMA). In a segment of their advisory on house design and construction in coastal zones, FEMA advises that construction techniques that make use of "wood-frame, light gauge steel or masonry walls on shallow footings or slabs" "are subject to damage when exposed to less than 3-foot breaking waves" (FEMA 2005, 1). They advise that new construction techniques take this into account, considering also the probability of such waves arriving, using a 1-in-100-years event as a benchmark.

The probability of a flood—and of waves that might crest at dangerous elevations—moves a statistical measure into the realm of human planning. Such probabilistic accountings are nothing new to coastal planning. In the Netherlands, for instance, since the 1960s, dikes have been generally built and dunes secured along the Dutch coast with the aim of protecting the country from 1-in-10,000-years flood and surge events, with such events defined as a water level exceedance of 5 meters above sea level (as measured at Amsterdam) (Voorendt 2016). Not all Dutch locales are given this same probabilistic measure for securing safety—in some places (e.g., Groningen) a 1-in-4,000-years probability is designated as the safety level. As Mark Voorendt summarizes the reasoning as it stood in the 1960s,

> The Delta Committee reasoned that a larger flood probability was acceptable for areas with a lower population density and higher ground levels (the north of the Netherlands) or smaller sub-areas (the southwestern part of the Netherlands) and the West Frisian Islands. For the north and the south-western part of the Netherlands a 2.5 times higher exceedance probability was considered acceptable because of the lower economical value of that part of the country. (2016, 25)

Built into such probabilities are the wave dynamics of run-up, overtopping, overflow (all, more or less, what they sound like), some descriptions of which have been in place for centuries, well before their probabilistic framing—as in the diagram by sixteenth-century dike warden Andries Vierlingh presented in figure 6.2.

Today's descriptions of waves are thoroughly mathematical and computational—and gathered by measurement instruments that are often connected to the internet—and it is these descriptions that become built into coastal regulation. Translocal standardized measures have been coded into widely distributed and internationalized informational infrastructure, thereby becoming critical determinants of *local* regulation.

Protecting the Waves

It is, then, at the shore where wave phenomena become most subject to legal attention. Sometimes, the waves *themselves* become objects for legal protection—rather than, as in the previous section, entities to be protected against. Waves

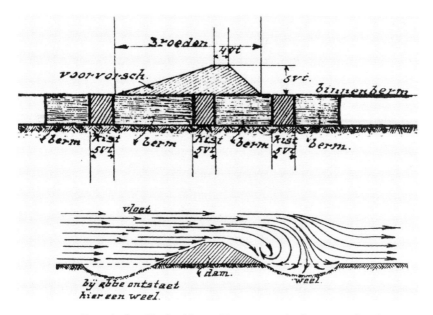

FIGURE 6.2. From Andries Vierlingh's 1578 *Treatise on Embanking*. Reproduced in Voorendt 2016.

are no longer simply entities to be survived, endured, prevented; much as coral reefs have gone from being experienced as *threatening* (to ships, for example) to being perceived as *threatened* (by scientists and ecotourists, for instance; see Braverman 2018; Sponsel 2018), so too with some kinds of coastal waves (think also of wolves, whales, or even sharks as other examples of entities once feared but now protected). Take, then, the case of the organization known as Save the Waves, an international nonprofit coalition dedicated to preserving the wave dynamics and profiles of select beaches (Save the Waves Coalition n.d.a). This organization, headed up by surfers interested in preserving waves on shorelines that might be subject to large-scale coastal engineering projects, seeks to protect waves from being modified or disappearing. They nominate, as part of their advocacy, entities they call "Endangered Waves," writing, "When an epic wave or coastline is under threat from poorly planned development or pollution, we mount campaigns to educate the public and take direct action through our Endangered Waves and Branded Campaigns" (Save the Waves Coalition n.d.a). The site lists a number of coastal sites around the world where the continued arrival and shape of desirable surfing waves is at risk (Save the Waves Coalition n.d.a). Save the Waves, contra King Canute, seeks to create the conditions by which waves can continue to operate as they have historically. Among the many strategies the organization uses (publicity, some direct action, et cetera) are legal ones. They work with local communities who hire lawyers to take a close eye to the legal frameworks behind real estate development projects. They push for environmental impact assessments. In the case of one beach in San Francisco, California, they have followed and supported the California Coastal Protection Network (CCPN), which has sued the city of San Francisco "for continued violations against the Coastal Act over the past 17 years for the illegal dumping of rock and unpermitted concrete and other debris on the shore at Ocean Beach" (Save the Waves Coalition n.d.d).

One project to which Save the Waves turned its attention in late 2016 was a seawall proposed to protect a golf course in Doughmore, Ireland. They reported on their website: "US President-Elect Donald Trump and his hotel company, Trump International Golf Links (TIGL), seek to build a massively controversial seawall on a public beach to protect his Trump Golf Resort in western Ireland" (Save the Waves Coalition n.d.c). The wall was meant to "run 2.8 kilometers, reach 15 feet tall, and consist of 200,000 tons of rock dumped in a sensitive coastal sand dune system" (Save the Waves Coalition n.d.c). Doughmore had earlier been designated a "Special Area of Conservation" by the European Union Special Habitats Directive, so there was an existing legal structure within which protection of the beach—and its waves—could work. Save the Waves reported,

> After a series of winter storms in February 2014, Donald Trump began to illegally dump boulders along the public beach at Doughmore without any permits to protect his golf course. Enraged local authorities quickly intervened and Trump was forced to cease his illegal revetment and is now required to obtain the legal permits. Trump has grown incensed that he needs to comply with the local planning regulations and has threatened to close the golf resort if his permit is not approved. Trump sought special permission from the Irish national government for the wall in March but was rejected in April. The local Clare County Council is now the responsible agency deciding the fate of Doughmore Beach. They have reviewed Trump's permit application and Environmental Impact Statement and have sent a Request for Further Information outlining 51 specific points that they want resolved or clarified. Trump has until December 2016 to submit the requested information. At that point, the Clare County Council will make a decision. All sides expect any council decision to be appealed, a process that will last several months more. (Save the Waves Coalition n.d.c)

FIGURE 6.3. #Nature
TrumpsWalls. From Save
the Wave Coalition n.d.c.

Here, Trump operates as the overreaching version of King Canute, seeking to control the waves that might compromise a property he owns. The wall is like Canute's throne, placed on the beach to enact a theory of sovereign power over the water.[9] In the event, Save the Waves (which collected 100,000 signatures) successfully blocked the proposed wall, following a #NatureTrumpsWalls campaign (figure 6.3) (Save the Waves Coalition n.d.b).

Beneath this story, however, is an odd wrinkle. Whereas Trump himself has famously dismissed the reality of climate change, his organization operates with climate change as part of its calculations and accounting. The environmental impact statement that Trump's people submitted in their original proposal for the Irish seawall read as follows:

> If the predictions of an increase in sea level rise as a result of *global warming* prove correct, however, it is likely that there will be a corresponding increase in coastal erosion rates not just in Doughmore Bay but also around much of the coastline of Ireland. . . . The existing erosion rate will continue and worsen, due to *sea level rise*, in the next coming years, posing a real and immediate risk to most of the golf course frontage and assets. (Partly quoted in Sherlock 2016; emphasis added)

This is not a shift to the wise and humble version of King Canute, recognizing the limits of human sovereignty. The theory of sovereignty here is, rather, a cynical one—opportunistically using coproduced legal and scientific language without regard to the truth claims it offers, but rather for the momentary rhetorical advantage it can enable. This may offer an intriguing complication to the analytic of the coproduction of science and law. Here, science and law are rhetorically coproduced at one moment and torn asunder at another (for a more general reflection on the concept of coproduction, one that points to how resistance, opposition, and friction characterize science-society relations just as much as collaborative coproduction, see Filipe, Renedo, and Marston 2017). Trump's aspiration to sovereign power (part of which he seeks to burnish by negating science [recall how he defiantly looked right at the sun during an eclipse, against the advice of ophthalmologists and astronomers!]) operates through attempting to decide when law/science will prevail and when it will not. This is not high-modernist control through data, but rather control through dissimulation and misdirection (though there is a parallel analysis to be written not about weather, but about the social field in which high-modernist control over social media data [surveillance] may be on the ascendant).

It may be no wonder that the figure of the (misguided, unwise) King Canute before the waves has been played upon in political cartoons that mock Trump's outsized denial of climate science.[10] And, at least with respect to the Save the Waves case (and a few other cases—such as Trump's travel ban), legal work has been able to push back Trump's sovereign fantasies (though this observation is not meant as a paean to law; after all, law is at once a tool, an instrument for diverse uses, and a figure that circulates widely in many arenas, with many possible politics and deployments).

In the time of Trump and attempts to roll back ocean monitoring as part of an attempt to dismantle the infrastructure that supports climate change science (Hiltzik 2017), one may fairly wonder how data about waves may fare. In early 2017, the Environmental Data and Governance Initiative (EDGI), an international network of academics and nonprofits addressing potential threats to federal environmental and energy policy, began to organize and sponsor what they called data rescue events aimed at marking specific US government databases as stores of valuable information (Schlanger 2017)—information that might be at risk, if not of erasure, then of not being properly cared for (Fortun 2005, 167, on "care of the data"; see also EDGI n.d.). EDGI's hope is that such data might be harvested by web crawlers and mirrored or saved in such repositories as the DataRefuge CKAN Repository, the Internet Archive's End of Term Archive, or Next GenClimate. As the Trump administration moves from data-oriented control to direct sovereign control over data (or its absence), attempting not to govern the waves but to govern information (or provide disinformation) about such environmental forces, the apt figure for thinking this through may not be King Canute, but rather that version of George Orwell's Big Brother that seeks to install a language that makes communication about actually existing conditions difficult to undertake and that seeks to wash away the vocabulary, data, and capacities that keep shared, responsible, and revisable accounts of the world in circulation.

Notes

1   The Alien Energy research group takes Denmark, Iceland, and Scotland as its case studies.
2   See the National Data Buoy Center's "Handbook of Automated Data Quality Control Checks and Procedures" (2009) for an accounting of data gathered by buoys.
3   Matters may become still more complex; depending on the buoy or the sensor employed, such a record may include such things as "maximum non-directional spectral density" or even "first and second normalized polar Fourier coefficients" (World Meteorological Organization 2011).
4   Thanks to sociologist of law Susan Silbey for helping me think through this point as well as others in this chapter.
5   See also Benjamin Bratton's claim that the planet's political ecology is now made of a range of interlocking "stacks" that govern and entangle states, environments, software platforms, and more (Bratton 2015).
6   The ECMWF is headquartered in the UK. This may remain the case even in the face of Brexit; however, the organization's supercomputing infrastructure may move elsewhere, with Italy a leading contender (Amos 2017).
7   Member states are Austria, Belgium, Croatia, Denmark, Finland, France, Germany, Greece, Iceland, Ireland, Italy, Luxembourg, the Netherlands, Norway, Portugal, Serbia, Slovenia, Spain, Sweden, Switzerland, Turkey and the United Kingdom. Co-operating States are Bulgaria, Czech Republic, Estonia, the former Yugoslav Republic of Macedonia, Hungary, Israel, Latvia, Lithuania, Montenegro, Morocco, Romania, and Slovakia (http://www.ecmwf.int/en/about/who-we-are/member -states).
8   The National Data Buoy Center, part of the US National Weather Service, was founded in 1967 and tasked with operating and maintaining a network of buoys around the waters not only of the United States, but also in extraterritorial waters around the planet. The most widespread of buoys today is called the Directional Waverider, created in the 1960s by a company called Datawell that is based in Haarlem, the Netherlands. This device, when deployed, must conform to legal and jurisdictional parameters. So, for example, the device requires a transmitter to relay its data to shore. The manual for the buoy reports that, "In case a transmitter is used within territorial waters a radio permit from the local authorities is obligatory." And, "The transmitting frequency band 28.0 MHz–29.7 MHz is reserved for amateur radio operators and needs to be avoided" (Datawell BV 2019, 3). So, right at the outset, this device for measuring waves sits within a legal framework.

9   And see Katherine Dow's study of the sociology of environment and ethics in Scotland, which has a short chapter titled "You've Been Trumped!" about Trump's efforts to build golf courses along an imperiled Scottish coast (Dow 2016).
10   See Tom Toles's cartoon in Bloom 2017.

References

Alien Energy. 2017. "Alien Energy: Social Studies of an Emerging Industry" (energy research project based at the IT University of Copenhagen). http://alienenergy.sand14 .com.

Amos, Jonathan. 2017. "Weather Supercomputing 'Heads to Italy.'" BBC News, March 3. http://www.bbc.com/news/science-environment-39144990.

Bloom, Jeremy. 2017. "Trump Is Pulling US out of Paris Climate Agreement—in FOUR YEARS." *Red, Green, and Blue*, June 1. http://redgreenandblue.org/2017/06/01/trump -pulling-us-paris-climate-agreement-four-years.

Bowker, Geoffrey C., and Susan Leigh Star. 2000. *Sorting Things Out: Classification and Its Consequences*. Cambridge, MA: MIT Press.

Bratton, Benjamin. 2015. *The Stack: On Software and Sovereignty*. Cambridge, MA: MIT Press.

Braverman, Irus. 2018. *Coral Whisperers: Scientists on the Brink*. Berkeley: University of California Press.

Cartwright, David. 2010. "Waves, Surges and Tides." In *Of Seas and Ships and Scientists: The Remarkable Story of the UK's National Institute of Oceanography*, edited by Anthony Laughton, John Gould, "Tom" Tucker, and Howard Roe, 171–81. Cambridge, UK: Lutterworth.

Datawell BV. 2019. *Datawell Waverider Manual*. Heerhugowaard: Datawell BV. http:// www.datawell.nl/Portals/0/Documents/Manuals/datawell_manual_dwr-mk3_dwr-g _wr-sg_2019-01-01.pdf.

Dow, Katherine. 2016. *Making a Good Life: An Ethnography of Nature, Ethics, and Reproduction*. Princeton, NJ: Princeton University Press.

ECMWF (European Center for Medium-Range Weather Forecasting). 2015. "Rules Governing the Distribution and Dissemination of ECMWF Real-Time Products." July 27. http://www.ecmwf.int/sites/default/files/Rules_real_time_products.pdf.

ECMWF (European Center for Medium-Range Weather Forecasting). 2016. "Set II— Ocean Wave Model High Resolution 10-day Forecast." December. https://www.ecmwf .int/en/forecasts/datasets/set-ii.

EDGI (Environmental Data and Governance Initiative). n.d. "About." EDGI website. Accessed March 2, 2019. https://envirodatagov.org/about.

Edwards, Paul. 2010. *A Vast Machine: Computer Models, Climate Data, and the Politics of Global Warming*. Cambridge, MA: MIT Press.

FEMA (US Federal Emergency Management Agency). 2005. "Design and Construction in Coastal A Zones." https://www.fema.gov/pdf/rebuild/mat/coastal_a_zones.pdf.

Filipe, Angela, Alicia Renedo, and Cicely Marston. 2017. "The Co-Production of What? Knowledge, Values, and Social Relations in Health Care." *PLoS Biol* 15 (5): e2001403-9.

Fortun, Mike. 2005. "For an Ethics of Promising, or: A Few Kind Words about James Watson." *New Genetics and Society* 24 (2): 157–73.

Gabrys, Jennifer. 2016. *Program Earth: Environmental Sensing Technology and the Making of a Computational Planet*. Minneapolis: University of Minnesota Press.

Gitelman, Lisa. 2013. *"Raw Data" Is an Oxymoron*. Cambridge, MA: MIT Press.

Helmreich, Stefan. 2015. "Old Waves, New Waves: Changing Objects in Physical Oceanography." In *Fluid Frontiers: New Currents in Marine and Maritime Environmental History*, edited by John Gillis and Franziska Torma, 76–88. Cambridge, UK: White Horse.

Helmreich, Stefan. 2016. "How to Hide an Island." In *New Geographies 08: Island*, edited by Daniel Daou and Pablo Pérez-Ramos, 82–87. Cambridge, MA: Harvard University Press.

Helmreich, Stefan. 2019. "Reading a Wave Buoy." *Science, Technology, and Human Values* 44 (5): 737–61.

Henry of Huntington. (1133–55) 1996. *Historia Anglorum: The History of the English People*. Edited and translated from the Latin by Diana Greenway. Oxford: Clarendon.

Hiltzik, Michael. 2017. "Trump's EPA Has Started to Scrub Climate Change Data from Its Website." *Los Angeles Times*, May 1. http://www.latimes.com/business/hiltzik/la-fi-hiltzik-epa-climate-20170501-story.html.

Irvine, David. 2002. "The Role of Spectra in Ocean Wave Physics." In *Oceanographic History: The Pacific and Beyond*, edited by Keith Rodney Benson and Philip F. Rehbock, 378–86. Seattle: University of Washington Press.

Jasanoff, Sheila, ed. 2004. *States of Knowledge: The Co-production of Science and Social Order*. London: Routledge.

Jasanoff, Sheila. 2008. "Making Order: Law and Science in Action." In *Handbook of Science and Technology Studies*, 3rd ed., edited by Edward J. Hackett, Olga Amsterdamska, Michael Lynch, and Judy Wajcman, 761–86. Cambridge, MA: MIT Press.

Joosten, Paul. 2013. *Datawell, 1961–2011: Riding the Waves for 50 Years*. Heemstede, Netherlands: Drukkerji Gravé.

Kohno, Nadao, 2013. "An Approach for Tough Navigation Sea Information." Paper presented at the Thirteenth International Workshop on Wave Hindcasting and Forecasting and Fourth Coastal Hazard Symposium, Banff, Alberta, October 27–November 1. http://waveworkshop.org/13thWaves/index.htm.

Longuet-Higgins, Michael. 2010. "Wave Research at Wormley." In *Of Seas and Ships and Scientists: The Remarkable Story of the UK's National Institute of Oceanography*, edited by Anthony Laughton, John Gould, "Tom" Tucker, and Howard Roe, 159–70. Cambridge, UK: Lutterworth.

Lord Raglan. 1960. "Canute and the Waves." *Man* 60 (January): 7–8.

Moran, John. 2014. "Lighting Northern New England with Water: A Comparative Analysis of Wave and Tidal Hydrokinetic Energy Regulation." *Ocean and Coastal Law Journal* 19 (2): 323–54. https://digitalcommons.mainelaw.maine.edu/oclj/vol19/iss2/6.

National Data Buoy Center. 2009. *Handbook of Automated Data Quality Control Checks and Procedures*. NDBC Technical Document 09-02. August. Hancock County, MS: Stennis Space Center.

Nolan, Bruce. 2009. "Stacy Head Has Rubbed Some People the Wrong Way, but Supporters Say Her Brash Style Is Misunderstood." *Times-Picayune*, April 8. http://www.nola.com/news/index.ssf/2009/04/stacy_head_photo_for_terry.html.

Postman, Neil. 1970. "The Reformed English Curriculum." In *High School 1980: The Shape of the Future in American Secondary Education*, edited by A. C. Eurich, 160–68. New York: Pitman.

Rheinberger, Hans-Jörg. 1997. *Toward a History of Epistemic Things: Synthesizing Proteins in the Test Tube*. Stanford, CA: Stanford University Press.

Save the Waves Coalition. n.d.a. "About Us." Save the Waves website. Accessed March 2, 2019. https://www.savethewaves.org/about-us.

Save the Waves Coalition. n.d.b. "Breaking News: Save the Waves and Irish Partners Defeat Trump's Irish Wall." Save the Waves website. Accessed March 2, 2019. https://www.savethewaves.org/stoptrumpsirishwall.

Save the Waves Coalition. n.d.c. "#NatureTrumpsWalls." Save the Waves website. Accessed March 2, 2019. https://www.savethewaves.org/stoptrumpsirishwall.

Save the Waves Coalition. n.d.d. "Save Sloat, San Francisco, USA." Save the Waves website. Accessed March 2, 2019. https://www.savethewaves.org/programs/endangered-waves/endangered-waves-sites/save-sloat.

Schlangher, Zoë. 2017. "Rogue Scientists Race to Save Climate Data from Trump." *Wired*, January 19. https://www.wired.com/2017/01/rogue-scientists-race-save-climate-data-trump.

Sherlock, Ruth. 2016. "Donald Trump Says Climate Change Is a 'Hoax' but Tries to Protect His Irish Real-estate from Its Impact." *The Telegraph*, May 25. http://www.telegraph.co.uk/news/2016/05/23/donald-trump-says-climate-change-is-a-hoax-but-tries-to-protect.

Sponsel, Alistair. 2018. *Darwin's Evolving Identity: Adventure, Ambition, and the Sin of Speculation*. Chicago: University of Chicago Press.

Standing Council on Transport and Infrastructure. 2012. *National Standard for Commercial Vessels*. Canberra, Australia: National Marine Safety Committee.

Tucker, Tom. 2010. "Applied Wave Research." In *Of Seas and Ships and Scientists: The Remarkable Story of the UK's National Institute of Oceanography*, edited by Anthony Laughton, John Gould, "Tom" Tucker, and Howard Roe, 182–90. Cambridge, UK: Lutterworth.

United Nations. 1980. "International Convention for the Safety of Life at Sea, 1974." Treaty No. 18961. Registered on June 30. In *Treaties and International Agreements*, vol. 1184. https://treaties.un.org/doc/Publication/UNTS/Volume%201184/volume-1184-I-18961-English.pdf.

von Storch, Hans, and Klaus Hasselmann. 2010. *Seventy Years of Exploration in Oceanography: A Prolonged Weekend Discussion with Walter Munk*. Berlin: Springer-Verlag.

Voorendt, Mark Z. 2016. "The Development of the Dutch Flood Safety Strategy." Technical Report, Department of Hydraulic Engineering, Delft University of Technology. December 11. Amsterdam: Bee's Books.

Watts, Laura. 2019. *Energy at the End of the World: An Orkney Islands Saga*. Cambridge, MA: MIT Press.

Watts, Laura, and Brit Ross Winthereik. 2017. "Ocean Energy at the Edge." In *Ocean Energy: Governance Challenges for Wave and Tidal Stream Technologies*, edited by Glen Wright, Sandy Kerr, and Kate Johnson, 229–46. London: Routledge.

Westcott, Kathryn. 2011. "Is King Canute Misunderstood?" *BBC News Magazine*, May 26. http://www.bbc.com/news/magazine-13524677.

Westwick, Peter, and Peter Neushul. 2013. *The World in the Curl: An Unconventional History of Surfing*. New York: Crown.

World Meteorological Organization. 2005. *World Weather Watch: Twenty-Second Status Report on Implementation*. Geneva: WMO.

World Meteorological Organization. 2011. *Manual on Codes: International Codes*. Volume I.1: Annex II to the WMO Technical Regulations, Part A Alphanumeric Codes. Updated 2016. Geneva: WMO.

7. ROBOTIC LIFE IN THE DEEP SEA

IRUS BRAVERMAN

In its report "Losing Humanity: The Case against Killer Robots," Human Rights Watch concluded that "fully autonomous weapons should be banned and . . . governments should urgently pursue that end" (Human Rights Watch 2012, 2). In 2016, two high-ranking United Nations experts on the Human Rights Council in Geneva issued a similar report that included a call to fully ban autonomous weapons, recommending that "autonomous weapons systems that require no meaningful human control should be prohibited" (Human Rights Watch 2016). Criticisms of killer robots have also spread to the academic community, with scholars cautioning that autonomous weapons are "[both] a progress toward humanizing war and an unprecedented danger to humanity" and that "the more autonomous these systems become, the less it will be possible to properly hold those who designed them or ordered their use responsible for their actions." Along these lines, it has also been pointed out that "the impossibility of punishing [the] machine means that we cannot hold the machine responsible" (Sparrow 2007, 74; see also Krishnan 2009, 4).

Because of the threats they pose to humans, killer robots are easily the most visible and contested unmanned weapons in the world. But what if such autonomous killer robots were to be deployed against nonhumans and operated only in those limited situations that benefit humans and ecological health? In particular, what if killer robots were deployed to save the increasingly imperiled coral populations of the Great Barrier Reef? Tuning into the applications of such drones in the nonhuman context focuses our attention not only on acts of killing, but also on the relationship between robotics and life. This chapter will indeed travel between "make die" and "make live" projects (my play on Michel Foucault's *let* die and make live) enabled by the marine use of robots.

I will note how make live projects are designed to extend human agency not only in acts of warfare, but additionally, and much more extensively so, within the emerging mundane eco-security regimes of the sea (see also Elizabeth R. Johnson, this volume; Jessica Lehman, this volume).

Sophisticated machines have already been used underwater for several decades, mainly for monitoring and surveillance purposes, and the future promises to present myriad further applications. More recently, scientists have access to a wide range of technologies that routinely carry them down to forty-five hundred meters (14,764 feet), enabling them to study the deepest parts of the ocean. I will describe the uses of human occupied vehicles (HOVs), remotely operated vehicles (ROVs), and automated underwater vehicles (AUVs) for producing knowledge about the deep sea. Finally, I will consider the humanoid OceanOne, the most recent development in marine robotics.

More broadly, this chapter will draw on in-depth interviews with marine biologists and engineers to explore the relationship between human scientists, nonhuman animals (e.g., crown-of-thorns starfish [COTS] as well as deep-sea and tropical corals), and the robotic entities mentioned above (namely: COTS-bots, ROVs, AUVs, and OceanOne robots). The chapter will also consider how the drives to ecological management are articulated through, and confined by, national and international law. I will conclude by asking whether it matters, physically, socially, and legally, if the acts of making live and making die are carried out by machines rather than by humans and, also, whether it matters that they target nonhuman animals. Some have cautioned, for instance, that a "starfish-killing robot may not sound like an internationally significant development, but releasing it on to the reef would cross a Rubicon" (*New Scientist* 2016). "These robots we build are not terminators," marine biologist Christian Voolstra, who helped design the OceanOne humanoid, told me in defense of this robot. "They are essentially an extension of the human. It's an avatar-driven robot. An avatar is a virtual projection of yourself in a different environment." These statements emphasize how the mechanization of knowledge production and management in the deep see displaces humans, creating the conditions for a kind of biopolitical gaze that extends not only beyond the human, but also beyond particular management sites to the entire ocean. At the same time, technology enables the virtual reinsertion of the human into a scene that was once considered human-less. Such technological developments thus both allow and reinforce a very particular perspective of planetary management. The oceans are at the forefront of ecosystem management, their transition signaling a broader move toward robotic management not only in the ocean, but also in planetary governance writ large.

Crown-of-Thorns Starfish: Life Blooms

The COTS (*Acanthaster planci*) is an unusually large starfish who can grow to more than one meter in diameter. The COTS has seven to twenty-three arms, all bristling with spikes. Native to the Indo-Pacific region, this starfish has one of the highest rates of fertilization recorded in any invertebrate: a large female starfish is capable of producing up to sixty-five million eggs over the spawning season (Braverman 2018, 177–81; Great Barrier Reef Marine Park Authority 2017). The coral-eating starfish has played an important role in increasing coral diversity, as it tends to feed on the fastest-growing corals, such as staghorns and plate corals, thereby allowing slower-growing coral species to form colonies. Currently, however, outbreaks of this venomous invertebrate pose a significant threat to the Great Barrier Reef: coral cover has declined by about 50 percent over the past thirty years, and the COTS have been deemed responsible for almost half of this decline (De'ath et al. 2012). Daunting images of the starfish show how it sucks the life out of corals, leaving them bleached (Living Oceans Foundation 2014).

Fighting back against these perceived attacks by the COTS, the Australian government identified this starfish as the number one enemy of Australian corals and published an instruction manual for their "culling." In "a program for the taking of animals, which pose a threat to the use and amenity of a particular area," the government advised that "the best practice method for undertaking COTS control is to use a modified drench gun to inject the starfish, using either the single-shot bile salts or the multi-shot sodium bisulfite method. These injection methods minimise the risk of breaking corals, and are safer than manual removal" (Great Barrier Reef Marine Park Authority 2017). At a cost of three cents per COTS injection, this is possibly the cheapest animal death ("removal") and, by extension, the cheapest animal life, on earth (Braverman 2018, 178). Furthermore, the law renders the COTS killable, celebrating this death as a way of making corals live. On the ground, this legal death sentence is executed by the trained human divers who perform the injections. While Australian law provides the broad framework for these procedures, the project mostly takes place through soft and less formal laws, such as administrative permits and professional guidelines.

David Wachenfeld is director of coral reef recovery at the Great Barrier Reef Marine Park Authority (GBRMPA). In our 2016 interview, Wachenfeld admitted that it is highly unlikely that conservation efforts will stop the outbreak of COTS altogether (see also Braverman 2018, 178). Instead, the rationale behind COTS killing, he told me, has been to create an in situ nursery that would later serve as a source for the repopulation of reefs. GBRMPA has prioritized twenty-one coral reefs, he said. "What we're hoping to achieve by tactically controlling the COTS is to create reefs where there is still good coral left that will [become] reproduction centers that will kick-start the next recovery phase." GBRMPA's main objective is not to kill starfish, Wachenfeld insisted, but rather to maintain the corals' capacity to reproduce. The problem facing the Great Barrier Reef, he further explained, is the accumulated impact of bleaching, cyclones, and COTS. "We can't stop bleaching and we can't stop cyclones. But we can do something about COT starfish" (interview, January 4, 2016).

The need to take action, coupled with the perceived inability to take action where it matters most (climate change), translate into a more easily obtainable and manageable target: starfish (see also Braverman 2017). Erasing humans from the climate change arena by shifting the blame to the starfish amounts to the first displacement of humans from the scene. Notably, the killing (or making die) is performed here by the state's various licensed agents, who operate within their sovereign capacity up to twelve nautical miles from the coast. The 1982 United Nations Convention on the Law of the Sea (UNCLOS) identifies this particular area as subject to the coastal state's sovereignty. The laws that govern the use of robotic and other vehicles in the high seas—namely, outside the nation-state's exclusive zones—are much less clear (see, e.g., Kraska et al. 2015).

COTSbot: The "Make Die" of Coral Biopolitics

In a recent turn of events, coral managers have been enlisting nonhumans in the war against the starfish and for the protection of corals, thereby instantiating a second displacement of humans from the scene. This time, humans are removed from actually killing these starfish, letting machines perform such acts in their place.

In 2015, researchers from Queensland University of Technology (QUT) were conducting final trials on a robot trained to administer the lethal injections to the starfish: the COTSbot (figure 7.1). They planned to send the robot out on the reef for up to eight hours at a time, delivering more than two hundred lethal shots a day. "It will never out-compete a human diver in terms of sheer numbers of injections but it will be more persistent," explained COTSbot designer Matthew Dunbabin (Australian Associated Press 2015; see also Braverman 2018, 179–81). This is especially true given that the bot can be deployed in conditions that are unsuitable for human divers, such as at nighttime and in inclement weather.

FIGURE 7.1. Researchers Matthew Dunbabin and Feras Dayoub (unseen) completing field trials of their COTS robot, which can navigate difficult reefs, detect COTS, and deliver a fatal dose of bile salts. Credit: Richard Fitzpatrick for QUT. Used with permission.

Dunbabin likens the training of the COTSbot to how dogs are trained to identify drugs. Using GPS and cruising a meter away from the seafloor, the COTSbot is taught to recognize the starfish through a sophisticated recognition system. The bot's attached camera uses sonar to determine long-range direction (Dunbabin 2008, 236). Dunbabin relies on a large collection of images to inform his robots about the starfish: at the outset, a data set of 3,157 images was created and sourced from publicly available YouTube footage of COTS captured by recreational and scientific divers (Dayoub, Dunbabin, and Corke 2015, 1924). To amass more images, Dunbabin attached GoPro cameras which captured close-up images of the many ways COTS orient on the coral, to the COTS divers' guns. This resulted in "hundreds of thousands of images of what COTS would look like under all sorts of different examples." Utilizing "deep machine learning" and computational models, the robots are "over 99 percent accurate at killing the starfish," Dunbabin told me (interview, January 20, 2016).

At the time of our interview, human approval was required for every lethal injection. Yet Dunbabin was hoping to move away from human verification and give the robot "as much autonomy as we can." The COTSbots photograph their targets, he explained. In cases of uncertainty, they would insert the injection only after a human verifies the photo. Such instances of uncertainty would also provide a training opportunity for the COTSbot: after verification, the photo would be added to the robot's arsenal of images to help it better distinguish between killable starfish and livable coral on its next outing. The robot's autonomy from humans in the context of governing the eco-security of the sea thus further removes humans from the killing scene and from responsibility for their acts.

Dunbabin pointed out, finally, the potential use of COTSbots by "citizen scientists." Specifically, he has been planning to design an easily accessible control system (for example, using a smartphone) to deploy the robots across oceans. If his vision materializes, a fleet of robots will soon roam the oceans, mapping the ocean floor, collecting images, and monitoring a variety of environmental "pests." The COTSbot, as well as other monitoring and surveillance technologies, could potentially be deployed by any interested party, which serves to highlight the contentious legalities of such projects across jurisdictional boundaries. Ultimately, Dunbabin was hoping to create a similar situation "like with drone aircrafts: if you can have millions that'd be awesome" (interview, January 20, 2016; see also Braverman 2018, 180).

Dunbabin's likening of COTSbots to drones speaks to his aspirations of granting robots yet more autonomy to kill. Nonetheless, he was careful to distinguish between the COTSbot and the highly criticized drone project. While the drone is designed to kill, he explained, the COTSbot is designed to save. According to Dunbabin, animal rights groups have not voiced protests against the culling of COTS and were in fact on board with the project. The institutional review boards that have authorized his project in university settings have also been silent on this front, he told me, explaining that "the starfish is an invertebrate, and there's only a couple of invertebrates that are considered animals in ethical review boards. One is an octopus, and I can't remember what the other one is. Maybe the coral. So it was very easy to get ethics approval for this project. Dolphins would be a different story" (interview, January 20, 2016). At the end of the day, then, the starfish are rendered by everyone (animal rights activists included) as a killable species (Braverman 2018).

Coralbot: The "Make Live" of Corals

Alongside the use of robots by conservation scientists and managers in configurations of threat, death, and mortality rates within the zones of the state's legal jurisdiction, a range of affirmative coral biopolitics have emerged through a robotic protection of corals. For example, marine biologists Murray Roberts and Lea-Anne Henry were both involved in the coralbot project, which was stopped short because of funding difficulties (Braverman 2018, 189). Unlike the COTSbot, which aims to kill, the coralbot was designed to rely on image-processing algorithms to directly restore broken pieces of coral to an orientation that will facilitate regrowth. The coralbots would thus serve as an army of repairmen that could potentially fix some of the damage caused by trawling in the deep sea, where trawl nets produce devastating impacts on deep-sea corals (interview, Sophie Arnaud-Haond, May 13, 2016).

This sort of restoration project again highlights how robotic technologies advance the goal of planetary management without requiring a change in human behavior or in broad societal structures. Under this way of thinking, humans can solve the ongoing devastation we have brought about through the management of nonhuman life and death, rather than through the management of our own human life. This erasure amounts to the first instance of human displacement from the planetary scheme. The second displacement instance takes place with the coralbot's ability to reach or work where and when the human cannot. "If you're restoring a tropical coral reef, a practical solution could be to send people in—they will do the job very effectively. But in the deep ocean that is absolutely impossible," Roberts told me (interview, January 28, 2016).

Although they are relatively new in the restoration context, robots and other machines have been used extensively to map, survey, collect data, and generally to monitor the underwater environment. Their use has been particularly acute in the context of deep-sea (or cold water) corals. Relative to tropical corals, deep-sea corals have largely been invisible to humans and researched by scientists only in the past couple of decades (Ocean Portal Team n.d.), which explains why some refer to them as Cinderella species. In Roberts's words: "We've been aware of them for a long time, but it takes the technology and the capacity we've had in the last decade really to reveal just how extensive they are." Alongside its unknown species, the deep sea also contains oil, gas, minerals, and other biomedical resources, as well as "important functions, including roles in gas and climate regulation, and waste absorption and detoxification" (Barbier et al. 2014, 476). Due to the remoteness of the deep sea and the technological sophistication required for its investigation, scientists have been central to the production of knowledge in this space (Ducker 2014, 12).

The Machine in the Garden: HOVs, ROVs, and AUVs

For twenty years, Murray Roberts, a deep-sea biologist at the University of Edinburgh, has mostly been using remotely operated vehicles (ROVs) for his coral research. In 1964, the *Alvin*—a human-occupied vehicle (HOV)—took its first free dive to 10.7 meters (35 feet) below the surface. HOVs like the *Alvin* transport

FIGURE 7.2. A science class ROV is launched to survey and sample the Mingulay deep-water coral reef complex in the Sea of the Hebrides in 2012. Courtesy of J Murray Roberts.

up to three people directly to the seafloor. Built to withstand the extreme pressures of the deep ocean, HOVs are equipped with robotic arms that scoop up marine creatures as well as seafloor sediments (Ocean Portal Team n.d.). Although it may seem advantageous for humans to personally experience the deep, Roberts prefers to stay above water in the ship that maneuvers the ROV, which can reach great depths for extended periods (see, e.g., figures 7.2 and 7.3).

A more recent development on this front are autonomous underwater vehicles (AUVs). These untethered robots are preprogrammed to collect data from particular parts of the deep ocean. Carrying mobile instrumentation platforms with actuators, sensors, and on-board intelligence, AUVs complete survey and sampling tasks with little or no human supervision (Bellingham 2001, 212). Over the past decade or so, the use of AUVs for oceanographic, commercial, and military missions has risen dramatically. A wide range of these machines have been developed, varying in dry weight from less than fifty to nearly nine thousand kilograms.

Finally, hybrid vehicles combine the features of ROVs and AUVs in that they can either be tethered to a ship and controlled by researchers or they can be

FIGURE 7.3. Subsea image showing the ROV manipulator opening a tube for a coral sample to be placed inside while a curious ling looks on. Courtesy of J Murray Roberts.

operated autonomously (Woods Hole Oceanographic Institution 2005; see also Jessica Lehman's chapter, this volume). In 2009, the hybrid vehicle *Nereus* traveled 10,902 meters (6.8 miles) below the surface to explore the Mariana Trench, the deepest point in the world's oceans. Five years later, the *Nereus* was lost in a dive into the Kermadec Trench northeast of New Zealand. Most likely, it imploded under pressure as great as sixteen thousand pounds per square inch, highlighting the perils of working at such extreme depths (Woods Hole Oceanographic Institution 2014).

Despite his excitement about the democratization of the deep sea through ROV research, Roberts is the first to admit that such vehicles are extremely costly and thus not as egalitarian as one might hope. For example, David Johnson, director of the Global Ocean Biodiversity Initiative, quoted $43,000 as the initiative's daily operating costs (interview, May 26, 2016). Typically developed and utilized by national governments and commercial companies, ROVs are indeed referenced as the Rolls Royce of deep-sea technology. As such, they are currently "only available occasionally, even in the most well-developed scientific economies" (Johnson, interview). The restricted accessibility of these machines highlights that, despite the facade of increased visibility, the deep sea is still inaccessible to most humans. The heightened dependence of scientific research on commercial interests is uniquely troubling when considering that the deep sea remains largely unregulated and thus vastly underprotected.

Zooming Out: Bathymetry Devices for Sonic Mapping

Alongside their capacity to monitor specific sites, robots operating in the deep sea are essential for any mapping of these areas, which are otherwise inaccessible and invisible to the human eye. Philip Weaver, scientific coordinator of the Global Ocean Biodiversity Initiative, likens surveying the ocean to "flying at night without any cities with lights on the ground." "You wouldn't see anything," Weaver told me. "You only have enough energy to light small areas. So you have to get very close to the seabed in order to see anything in terms of camera work" (interview, May 26, 2016). Instead of vision, then, deep ocean mapping is performed through remote sensing by bouncing sound waves off the seabed. According to Weaver, current technology determines both the topography and the reflectivity factors in order to construct a "bathymetry of the whole ocean floor."

Because of the vastness and remoteness of the seabed in the high seas, such detailed mapping is limited to small areas. Here, again, ROVs have become invaluable. Using ROVs, "you can do the map and see if there are corals at the same time, so it's quite effective" (Johnson, interview). To determine where to focus the high-end explorations, surveyors undertake what they call "predictive habitat mapping." This preliminary survey through sound waves assesses the location of coral gardens and other vulnerable deepwater ecosystems. "So you've got to use particular knowledge and a lot of intuition to work out your predicted habitat map," Weaver told me. "It's called 'ground truthing': you go out and verify what you've predicted," Johnson further explained. The Norwegian government plans to map the entire Norwegian territorial off-shore waters using this technology (MAREANO 2017). Similarly, the European Commission has been creating a digital seabed map of European waters by consolidating all existing data into one coherent and freely accessible database, a project scheduled for completion by 2020 (European Commission 2012).

In the meantime, the number of expeditions to the deep sea using ROVs and other devices has been growing steadily. For example, the Nekton Foundation launched its first deep-sea expedition in summer 2016. According to its website, members of the team "will be diving in human-operated submersibles with the world's leading scientists and storytellers to bring the deep ocean to you" (Nekton n.d.; see also Deep Links Project 2016). By promoting ocean literacy, Nekton catalyzes what its operators refer to as the blue economy (see also Amy Braun, this volume; Katherine G. Sammler, this volume). In another expedition, this time to explore deep-sea corals in the Gulf of Maine, an ROV called ROPOS (remotely operated platform for ocean science) documented significant concentrations of centuries-old cold water corals. Over the course of 12 days, ROPOS conducted 16 dives, visited 7 dive sites, and accumulated 168 hours of underwater time, providing the research team with 68 video transects, 236 physical samples, 7.5 terabytes of HD video, and more than 1,000 digital stills (ROPOS 2014). This extensive data has led to the identification and protection of two new sensitive benthic areas.

Increasingly, images from the bottom of the deepest sites within the deep sea are also making grand appearances in the mainstream media (e.g., Carrington 2017), emphasizing not only the reach of human pollution to the most remote points on earth, but also the making of an all-encompassing planetary imaginary that leaves nothing out of sight.

OceanOne: The Humanoid Robot

The humanoid robot OceanOne represents the latest in deep-sea technological advances. In OceanOne, scientists hope to erode the gap between robot and human in order to create a "robotic submarine [that] could dive with the skill and care of a human diver" (Carey 2016). Christian Voolstra is an assistant professor of marine science at the Red Sea Research Center at King Abdullah University of Science and Technology. Voolstra has been involved with the development of OceanOne as part of his research in the nexus of coral genetics and conservation. He described the feeling of working with OceanOne as a "glove you put on," explaining that the glove-wearer's hands and movements translate to the robot's pinching device and that the robot precisely copies the above-water controller in its actions underwater (King Abdullah University of Science and Technology 2015). With the use of haptic technology, the sense of touch is communicated through the robot to the human controller, the connection between the two depicted as "direct and instantaneous" (King Abdullah University of Science and Technology 2015). OceanOne's advanced artificial intelligence allows it to actively respond to ocean conditions and adjust its movement accordingly, purportedly making it one with both the human and its ocean environment.

The Red Sea has been a particularly important research site to coral scientists documenting the impact of climate change on coral ecosystems. Because the deep waters of the Red Sea are warmer than usual, they are also more oxygen-deprived, nutrient-deficient, and high in salinity. Although such physical conditions were previously thought to be detrimental to their survival, a variety of deep-sea corals were recently found thriving there (Roder et al. 2013). An understanding of how Red Sea corals exist in such warmer waters could serve as a model for scientists to artificially increase adaptation in coral species that reside in other, increasingly warming, seas. The OceanOne humanoid robot has been deployed in research on these and other coral-related questions.

Voolstra's involvement with OceanOne started due to his frustration when using ROVs in the field. "I was surprised how clunky [the ROV] is," he told me. "You don't have a good way of targeting what you want to do . . . . It's like those machines where you throw in one dollar and try to grab a teddy—and you never get it" (interview, May 12, 2016). In addition to the difficulty of maneuvering ROVs, Voolstra found them to be insufficient for performing in-depth scientific research because they only facilitated research "in a foreign environment," for example by providing extracted samples for analysis in a terrestrial lab. "Things behave differently out of context," he explained, emphasizing the importance of research that can take place in situ rather than outside the ocean.

The technical limitations of ROVs also dictate what kind of research can be carried out using these machines. Voolstra explained that with a "robotic arm with 3–4 degrees, you're limited with how, what, and where you sample. You have a tiny little screen, and you are monitoring what is happening three thousand feet below. The ROVs are [tethered] so there's that physical limitation, too" (interview, June 20, 2016). Furthermore, an engineer must be present to operate the ROV in a detailed manner: "Lift the left leg, put down the leg, then lift the right leg, put down the leg." By contrast, with OceanOne it is like "you yourself," Voolstra told me. "If you go diving, you don't try to coordinate both arms: one arm moves to a rock, the other arm takes it." And although Ocean-One is still tethered due to voltage constraints, it will likely soon become wireless. Voolstra summed up the benefits of this humanoid as follows: "You have a robot that can do things in the natural environment and study them. You [have] tactility, the delicacy of handling things, [and] control over how hard you touch things. This robot operates through haptic control. You can literally feel the ocean. You can feel the resistance. You can pick up an egg or apple, and you will feel the difference." Oussama Khatib of Stanford's Robotic Lab, the central human behind the development of this nonhuman, told me along similar lines:

> Why is this the robot we need? If you go all over the world and look at the robots used underwater, you can characterize them as robots that can see, but that cannot do. They can observe, map, but they have no capability of doing things because they don't have arms, hands, and the autonomy to manipulate underwater. The main thing about OceanOne is that

it is bringing the capability of doing—of performing tasks underwater—because the robot has hands, arms, visual feedback, sensors, touch. (Interview, May 31, 2016)

Humanoid robots are programmed to "understand" and "correspond with" different environments. They are designed to work in minuscule structures such as the wing of an airplane or in hazardous industrial situations such as the Fukushima nuclear plant—namely, environments that are otherwise inaccessible to humans. Unlike the remotely controlled robot, the humanoid robot allows the human scientists to "immerse the robot into an environment but still move freely without having the restriction that you would need to control the robot, because the robot controls itself" (Voolstra, interview, June 20, 2016). Arguably, the robot's humanlike features enhance human intimacy, both with the machine and, in the case of OceanOne, with the ocean in which it is embedded (see also Elizabeth R. Johnson, this volume).

Humanoid robots are also important for facilitating scientific communication with laypeople, as they help to relay and make visible the importance of deep-sea research. Voolstra told me accordingly: "You need to make them agree with you on an emotional level that this is an important endeavor. The robot makes this happen, so that humans can better connect with this outer space–like environment. It's important that saving species is not only [something that] a crazy group of environmentalists needs to do. . . . It's not a luxury [for] crazy people out there, it's all of our responsibility" (interview, June 20, 2016).

Nonetheless, many scientists, including Voolstra himself, are skeptical about the use of such robots for coral restoration. "Humanoids for restoration? You're talking to the wrong person," he told me point blank. From his evolutionary perspective, restoration doesn't make sense until we change the basic conditions that have led to the devastation in the first place—namely, climate change and ocean acidification. In his words: "If something got lost, it got lost for a reason. If you don't change the factors and just restore, it will have the same destiny or fate. You think you've restored a coral reef—it looks like a coral reef, but in the majority of cases, it's not (if you look at organism diversity and so on). Restoration implies you can fix it. I don't think that's possible" (interview, June 20, 2016). Relatedly, Voolstra insists that we cannot save corals by displacing either the cause of their demise or the solution to this issue into technological means. In this sense, his position is different from that of the designers of the COTSbot, who seem to suggest that we can fix the reef by displacing the cause from human industry and climate change into the starfish (and, thereby, its solution away from climate mitigation into acts of killing by the COTSbot).

Deep Ocean Legalities

Whereas the acts of killing starfish near the coastal shores of Australia are governed by state law and executed by such administrative bodies as GBRMPA, the legalities of benthic mapping projects by ships and such research expeditions using HOVs and ROVs in the depth of the high seas are much less clear. In these areas, international law prevails, at least formally, and UNCLOS's complicated apparatus is gospel.

Parts XIII and XIV of UNCLOS contain almost 100 of the Convention's 320 articles—that is, about one-third. These articles deal with marine scientific research and with the transfer of marine technology. While Article 238 defines the basic right of all states to conduct marine scientific research, subsequent clauses subordinate this right to permission by the coastal state when conducted within its territorial waters and exclusive economic zone (EEZ) and on its continental shelf (UNCLOS Articles 245, 246). In any case, adequate research can only be carried out by nation-states or by recognized international organizations and for peaceful purposes (UNCLOS Article 240). States and organizations also have a duty to promote the flow of scientific knowledge that results from marine scientific research, especially to developing states, and to strengthen their "autonomous" marine scientific research capabilities through training and education programs (UNCLOS Article 244(2)). As for the high seas, scientific research is a freedom of all states, subject to the rights of the coastal state to give or withhold consent to research on its continental shelf or EEZ (UNCLOS Article 87(f)).

This lack of direct regulation of marine research on the high seas stands in stark contrast to the detailed regulation that prevails in the ocean's national jurisdictions and has resulted in voluntary, or "soft," codes of conduct for the deep sea. For example, the OSPAR Code of Conduct for the North East Atlantic (OSPAR Commission 2008) stipulates that "because of the specialized nature of the equipment required to work in the deep-sea, such as manned and unmanned research submersibles, scientists are the primary group of people who have had the opportunity to visit and value these extraordinary habitats." The Code of Conduct includes rules such as "avoid, in the course of scientific research, activities which could lead to long-lasting changes in regional populations or substantially reduce the number of individuals present" (OSPAR Commission 2008).

The autonomous nature of AUVs exposes the gap at the heart of the national and international legal regimes pertaining to the sea (Showalter n.d.).

When tethered to a vessel, ROVs are regulated as part of the vessel. Commonly referred to as the rules of the road, the 1972 International Regulations for Preventing Collisions at Sea (COLREG) include special signaling requirements for surface vessels conducting underwater operations. However, these regulations apply only to vessels operating *on* the water and do not pertain to underwater vessels (Showalter n.d.). Furthermore, under US federal law, research AUVs are unlikely to be considered vessels because they are not used for commerce or navigation. Due to the newness of the technology and the unwillingness of overburdened federal agencies to incur additional responsibilities, AUVs are exempt from US maritime laws. As a result, the use of these vehicles remains virtually unregulated.

Marine scientists have lamented more broadly the lack of universal authority to consider ecosystem protection in international waters. In a 2014 comment in *Nature*, Lea-Anne Henry and colleagues expressed a specific concern about the damage caused by trawling in the deep sea, calling for "formal governance structures and funds to be put in place by 2020 to create networks of deep-sea reserves that maintain and restore biodiversity and function in this vast and important biome" (Barbier et al. 2014, 475). Henry and her colleagues argued that a "global strategy must be framed under the aegis of national governments and an international body." For areas that are beyond national jurisdiction, they offered that the International Seabed Authority (ISA) is best suited to this task (Barbier et al. 2014, 475). Finally, these scientists have been advocating to add a biodiversity conservation agreement to the UNCLOS (Barbier et al. 2014, 476).

Asking to remain anonymous, a prominent government official on the US Workforce for UNCLOS disagreed with the claim that the deep sea could use more regulation. "If I had a penny for each time I've been told that the deep sea is the 'Wild West' in terms of regulation, I'd already be able to afford my retirement," she told me. The high seas are anything but lawless, she argued, explaining that the United States has been opposed to negotiating new treaties precisely because such laws are already in existence. At the same time, she admitted that the sectorial and fragmented nature of the existing laws can be challenging.

Responding to the various calls for action and despite the US's explicit objections to this move, the United Nations created the Ad Hoc Open-ended Informal Working Group and tasked it with assessing the feasibility of a new treaty. Decided in 2015, UN Resolution UNGA 99/292 formalized the recommendations made by the ad hoc working group, convening an intergovernmental negotiating conference to finalize the terms of the new treaty (United Nations General Assembly 2015).

Conclusion

The deep sea is home to a multitude of previously unknown and still undiscovered forms of organic life. Increasingly, it is also home to numerous forms of machine and robotic life and, by extension, to their myriad human operators. This chapter has explored the recent attempts by conservation agencies to enhance their capacities of knowing the deep sea, often referred to by these agencies as "ocean literacy." Visibility to the human eye has been critical for all forms of scientific knowledge, which explains the increased efforts of scientists to render the deep sea visible through surveys, mapping projects, and expeditions. The current efforts by the United Nations to set preconditions for negotiating a new treaty that will centralize high seas management will probably add even more momentum to scientific explorations of the deep sea.

Because humans are physically unable to visit the depths of the oceans, over the years we have conscripted an army of robots to perform this task. Remote and automated vehicles as well as more advanced humanoid technologies have been programmed not only to map, document, and make visible, but also to collect and make physically tangible bits and pieces of the deep sea. Beyond their use for data collection, I have described the deployment of robots for conservation purposes, such as the restoration of coral reefs. Such attempts, while currently in their infancy, will likely proliferate in the coming years as robotic technologies become yet more widely available and affordable.

Arguably, the growing use of robotic technologies in the deep sea signals the potential uses of such technologies in a vast range of other conservation management contexts. Beyond their physical capacity to perform tasks that humans cannot perform, and therefore to bring us virtually and emotionally closer to the oceans, robots at the same time serve as displacers, their use removing human responsibility for the violence inflicted in these spaces by enlisting other, typically nonhuman, creatures as perpetrators in their place. This, I have argued here, is what the coralbot restoration project is about.

More controversial than the use of robots for making coral life is the deployment of robots to kill. Because the target of this killing has been a designated pest, the crown-of-thorns starfish, and because the purpose of the killing has been to save the increasingly vulnerable coral, the use of the killer robot has mostly gone unnoticed. This chapter calls for a more comprehensive scholarly consideration of the biopolitical enlisting of robots both to make die and to make live. On the table for this discussion should be the metrics through which humans assign particular values to certain, but not to other, forms of life as well as a reflection on how deploying machines influences these metrics.

References

Australian Associated Press. 2015. "Robotic Killer Being Trialed to Rid Great Barrier Reef of Crown-of-Thorns Starfish." September 3. http://www.theguardian.com/environment/2015/sep/03/robotic-killer-being-trialled-to-rid-great-barrier-reef-of-crown-of-thorns-starfish.

Barbier, Edward B., David Moreno Mateos, Alex David Rogers, James Aronson, Linwood Pendleton, Roberto Danovaro, Lea-Anne Henry, Telmo Morato, Jeff A. Ardron, and Cindy Lee van Dover. 2014. "Ecology: Protect the Deep Sea." *Nature* 505 (7484): 475–77.

Bellingham, James. 2001. "Autonomous Underwater Vehicles." In *Encyclopedia of Ocean Sciences*, edited by John H. Steele, Steve A. Thorpe, and Karl K. Turekian, 212–16. Cambridge, MA: Academic Press. http://www.curry.eas.gatech.edu/Courses/6140/ency/Chapter11/Ency_Oceans/AUVS.pdf.

Braverman, Irus. 2017. "*Bleached!* Managing Coral Catastrophe." *Futures* 92 (September): 12–28.

Braverman, Irus. 2018. *Coral Whisperers: Scientists on the Brink*. Berkeley: University of California Press.

Carey, Bjorn. 2016. "Maiden Voyage of Stanford's Humanoid Robotic Diver Recovers Treasures from King Louis XIV's wrecked Flagship." *Stanford News*. April 27. https://news.stanford.edu/2016/04/27/robotic-diver-recovers-treasures/.

Carrington, Damian. 2017. "'Extraordinary' Levels of Pollutants Found in 10km Deep Mariana Trench." February 13. https://www.theguardian.com/environment/2017/feb/13/extraordinary-levels-of-toxic-pollution-found-in-10km-deep-mariana-trench.

Dayoub, Feras, Matthew Dunbabin, and Peter Corke. 2015. "Robotic Detection and Tracking of Crown-of-Thorns Starfish." Paper presented at the 2015 IEEE/RSJ International Conference on Intelligent Robots and Systems (IROS), Congress Center, Hamburg, September 28–October 2.

De'ath, Glenn, Katharina E. Fabriclus, Hugh Sweatman, and Marji Puotinen. 2012. "The 27–Year Decline of Coral Cover on the Great Barrier Reef and Its Causes." PNAS 109 (44): 17995–99.

Deep Links Project. 2016. "Sampling the Deep—Processing and Preservation." Deep Links website, May 20. https://deeplinksproject.wordpress.com/2016/05/20/sampling-the-deep.

Ducker, Erik. 2014. *News from an Inaccessible World: The History and Present Challenges of Deep-Sea Biology*. Enschede, Netherlands: Gildeprint.

European Commission. 2012. Seabed Mapping: New Opportunities for Blue Growth and Jobs in Seas and Oceans. Press release. August 29. http://europa.eu/rapid/press-release_IP-12-920_en.htm.

Great Barrier Reef Marine Park Authority. 2017. "Crown-of-Thorns Starfish: Control Guidelines." 2nd ed. http://elibrary.gbrmpa.gov.au/jspui/bitstream/11017/3162/1/COTS-control-guidelines-update-2017.pdf.

Human Rights Watch. 2012. "Losing Humanity: The Case against Killer Robots." Human Rights Watch website. https://www.hrw.org/report/2012/11/19/losing-humanity/case-against-killer-robots.

Human Rights Watch. 2016. "Killer Robots and the Concept of Meaningful Human Control: Memorandum to Convention on Conventional Weapons (ccw) Delegates." Human Rights Watch website, April 11. https://www.hrw.org/news/2016/04/11/killer -robots-and-concept-meaningful-human-control.

King Abdullah University of Science and Technology. 2015. "Deep Sea Coral Reefs More Accessible with Touch-Sensitive Underwater Robotic Platform." http://www.kaust .edu.sa/latest-stories/robotic-diver-expands-underwater-research.html.

Kraska, James, Guillermo Ortuño Crespo, and David W. Johnston. 2015. "Bio-Logging of Marine Migratory Species in the Law of the Sea." *Marine Policy* 15: 394–400.

Krishnan, Armin. 2009. *Killer Robots: Legality and Ethicality of Autonomous Weapons.* Farnham, UK: Ashgate.

Living Oceans Foundation. 2014. "Deadly Starfish Eats Corals: Crown of Thorns Starfish (cots) Crisis." Living Oceans Foundation website, February 15. https://www .livingoceansfoundation.org/video/crown-thorns-starfish-cots-crisis.

mareano Programme. 2017. "About mareano." Mareano website, June 6 update. http://www.mareano.no/en/about_mareano.

Nekton Foundation. n.d. "About Nekton Foundation." Accessed March 2, 2017. https:// www.charityjob.co.uk/recruiter/nekton-foundation/29061.

New Scientist. 2016. "Killer Robots: It's Time to Decide Who Pulls the Trigger." January 13. https://www.newscientist.com/article/2073157-killer-robots-its-time-to-decide -who-pulls-the-trigger.

Ocean Portal Team, Smithsonian National Museum of Natural History. n.d. "Deep Sea Corals." Smithsonian website. Accessed March 2, 2019. http://ocean.si.edu/deep-sea -corals.

ospar Commission. 2008. "The ospar Code of Conduct for Responsible Marine Research in the Deep Seas and High Seas of the ospar Maritime Area." August 24. https://www.google.com/search?q=OSPAR+code+of+conduct+for+deep -sea+science&ie=utf-8&oe=utf-8.

Roder, Cornelia, Michael L. Berumen, Jessica Bouwmeester, Evangelos Papathanassiou, Abdulaziz Al-Suwailem, and Christian R. Voolstra. 2013. "First Biological Measurements of Deep-Sea Corals from the Red Sea." *Scientific Reports* 3: 2802–12.

ropos. 2014. "ropos Helps Protect Sensitive Benthic Areas." http://www.ropos.com /index.php/news-and-media/37-ropos-helps-protect-benthic-areas.

Showalter, S. E. n.d. "The Law Governing Autonomous Undersea Vehicles: What an Operator Needs to Know." Unpublished ms.

Sparrow, Robert. 2007. "Killer Robots." *Journal of Applied Philosophy* 24 (1): 62–77.

United Nations General Assembly. 2015. Resolution unga 99/292. June 25. http://www .un.org/ga/search/view_doc.asp?symbol=A/69/L.65.

Woods Hole Oceanographic Institution. 2005. "*Nereus* Frequently Asked Questions (faqs)." http://www.whoi.edu/main/nereus/faqs.

Woods Hole Oceanographic Institution. 2014. "Robotic Deep-Sea Vehicle Lost on Dive to 6-Mile Depth." May 10. https://www.whoi.edu/news-release/Nereus-Lost.

8. THE TECHNOPOLITICS OF OCEAN SENSING

JESSICA LEHMAN

New ocean visual imaginaries, such as Google Ocean, as well as enhanced visuals of global ocean temperatures, salinity, productivity, and others, give the impression of a real-time, high-resolution snapshot of global ocean properties (Helmreich 2011; Jue 2014). However, even a cursory look below the surface shows them to be thin digital skins stretched over a mass of data collected using a wide variety of new and old sensing methods. This chapter focuses on the geopolitical and legal dimensions of new robotic, autonomous, and/or remotely operated ocean sensors, which herald a step away from ship-based methods of ocean measurement that have defined the discipline since its inception. New sensing technologies, such as satellites and remotely operated and autonomous instruments, have elicited much critique in the social sciences and humanities for their distancing and abstracting views that can make nature exponentially more available to the uses of capital and empire (see, for example, Dodge and Perkins 2009; Haraway 1988; Helmreich 2011; Jue 2014; Litfin 1997; Loftus 2015; Lövbrand, Stripple, and Wiman 2009). Yet by largely leaving out the geopolitical implications of their deployment, these authors do not fully account for the world-making practices of new ocean observing technologies. The challenges and controversies that new observing technologies produce within existing geopolitical dynamics are not simply matters of technicality. They pertain to key questions: What is marine scientific research? Whom does it serve? What is the role of the nation-state in governing the collection of environmental data? Who is responsible when machines have lives of their own?

This chapter analyzes the legal and geopolitical dimensions of new techniques of ocean observation, especially Argo, a program of drifting floats. Drawing from interviews with over forty scientists and science bureaucrats,

I argue that contemporary observations for ocean governance emerge at the legally and politically fraught juncture of two seemingly contradictory imaginaries. On one hand, new paradigms and practices of ocean sensing imagine the ocean as devoid of legal and territorial boundaries, a necessarily smooth space for the advancement of science amid environmental crisis. On the other hand, these changes in the conduct of ocean science can seem to indicate that the measurement of the ocean is both predicated on and productive of territorial boundaries and inequalities. As this volume suggests, that these imaginaries seem paradoxical may well be rooted in the terrestrial assumptions that frequently undergird our analysis of ocean space. By attending to changing ways of knowing the ocean more closely, we can see that these apparently contradictory imaginaries create a space for complex and overlapping regimes of governance. At the same time, these imaginaries do not encompass all possibilities for how ocean space is imagined and enacted, despite looming large in dominant analytical frameworks. As evidenced in this volume, at stake in understanding these imaginaries and their limitations is not simply what we imagine the ocean to be, but also what actions (by private or public actors, at various scales) are authorized to control, monitor, occupy, traverse, and/or exploit the sea and what we understand our human responsibilities toward the sea to be. While the United Nations Convention on the Law of the Sea (UNCLOS) attempts to draw distinctions between pure and applied science, which are often echoed in policy documents and by scientists themselves, knowledge, technology, and geopolitics are woven together in how questions of ocean governance are framed and, potentially, answered.

Observing the Ocean

The Google Earth Argo layer shows the Argo oceanographic floats drifting through the globe's seas. By clicking on any float, indicated by a glowing blue dot, the user can learn about the float's design, country, and institute of origin; the data it has collected; and more. The Google Earth Argo layer, then, corresponds to a vision of Argo floats as intrepid explorers on a friction-free journey through the seas, constrained only by the currents that carry them. However, when talking with the people charged with running Argo a different story emerges. The machinations of the Argo program reveal geopolitical tensions around marine sovereignty and unequal access to international oceanography despite the program's seemingly almost radical democratic nature. Argo thus provides crucial insight into the contemporary legal and political issues that are imbricated with the tantalizing promises of new methods of sensing the sea.

Many scientists agree that Argo is transformative for oceanography, but its novelty draws on a history of ocean observations that have always been the bread and butter of the discipline (Cai et al. 2015). While other disciplines prioritize theoretical or experimental practices, oceanography relies on the widespread and coordinated collection of observational data to describe and analyze the characteristics of the sea. This is especially true in the earth science component of ocean science (as opposed to marine biology). Until recent decades, nearly all oceanographic observations were taken by scientists aboard research vessels and commercial ships of opportunity or through the use of equipment such as moorings, which consist of various instruments suspended between the ocean's surface (or subsurface) and the ocean floor (Lehman 2018). Such techniques are expensive, require massive labor inputs, and are necessarily limited in their spatial and temporal resolution—ships can sample only a small portion of the ocean and usually, at most, once every few years, and mooring studies usually consist of a few sets of instruments arrayed along a particular latitude, longitude, current, or other feature.

Oceanography's contemporary technological revolution began in the 1980s with the development of satellite measurements, which created an unprecedented amount of ocean data (Conway 2006). Satellites are now accompanied by advanced in situ technologies, including distributed networks of sensors that report their data via satellite as well as remotely operated and autonomous undersea vehicles (ROVs and AUVs), more details about which are provided below. These days, scientific information about the ocean is created through a complex and iterative relationship between satellites, models, remotely operated and robotic sensors, and ship-based measurements or other traditional methods (see also Edwards 2010; Lehman 2016, 2018). Many scientists have tracked a reduction in ship-based sensing due to its high and rising cost and the relative difficulty of obtaining data compared to other methods. One scientist even told me, "I think the push now is to go into this sort of robotic state" (Isabelle Ansorge, interview, November 18, 2014). This shift to remote and robotic sensors has had many implications; perhaps chiefly it has led to the production of significantly more oceanographic data with greater spatial extent and resolution, especially real-time results that are freely available on the internet. This surge of data not only contributes vitally to new discoveries about ocean characteristics; it also provides increased capacity to monitor the ocean's shifting properties on a variety of scales in an era of planetary environmental uncertainty and change (Lehman 2016).

If a coconstitutive relationship can be drawn between ocean observations and oceanographic science, a comparable relationship may then be suggested between oceanography and ocean governance. Of course, akin to the strong relationship between cartography and colonial expansion, oceanographic surveys and mapping (both coastal and bathymetrical) have long been key to the governance of the sea, as perhaps best evidenced by strong military support for oceanography in many countries (see also Mukerji 1990; Steinberg 2009; Elizabeth R. Johnson, this volume). While even the pursuit of "pure" ocean science has perhaps always been entangled with national interests, there is now increasing pressure to make science relevant to societal needs, particularly in a time of global-scale environmental crisis to which the ocean is central (see also Boesch 1999). Similarly, visions of the sea as common space outside territorial control have frequently authorized seemingly contradictory practices regarding territorial expansion and resource exploitation (see Jennifer L. Gaynor, this volume; Zsofia Korosy, this volume). Science plays a key role in this pattern of governance; understandings of the sea formed by ocean observations are never divorced from geopolitical contexts. Hence, ocean observations and governance are connected through political and legal regimes at the same time as they shape them, and new robotic sensing technologies configure this relationship in novel ways even as they build on historical legacies.

Global ocean observations are the focus of a number of international organizations, including the World Climate Research Program, which links them with climate science, and the Partnership for Observing the Global Ocean, which "offers a venue for discussion and collaboration on ocean observing" and promotes capacity-building efforts (Cai et al. 2015, 4). Ocean observations are perhaps most broadly overseen on a legal and geopolitical basis by the Intergovernmental Oceanographic Commission (IOC), which falls under the purview of the United Nations Educational, Scientific, and Cultural Organization (UNESCO) and is headquartered in Paris. The IOC has a range of duties related to the international coordination and regulation of oceanographic research, capacity-building, and data sharing under UNCLOS. The IOC is the governing and coordinating body of the Global Ocean Observing System (GOOS), which is part of the Global Earth Observing System of Systems (GEOSS). It is important to point out that these new ocean sensing technologies cannot be considered apart from the networks that coordinate their deployment and the storage and sharing of the data they produce. While the GOOS and many other systems remain loosely connected assemblages made up of many components administered by various governments and research institutions, overarching goals for comprehensive global data connection and frameworks of global-scale ocean governance are crucial to understanding contemporary marine politics.

For many years, the main goal when it came to ocean observations was simply to gather as much basic data as possible. Global ocean observations are now organized by the Framework on Ocean Observing (FOO), which emerged from a 2009 conference called OceanObs'09. Rather than simply advocating for the collection of as much data as possible, this framework asserts that measurements should be guided by the identification of Essential Ocean Variables (EOVs) determined by "international decision-makers, and the public at large" and thus be driven by societal concerns rather than pure science questions (UNESCO 2012, 5). In the words of one IOC officer, "You can't measure everything, and there's no point in just cataloging everything, you've actually got to do what is relevant for the questions that you want to ask" (Sarah Grimes, interview, March 11, 2014).

While ocean science has of course long been tied to issues of governance and resource exploitation, the FOO indicates a new approach to ocean observations that seeks to explicitly tie societal concerns to the collection of the most fundamental of ocean data (see also Lehman 2016). This new orientation toward science has been observed in many disciplines. In a well-known article, Jane Lubchenko (1998) explains that the postwar "social contract for science," in which scientists were understood to have free rein to seek answers to their own questions in exchange for the accumulation of knowledge and technological innovation, is required to change in the twenty-first century. The new social contract for science requires scientists to more explicitly address societal concerns, which could mean more directly serving the interests of state and capital, just as it could mean addressing new and compounded societal risks under environmental crisis. The FOO can be read as a policy directive for this new social contract, mandating the reorganization of ocean observations to not only streamline expensive measurements, but also to more immediately serve data users, however loosely defined.

New Methods of Ocean Observing

As already suggested, three types of measurements are most relevant as alternatives to ship-based sensing. Satellite measurements are the most well-established, and the impact that they have had on oceanography, as in many sciences, is difficult to overstate. In the words of one oceanographer, "The ability to image the entire sea surface every week maybe, through . . . compositing satellite tracks, was a real revolution" (Albert Pluedemann, interview, April 22, 2014). Satellites measure a wide variety of oceanographic variables, including sea surface height (altimetry), temperature, color, and perhaps most recently, salinity. Satellite measurements make it possible to get a view of the entire ocean at once, to envision a truly global ocean. They are limited, however, because satellites can only measure the surface, so they miss much of what is going on in the ocean, such as the processes of vertical mixing, deepwater formation, and subsurface currents that are of great interest to scientists. Therefore, while satellite measurements are now indispensable in oceanography, they are not sufficient on their own.

A second category of alternatives to ship-based measurements is distributed sensing networks, which make in situ measurements of ocean properties. Chief among these, and a key example in this chapter, is Argo, a program of more than thirty-five hundred drifting floats that measure temperature and salinity in the upper two thousand meters of ocean every ten days (Roemmich et al. 2001; Wilson 2000). To do this, the floats descend using a simple mechanism to a predetermined depth (usually a thousand meters), where they drift for a prescribed number of days (usually ten). As they rise to the surface, they make a temperature and salinity profile and then communicate this data, along with their position, to satellites. With a large number of floats and new ice-sensing technology, Argo has been able to achieve near-global coverage, making it a proxy for satellite coverage under the ocean. New developments are underway to extend Argo's capacities to the deep seas and to include biological and geochemical sensors. Argo data is automatically reported via satellite and made available for free to online users in two forms: uncorrected real-time data and quality-controlled delayed mode data (see figures 8.1 and 8.2).

In many ways, Argo, along with satellites, have transformed oceanography, bringing it rapidly into a regime of big data. Where previously scientists had to rely on only a few measurements taken over periods of fifty years or longer using different instruments to draw conclusions about the ocean's complex behavior, they now have streams of constantly updated data at their fingertips; more than one million Argo profiles are now in use (Cai et al. 2015; Steven Piotrowiscz, interview, July 12, 2017). But the floats themselves are increasingly divorced from their human leaders. Human labor is necessary at a few steps in the process: deploying the floats, which is usually done from a research, commercial, or sometimes sport vessel, or even by airplane; quality control, which takes an international team of data experts; and in analysis and processing for various outputs, including models. Yet the instruments themselves drift through the seas with no plans for recovery at the end of their lives or otherwise; the costs even to fix broken or malfunctioning floats are considered to be too great.

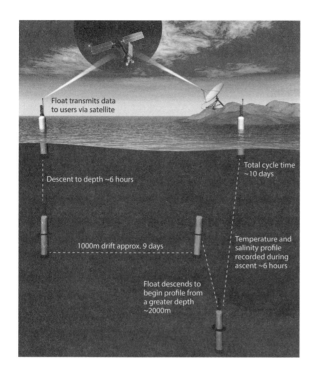

Float transmits data
to users via satellite

Descent to depth ~6 hours

Total cycle time
~10 days

1000m drift approx. 9 days

Temperature and
salinity profile
recorded during
ascent ~6 hours

Float descends to
begin profile from
a greater depth
~2000m

FIGURE 8.1. Diagram
of Argo data collection
cycle. Source: Argo
Project, UCSD. Repro-
duced with permission.

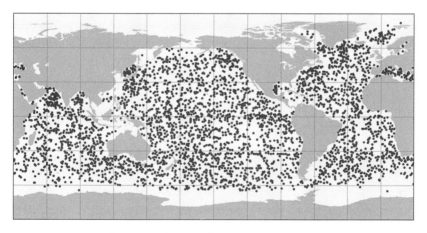

FIGURE 8.2. Map of 3,827 Argo floats as of October 10, 2017. Source: Argo Project,
UCSD. Reproduced with permission.

The third kind of sensors encompasses the closely related, remotely operated vehicles (ROVs) and autonomous underwater vehicles (AUVs). ROVs and AUVs are forms of in situ sensing with different scales and purposes than distributed sensing networks, such as Argo. ROVs generally are "driven" by a human operator and have a much higher cost than Argo's drifting floats, though some generate their own power by harnessing the energy of ocean waves. Rather than aim for large-scale coverage, usually they are used exclusively by researchers, and on shorter spatial and temporal scales, to understand smaller-scale processes and the intricacies of fluid dynamics that can shed light on larger-scale processes or dynamics in other locations. ROVs, then, can be understood as types of undersea drones, operating under the same dynamics as those described by Elizabeth R. Johnson (this volume), if toward different ends.

As is perhaps already evident, these new sensing technologies do not simply produce more data at more ambitious spatial and temporal scales. They have the potential to produce new environmental sensibilities as well as new relationships between scientists, technologies, and environments (see, for example, Gabrys 2016; Helmreich 2009; Lehman 2018; Vertesi 2012). New sensing technologies and the computational practices they enable "hold the promise of extending the threshold for human perception and cognition" (Amoore and Raley 2017, 4). Yet these new possibilities are never divorced from questions of utility, governance, and sovereignty that always accompany scientific practice and that are amplified in international projects seeking comprehensive knowledge of global systems (see also Lövbrand, Stripple, and Wiman 2009). Sensing the sea becomes a practice enacted by a "composite figure of distributed human and nonhuman agency," raising questions of culpability that Irus Braverman also discusses in this volume (see also Amoore and Raley 2017, 7). Responsibility for the ways in which new sensing practices and technologies shape and interact with geopolitical relations and legal regimes is diffuse, and new and frequently ad hoc networks of experts have arisen to address these challenges.

Legal Troubles

The 1982 United Nations Convention on the Law of the Sea aimed to comprehensively cover all issues relating to the sea. Therefore, it is not surprising that it covers marine scientific research (in Part XIII) and is considered the governing legal authority on the conduct of research at sea. However, UNCLOS does not give a definition of what constitutes marine scientific research. Some authors have commented that this lack of definition arose over disagreement about the difference between fundamental and applied science (Hofmann and Proelss

2015). Here we can assume that fundamental research should be given special provisions because it is meant to answer scientific rather than political questions. Applied research is generally executed for the political or economic gains of individual actors, whether corporations or nation-states, and thus would not fall under the more permissive guidelines that govern marine scientific research. As evidence, UNCLOS states in Part XIII, Article 240, that "marine scientific research shall be conducted exclusively for peaceful purposes" and in Article 241 that "marine scientific research activities shall not constitute the legal basis for any claim to any part of the marine environment or its resources" (UNCLOS 1982). Marine scientific research, the UNCLOS states, is to be "for the benefit of all mankind" (UNCLOS 1982, Article 241).

UNCLOS affords many allowances for the execution of marine scientific research. In general, though states must ask permission to conduct research in another state's territorial waters or exclusive economic zone (EEZ), states are not permitted to withhold consent except in a few circumstances. In fact, UNCLOS seems to actively promote marine scientific research, as it includes provisions that exhort states to "create favorable conditions for the conduct of marine scientific research in the marine environment and to integrate the efforts of scientists in studying the essence of phenomena and processes occurring in the marine environment and the interrelations between them" and asserts that states, "both individually and in cooperation with other States and with competent international organizations, shall actively promote the flow of scientific data and information and the transfer of knowledge resulting from marine scientific research" (UNCLOS 1982, Article 244). There are also considerable efforts in UNCLOS to advance the scientific capacities of what it calls "developing States."

Nonetheless, certain procedures must be followed. As mentioned above, permission is required for the conduct of marine scientific research within any state's EEZ. While states are expected to consent to marine scientific research in their waters, they can refuse based on a number of reasons, including the belief that such research may result in the exploitation of marine resources for economic or political profit or be for not wholly peaceful purposes. States are also obligated to share the results of the research they conduct with the state whose marine environment they have studied. Perhaps most radically, states are required to allow representatives of the coastal state to observe the research process "especially on board research vessels and other craft or scientific research installations" without financial obligations on either party (UNCLOS 1982, Article 249).[1]

Both the affordances and restrictions as well as, it could be argued, the category of marine scientific research itself, assume that research will be carried out via ships or via relatively stable equipment, such as moorings, which remain under the control and supervision of scientists or technicians. New ocean observing technologies present different challenges. Many distributed sensor networks, such as Argo, drift with the ocean currents, meaning that scientists cannot control whether or when they enter another country's territorial seas. Autonomous vehicles, such as wave gliders, introduce similar issues (Hofmann and Proelss 2015). And remotely operated vehicles, analogous to undersea drones, can enter territorial waters covertly even if their trajectories are managed by human pilots.

Even if nations object to the use of drifting floats and remotely operated and autonomous vehicles in their waters, and these objections are found to have legal basis, restrictions can be difficult to enforce. In many cases it would not be worth the resources required for either state to find and divert or destroy the offending equipment; it may even be impossible. In general, states can only request that equipment be turned off if it enters their waters or that the data collected there be destroyed. Here is what an IOC officer told me in 2014: "So as far as I know, no one has yet deployed an Argo float or a glider with any of these off switches, but that's the kind of message we're getting loud and clear from the community; they're saying as these things get smarter, we want the right to be able to say switch it off as it goes through [our] water" (Steve Hall, interview, February 18, 2014).

What's more, these technologies gather data that muddles the already-unclear distinction between marine scientific research for the benefit of all humankind and research for economic or militaristic gain. For example, measurements of dissolved oxygen indicate ocean primary productivity, which is relevant to a number of biological processes in the sea, including the productivity of fisheries. Moreover, basic data on how temperature and salinity vary with depth provides the fundamentals both for climate modeling and for understanding the structure of the sea for the purpose of submarine warfare; as Johnson writes (this volume), these measurements are key in the configuration of the ocean as a three-dimensional space in which physical properties and technological threats circulate. Indeed, several scientists mentioned to me that the US Navy is the most significant user of Argo data, though the navy largely stays out of the program's execution.

How, then, should distributed sensors, AUVs, and ROVs be regulated? Arguably, the most obvious solution would be to regulate them as ships are regulated. Hofmann and Proelss (2015) point out that UNCLOS itself never defines "ship" or "vessel." However, after reviewing definitions of these terms in other international agreements, they conclude that gliders (a form of ROV) cannot properly be considered ships, as they fall short in such metrics as self-propulsion and the ability to be used for marine navigation and transport of people or cargo. Certainly Argo floats and other new ocean observation technologies similarly cannot be considered ships or vessels. Aside from discrepancies in their basic characteristics, it would be impossible for them to comply with the UNCLOS stipulations for ship-based research. For example, as one IOC representative told me, "If it's sort of a glider the size of this table, there's no space for, there's no observer's berth" (Hall, interview). Gliders and other ROVs and AUVs, as Hofmann and Proelss (2015) argue, are instead regulated as marine science research equipment. Countries wishing to deploy them in another nation's waters must request permission, which can only be withheld based on the requirements laid out in UNCLOS.

Argo presents different challenges, as the floats cannot be controlled by humans after they are launched. Their trajectories can be difficult to predict because they move throughout the water column and are thus subject to different currents and winds. Furthermore, because their purpose is generally broadscale monitoring for climate change modeling, many scientists believe they should be treated in the same way as meteorological monitoring equipment, which under agreements through the World Meteorological Organization (WMO) is permitted to be deployed worldwide without special permission, including on the surface of the ocean. The then-president of the IOC explained it to me like this: "Some of the technology that the WMO puts out, . . . they have this global sort of agreement so it's no big deal. They can send things into territories to gather data and that's okay, but [the IOC doesn't] have the convention, so we are obligated to inform whenever a float is drifting into somebody's territorial waters" (Wendy Watson-Wright, interview, March 10, 2014).

In 2003 the Advisory Body of Experts on the Law of the Sea was convened under IOC auspices to analyze and provide a legal framework for the automated collection of data in the EEZs of nation-states. After several years of debate and disagreement, a subgroup developed a plan that was later adopted by the IOC Executive Council due to an assessment of one highly ranked individual that it "[didn't] meet the letter of the law of the sea, but it [met] the spirit of it" (Steve Piotrowicz, interview, August 6, 2014). According to this agreement, the national Argo coordinator in each nation is automatically notified when one of their nation's Argo floats approaches within a hundred miles of another nation's EEZ. They are then required to notify that nation if they have requested notification. As of 2014, only eleven nations had requested notification (Piotrowicz, interview).

While this resolution seems rather straightforward, the amount of debate it garnered shows that these issues relate not only to the limits of any legal document to adapt to technological changes, but also to some central tensions of oceanographic science. Whom is science supposed to serve? What shape will the always-present entanglements between governance, resource exploitation, and ideals of pure science take? Here notions of the sea as a borderless space resound with implications for a science that could benefit all of humanity. Yet these notions are in fact central to strategies of governance that seek to impose systems of governance and regulation on such space, as others have shown in this volume. Relatedly, arguments that marine scientific research benefits all humankind assume that there is a unitary notion of the human, which should override the inevitable fact that not all humans will benefit equally and, in some cases, may even be harmed. This tension is reflected in recent debates in critical literature on the Anthropocene, the very idea of which asserts a unitary humanity even as its fractures are shown in relief by both historical effects on the environment and damages to come (see, for example, Malm and Hornborg 2014).

Geopolitical Turbulence

The legal debates surrounding new ocean observing technologies show the ways in which the field of ocean science is not only connected to national sovereignty but both shapes and is shaped by geopolitical inequalities within science and without. The geopolitical dimensions of global ocean observations reveal similar tensions. On one hand, the ocean is imagined as a common resource and global environment that should be the provenance of all humankind. From this perspective, oceanography is understood as inherently and necessarily international, given that the phenomena it studies cross territorial boundaries and are capable of affecting life categorically on the planet (Jappe 2007). On the other hand, global-scale oceanography is frequently expensive and exclusive. Furthermore, the GOOS and most other global systems are largely financed piecemeal by the nations that sponsor them rather than by an international body or fund. Therefore, for the most part, countries must pay to play when it comes to international oceanography. My inquiry here into the geopolitics of new ocean observing systems focuses on Argo. It uses two questions as an entry into issues of inequality and global-scale oceanography: First, if Argo aims for universal coverage and shares data freely on the internet, what incentive do nations have to actively participate, for example, by buying and launching Argo floats? Second, if all Argo data is shared freely, why would nations object to the program collecting data in their waters?

The second question proves somewhat easier to address than the first, while both show unevenness in the global oceanographic community. Nonetheless, international objection to Argo's operation in territorial waters has multiple dimensions. First, although the data is equally available to anyone, not every nation is able to use the data in the same way. Not only may some users not possess the expertise necessary for turning data into information, but they may also not be able to exploit the information they are able to obtain. For example, even if they have the technical ability and computing power to process raw Argo data using computer models, they may not have the fleet capacities to act on potential economic opportunities the models reveal, such as the location of productive fishing grounds.[2] Second, marine claims continue to be central to assertions of sovereignty in many nations (see, for example, Dodds and Benwell 2010). Finally, and relatedly, whether justified or not, nations may believe that Argo floats contain undisclosed sensors that give operating nations military or economic advantages. Steve Hall shared some illustrative insights regarding his time representing the United Kingdom on the IOC: "I remember an informal conversation with the Iranian delegate some years ago, who was very unhappy about things like Argo et cetera, into their waters. He said, 'Well you're just using them to you know, sense chemicals and particulates in our waters that might be used as evidence that we've got a weapons program or something. And how do we know that all you're doing is measuring temperature and salinity?' So he said, 'Of course we're not going to say yes'" (Hall, interview).

Sovereignty was frequently cited by the science bureaucrats with whom I spoke as the main reason that nations objected to the operation of research equipment in their waters. But concerns over sovereignty take different forms for different nations. Sarah Grimes, an IOC officer, said that Pacific Island nations were initially skeptical of Argo: "Unfortunately for the island communities they get so many people coming in and trying to take things, or do things, they are very isolated in the world and you get big dominant corporations coming in and just making decisions for them" (Sarah Grimes, interview). For these states to decide to allow Argo floats in their waters, the scientists needed to not only provide the raw data, but make it into information that was of obvious social relevance to the nation (Grimes, interview). Pacific Islanders have good reason to be suspicious of international scientific projects; for example, their initial inclusion in global techno-scientific networks resulted from being the coerced hosts of nuclear tests in the Pacific (see, for example, Davis 2015; DeLoughrey 2013). Likewise, in this volume, Zsofia Korosy details links between private and public oceanic enterprise and the expansion of the British Empire into the Pacific. *Sovereignty* is thus not a generally defined ideological concern, but one that emerges out of concrete experiences and justifiable suspicion of what might be seen as imperial information-collecting projects, even if on the surface they purport to be for the benefit of humankind.

As for my second guiding query, the issue of why nations choose to participate in Argo seems simple on the surface but gets to the core of what is meant by global scientific community. The scientists and bureaucrats with whom I spoke mentioned two main reasons why nations with limited resources for oceanographic research might choose to participate in Argo and related programs even though they can access the data for free without making any commitments to the program. First, although Argo aims for universal data coverage and currently has more than thirty-five hundred floats deployed, these floats are not evenly distributed. If a nation buys floats and launches them in their territorial waters, they are more likely to obtain higher-resolution data that may advance their interests, whether that is answering scientific questions, predicting weather and climate, or serving economic or security interests.

Argo, and even more expensive ROVs and AUVs, are considerably cheaper than ship-based sensing. While the United States owns most of the Argo floats, any nation can purchase a float from a variety of approved manufacturers in the US, France, and Japan, among others, and participate in the agenda-setting and governance of Argo. The cost of using a world-class research vessel at sea can be, according to the estimate of one science bureaucrat, $55,000 US per day. In contrast, an Argo float costs only about $16,000 over its entire life, and purchasing it provides the owner with entry into the Argo community, including a place at the table for setting the research agenda (Dean Roemmich, interview, April 8, 2016).

With about thirty countries participating, Argo is frequently presented as a model of international collaboration in oceanography (e.g., Cai et al. 2015). Nonetheless, while good-faith efforts are made to involve other nations, and to promote capacity-building through workshops and other training sessions, the US continues to own and operate most of the Argo fleet, and the data, while of broad interest to the scientific community, is directly relevant to the interests of the US Navy. Furthermore, although the US seems to be promoting international oceanography by championing Argo, we must remember that it never ratified UNCLOS. The relevance of this fact emerged, for example, when I asked NOAA climate program officer and US Argo program manager Steven Piotrowicz whether UNCLOS should be amended to address the challenges of new technologies:

> SP: It's better to keep it under the radar so we can do it in these exceptions. Does the Law of the Sea need [to be] re-negotiated? The United

States hasn't even ratified it yet. They've adopted it but they haven't ratified it . . . there are a couple senators that are basically saying over our dead bodies, two of which don't even have a coastline [laughing].

JL: Why are they so resistant to it?

SP: Sovereignty. This is America [laughing].

Consternation over sovereignty may seem ill founded when it comes to Argo. After all, Argo is only able to make the most basic of ocean observations, and it does so in a seemingly transparent manner, from float deployment to data sharing. Argo operations are highly unlikely to compromise national security or even lead to direct economic advantages. Furthermore, the data that Argo collects is fundamental to climate change modeling, which is framed as a self-evidently universal concern. Yet, again, concerns over Argo's potential risks to marine sovereignty do not just come from weak or petty nations unequipped to deal with oceanographic data or lacking understanding of its importance. Moreover, Argo replicates an unequal division of international labor as hegemonic nations like the US and the UK guide the program and possess the expertise while less developed nations are charged with catching up, setting aside concerns about their own marine sovereignty and ocean science priorities in the name of global climate research.

Conclusion

While new data feeds ocean models and the resulting representations of the ocean garner critical attention, the legal and geopolitical elements of collecting this data have been underexamined. Yet they reveal the complex contours of marine environmental politics in the contemporary era. The issues raised by new ocean observing practices and accompanying technologies are not simply practical, involving the allotment of research dollars and the focus of capacity-building efforts. They also pertain to core issues regarding the definition of socially relevant ocean science as well as geopolitical inequalities and tensions.

The ocean was once considered a sort of no-man's land, of interest only for marine passage and the possibility of resource exploitation. Through a complex host of changes, including, perhaps chiefly, the realization of the ocean's role in climate, the sea has become of crucial importance to contemporary global society (Oreskes 2014). As other authors in this volume explain, through entangled relationships between state governments and private interests, a complex governance structure regarding the sea has emerged whereby such notions as jurisdiction and exclusive economic rights complicate a clean division between sovereignty and freedom (see especially Elizabeth R. Johnson, this volume; Zsofia Korosy, this volume). A look at the development of ocean observations reveals further (though not unrelated) complications to notions of oceanic territoriality and control. The new organization of ocean observations shows how a vision of the ocean as unbounded both in its global impact and as a space for science in fact legitimizes and reinforces efforts to regulate the sea and to assert sovereignty and territorial control.

But if new ocean observations complicate the distinction between these two notions of the sea, they might also suggest that there are other ways of conceptualizing the ocean that are now gaining traction and to which legal frameworks must adapt, however clumsily. Perhaps most broadly we can see that the ocean is now seen not as a static entity, the "outside" to territorial claims and indeed to terrestrial life, but as a source of great potentiality, including the potential to threaten the conditions of possibility for life on earth (Lehman 2016). This potentiality introduces new dimensions of uncertainty and demands constant monitoring, not only cutting across traditional academic disciplines and international institutions, but also scrambling the already weak distinction between pure and applied science. While the practices of making and governing contemporary ocean observations reflect seemingly contradictory visions of the ocean as gridded territory and as a common space of flows, we may see both approaches as strategies for dealing with this perceived potentiality. Indeed, they may not be contradictory; they may be necessary as existing modes of governance are pressed to account for new understandings of the ocean's role in life on earth.

Notes

1   Research on the high seas (international waters) is exempt from all the requirements cited above (UNCLOS 1982, Article 249).
2   Locating fishing grounds is not currently in the capacity of most Argo floats, but there is widespread agreement that this development is imminent.

References

Amoore, Louise, and Rita Raley. 2017. "Securing with Algorithms: Knowledge, Decision, Sovereignty." *Security Dialogue* 48 (1): 3–10.
Boesch, Donald. 1999. "The Role of Science in Ocean Governance." *Ecological Economics* 31 (2): 189–98.
Cai, Wenju, Susan Avery, Margaret Leinen, Kenneth Lee, Xiaopei Lin, and Martin Visbeck. 2015. "Institutional Coordination of Global Ocean Observations." *Nature Climate Change* 5 (1): 4–6.

Conway, Erik M. 2006. "Drowning in Data: Satellite Oceanography and Information Overload in the Earth Sciences." *Historical Studies in the Physical and Biological Sciences* 37 (1): 127–51.

Davis, Sasha. 2015. *The Empire's Edge: Militarization, Resistance, and Transcending Hegemony in the Pacific.* Athens: University of Georgia Press.

DeLoughrey, Elizabeth. 2013. "The Myth of Isolates: Ecosystem Ecologies in the Nuclear Pacific." *Cultural Geographies* 20 (2): 167–84.

Dodds, Klaus, and Matthew C. Benwell. 2010. "More Unfinished Business: The Falklands/Malvinas, Maritime Claims, and the Spectre of Oil in the South Atlantic." *Environment and Planning D: Society and Space* 28 (4): 571–80.

Dodge, Martin, and Chris Perkins. 2009. "The 'View from Nowhere'? Spatial Politics and Cultural Significance of High-Resolution Satellite Imagery." *Geoforum* 40 (4): 497–501.

Edwards, Paul. 2010. *A Vast Machine: Computer Models, Climate Data, and the Politics of Global Warming.* Cambridge, MA: MIT Press.

Gabrys, Jennifer. 2016. *Program Earth: Environmental Sensing Technology and the Making of a Computational Planet.* Minneapolis: University of Minnesota Press.

Haraway, Donna. 1988. "Situated Knowledges: The Science Question in Feminism and the Privilege of Partial Perspective." *Feminist Studies* 14 (3): 575–99.

Helmreich, Stefan. 2009. "Intimate Sensing." In *Simulation and Its Discontents*, edited by Sherry Turkle, 129–50. Cambridge, MA: MIT Press.

Helmreich, Stefan. 2011. "From Spaceship Earth to Google Ocean: Planetary Icons, Indexes, and Infrastructures." *Social Research* 78 (4): 1211–42.

Hofmann, Tobias, and Alexander Proelss. 2015. "The Operation of Gliders under the International Law of the Sea." *Ocean Development and International Law* 46 (3): 167–87.

Jappe, Arlette. 2007. "Explaining International Collaboration in Global Environmental Change Research." *Scientometrics* 71 (3): 367–90.

Jue, Melody. 2014. "Proteus and the Digital: Scalar Transformations of Seawater's Materiality in Ocean Animations." *Animation* 9 (2): 245–60.

Lehman, Jessica. 2016. "A Sea of Potential: The Politics of Global Ocean Observations." *Political Geography* 55 (November): 113–23.

Lehman, Jessica. 2018. "From Ships to Robots: The Social Relations of Sensing the World Ocean." *Social Studies of Science* 48 (1): 57–79.

Litfin, Karen. 1997. "The Gendered Eye in the Sky: A Feminist Perspective on Earth Observation Satellites." *Frontiers: A Journal of Women Studies* 18 (2): 26–47.

Loftus, Alex. 2015. "Violent Geographical Abstractions." *Environment and Planning D: Society and Space* 33 (2): 366–81.

Lövbrand, Eva, Johannes Stripple, and Bo Wiman. 2009. "Earth System Governmentality: Reflections on Science in the Anthropocene." *Global Environmental Change* 19 (1): 7–13.

Lubchenco, Jane. 1998. "Entering the Century of the Environment: A New Social Contract for Science." *Science* 279 (5350): 491–97.

Malm, Andreas, and Alf Hornborg. 2014. "The Geology of Mankind? A Critique of the Anthropocene Narrative." *Anthropocene Review* 1 (1): 62–69.

Mukerji, Chandra. 1990. *A Fragile Power: Scientists and the State.* Princeton, NJ: Princeton University Press.

Oreskes, Naomi. 2014. "Scaling Up Our Vision." *Isis* 105 (2): 379–91.

Roemmich, Dean, Olaf Boebe, Yves Desaubies, Howard Freeland, Kuh Kim, Brian King, Pierre-Yves Le Traon, Robert Molinari, Breck Owens, Stephen Riser, and Uwe Send. 2001. "Argo: The Global Array of Profiling Floats." In *Observing the Oceans in the 21st Century: A Strategy for Global Ocean Observations*, edited by Chester Koblinsky and Neville R. Smith, 248–57. Melbourne: GODAE Project Office, Bureau of Meteorology.

Steinberg, Phillip E. 2009. "Sovereignty, Territory, and the Mapping of Mobility: A View from the Outside." *Annals of the Association of American Geographers* 99 (3): 467–95.

UNCLOS (United Nations Convention on the Law of the Sea). 1982. http://www .refworld.org/docid/3dd8fd1b4.html.

UNESCO (United Nations Educational, Scientific and Cultural Organization). 2012. "A Framework for Ocean Observing." Report no. IOC/INF-1284. http://www .oceanobs09.net/foo/FOO_Report.pdf.

Vertesi, Janet. 2012. "Seeing Like a Rover: Visualization, Embodiment, and Interaction on the Mars Exploration Rover Mission." *Social Studies of Science* 42 (3): 393–414.

Wilson, Stan. 2000. "Launching the Argo Armada: Taking the Ocean's Pulse with 3,000 Free-Ranging Floats." *Oceanus* 42 (1): 17–19.

9. THE HYDRA AND THE LEVIATHAN

Unmanned Maritime Vehicles and the Militarized Seaspace

ELIZABETH R. JOHNSON

God, having set forth the great power of Leviathan, called him king of the proud. "There is nothing," saith he, "on earth to be compared with him. He is made so as not to be afraid. He seeth every high thing below him; and is king of all the children of pride."
—THOMAS HOBBES, *Leviathan*

[T]he boat is a floating piece of space, a place without a place, that exists by itself, that is closed in on itself and at the same time is given over to the infinity of the sea.
—MICHEL FOUCAULT, "Of Other Spaces"

For Thomas Hobbes, the Leviathan was a fitting metaphor for sovereignty not because it was monstrous or came from the sea, but because it derived from the Hebrew word *liwyāthān,* meaning to join or twine. Hobbes insisted that the primary virtue of the sovereign body lay in its power of unification, its ability to amplify the capacities of the people and thereby constitute a commonwealth. Without a sovereign to rule them, Hobbes declared, humans would remain brutish, engaged in a war of "every one against every one" (Hobbes [1651] 1982, 80). Hobbes's Leviathan therefore named a people unified, saved from their monstrous selves by the sovereign.

While Hobbes's sovereign power invoked the people as the subject of governance, Michel Foucault's biopolitics drew attention to populations (1990, 1995). As Foucault described, institutions of medicine and learning, technologies of security and social life, and management of physical bodies reconfigured techniques of governance throughout the nineteenth and twentieth centuries. Alongside industrial and postindustrial capitalism, disciplinary and biopower diffused political power across the social body. While the techniques of sovereign governance characterized by Hobbes's Leviathan persist in many aspects of today's nation-states, the many-headed Hydra of Greek mythology seems the more apt oceanic metaphor for the recently ascendant forms of political governance that Foucault described.

The Leviathan and Hydra are not much more than mythic metaphors in these political theories. Hobbes did not take the actual oceans very seriously, unashamedly grounding his political treatise in the lands of Europe. Foucault gave the oceans slightly more thought. In his essay "Of Other Spaces" (1986), the seas exemplified his concept of "heterotopia," or "counter-sites" where alternatives to prevailing hegemonic norms were possible (Saldanha 2008). While he would later abandon the concept, Foucault famously referred to sea-faring ships as the "heterotopia par excellence" (1986, 27). Operating outside the normative social and legal structures that govern landed society, the ship was a space "unto itself" that was "given over to the infinity of the sea" (Foucault 1986, 27).

Just as the Hydra and Leviathan signal very different modes of governance and different visions of the commonwealth, Foucault's essay envisions the sea and its ships as radically other to the workings of government on land. Within Foucault's writings, however, the seas themselves remain abstracted, primarily serving as a space unburdened by the matters and histories of territory, where one might imagine alternative political formulations. What might happen to these considerations of sovereignty and the commonwealth when we take the three-dimensional space of the ocean more seriously?

In what follows, I consider this question by following how the US Department of Defense (DoD) is developing machinic technologies—notably endowed with the moniker Hydra—that would enable a more distributed geopolitical security apparatus at sea. I ultimately trouble the claims that ocean and land, as well as Hydra and Leviathan, are oppositional in governance, finding instead that they are interactive and coconstitutive—materially, legally, and symbolically. This, I suggest, raises questions about the nature of sovereignty and the future of what Hobbes referred to as the commonwealth.

Entangled Seas, Entangled Futures

The mission of the Defense Advanced Research Projects Agency (DARPA), the DoD's research and development arm is to create "breakthrough technologies for national security."[1] But the agency's role is perhaps best captured by the epigraph on its "About" web page, a quote by composer Franz Liszt that reveals DARPA's true purpose is to "cast a javelin into the infinite spaces of the future." As the placement of Liszt's quote suggests, DARPA is a national defense agency unlike any other: rather than predicting and responding to an imagined political landscape to come, DARPA seeks to chart a course into the "infinite spaces of the future." By seeding science and innovation, they also direct them and, thereby, hope to give our collective future definition through scientific and technological enhancement.[2]

With what kinds of technologies is DARPA hoping to shape the "spaces of the future"? What futures—indeed, what worlds—does it seek to build for our collective inhabitation? The media and academy have lavished attention on the ways that aerial drone technology has reshaped warfare as well as geopolitical borders (Chamayou 2015; Kindervater 2017; Shaw 2016; Shaw and Akhtar 2012). But new programs are also expanding into the spaces on, below, and above the ocean's surface. Under the moniker of the Hydra program, DARPA is working to build unmanned autonomous vehicles (UAVs) capable of performing surveillance and reconnaissance, detonating underwater mines, and delivering various payloads in international waters. Launched in 2013, Hydra is one of many research and development programs in unmanned maritime vehicle (UMV) technologies. It is meant to ameliorate the core problem faced by the US Navy: the seeming imperative to "cover vast regions of interest around the globe" while fewer forces and budget restrictions shrink the size of the fleet overall (DARPA n.d.b). DARPA's Hydra program envisions a floating, unmanned infrastructure of modular, interchangeable parts. In the words of the DARPA project description, Hydra would enable "faster, scalable and more cost-effective deployment of assets wherever needed" (DARPA n.d.b). In what follows, I chart a transition in sovereign imaginaries of and on the sea. Rather than emanating from territorial land, I find that sovereign power increasingly attaches to technological objects and the algorithms that operate them.

Throughout this chapter, I analyze DARPA program calls and descriptions as well as naval planning documents and technoscientific publications germane to US naval strategies. The documents that imagine those technologies utilize and challenge existing ocean legalities and visions of sovereignty. Contrasting DARPA's Hydra project with conventional understandings of sovereign power and the commonwealth, I consider how the rise of machinic warfare is reshaping ocean space and statecraft.

DARPA seeks to bring future visions to life through the creation of UMV technologies. These technologies are part of efforts to "secure the volume" (Elden 2013b) of underwater space and extend the dominance of the US military across and among the continents. Yet military technologies and the forms of spatial dominance to which they strive are fragile compositions at sea (as well as elsewhere). Following Philip E. Steinberg and Kimberley Peters's call to consider the "turbulent materialities" of the ocean (2015, 247), I think in this chapter with the militarized sea as a three-dimensional space. But the material processes of the militarized ocean also connect with turbulent materialities and imaginaries well beyond the seas. DARPA's ocean technologies take shape in laboratories and research sites in connection with the "underlying churn" (Peters 2015, 248; see also the introduction to this volume) of military histories, fears of the deep, and transnational legal infrastructures, none of which are stable. Far from infinite, therefore, these militarized "spaces of the future" are tightly tied to matters, technologies, and legal frameworks created at temporal and spatial distance.

Paying attention to this turbulent churn of imaginaries, materialities, and legislative infrastructures raises important questions about who and what is brought together into a common world by DARPA's innovations. The rise of autonomous technologies is a process that seems to decenter the human in the making of machines and engender a security apparatus that appears to be predominantly composed of nonhuman actions (Shaw 2016). But machinic technologies do not remove human actions from geopolitical engagements. Rather, they distance the work of humans from the immediacy of battle to civilian sites of anticipatory innovation. And though the military's future imaginaries and technologies are far from a fait accompli, they play a significant role in reconstituting sovereignty and the commonwealth by silently migrating ocean warfare not only into technological devices, but into the laboratories that make them (see also Irus Braverman, this volume).

Reshaping Warfare, Reengaging the Seas

Since the conclusion of the Cold War, the US military has been unmatched in size and strength. Even as the number of military personnel is almost half of what it was in 1955, the US military's global dominance remains unrivaled. To maintain strength in capacity, the US has turned to drones and other UAVs to act as "force multipliers" on the labor of the military workforce (US Department of the Navy 2004, 13). By replacing human life with the machines, the DoD aspires to "maintain global dominance by doing far more with less" (David Vine, quoted in Shaw 2016, 38).

As many writing on aerial drone technology have shown, advanced machinery like UMVs does not merely intensify existing military strategies; it transforms them (Chamayou 2015; Gregory 2011; Kindervater 2017; Shaw 2016). Displacing the battlefield as the site of military engagement, the machinery of the drone has engendered what Derek Gregory has called an "everywhere war"

(2011). If battlefields were once geographically distinct, Gregory argues, their borders have now been eroded. Effecting a particular bio- and geopolitical calculus, endangerment and risk in the drone's surgical strike are felt only on one side of this everywhere war. The executers of drone strikes sit removed, safely distanced from the action, while bombs are dropped in Pakistan, Yemen, Iraq, Afghanistan, and Somalia. There, the distinction between civilian and enemy combatant or militant is made more or less indistinct. There, one's life is constantly at risk. For this reason, Grégoire Chamayou refers to this warscape of aerial drones not as an everywhere war, but as a planetary "hunting ground" (2015, 52).[3]

Just as aerial drones shifted the logics and spaces of war, seagoing autonomous vehicles are changing military engagement at sea. The future ocean at work in DARPA's designs is not one of climate change and rising sea levels, resource contraction or expansion in the form of subsurface minerals or fisheries (see Zsofia Korosy, this volume; Alison Rieser, this volume), or dramatic losses in biodiversity and dying coral reefs (see Irus Braverman, this volume). Instead, the oceans are one of several milieus of military engagement, where security and warfighting capacities might be enhanced by technological innovation. At play in military imaginaries are multiple marine epistemologies that can ostensibly anticipate future actions (Anderson 2010) as well as the reemergence of remembered threats.

DARPA's Hydra program developed in response to the US Navy's master plan for research into unmanned undersea vehicles (UUVs) released in 2004. The eighty-page document reveals the navy's strategic imaginary. The cornerstone of that imaginary is the production of "network-centric warfare," what the navy refers to as a Force Net (US Department of the Navy 2004). The Force Net and other elements of the DoD's marine spatial imaginary reflect that of its aerial and territorial counterparts and ensure access to land. As the navy's UUV 2004 master plan establishes, autonomous technologies are designed to ensure that "the Navy be able to achieve and maintain access to all the world's littoral at the times and places of its choosing" (US Department of the Navy 2004, 31).

The Office of Naval Research (ONR), often in conjunction with DARPA, has been experimenting with robotic technologies for decades. Throughout the 1990s and early 2000s, DARPA funded the development of an assortment of small-scale UUVs, many of which operate on principles of biomimicry (Johnson 2015). Robotic lobsters, clams, tuna, and crabs have marched (or swum) forth from DARPA's coffers to demonstrate the potentials of robotics in military security. Although many of these technologies never advanced past prototype, new UUV technologies are less experimental and more real-world ready.

DARPA is building on those earlier projects to reimagine the potential of autonomous robotic engagement within a wider ocean space and amid a broader range of war-fighting capacities.

DARPA's UUVs operate according to a somewhat different calculus of life, death, and geopolitical risk than do aerial drones. For the US naval and marine forces, securing the spaces of the sea with our terrestrial-bound human bodies has long been a challenge. Basic human needs for air, fresh water, food, and space have always limited movement across the seas. Warships, aircraft carriers, and submarines—until recently technologies necessary to sustain life and warfare on or beneath the waves—represent some of the most capital-intensive infrastructure used by the US military. Traditional warships, for example, cost upward of $700,000 US per day to operate (Merchant 2015). Such a fleet is not only costly, but ponderous: aircraft carriers and warships are incompatible with an ongoing, globally distributed war that calls for "just in time" capabilities. Replacing peopled warships with autonomous systems could save millions: one report estimates that autonomous systems could operate at only $15,000 to $20,000 per day.

DARPA's Hydra is imagined as a network of machinic agents capable of patrolling the waters without necessary input from a central command. The nine-headed serpent of Greek mythology with the powers of regeneration serves as its emblem. Hydra would create a coordinated modular system of networked autonomous vehicles and weapons capable of engaging sea, air, and land. As the original agency announcement on the program explained, Hydra would provide "a novel delivery mechanism for insertion of unmanned air and underwater vehicles into operational environments" (DARPA, n.d.b). If successful, the program would result in the deployment of a fungible container vehicle, referred to as the mothership, capable of coordinating smaller UMV and UAV operations in sea and air space. Several related projects are also part of the Hydra mission, including DARPA's Tactically Exploited Reconnaissance Node (TERN) program and the Raytheon-produced six-pound Switchblade drone that can morph from an underwater submersible to a workable aerial drone capable of taking flight from the surface of the sea (figure 9.1).

If DARPA's javelin into the future is reshaping the space of naval battlefield, it is also shifting governance and broader geopolitical strategies. In doing so, DARPA utilizes and responds to existing ocean legalities as well as the turbulent movement of the seas. In DARPA's strategic documents, the oceans appear on two registers. In the first, the high seas serve as a *surface* of engagement. There, UMV technologies extend not only the capacities of human warfighters, but also sovereign control over global space. Extended via seacrafts networked

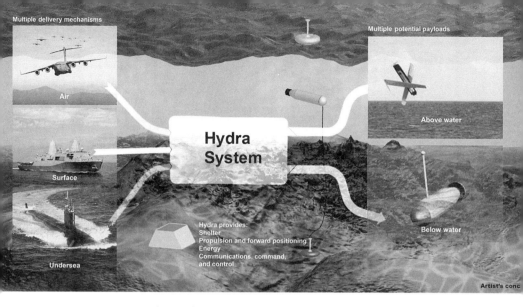

Hydra System

FIGURE 9.1. Artist rendition of DARPA's proposed Hydra System and component parts. Source: DARPA.

across the earth, the imagined future US naval fleet will utilize the legal status of the high seas to expand its access to distant regions. In the second, the DoD builds strategies and technological futures around the materials *within* the sea. Here, the sea appears as a three-dimensional or volumetric space (Elden 2013b), "churning," as Steinberg and Peters have written, with material and temporal dynamics that must be abided. In the two sections that follow, I show how the Hydra program and the DoD's wider efforts to produce a future of autonomous warfare are hitched to these two visions of the sea.

Seacrafts and Statecrafts: Buoying Empire on the Surface

United States territory hosts no foreign armies, yet it operates bases in almost eight hundred locations. These bases produce a network of US military forces that span the globe, effecting an empire of "lily-pads" from which the US can launch military operations on a just-in-time basis (Vine 2015a). As David Vine has noted (2015a), maintaining such a network is resource heavy and fraught with tension. International base infrastructure requires constant diplomatic negotiation with host nations and often results in international pressures as well as anti-American sentiment in host countries. In some cases, US bases are housed within the territories of dictatorial and autocratic regimes. In others, the governmental arrangements that permit US bases on foreign soil are ludicrously complex and decidedly undemocratic. In Thailand, for example, private contractors—and not the Thai state—negotiated the creation of Utapao Naval Air Base south of Bangkok (Vine 2015b). With the UMVs of the Hydra program, the DoD hopes to turn the international status of the high seas into a tactical opportunity capable of circumventing these issues.

The United Nations Convention on the Law of the Sea (UNCLOS)—which is in effect, although the US has never ratified it—divides the ocean into seven zones. Of them, five are subject to the jurisdiction of coastal nation-states to varying degrees: internal waters, the territorial sea, contiguous zones, exclusive economic zones (EEZs), and continental shelves. As noted elsewhere in this volume, coastal states have full sovereign control over their territorial seas, which extend twelve miles from the coastline and include everything from the air above the water to the seabed and subsoil (UNCLOS 1982). Here, "ships of all states," including submarines, warships, and (presumably) UMVs, maintain the "right of innocent passage." That is, they may traverse the surface of the sea, their flag in view, in ways that are not "prejudicial to the peace, good order or security of the coastal State" (UNCLOS 1982, Article 31). Behaviors considered "prejudicial" obviously include the threat of force, exercise of weapons, or launching of aircraft. But UNCLOS also prohibits the collection of information, the carrying out of research, or any activity that would jeopardize the environment of the coastal state (UNCLOS 1982; see also Jessica Lehman, this volume).

The final two zones, the high seas and the deep seabed, are not subject to the jurisdiction of any one state. These vast expanses of ocean space remain governed as a common in accordance with Hugo Grotius's principle of *mare labarum* (see Alison Rieser, this volume). There, all ships—whether fishing boats, warships, or UMVs—"have complete immunity from the jurisdiction of any State other than the flag State" (UNCLOS 1982, Article 59). Accordingly, UMVs can operate a range of missions, from research to military exercises, without the express permission of other states (Showalter and Manley 2009). The hope is that, by using UMV technologies to fan out across the high sea, a combination of UMVs and aerial drone technologies will allow the US Navy access to the world's coasts (at least, at a distance of only two hundred miles), where they might respond to threats as they emerge. That is, they hope to create the conditions for constant and continuous surveillance of the shorelines of every continent.

Envisioned through the Hydra program, therefore, is not only a global empire of military power, but also a decoupling of warfare and sovereign territory. In this military imaginary, the production of a networked, floating infrastructure of autonomous components would unground the navy's and air force's war-fighting capacities: territorial bases and resource-intensive aircraft carriers would no longer be needed as operation launch sites for weapons or drones. Hydra would network the globe into a system of floating, mobile bases capable of rapid response. By utilizing the status of the high seas, the US dreams of breaking the links between military might and diplomacy.

Ian Shaw has written that aerial drone strikes show how the "reach of state power is clearly not tied to the fixed territory of the state," but, rather, is "mobile and global" (2016, 14). The rise of UMVs take this even further, to demonstrate how state power also operates on the back of material objects that float through the fluid substrate of the sea and the broad legal infrastructure that is UNCLOS. Requiring neither land nor diplomatic agreements with other nations states, UMV programs would, contra Shaw, not render US geopolitical reach "boundless" (Shaw 2016, 146). They would instead affix US military force to material technologies rather than land masses. This is a machinic, mobile extension of the surface logics of landed territory mapped over the legal status of the high seas. Here, sovereignty and geopolitical power are made *on top of* technological objects and the algorithms that operate them. By ungrounding military power and loosening the constraints of sovereign territory, land is not rendered irrelevant but is redistributed to the sea through these floating objects of military significance. The imagined future built by UMV technologies thus promises to shift geopolitical space and retie the knots between land and sovereignty on the back of mobile technologies.

Turbulent Oceans, Anticipatory Threats

The strategic and tactical advantage of UMV technologies goes beyond the extension of sovereignty onto adrift technological objects. Through machinic innovation, the DoD also exemplifies Stuart Elden's volumetric geopolitics (2013b), showing how the nation-state mobilizes political power below the surface as well as on it. The Navy's UMV master plan and DARPA's program documents envision sea depths as a stratum of threats—both known and potentially emergent. Here, we find that the oceans are, indeed, a "hunting ground." But unlike sites of engagement in air and over land, the objects of the hunt are more diverse and predominantly nonhuman. Other autonomous seacrafts, submarines, missiles, and underwater mines—recently laid and long buried—are the DoD's primary concerns.

Consider, for example, one of DARPA's most successful autonomous marine programs to date: the Anti-Submarine Warfare Continuous Trail Unmanned Vessel (ACTUV) program. In 2016, ACTUV unveiled *Sea Hunter*, a ship currently undergoing field testing. While it glides across the surface of the sea "under sparse remote supervisory control," it monitors what lies beneath. *Sea Hunter* was designed to detect hard-to-sense diesel electric powered subs by performing unmanned missions spanning "thousands of kilometers of range and months of endurance" (DARPA n.d.a). Brought to fruition by the national security and healthcare company Leidos, the *Sea Hunter* is reportedly capable of autonomously complying with "maritime laws and conventions for safe navigation" as well as interacting with "an intelligent adversary" (DARPA n.d.a).

In the context of ACTUV and other UMV development programs, the oceans and seas appear as "vast sanctuaries" for potentially emergent threats, including stealth submarines and nuclear missiles (Holmes 2016: 228). More than a container in which action might occur, the ocean becomes a milieu within which the unexpected might at any time emerge. Here, the deep sea appears as what it has long been: a site where fears of the monstrous lurk. Within both near-term and long-range naval strategy, the sea therefore becomes an arena for what Ben Anderson has referred to as anticipatory actions (Anderson 2010). This anticipatory posturing toward the future is not abstract; futures are produced through engagement with logics of "precaution, preemption and preparedness" (Anderson 2010, 792). Even as the US naval fleet is by far the most well-heeled and technologically advanced in the world, the DoD approaches the sea through the lens of future catastrophes, some imminent and others improbable. As several looming threats build—for example, as North Korea brashly develops nuclear capacities, China modernizes its naval fleet and Russia postures aggressively toward Arctic oil reserves—the threat of traditional and nuclear war looms ever larger in the DoD's imaginary (Gramer 2017; O'Rourke 2018; Pellerin 2017). In the short term, the DoD has planned to buttress existing naval strategies by building warships, equipping aircraft carriers, and developing longer-range land missiles. The long-term strategy, however, imagines a network of autonomous vehicles capable of near-constant surveillance and rapid response.

Developing strategies for preemption and preparedness at sea requires knowing what lies beneath the surface to effectively maneuver within it: how to communicate, navigate, lay cable on the ocean floor, and detect and neutralize threats. By doing so, the navy reimagines the sea as a space for "operational battlespace preparation" (US Department of the Navy 2004, xx). Through this lens, the sea becomes subject to particular epistemologies. To operationalize the oceans, DARPA and the US Navy must first abide the unique qualities of the sea. As Steinberg and Peters have written, the material conditions of the oceans differ dramatically from the conditions of the air (2015). Ocean water as a medium is exceedingly difficult to penetrate, sense, and know; its very nature threatens to limit or thwart military operations at every turn. Large bodies of water diffuse, refract, and attenuate sound and light. Indeed, electromagnetic emissions of all types are subject to fluid dynamics.

Steinberg and Peters's notion of "turbulent materiality" (Steinberg and Peters 2015, 247) is particularly salient here: changes in temperature, pressure, and salinity bend light and sound, playing tricks on eyes as well as sonar operators (Holmes 2016). Threats can hide in the three-dimensional space of the water, above and below, "disguising their presence even from nearby foes" (Holmes 2016, 228). The *Sea Hunter* and other UMV technologies must therefore do more than merely sense what lurks in the depths of the ocean: they also require the capacity to sense *through* the material substrate of the sea.

For this reason, many of the navy's existing and envisioned UMVs are meant to facilitate the production of knowledge of what lies beneath and above the surface, to render transparent the ocean's contents and physical conditions so that movement through that substrate can be ensured. To produce such knowledge, UMVs are required to perform feats that are impossible for the human body. Like the research vessels described by Jessica Lehman and Irus Braverman (this volume), the military is producing UMVs capable of the deep-sea and long-range missions necessary to map the seafloor and gather data on the physical components of the sea: bathymetry, water column characterization, salinity profiles, measures of bioluminescence as well as chemical, biological, and nuclear weapons detection and tracking. This information can be gathered and used in "near real-time for tactical support" or archived and "provided in rapid-turnaround mode for operational battle space preparation" (US Department of the Navy 2004, 39).

The DoD engages in a world made murky by more than its material turbulence. The history of maritime warfare has given life to a class of weapons that seem to continually resurface even after they fade from memory. Perhaps surprisingly, today's Navy considers traditional underwater mines and underwater improvised explosive devices (UIEDs) the "quintessential naval asymmetric threat" (US Department of the Navy 2004, 31). Mine warfare resurfaced after the conclusion of the Cold War as one of the "most problematic of the missions" faced by the US Navy (US Department of the Navy 2004, 24). Their proliferation, international availability, and ease of employment make them a key component of what the DoD often refers to as a "poor man's army" (Truver 2011). Formal mine technologies are produced today by thirty countries and exported by a third of those (Truver 2011). UIEDs are easy to build even as a do-it-yourself technology. For aging arsenals, retrofitting old mines with updated components is highly effective as well as cost-saving. In some cases, such updates are not necessary: in 1988, a US tanker in the Arabian Gulf sustained

$96 million in damage after striking a mine that was designed during World War I. The oceans and their troubled histories mean that even past threats may reemerge at any time (see also Astrida Neimanis, this volume).

Mine countermeasures (MCM) have been a cornerstone of the development of UMV technologies. Calls for UMV development often reference the history of mine warfare. Strategists often recall when, in 1991, Iraqi forces sowed thirteen hundred mines in the Arabian Gulf during the Desert Storm conflict. Or when North Koreans embedded over three thousand mines off their eastern coast to deter an attack on the city of Wonsan in 1950. Rear Admiral Allen E. Smith, commander of that thwarted attack, had this to say about the power of mine warfare in the twentieth century: "We have lost control of the seas to a nation without a navy, using pre–World War I weapons, laid by vessels that were utilized at the time of the birth of Christ" (quoted in Truver 2011, 31). And while we often think of underwater mines as a line of defense used to prevent enemy invasion, they are also an effective tool for encircling one's enemy. In 1945, more than twelve thousand US mines placed along Japanese shipping routes damaged approximately 670 Japanese ships to cut off supply lines as part of what was referred to as Operation Starvation.

Underwater mines may be considered the first autonomous underwater technology, one of the earliest means of taking humans out of the loop in the deployment of weapons. While scientists and engineers attempt to develop the capacities for communication, surveillance, and navigation in the undersea environment, these early forms of unmanned weaponry require only the capacity to persist as potential explosives. Indeed, nearly every military document and white paper on mines begins with the same refrain: "a mine is a terrible thing that waits" (LaGrone 2014a, 2014b; Truver 2014). These weapons are therefore both a material and immaterial threat: an imagined minefield can be just as effective in deterring enemy forces as the laying of actual mines (US Department of the Navy 2004).

By building networked UMV technologies with the capability of reliably sensing the three-dimensional, turbulent materiality of the seas, DARPA promises to build the capacity to eliminate both real and feared threats. In doing so, the agency seeks to eradicate the very possibility for ignorance in what lies beneath. But what is rendered transparent by military science and imaginary is heavily constrained—there are no ecologies or forms of life here. By imagining and enhancing the capacity to know the seas' movements and sense what lurks beneath the waves, the US military only seeks to render the ocean operational for anticipatory action. Knowledge of the seas is shaped accordingly, as it is oriented to threats, preemption, and geopolitical preparedness.

Mechanizing Sea Monsters, Reshaping the Commonwealth

The US military's efforts to make the ocean an operational space are consistent with their decades-long desires to achieve full-spectrum dominance on the battlefield. The dream of full-spectrum dominance has long spurred military innovation, but it has far from materialized. As the previous sections have shown, DARPA's "javelin" does not encounter the "infinite" space of either sea or future; it is deeply entangled with multiple pasts and legal infrastructures that constrain it. While the US Navy may never achieve its visions of geopolitical dominance at sea, in this final section I return to questions of the relationship between governance and Hobbes's notion of the commonwealth. I consider how the DoDs' dreams prefigure changes in how our human lives are composed with and in relation to the sea.

Just as manufacturing has replaced human labor with machines, DoD technologies promise to eliminate human life—not from the ranks of enemy forces, but from the US's own front lines of warfighting. Before the end of the Cold War, spatial configurations of the battlefield largely remained rooted in territoriality and the disciplined behaviors of bodies that dealt in and were made subject to death on the battlefield (Elden 2013a; Wilcox 2015). Conscription and the draft sourced bodies from a general, if primarily underclass, population. But as Ian Shaw has noted, the biopolitical, technologically enabled state engages in warfare differently: life and the cost of military labor are no longer as cheaply spent as they once were (Shaw 2016).[4] Mobilizing human bodies and the materials necessary to sustain them is economically and politically costly.

The advancement of machinic technologies also means that humans are no longer required to do inhuman things, at least not in the flesh. Or, as Grégoire Chamayou has put it, "the sacrifice of vile bodies [is] no longer necessary" to advance the security aims of the militarized state (2015, 22). The institution of this new regime of warfare has not constituted a break from past forms of military engagements but has taken shape gradually as technologies and advanced weaponry have made it ever easier to distance bodies from battlefields. While geopolitical strategies and military conflicts have long been made in advance of battle at sites of weapons manufacturing, today the innovations of war and machinic engineering are eclipsing the soldier, the medic, and the logistics officer, all of whom orchestrate on-the-ground invasions. This gradual distancing continues as the seas appear in the DoD's strategic visioning to be evacuated of human and other life-forms. Machinery and physical matter take over as the primary elements of concern in the operational environment. This seems a very different sovereignty and corresponding commonwealth than those that

Hobbes imagined. Whereas in his vision nonhumans and forces of production were relegated to the background, in the DoD's imaginary, humans in the form of military personnel, politicians, and populations retreat from view.

In his work on aerial drones, Shaw argues that autonomous weapons serve the interests not of a people or the health of a population, but of a world that is "predominantly nonhuman" (2016, 39). Indeed, to make the sea an operational environment, the DoD has come to rely on technological craft and scientific research. In doing so, geopolitical governance is redistributed away from the control of territory, land, and space and toward the management of knowledge and machinic production. However, much like territory, human action does not disappear in these experimental futures—and we can scarcely consider them nonhuman. Rather, humans are redistributed, displaced. Machinic warfare does not simply reshape the battlefield; it also reconditions the labor of war, reshaping what we have in common by reshaping what we know and how we produce technologies that engage with our environment.

If DARPA's calculus is correct, warfare at sea will become a tournament of machines. Humans are not erased from such a tournament; they prefigure it. This is DARPA's javelin into the spaces of the future: the behaviors of its actors—autonomous technologies—are built in anticipation of engagement. Through these investments in innovation, the front line runs ahead of conflict itself, in laboratories and algorithms in anticipation of geopolitical threats. If, as Amoore has written, *who* we are flows into the algorithms that govern autonomous technologies (Amoore 2017), *where* we are is displaced into the movement of mechanical bodies at sea as well as the laboratories that build them.

DARPA has awarded more than $22 million in contracts to develop the UAV, UMV, and communication technologies that would make up Hydra's floating base infrastructure. This changing atlas of war finds the navy's most crucial sites of engagement not in the sea itself, but in the sites of research and development: at Johns Hopkins University, Woods Hole Oceanographic Institute, and MIT, and in the laboratories of Leidos, Raytheon, Northrup Grumman, and Aero-Vironment, where UMVs are imagined and put into production. The battlefield is thus not only where technologies are used, but also where they are produced.[5] In the process and as Louise Amoore and Rita Raley have noted, the military's technological programs shift responsibility away from human bodies and into experimental programming (2017). The construction of UMV technologies and responsibility for the shape and outcomes of warfare are therefore distributed among civilians, researchers, and the archives of science and engineering.

In the making of these military technologies, warfare is again increasingly distributed across the social body into innovation, just as Foucault described when he charted the rise of regimes of disciplinary and biopower. Now, however, the commonwealth is not constituted through its health or collective well-being, but through its productivity and capacity for innovation. It has become a commonwealth that is measured through the advance of a techno- rather than bio-power. As the labor of engineering has become the force of the military, the might of the nation-state has come to reside in the minds of scientists, engineers, and programmers as well as in the conditions of their employment.

Conclusion

The javelin into the future that DARPA throws in the form of UMV technologies attempts to remake ocean spaces as operational platforms. And although these militarized marine technologies and epistemologies are often more fragile than they seem, they reshape who and what constitutes our common world—and our future. Programs in technological advancement engage not a people or a population, but a multitude of capacities, intellectual and material (Virno 2004). If the wealth that is held in common is our knowledge of the conditions of the world, much of this knowledge is currently shaped, harnessed, and wielded in the making of the global military state. Rather than DARPA's imagined network of autonomous machinery, we might consider the true Hydra and Leviathan to be entwined in the labor of lives on land and at sea.

Unlike the Leviathan in Hobbes's imaginary, however, the US military's monstrous creations do not save the people from a brutish state of nature. Instead, they unite labor in creating and extending a militarized epistemology that, in this case, reimagines the planetary seas. In the process, the turbulent ocean and how we come to know it—how we come even to know its conditions of turbulence—are therefore conditioned by imagined and anticipatory futures as well as histories of state violence that continue to circulate on- and offshore.

Mapping these arrangements and technologies reveals that sites of experimentation—distributed across the US and the world—are where the force of the US military apparatus might be challenged. In those sites of production, we might reimagine and recompose to engage with richer marine epistemologies in the service of a wider common world.

Notes

Epigraphs: Hobbes (1651) 1982, 362; Foucault 1986, 27.
1   The Advanced Research Projects Agency, later to become DARPA, was established by the Eisenhower administration in 1958 after the Soviet Union's Sputnik satellite

orbited Earth, a technology that caught the US completely off guard. Its mission then was to "prevent technological surprise." In the intervening years, it has done so largely by facilitating some of the country's most transformative technologies, including the internet (originally ARPANET) and, more recently, driverless cars, which are the consumer beneficiary of DARPA's push for unmanned autonomous vehicles of all kinds.

2   DARPA's annual budget typically hovers just under $3 billion US. At approximately five-tenths of one percent of the DoD's total annual allocation (582 billion in 2017), it is minor arm of the broader US defense program. But in the world of technological research and development, the amount it allocates in grants to industry and university researchers has a significant impact on the direction of cutting-edge innovation. The National Science Foundation, by comparison, has a budget of approximately $7 million.

3   While data on the number of drone-related deaths is notoriously difficult to assess, the Bureau of Investigative Journalism estimates that US drones were used to kill somewhere between 5,734 and 8,853 people between 2002 and January 2017 in Pakistan, Yemen, Afghanistan, and Somalia. The website Airwars reports that American-led airstrikes were responsible for approximately thirty-one hundred civilian deaths in Mosul and Raqqa, Syria, from August 2014 to March 2017 (Almukhtar 2017). These deaths mark an erosion of conventional forms of military engagement characterized by front lines and the invasion of geographic territory.

4   The number of active-duty personnel in the US military in 2011 had dropped to fewer than half of 1955 rosters and fifty thousand fewer than in 1995 (Coleman n.d.).

5   This is not novel, but an extension of the experimental landscapes of the Bikini Atoll and the Nevada desert, where scientists tested the most devastating experiments of all time.

References

Almukhtar, Sarah. 2017. "US Airstrikes on ISIS Have Killed Hundreds, Maybe Thousands of Civilians." *New York Times*, May 25. https://www.nytimes.com/interactive /2017/05/25/world/middleeast/airstrikes-iraq-syria-civilian-casualties.html.

Amoore, Louise. 2017. "What Does It Mean to Govern with Algorithms?" Antipode Foundation.org, May 19. https://antipodefoundation.org/2017/05/19/algorithmic -governance.

Amoore, Louise, and Rita Raley. 2017. "Securing with Algorithms: Knowledge, Decision, Sovereignty." *Security Dialogue* 48 (1): 3–10.

Anderson, Ben. 2010. "Preemption, Precaution, Preparedness: Anticipatory Action and Future Geographies." *Progress in Human Geography* 34 (6): 777–98.

Chamayou, Grégoire. 2015. *A Theory of the Drone*. New York: New Press.

Coleman, David. n.d. "US Military Personnel 1954–2014." Accessed October 16, 2017. http://historyinpieces.com/research/us-military-personnel-1954-2014.

DARPA. n.d.a. "Anti-Submarine Warfare (ASW) Continuous Trail Unmanned Vessel (ACTUV)." Accessed June 2, 2017. http://www.darpa.mil/program/anti-submarine -warfare-continuous-trail-unmanned-vessel.

DARPA (Defense Advanced Research Projects Agency). n.d.b. "Hydra." Accessed June 2, 2017. http://www.darpa.mil/program/hydra.

Elden, Stuart. 2013a. *The Birth of Territory*. Chicago: University of Chicago Press.

Elden, Stuart. 2013b. "Secure the Volume: Vertical Geopolitics and the Depth of Power." *Political Geography* 34 (May): 35–51.

Foucault, Michel. (1984) 1986. "Of Other Spaces." *diacritics* 16 (Spring): 22–27.

Foucault, Michel. 1990. *The History of Sexuality: An Introduction*. New York: Vintage Books.

Foucault, Michel. 1995. *Discipline and Punish: The Birth of the Prison*. New York: Vintage Books.

Gramer, Robbie. 2017. "Here's What Russia's Military Build-Up in the Arctic Looks Like." *Foreign Policy*, January 25. https://foreignpolicy.com/2017/01/25/heres-what-russias-military -build-up-in-the-arctic-looks-like-trump-oil-military-high-north-infographic-map.

Gregory, Derek. 2011. "The Everywhere War." *Geographical Journal* 177 (3): 238–50.

Hobbes, Thomas. (1651) 1982. *Leviathan*. Harmondsworth, UK: Penguin Classics.

Holmes, James. 2013. "China's Selective Access-Denial Strategy." *National Interest*, December 3. http://nationalinterest.org/commentary/chinas-selective-access-denial -strategy-9482.

Holmes, James. 2016. "Sea Changes: The Future of Nuclear Deterrence." *Bulletin of Atomic Scientists* 72 (4): 228–33.

Johnson, Elizabeth R. 2015. "Of Lobsters, Laboratories, and War: Animal Studies and the Temporality of More-Than-Human Encounters." *Environment and Planning D: Society and Space* 33 (2): 296–313.

Kindervater, Katharine. 2017. "Drone Strikes, Ephemeral Sovereignty, and Changing Conceptions of Territory." *Territory, Politics, Governance* 5 (2): 207–21.

LaGrone, Sam. 2014a. "The World's Most Dangerous Naval Weapon." *Popular Science*, April 21. http://www.popsci.com/blog-network/shipshape/worlds-most-dangerous -naval-weapon.

LaGrone, Sam. 2014b. "A Terrible Thing That Waits (under the Ocean)." *Popular Science*, May 19. http://www.popsci.com/blog-network/shipshape/terrible-thing-waits-under -ocean.

Merchant, Brian. 2015. "DARPA Is about to Start Testing an Autonomous, Submarine-Hunting Ocean Drone." *Vice: Motherboard*, November 10. https://motherboard.vice .com/en_us/article/darpa-is-building-an-autonomous-submarine-hunting-drone-boat.

O'Rourke, Ronald. 2018. "China Naval Modernization: Implications for US Navy Capabilities—Background and Issues for Congress." Congressional Research Service Report. https://fas.org/sgp/crs/row/RL33153.pdf.

Pellerin, Cheryl. 2017. "Mattis, Dunford Brief President on Military Options Available to Deal with North Korea." DoD News, Defense Media Activity, September 3. https:// www.defense.gov/News/Article/Article/1298855/mattis-dunford-brief-president-on -military-options-available-to-deal-with-north.

Saldanha, Arun. 2008. "Heterotopia and Structuralism." *Environment and Planning A: Economy and Space* 40 (9): 2080–96.

Schmitt, Carl. 2003. *The Nomos of the Earth: In the International Law of the Jus Publicum Europaeum*. New York: Telos.

Shaw, Ian. 2016. *Predator Empire: Drone Warfare and Full Spectrum Dominance*. Minneapolis: University of Minnesota Press.

Shaw, Ian, and Majed Akhtar. 2012. "The Unbearable Humanness of Drone Warfare in FATA, Pakistan." *Antipode* 44 (4): 1490–1509.

Showalter, Stephanie, and Justin Manley. 2009. "Legal and Engineering Challenges to Widespread Adoption of Unmanned Maritime Vehicles." Paper presented at the OCEANS 2009 Conference, November 9. https://www.researchgate.net/publication/224119483_Legal_and_engineering_challenges_to_widespread_adoption_of_unmanned_maritime_vehicles.

Steinberg, Philip E. 2011. "Free Sea." In *Spatiality, Sovereignty and Carl Schmitt: Geographies of the Nomos,* edited by Stephen Legg, 268–75. London: Routledge.

Steinberg, Philip, and Kimberley Peters. 2015. "Wet Ontologies, Fluid Spaces: Giving Depth to Volume through Oceanic Thinking." *Environment and Planning D: Society and Space* 33 (2): 247–64.

Truver, Scott. 2011. "Taking Mines Seriously: Mine Warfare in China's Near Seas." *Naval War College Review* 65 (2): 30–66.

Truver, Scott. 2014. "An Act of War? The Law of Naval Mining." *War on the Rocks*, October 22. https://warontherocks.com/2014/10/an-act-of-war-the-law-of-naval-mining.

UNCLOS (United Nations Convention on the Law of the Sea). 1982. http://www.un.org/depts/los/convention_agreements/texts/unclos/part7.htm.

US Department of the Navy. 2004. "The Navy Unmanned Undersea Vehicle (UUV) Master Plan." November 9. http://www.navy.mil/navydata/technology/uuvmp.pdf.

Vine, David. 2015a. *Base Nation: How U.S. Military Bases Abroad Harm America and the World*. New York: Metropolitan Books.

Vine, David. 2015b. "Our Base Nation." *TomDispatch* blog, September 13. http://www.tomdispatch.com/blog/176043/tomgram%3A_david_vine%2C_our_base_nation.

Virno, Paolo. 2004. *A Grammar of the Multitude: For an Analysis of Contemporary Forms of Life*. Cambridge, MA: Semiotext.

Wilcox, Lauren. 2015. *Bodies of Violence: Theorizing Embodied Subjects in International Relations*. New York: Oxford University Press.

10. *CLUPEA LIBERUM*

Hugo Grotius, Free Seas, and the Political Biology of Herring

ALISON RIESER

There is an origin story in the historiography of the law of the sea that satisfies most legal scholars but disappoints geographers. It emphasizes the seventeenth-century competition between two legal ideas: on the one hand, the idea that the seas should be free for use by all humankind and, on the other, that they should be subject to sovereign control and regulation by the adjacent nation-state. The story portrays this juridical controversy as a "battle of books" written by the leading legal minds of Western Europe, ending with the eventual victory of the freedom of the high seas doctrine over the doctrine of maritime sovereignty (Bederman 2012). Revisionist historians have located the geopolitical context of this ideational battle (Armitage 2004; Ittersum 2016; Weindl 2009). But legal historians have so far failed to contextualize the battle in the competition between the Dutch and the English for control of the vast fisheries wealth of the North Atlantic.

This is a serious shortcoming. After free seas became the dominant norm of international ocean law, it ossified a regime of overexploitation and inefficient resource use (Barnes 2010, 87). This chapter seeks to correct this lacuna by introducing *Clupea harengus*, Atlantic herring, the marine-life protagonist whose exploitation fueled the competing doctrines at the heart of the battle. My goal is to show how herring, with its particular habits and biological properties, can be said to have coproduced the freedom of the seas as that doctrine emerged in early modern European legal culture. The herring's seemingly intentional arrivals and disappearances were part of the oceanic imaginaries of the competing polities of the North Sea basin, where new legal institutions were emerging to undergird their rapidly changing economies.

FIGURE 10.1. John Selden's map of the British Seas, from the Amsterdam edition of *Mare Clausum* (1636). Courtesy of Imaging Services, Huntington Library, Pasadena, CA.

Herring is the first fish in recorded history to have triggered a war fought with ships and cannons: the Anglo-Dutch war of 1652–54 (Benson 2015; Wilson 1978, 26). I contend that herring also sparked the ideational battle that was a prelude to this warfare. This contest was between the books *Mare Liberum* (*The Free Seas*) and *Mare Clausum* (*The Closed Seas*), written by the leading Dutch and English lawyers Hugo Grotius and John Selden, respectively. To make this case, I first describe the habits and behavior of Atlantic herring, the proximate object of Dutch and English-Scottish rivalry, and the laws these antagonists enacted to promote and protect herring fisheries. I then recount the Grotius-Selden debate in the context of the living marine-resource conflict between England and Scotland, on the one hand, and the Dutch Republic, on the other.

Drawing on textual and circumstantial evidence, I conclude that of the two doctrines, Grotius's *mare liberum* was the most influenced by herring. Herring was the mother-trade in the economy of the newly established Dutch Republic. Migrating shoals of herring, like armies or armadas, were important to the oceanic imaginaries of Grotius, his clients in the merchant and political classes of Delft and The Hague, and his intellectual colleagues at the University of Leiden. With Holland's *grote visserij* (great fishery) not far from his mind, Grotius crafted a new, secular law of nations based upon the natural properties of the seas and its herring. Exhaustion of the great shoal was impossible; its return to its ancient haunts in the North Sea reflected rhythms and patterns that were the voice of God speaking through nature.

John Selden also held a vision of the great shoals of herring. His theory of British sovereignty over the seas, the *mare clausum* surrounding the British Isles, as illustrated in figure 10.1, was based also on a conception of natural law, but one that could be modified by human institutions (Lesaffer 2017). In his mind's eye he saw herring, but he also saw legal precedents: British claims to sovereignty at sea dating back to pre-Norman times. To Selden, too, herring was a silver mountain, a rich vein that ran around the British Isles. The British right to this resource was not a gift of Providence, but a product of parliaments, which, from before the Magna Carta, the great English charter controlling the powers of kings, had enacted laws to prevent herring's exhaustion and deliver its wealth to the kingdom.

The Natures of Herring

A small, pelagic schooling fish, since time immemorial herring have migrated from wintering grounds in deep troughs of the Northeast Atlantic to shallow spawning grounds along the coasts of Scandinavia and Britain. These herring shoals, or schools, were many fathoms deep, extending for miles at the surface. The herring's seasonal arrivals to nearshore waters attracted lucrative fisheries and trade, which in turn inspired polities along the herring's route to make laws controlling access to and commerce with the shoals (Dodd 1752; Elder 1912; Jackson 2000). By authorizing the collection of taxes, tolls, and tithes, these laws channeled the wealth of the oceans to landowners, merchants, and monasteries in England and Scotland and to northern kingdoms adjacent to the spawning grounds. The longest surviving and most consequential of these laws is the principle that the seas beyond the horizon and the fisheries they support are open to all nations; they cannot be owned by any one sovereign for the exclusive use by one state's people.

The Atlantic herring, *Clupea harengus*, is a medium-sized (45 cm), blue-gray to silver fish that gathers in enormous schools for feeding and spawning.

A vertically migrating plankton eater, the herring inhabits waters near the surface at night but spends daylight hours at depths where the seas are dark and it can hide from its many predators. The species is widely distributed in the North Atlantic and its adjacent seas, ranging from the Bay of Biscay, off France and Spain, to the west coast of Spitzbergen north of Norway, but is absent from the Mediterranean (Jenkins 1927, 13–14). A member of the Clupeoid family of bony fishes, the herring has cousins known as sprats, pilchards, and shads. The herring, however, has been its family's most important member in terms of providing food and commerce for humankind and forage to other species in the oceans. When the great Swedish naturalist Carl Linneaeus gave herring its genus and species name in 1758, he described it as *copiosissimus piscis*, the most prolific fish (Stephenson 2001, 3, quoting Linneaeus [1758], 318).

Natural histories of herring agree that it was one of the first marine fishes caught and subsisted on after European tribes traded their nomadic existence for life in coastal settlements (Jenkins 1927, v). Herring are found on both sides of the North Atlantic, with Scandinavian stocks ranging to the Faroe Islands and Iceland and American stocks ranging from Labrador to Cape Cod. The largest concentrations of herring in Europe have always been found off the coasts of Britain and Ireland and in the North Sea between Scotland and Norway, John Selden's *mare clausum* (as illustrated in figure 10.1). Covered in small, soft scales, the herring has a single, short dorsal fin near the center of its back and a large mouth. It strains its food from the same water from which it draws oxygen, passing the plankton-rich waters through its mouth and over its gills. The herring deposits its eggs on the seafloor, sticking them to gravel on underwater banks formed by ancient river beds, subsurface features that once dominated the central North Sea seascape (Jenkins 1927, 1–2).

From the headlands, herring can be seen in large aggregations during spawning season. They arrive after spending the winter months in deep water waiting for the spring plankton bloom that will feed the larvae that hatch from the eggs nested on the seafloor. In medieval Scandinavian fisheries the herring came so close to shore and in such densities that the text accompanying a sixteenth-century historical atlas depicts Baltic fishermen scooping them up in buckets and standing an ax upright in the shoal (Magnus 1998). In later centuries scientists used morphology and then genetic markers to define separate races of herring in the North Sea, each with multiple spawning seasons (Hjort 1914; Huxley 1881, 609–10; Sinclair 2009). Before these separate races became general knowledge, people believed herring was one vast population with one great migration, traveling south from the polar seas above the Arctic Circle and then

204 · Alison Rieser

separating into eastern and western brigades to populate the fjords, inlets, and bays of Scandinavia and the British Isles (Jenkins 1927, 13–14).

Herring's immense value to the kingdoms of Europe made it an early subject of investigation. Philosophers and merchants alike sought to understand its periodic disappearance, such as in the early fifteenth century when the great shoal migrated from the Baltic to the North Sea (Wilson 1978, 2). Whenever the herring did not appear as expected, their loss was attributed to God's punishment for fishers and merchants who had become "rich and *ubermutig*" (boisterous and arrogant) or who had polluted the seas with whale oil and the noise of cannon fire. Dutch fishermen believed the disappearance was due to failure to release the *Heringskonig*, or king of herring, the steering fish that led the herring shoals south from the polar seas (Stephenson 2001, 9–10; quoting William Marshall, *Die Deutschen Meere und ihre Bewohner* [*The German Seas and Their Inhabitants*] [1895]).

Noting that herring are capricious in their motions, Thomas Pennant, a prominent, early British zoologist, described this behavior as a providential instinct (Pennant 1776, 338):

> Were we inclined to consider this partial migration of the herring in a moral light, we might reflect with veneration and awe on the mighty Power which originally impressed on this most useful body of his creatures, the instinct that directs and points out the course, that blesses and enriches these islands, which causes them at certain and invariable times to quit the vast polar deeps, and offer themselves to our expecting fleets.

This instinct was really a key biological adaptation to the changeable environment of the North Atlantic. The herring's forerunner had evolved into many subpopulations, each with different spawning seasons; the length of the incubation period for their eggs varies depending on the ambient water temperature. A cloudy spring when little sunlight reaches and warms the sea surface will delay the hatching of herring eggs. The greatest number of herring larvae survives to replenish the adult population when they emerge near to or during the plankton bloom. This is when tiny drifting plants and animals are available in the surface waters to feed the growing herring. With so many different seasons and subpopulations, or races, the shoals remain catchable by humankind even as the population is diminished in overall size. Fishermen are thus tempted to believe there always will be herring somewhere to be caught; any signs of overfishing are masked by the appearance of shoals along another shore. Herring's shoaling behavior is an evolutionary trait, one that protects the fish from its many predators but makes them too easy for humans to catch, whether by basket in the Middle Ages, the herring buss in the Dutch Golden Age, or the modern purse seine today.

The Laws of Herring

Herring die the minute they are taken from the seas. Because they spoil quickly, to be palatable they must be eaten soon after landing or preserved for long storage or for transport to market. The localities that Providence favored with shoals of herring thus became the sites of some of the earliest international trade. Foreign dealers would visit sites like Skäne, in southern Sweden, to buy herring from the merchants camped along the shore. Their workers meanwhile (usually women) filled more barrels, gutted the herring, and pickled it with salt mined nearby in preparation for shipment to markets via the Baltic and the English Channel.

The northern coastal towns of the Netherlands developed a fishery early in the Middle Ages that did not depend upon the herring making a close approach to the shore where competing merchants were waiting (Jenkins 1927, 10). Dutch fishermen converted timber carriers used in the Baltic trade into herring busses, decked fishing vessels of forty to seventy tons. These ships could carry a crew and the materials needed to build and fill barrels with herring that swam into the surface-drifting nets deployed from the vessels' bows. Fleets of these vessels began traveling to the herring spawning grounds around the Shetland Islands, hundreds of miles away from the towns in Holland that owned these vessels (included Hugo Grotius's hometown of Delft).

By the early sixteenth century, the Dutch had taken control of the ancient trade between northern and western Europe from the Hansa towns and the Danish kingdom (Cameron and Neal 2002; Wilson 1978, 2). To maintain their hard-won share and to protect the industrial secret they believed was the key to their success, Dutch port towns adopted ordinances to maintain the value of the Dutch brand (Unger 1980, 260–61). These laws set strict fishing seasons to ensure fish were caught in peak condition. They also required that only the best qualities of salt and wood be used to pickle the herring and that the fishers gutted the herring using the method invented by Willem Beukels, the fisherman who became a Dutch national hero (Beaujon 1884, 62; Unger 1978). The towns formed a collective, the College of the Great Fishery, to oversee compliance with these standards and fund naval escorts protecting the herring busses as they sailed to and from the North Sea (Cushing 1988, 89; Tracy 1993; Unger 1980). When the barrels of herring were brought back to port, merchants watched the repacking process to ensure compliance with the quality-control ordinances, to maintain the value of the Dutch brand. When in the mid-sixteenth century the Dutch provinces declared their independence from the Spanish Catholic kingdom, one of the first acts of their new legislative assembly was a law codifying the herring trade quality standards.

In England, too, laws controlling the herring trade were an early subject of parliaments and privy councils. The parliament during the reign of Edward III enacted the Statute of Herring, confirming the ancient right of Great Yarmouth in Norfolk, adjacent to the autumn spawning grounds, to hold a free fair (market) when the shoals arrived. This privilege allowed Yarmouth to appoint bailiffs and judicial officers to collect tolls and customs duties from any ship unloading herring within seven leagues of the harbor. Merchants and fishers from other towns tried to evade the landing fees, such as when the mouth of the River Yare shifted or, in the 1590s, when the shoals failed to arrive. The resulting fines and vessel seizures triggered petitions for relief to the Privy Council (Dean 1990, 41, 44). In the last two decades of her reign, Elizabeth vetoed bills passed by the House of Commons to maintain Yarmouth's privilege (Dean 1990, 57–58).

The most unpopular law of the herring laws was the so-called Political Lent. In 1563, William Cecil, Lord Burley, chief advisor to Elizabeth and later her Lord Treasurer, realized that England's herring fishing towns had decayed since Henry VIII's break with the Catholic Church (Kitch 2013, 89–90). To restore the observance of Lent and the attendant consumption of fish, Cecil, via the Privy Council, enacted a decree requiring people to abstain from eating flesh every Wednesday, in order to increase the number of fishermen who could defend (and expand) the realm (Borneman and Littlejohn 2015).

Cecil's law was, in essence, a secular duty to eat more herring, fresh when it was in season, and preserved when it was not. A proviso in the law made it a crime to spread rumors that the fish-day decree was a plot to reinstate the Catholic pope as the authority over England:

> Because no person should misjudge the intent of the statute, which is politically meant only for the increase of fishermen and mariners, and not for any superstition for choice of meats; whoever shall preach or teach that eating of fish or forbearing of meat is for the saving of the soul of man, for the service of God, shall be punished as the spreader of *false news*.
> (Borneman and Littlejohn 2015, quoting Cecil [1563]; emphasis added)

The English citizenry hated the decree, and it was abolished in 1584. By that time, however, another proposal to rebuild English fisheries was afoot: political pamphleteers were lobbying Elizabeth I to establish a royal fishing company.

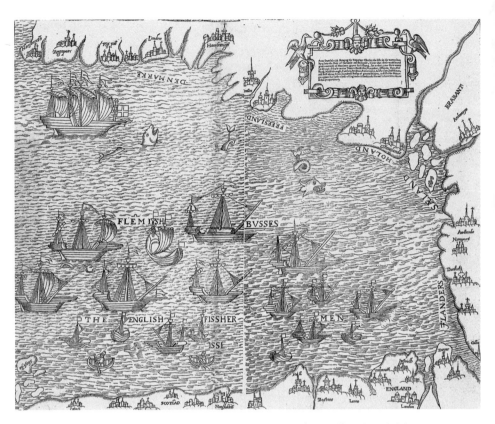

FIGURE 10.2. Similitude of contrasting scales of Dutch (Flemish) and English herring fisheries along England's east coast, from Hitchcock's *Pollitique Platt* (1580). Courtesy of Imaging Services, Huntington Library, Pasadena, CA.

They sought government financial subsidies known as bounties to build a fleet of English herring busses that could reclaim Britain's fishing grounds from the Dutch. In *A Pollitique Platt for the Honor of the Prince*, Robert Hitchcock argued that, in the spirit of Protestant internationalism, an English fleet was needed in order to share in the North Sea's herring wealth (Kitch 2013, 83). Hitchcock did not ask the queen to oust the Dutch, whose fishing vessels dwarfed the small, English fishing skiffs, as illustrated in figure 10.2. A retired warrior and generous in spirit, Hitchcock believed there were enough herring in the northern seas for all, even if the Dutch deployed a thousand busses (Fulton 1911, 98–99).

In any event, Elizabeth I was not inclined to claim sovereignty over the seas in which the herring grounds were located (Smith 1977, 357). She was an ardent proponent of *mare liberum* and Britons' use of distant fishing grounds. She chastised the Danes for claiming *mare clausum* to exclude English fishermen from waters extending from Iceland to Norway. Her successor to the Crown, however, was of a different mind. Reflecting Scotland's long practice of maritime sovereignty, James I broke with Elizabeth's free-seas policy and in 1609 proclaimed British sovereignty at sea and the power to tax all foreign fisheries (Vervliet 2009, xxi).

Herring at the Battle of the Books

When the Dutch embassy in London heard that a great fishery edict was under consideration, messages to Holland suggested a full-throated legal response was warranted. A month before the king's edict was announced, a pamphlet was published in Holland; it was an instant best seller (Ittersum 2006a). The little book that caused such a stir was *Mare Liberum*, written by Hugo Grotius as a chapter of a larger work. Never published in Grotius's lifetime, the larger work would come to be known as *De Jure Praedae Commentarius* (Commentary on the Law of Prize and Booty), a treatise on war and the moral basis for Dutch trade with the Indian Ocean world. At the urging of his political associates, Grotius rushed his chapter into publication to influence treaty negotiations between the Dutch provinces and Spain (Ittersum 2016). His patrons were worried that Dutch negotiators, in exchange for recognition of their independence, were about to concede the Spanish kingdom's exclusive right to engage in overseas trade.

In *Mare Liberum* Grotius had sought to undermine the validity of the *Inter caetera* (Among Other Laws), a papal decree giving Spain and Portugal an exclusive right to trade with the non-Catholic world. He argued that the seas were free for the use of all nations and could not by their nature be subject to the exclusive use or ownership of one sovereign. In fact, their natural conditions made any ownership impossible. The seas were incapable of occupation, as boundaries could not be marked in them with stakes, nor were they capable of exhaustion when humankind used the seas for navigation and fisheries, the natural right of all peoples and nations. The oceans were, by their nature, immune from claims of dominion (Bederman 2012).

Grotius's concern in *Mare Liberum* was with God's authority, not the authority of kings. He was not thinking about herring, or taxes, or the fishery edict that James I had been about to announce to the North Sea world (Ittersum 2006b, 388). The pamphlet appeared too late, however, to influence the treaty negotiations (Gordon 2008, 257). But across the North Sea, Scottish fishermen and their sovereign believed the free-seas argument had been aimed at them. Even though not a single argument in *Mare Liberum* had mentioned fishing rights in the North Sea, they believed Grotius was using his prodigious knowledge of classical texts and continental scholarship to justify Dutch poaching.

James I of England, as mentioned above, was also James VI of Scotland. Dutch herring fisheries were never popular with his Scottish subjects, and he had tried and failed to establish a Scottish fishing colony in the Hebrides (Mitchell 1864, 154). After learning that Holland's leading legal mind was at work on behalf of Dutch commerce, he encouraged William Welwood (1578–1622), a Scottish jurist, to revise and expand his treatise *An Abridgement of All Sea-Lawes* (1613) (in Grotius 2004) to rebut *Mare Liberum*, especially its notion of a free fishery (Alsop 1980).

A former professor of civil law at the University of St. Andrews, Welwood was now in London, out of work and eager to oblige. He took strong exception to Grotius's reasoning that the seas could not be owned because borders could not be put upon them. Grotius had relied upon the wrong legal authorities, on "old poets, orators, philosophers, and jurisconsults" rather than the greatest authority of all, the Creator (Somos 2007, 148, quoting Welwood 1613 at 71, 72). God was the first author of the distinction between land and sea. He had purposefully designed the seas to remain in one place, giving to men an understanding heart with which to measure nature and construct artificial boundaries for states (Garry 1995, 208–9).

Grotius had written in chapter 5 of *Mare Liberum* that "everyone admits that if a great many persons hunt on the land or fish in a river, the forest is easily exhausted of wild animals and the river of fish, but *such a contingency is impossible in the case of the sea*" (emphasis added). To this, Welwood had replied, "By the near and daily approaching of the buss-fishers the shoals of fishes are broken and so far scattered away from our shores and coasts that no fish now can be found worthy of any pains and travails, to the impoverishing of all the sort of our home fishers and to the great damage of all the nation" (Welwood 1613, in Grotius 2004, 74).

Welwood was a comparative law scholar but also an academic embroiled in his own dangerous political and religious rivalries; he pursued controversy (Ford 2013; Furdell 1998, 33). He most certainly understood the political implications of *mare clausum* for James I and for his queen consort, Anne of Denmark. Her Danish relatives were encouraging her to obtain the patent right to receive the income from the Dutch herring fishery (Alsop 1980). But he had ample legal precedents for asserting sovereignty over the British seas where the Dutch busses were fishing. Scottish law required foreign fishing fleets to stay at least one land-kenning from the shore, a distance that can be seen from the top of the mast of the herring buss. This law in effect created an exclusive fishing zone of several marine leagues for Scottish fishermen, perhaps reflecting the folk-zoological belief that herring would abandon local fishing waters if the boisterous and clamorous Dutch were allowed to fish too close to shore (Fulton 1911, 77).

Grotius learned of Welwood's criticism while on a commercial-diplomatic mission to London in 1613. One purpose of the mission had been to defend the Dutch whale oil monopoly in eastern Greenland against English penetration (Vervliet 2009). But the English counsellors had insisted on bringing to the table the matter of the king's herring tax (and the queen's patent) and the right to trade with the East Indies (Ittersum 2006a). The English argued that under the notion of *mare liberum* they were free to enter both the whaling and spice trades and compete with the Dutch. Grotius did little to advance his clients' cause. He argued that his countrymen had won the exclusive right to trade with the East Indies. Having ousted the Portuguese traders, at their own expense, the Dutch were entitled to enter into exclusive trading agreements with eastern polities. Their rulers, after all, enjoyed a freedom of contract under the law of nations. Aware that it was Grotius who had written the infamous *Mare Liberum*, the English, understandably, were not impressed by his disquisition (Knight 1919).

Grotius had obtained on the trip a Latin translation of Welwood's book. On his return to Holland, he wrote his rebuttal. Perhaps realizing he had undermined *Mare Liberum* with his flexible interpretation, Grotius (2004, 87) wrote:

> If the British please, they can not only fish beside the [Dutch], but also outstrip the[m], since they themselves are nearer the sea where fish are plentiful. But if they weary of the great labor, weary of the expense which with the greatest frugality nevertheless frequently eats up all the profit, why begrudge the fact that what is neglected by themselves is taken by their neighbors?

In this passage, Grotius reveals knowledge of both the seasonal migration routes of the main shoal of herring and the economics of the herring fishery. He notes the proximity of the herring fishing grounds to the Scottish shore, from which fishing vessels could be launched and the herring cured at a cost much lower than that of operating the Dutch herring buss fleet. In *Mare Liberum* he had written (as a jab to the always impecunious James I?) that any sovereign who tried to restrict the right of free fishery, on the notion that nature in general and fisheries in particular have their limits, could be rightly accused of "brainsick covetousness" (Grotius 2004, 32).

Grotius never published his defense of *Mare Liberum* or sent it to London. By this time, for other reasons, James I had decided against exercising his maritime sovereignty. He did not want to antagonize his brother-in-law, the Danish king, from whom he was negotiating a loan. It would fall to Charles I, the son of Anne of Denmark and James I and the most ill-fated of the Stewart kings, to collect the herring tax when he too ran short of money.

Mr. Selden's Assignment

As his father, had done, Charles, too, issued a proclamation intended to restore the herring fisheries to the English (Mitchell 1864, 158–59). To bolster the legal basis for taxing the Dutch fishery, Charles engaged John Selden (1560–1655), a noted legal historian and antiquarian whom his father had previously asked to write a rebuttal to *Mare Liberum*. Charles requested that Selden expand his earlier rebuttal, proving with an even lengthier scholarly discourse that the oceans were capable of enclosure (Thornton 2006, 107–8). Selden completed the assignment and published *Mare Clausum* (*Of the Dominium; or, Ownership of the Sea*) in 1635.

Selden's treatise differed in significant ways from *Mare Liberum*. Whereas Grotius's imaginary had been of the seas beyond the horizon, Selden's was of the seas surrounding the British archipelago, where a tax or license fee on foreign fishing could help the treasury and reduce the burden of taxes and tithes on working people. Selden summarized his argument in a preface: "There remains not in the nature of the Sea itself, or in the Law either Divine, Natural or of Nature, anything which may so oppose the private dominion thereof." By this he meant that, regardless of whether divine or natural law applied, the seas were capable of being owned (Lesaffer 2017).

Mare Clausum was published in two books. The first was an elaborate response to the natural law theory of Grotius. In the second book, Selden cited precedents dating back to before the Norman invasion of England. These precedents, in his view, showed that Britain had always claimed and exercised sovereignty over the seas around the British Isles, to the east as far as the coasts of Denmark, the Netherlands, and France (Nellen 2015, 495).

Selden's arguments were as scholarly as Grotius's but stronger in one sense. Selden's assignment did not require him to walk the same rhetorical tightrope; Grotius had had to quote Holy Scripture, to satisfy his intended audience of devout Protestants, while at the same time try to reduce scripture's ranking in the hierarchy of authorities. By constructing a natural law of nations, Grotius was attempting a grand project of secularization, of elevating humankind's ideas and principles in political discourse (Somos 2007, 148–49). Selden's theory of *mare clausum* also relied on natural law, but a type of natural law that was based on human consent, one that could be modified by lawmakers. Selden emphasized that other nations had consented to British assertions of maritime sovereignty, again showing that laws and principles are made by human institutions (Lesaffer 2017). Selden also echoed Welwood's vision of the herring shoals broken by the boisterous busses.

Selden's book set off alarm bells in the herring towns of the Dutch Republic and it, too, became a best seller. A new publishing house in Amsterdam owned by the Elsevier brothers printed side-by-side, unauthorized editions of *Mare Liberum* and *Mare Clausum* (Lucas 2001). By this time, lawmakers in Holland were gravely concerned that they would soon have to pay tribute and a hefty herring tax to Charles I (Fletcher 1933; Lesaffer 2017). They looked to Grotius to rebut Selden. But the champion of the Dutch freedom to use the seas, and their greatest living scholar, was no longer in Holland. Shortly after returning from commercial conferences with the English in 1618, Grotius had been arrested and tried for treason, along with his political mentor, Johan Oldenbarnevelt, a former leader in Holland's government, in a coup d'état fueled by a doctrinal dispute among Holland's Protestant sects.

In his disgrace, Grotius, champion of the free-seas doctrine, suffered the fate of the free herring: predation. When the press satirized his trial, a caricature appeared on an engraving illustrating a famous Netherlandish proverb, "It's the big fish that always eats the small fish," shown in figure 10.3 (Grotius's name is in mirror writing). This time, Grotius was the small fish, along with the Oldenbarnevelt's other allies (Nellen 2015, 50). Imprisoned for life after a humiliating show trial, Grotius was able to escape after serving only three years. While in exile, he wrote much of what was to be his major work on international law. In *On the Law of War and Peace* (1625), Grotius seemed to soften his position on *mare liberum*, suggesting that sovereignty for the purposes of stewardship may be warranted in straits and bays where fishing grounds are located.

The merchants and lawmakers of Holland could do nothing to convince Grotius to refute John Selden. By 1635, Grotius was fully ensconced in Paris, representing the Queen of Sweden at the French court. Sweden's sovereign supported a *mare clausum* of her own in the Baltic. She may have hoped her maritime sovereignty would protect the Swedish fishery in those good years when the coast at Skäne was again alive with herring and they could be harvested close to the shore and the former beachfront marketplace. Alerted to

FIGURE 10.3. Caricature of Hugo Grotius as a small fish being eaten (and disgorged) by his political mentor, Johan Oldenbarnevelt, in an engraving published at the time of their joint trial for high treason in 1618 (Nellen 2015, xxiv). Courtesy of Rijksstudio Online Collection, Rijkmuseum, the Netherlands.

the publication of *Mare Clausum* by his English contacts, Grotius wrote of the entreaties from Holland, "Let the Batavians respond [to Selden], I am looking after Swedish interests now" (Nellen 2015, 495).

Grotius may have been reluctant to attack Selden as fiercely as he had Welwood. In *Mare Clausum*, Selden had been complimentary of Grotius's scholarship, even quoting Grotius's poem to James I. Written in 1603 to celebrate his ascendancy to the joint thrones of England and Scotland, the youthful Grotius had lauded the new king's worthiness to be considered a sovereign of the seas (Nellen 2015, 495). Selden may have detected an ambivalence about empire in *Mare Liberum*'s poetic references (Jones 2011). And, having closely studied Grotius's more mature work, the 1625 treatise *On the Law of War and Peace*, Selden composed book I of *Mare Clausum* with knowledge that Grotius was of at least two minds on the freedom of the seas (Thornton 2006, 127).

In England, Charles I was in dispute with his parliament over his authority as king. Without its approval, he charged his subjects a tax called ship money and used the revenue to build a ship with a hundred cannons. With this he planned to collect at last the fishing license fees and taxes the Dutch had promised to pay. When Oliver Cromwell tried to enforce a thirty-mile exclusive fishing zone along the coast, war broke out between the Dutch and the British, and dozens of Dutch herring busses and hundreds of fishermen were lost (Benson 2015; Wilson 1978). By the time the first Anglo-Dutch War ended, the great herring fishery had started to decline.

By the end of the Dutch wars, the herring fishery in England and Scotland was finally poised to take off. Climate conditions were favorable for successful herring spawning, and the fishery once again looked very promising. The British parliament enacted in the early 1700s the white-herring bounties, a program of mercantilist subsidies for offshore herring fisheries that lasted for over a hundred years (Rieser 2017). The human capacity for lawmaking that Selden had championed would eventually build a domestic herring fishery that would dominate global fisheries until the outbreak of World War I. The herring again became a staple food in England and in Britain's overseas colonies, where it fed the plantations of enslaved people. After British fishing and curing methods improved, herring became the popular kipper of the British breakfast table. Britain built distant water fishing fleets to scour the banks of Iceland and North America, abandoning *mare clausum* as it championed the freedom of the seas doctrine.

Grotius did not live to see the vindication of his doctrine of free seas or its refinement by fellow Dutchman Cornelius van Bynkershoek, proponent of the marginal seas and cannon-shot rules (Fulton 1911, 21). He also did not live to witness the first Anglo-Dutch war that decimated the herring buss fleet. He died in 1645, before Britain became an adherent to the doctrine. He was shipwrecked in the Baltic while still ambassador to Paris for Sweden, having never convinced his countrymen that despite his wish for peace among religious sects, he was first and foremost a loyal son of the Dutch Republic (Nellen 2015, 760). Centuries later, when scholars and diplomats christened Grotius the father of international law, he would be declared the victor of the battle of the books (Ittersum 2016).

Conclusion

This excursion through the material representations and imaginaries of herring and herring fisheries in the era of *Mare Liberum* and *Mare Clausum* suggests that the free-seas doctrine crafted by Hugo Grotius was influenced by what he had learned from wealthy herring merchants and fishmongers alike of the

Dutch Republic's silver mountain, the Atlantic herring. Their fortunes had been won in the great climate lottery, which distributes wealth and poverty without regard to politics or faith, when the herring left the Baltic and built up its spawning grounds in the North Sea. Investors in the College of the Great Fishery had seen and profited from fluctuating herring catches and abrupt changes in migratory patterns with climate. But because they were involved in political struggles for independence and for commercial success that relied on overseas industries, they crafted legends and patriotic explanations for the superiority of the Dutch brand and its economic model. The natural law right of free seas and fishery had many sources in biblical scripture, Roman law, and learned writers, but it too was a legend. It was a convenient truth, a bit of social technology that helped protect the Dutch hegemony over trade in herring and between the North Sea coasts and the peoples of the European interior. The battle of the books was won by *Clupea liberum*.

References

Alsop, J. D. 1980. "William Welwood, Anne of Denmark, and the Sovereignty of the Sea." *Scottish Historical Review* 59 (168, pt. 2): 171–74.

Armitage, David. 2004. "Introduction." In Hugo Grotius, *The Free Seas* [1609], translated by Richard Hakluyt, with William Welwod's critique and Grotius's reply, edited by David Armitage. Indianapolis, IN: Liberty Fund. http://oll.libertyfund.org/titles/859.

Barnes, Richard A. 2010. "Entitlement to Marine Living Resources in Areas beyond National Jurisdiction." In *The International Legal Regime of Areas beyond National Jurisdiction: Current and Future Developments*, edited by A. G. Oude Elferink and E. J. Molenaar, 83–141. Leiden: Martinus Nijhoff.

Beaujon, A. 1884. "The History of the Dutch Sea Fisheries: Their Progress, Decline and Revival." In *Fisheries Exhibition Literature*, vol. 9, pt. 2. London: Clowes & Sons.

Bederman, David J. 2012. "The Sea." In *The Oxford Handbook of the History of International Law*, edited by Bardo Fassbender and Anne Peters, 359–79. New York: Oxford University Press.

Benson, J. D. 2015. "England, Holland, and the Fishing Wars." *Philosophy Study* 5 (9): 447–52.

Borneman, Adam, and Brad Littlejohn. 2015. "Lent, the Maintenance of Seafaring Men, and the Politics of Fasting." *Political Theology* blog, March 19.

Cameron, Rondo E., and Larry Neal. 2002. *A Concise Economic History of the World: From Paleolithic Times to the Present*. New York: Oxford University Press.

Cushing, David H. 1988. *The Provident Sea*. New York: Cambridge University Press.

Dean, David M. 1990. "Parliament, Privy Council, and Local Politics in Elizabethan England: The Yarmouth-Lowestoft Fishing Dispute." *Albion* 22 (1): 39–64.

Dodd, James Solas. 1752. *An Essay towards a Natural History of the Herring*. London: Vincent.

Elder, John R. 1912. *The Royal Fishing Companies of the Sixteenth Century*. Glasgow: Maclehose & Sons.

Fletcher, Eric G. M. 1933. "John Selden (Author of Mare Clausum) and His Contribution to International Law." *Transactions of the Grotius Society* (19): 1–12.

Ford, J. D. 2013. "William Welwod's Treatises on Maritime Law." *Journal of Legal History* 34 (2): 172–210.

Fulton, Thomas Wemyss. 1911. *The Sovereignty of the Sea*. Edinburgh: W. Blackwood and Sons.

Furdell, Elizabeth L. 1998. "The Dangerous Academy: William Welwood at the University of St. Andrews." *European Studies Journal* 15: 21–39.

Garry, Edmond. 1995. "The Freedom of Histories: Reassessing Grotius on the Sea." *Law Text Culture* 2: 179–217.

Gordon, Edward. 2008. "Grotius and the Freedom of the Seas in the Seventeenth Century." *Willamette Journal of International Law and Dispute Resolution* 16: 252–69.

Grotius, Hugo. 2004. *The Free Sea*. Translated by Richard Hakluyt, with William Welwod's Critique and Grotius's Reply. Edited by David Armitage. Indianapolis, IN: Liberty Fund. http://oll.libertyfund.org/titles/859.

Hjort, Johan. 1914. *Fluctuations in the Great Fisheries of Northern Europe*. Rapports, Conseil Permanent International pour Exploration de la Mer 20.

Huxley, Thomas Henry. 1881. "The Herring." *Nature* 23: 607–13.

Ittersum, Martine J. van. 2006a. "Mare Liberum versus the Propriety of the Seas? The Debate between Hugo Grotius (1583–1645) and William Welwod (1552–1624) and Its Impact on Anglo-Scotto-Dutch Fishery Disputes in the Second Century of the Seventeenth Century." *Edinburgh Law Review* 10: 239–76.

Ittersum, Martine J. van. 2006b. *Profit and Principle: Hugo Grotius, Natural Rights Theories and the Rise of Dutch Power in the East Indies, 1595–1615*. Brill Studies in Intellectual History, vol. 139. Leiden: Brill.

Ittersum, Martine J. van. 2016. "Hugo Grotius: The Making of a Founding Father of International Law." In *Oxford Handbook of the Theory of International Law*, edited by Anne Orford and Florian Hoffman, 82–100. New York: Oxford University Press.

Jackson, Gordon. 2000. "State Concern for the Fisheries, 1485–1815." In *England's Sea Fisheries: The Commercial Sea Fisheries of England and Wales since 1300*, edited by David J. Starkey, Chris Reid, and Neil Ashcroft, 46–53. London: Chatham.

Jenkins, James T. 1927. *Herrings and the Herring Fisheries*. London: P. S. King & Son.

Jones, Stephanie. 2011. "The Poetic Ocean in *Mare Liberum*." In *Law and Art: Justice, Ethics and Aesthetics*, edited by Oren Ben-Dor, 188–203. Abingdon, UK: Routledge.

Kitch, Aaron. 2013. *Political Economy and the States of Literature in Early Modern England*. Abingdon, UK: Ashgate.

Knight, W. S. M. 1919. "Grotius in England: His Opposition There to the Principles of the *Mare Liberum*." *Transactions of the Grotius Society* 5: 1–38.

Lesaffer, Randall. 2017. "Mare clausum (The Closure of the Sea or The Ownership of the Sea) 1635 John Selden (1584–1654)." In *The Formation and Transmission of Western Legal Culture: 150 Books That Made the Law in the Age of Printing*, edited by Serge Duachy, Georges Martyn, Anthony Musson, Heikki Pihlajamäki, and Alain Wijffels. Studies in the History of Law and Justice, vol. 7, 190–94. Cham, Switzerland: Springer.

Lucas, Peter J. 2001. "Printing Anglo-Saxon in Holland and John Selden's *Mare Clausum seu de Dominio Maris*." *Quaerendo* 31 (2): 120–36.

Magnus, Olaus. 1998. *History of the Northern Peoples, Rome 1555*. London: Hakluyt Society.

Mitchell, John M. 1864. *The Herring: Its Natural History and National Importance*. Edinburgh: Edmonston and Douglas.

Nellen, Henk. 2015. *Hugo Grotius: A Lifelong Struggle for Peace in Church and State, 1583–1645*. Translated by J. C. Grayson. Leiden: Brill.

Pennant, Thomas. 1776. "Herring." *British Zoology* 3: 335–43. http://www.biodiversitylibrary.org/item/126997.

Rieser, Alison. 2017. "The Herring Enlightenment: Adam Smith and the Reform of British Fishery Subsidies, 1783–87." *International Journal of Maritime History* 29 (3): 600–619.

Selden, John. 1635. *Mare Clausum seu de Dominio Maris* [The Closed Sea; or, Of the Dominion, or Ownership of the Sea: Two Books]. https://archive.org/details/ofdominionoroweooseld.

Sinclair, Mike. 2009. "Herring and ICES: A Historical Sketch of a Few Ideas and Their Linkages." *ICES Journal of Marine Science* 66 (8): 1652–61.

Smith, George P. 1977. "The Concept of Free Seas: Shaping Modern Maritime Policy within a Vector of Historical Influence." *International Lawyer* 11: 355–63.

Somos, Mark. 2007. "Secularization in *De Iure Praedae*: From Bible Criticism to International Law." *Grotiana* 26 (1): 147–91.

Stephenson, R. L. 2001. "The Role of Herring Investigations in Shaping Fisheries Science." In *Herring: Expectations for a New Millennium*, edited by F. Funk, J. Blackburn, D. Hay, A. J. Pual, R. Stephenson, R. Toresen, and D. Witherell, 1–20. Fairbanks: University of Alaska Sea Grant.

Thornton, Helen. 2006. "John Selden's Response to Hugo Grotius: The Argument for Closed Seas." *International Journal of Maritime History* 18 (2): 105–27.

Tracy, James D. 1993. "Herring Wars: The Habsburg Netherlands and the Struggle for Control of the North Sea, ca. 1520–1560." *Sixteenth Century Journal* 24 (2): 249–72.

Unger, Richard W. 1978. "The Netherlands Herring Fishery in the Late Middle Ages: The False Legend of Willem Beukels of Biervliet." *Viator* 9: 335–56.

Unger, Richard W. 1980. "Dutch Herring, Technology and International Trade in the Seventeenth Century." *Journal of Economic History* 40 (2): 253–79.

Vervliet, Jeroen. 2009. "General Introduction." In *Hugo Grotius Mare Liberum, 1609–2009*, edited by Robert F. Feenstra, ix–xxviii. Leiden: Brill.

Weindl, Andrea. 2009. "Grotius's *Mare Liberum* in the Political Practice of Early-Modern Europe." *Grotiana* 30 (1): 131–51.

Welwood, William. 1613. "Of the Community and Propriety of the Seas" (Chapter 27 of *An Abridgement of All Sea-Lawes* [London 1613]). In Grotius (2004), *The Free Sea*, translated by Richard Hakluyt, with William Welwood's critique and Grotius's reply, edited by David Armitage. Indianapolis, IN: Liberty Fund. http://oll.libertyfund.org/titles/859.

Wilson, Charles H. 1978. *Profit and Power: A Study of England and the Dutch Wars*. The Hague: Martinus Nijhoff.

11. WHALES AND THE COLONIZATION
OF THE PACIFIC OCEAN

ZSOFIA KOROSY

Captain James Colnett lived an adventurous life. Born in the mid-eighteenth century, he was a member of the royal navy, midshipman to Captain James Cook on *Resolution* during Cook's second expedition to the South Pacific between 1772 and 1775, and master of the British naval ship *Discovery* during the American Revolution (Burroughs 2010, 55; Cook 1973, 104). In the postwar quiet, Colnett took leave from the Admiralty. Joining a fur-trading expedition under the auspices of the Etches trading company, he sailed to Nootka Sound, a Pacific Ocean inlet on what is now Vancouver Island, Canada. His arrest there by Spanish forces was one of a series of events that almost precipitated a war between Spain and Britain. Upon his release, he became the first Englishman in a century to trade in Japan before being hired by the British Admiralty on the recommendation of Samuel Enderby, of the Samuel Enderby & Sons whaling company, to chart the coastlines of the southern Pacific in order to establish a whaling industry there. The first Englishman to explore the Galapagos Islands, he went on to captain a naval ship transporting convicts to the fledgling Australian colony of New South Wales (Burroughs 2010, 56–58; Colnett 1968, vii–viii).

Colnett embodied the commitments of the mercantilist age of discovery in which he lived. Both private merchant and agent of his state, he undertook exploratory voyages for personal and national benefit. Skilled in the navigational and cartographic technologies of his time, Colnett accrued valuable knowledge of distant oceans and extended the edges of the British Empire into them. This chapter explores the iterative and mutually reinforcing dynamics of merchant whaling and British claims of legal authority in the Pacific Ocean in the closing decades of the eighteenth century. Colnett lived those dynamics: in the territorial conflict over Nootka Sound and the broader implications of that conflict for colonial control in the Pacific Ocean, and in the endeavors by Enderby and other commercial actors to establish whaling rights in theretofore uncharted seas.

In examining the processes by which colonial powers staked out legal authority in Pacific Ocean space, my focus is on British expeditions and, where relevant, on the interactions between those expeditions and Britain's key external antagonist in this context—Spain. Though not the only European power to explore and colonize Pacific territories, the British were significant actors in this space in the late eighteenth century and were primary proponents of the spread of a European whaling industry to Pacific waters. This chapter focuses on the role that the quest for whales had in the negotiation of the larger questions of colonial legal control over the ocean. The need to satisfy a burgeoning domestic demand for whale products drove the state to make new legal claims over distant oceans: claims that the activities of the whaling enterprises themselves helped propagate. Sovereign claims could thus follow in the wake of mercantilist impulses that were generated by private actors, as well as by the state itself.

Although the events forming the focus of this chapter occurred centuries ago, they illustrate contestations over control of ocean space and its resources, and the legal regimes that allocate this control, that continue to resonate today. Other chapters in this volume elaborate the contemporary manifestations. Jennifer L. Gaynor, for instance, examines confluences of interest between the state and local and international elites and business concerns in land reclamation activities in Southeast Asia. In some cases, as she notes, these activities have had broader consequences for the effectiveness of states' legal claims in surrounding ocean space. Philip E. Steinberg, Berit Kristoffersen, and Kristen Shake's description of Norway's delimitation of the ice edge in the Barents Sea and the consequent demarcation of zones of permissible oil drilling highlights a correspondence of interest between the Norwegian Ministry of Petroleum and Energy and the oil industry. The government's position on ice edge delimitation has moved closer to that favored by the Ministry and industry, suggesting the intermingled roles that public and private actors play in shaping state policy on ocean use.

The maritime activities with which these chapters are concerned principally take place in states' territorial waters. This chapter complements those analyses by showing that these forms of territorial contestation have long pedigrees and can take place in waters far from the territory of the claimant state. While factors such as the rise of conservationism and the end of whale products as commercially significant commodities may mean that whales no longer motivate states to make territorial claims, the relationship between oceanic borderlines and quests for resources continues to be closely intertwined.

In this chapter I demonstrate how the state negotiated, represented, and enforced areas of control in the oceans. By control, I mean a patchwork of claims encompassing such things as rights to fishing, trade, or navigation. As Alison Rieser (this volume) outlines, Hugo Grotius's conception of the freedom of the high seas was to prove of enduring importance in circumscribing the extent of such control, which could be fragmented and was often not exclusively vested in one state. Different states or their agents exercised different claims over the same space. At various times, such concepts as *jurisdiction* and *sovereignty* have been used to describe the different kinds of legal control applied to the oceans (see Benton 2010, 125, 129, 135–36; Dorsett and McVeigh 2012, 36–37; Grotius 1950, 232–38). I do not seek to define or distinguish between those terms in any detailed way in this analysis. I examine various kinds of legal authority or control deployed over ocean space, the precise nature of this control depending on the circumstances.

From the mid-eighteenth century, European whaling centered on the northern Atlantic and Arctic Oceans and was dominated by the Netherlands, Britain, France, and, perhaps most significantly, by fleets from British North American colonies (see Ellickson 1989, 85; Jackson 2005, 44, 50–51, 63). The significance of whaling to the larger project of British imperial expansion derived from the economic centrality of whaling products to industrial revolution Britain. Whale oil provided street lighting, candles, and machine lubricants; was used in the processing of certain fabrics; and was an ingredient in soaps, paints and varnishes, perfumes, and explosives (Harlow 1964, 293; Jackson 2005, xiv; Sanger 2003, 154). Baleen, the flexible bonelike plates inside the mouths of most commercially hunted whale species (sperm whales are an exception) had numerous household applications, such as in shaping corsetry (Sanger 2003, 156). Spermacetti, the waxy substance found inside the head cavity of sperm whales, was in high demand for candles (Jackson 2005, 42).

For decades, Britain had relied on its New England colonies for whaling products (Jackson 2005, 44). Then, following the outbreak of revolutionary war there in 1775, tariff protection effectively kept American whale products out of Britain's domestic market. Britain sought to make up the shortfall by expanding its own whaling industry, particularly in sperm whale oil (Harlow 1964, 294–95; Stackpole 1972, 1–13). The South Seas, especially the Pacific as newly charted by Captain Cook, were the target of this exploration. This expansion was not solely government-driven. Entrepreneurs, mostly modestly sized, pushed government to facilitate their endeavors, while the government found correspondence between these efforts and the broader national interest.

There were few such entrepreneurs (A. G. E. Jones 1981, 90). Chief among them was Samuel Enderby, founder of the whaling house Samuel Enderby & Sons, described admiringly in *Moby-Dick* (Melville [1851] 1985, chap. 101). Also important were Alexander Champion and his son (Jackson 2005, 81). Enderby, Champion, their two sons, and another whaler, John St. Barbe, together formed the Committee of South Whalers from London and became an influential lobby during the establishment of the British South Seas industry (Harlow 1964, 310). Enderby and others agitated, with some success, for government support in establishing a southern whale fishery (Harlow 1964, 303). Already, however, when European exploration of the Pacific was in its infancy, the whalers could not take whales at will. Restrictions on fishing, trading, and navigation rights existed between states and within states through the allocation of such rights to domestic entities. As the following historical examples show, the articulation of these restrictions was mediated by cartography and the ways in which it was deployed, by the state and its agents, to serve particular interests. Through cartography and other means, those agents, acting variously in their own interests and as representatives of Britain, motivated the negotiations over how the ocean would be marked by zones of legal authority.

The first part of this chapter provides an overview of the historical clash between Britain and Spain over rights to Pacific Ocean space adjoining Nootka Sound. The second part analyzes two practical mechanisms by which such colonial powers as Britain propagated their legal authority over space: mapping and human agency. Mapping was used both to render unknown spaces knowable to those seeking to colonize them and to disseminate legal authority over those spaces. Alongside mapping, the activity of private human agents carried legal authority into dispersed spatial realms. This analysis is then applied to the events at Nootka Sound. Finally, I explore a different form of negotiation of legal authority over ocean space: the tussle, within the outlines of the British state, between whaling entrepreneurs such as Enderby, the British government, and the British East India Company (EIC) for control over trade and navigation rights in the Pacific Ocean. The EIC's claim to those rights originated from the company's very foundations. Its establishing charter, issued in 1600 by Elizabeth I, gave the EIC monopoly trading rights (as against all other British merchants) extending across the Indian and Pacific Oceans from the Cape of Good Hope east to the Straits of Magellan (Sherman 1976, 332). While the broader significance of the EIC for British colonial endeavors is not the concern of this chapter, its close intertwining with the British Crown (see, e.g., Lawson 1993, 22–23) complicated its role as a formidable player in the negotiation of legal control, as between British agents, in Pacific Ocean space.

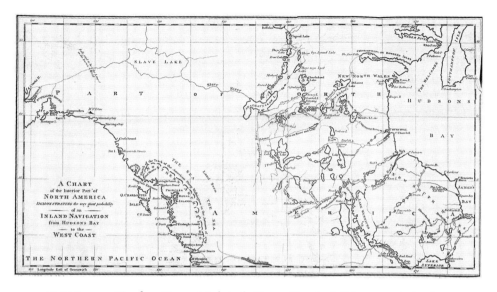

FIGURE 11.1. Map from *Voyages Made in the Years 1788 and 1789* (Meares 1791), showing Nootka Sound (bottom left). Image courtesy of Hill Collection, Special Collections and Archives, UC San Diego Library.

Nootka Sound

By the 1780s, Nootka Sound on modern-day Vancouver Island, Canada, had become a crucial post of the lucrative fur trade between North America and China. For this reason, both Britain and Spain attempted to lay claim to it. In 1790, as the following brief account of a contested sequence of events sets out, these conflicting claims almost precipitated a war.

The British settler presence at Nootka Sound dated from 1788, when Captain John Meares, a (possibly retired) British naval lieutenant, purportedly purchased land at Nootka Sound from Maquinna, a chief of the Nuu-chah-nulth peoples, and built a house on it, along with a small ship—the *Northwest America* (Clayton 2000b, 23, 170–71, 179; Cook 1973, 137–41, Frost 1993, 107; Manning 1905, 286–87, 290–91; Mills 1925, 110). Accounts differ as to whether Meares was acting solely as a merchant captain or also in his naval capacity and on behalf of the British sovereign (see Cook 1973, 137; Frost 1993, 116). Meares disguised his ships as Portuguese, which had, among other purposes, a possible intention of avoiding the monopolies of trading companies such as the EIC, as discussed below (Cook 1973, 137; Manning 1905, 288–89; Mills 1925, 111).

In 1789, Meares sent four ships to establish a more permanent settlement at Nootka Sound (Mills 1925, 110–11). Although British, the ships again pretended to sail under Portuguese authority. The activities of Meares and other fur traders seeking to establish a foothold at Nootka Sound coincided with British government policy to extend trade with China by sourcing a reliable supply of furs (Frost 1993, 105–16; see also Clayton 2000b, 178–79). The events at Nootka Sound centered on this trade but also were a valuable pretext for Britain to resist claims of Spanish dominion in the Pacific, motivated in no small part by British designs on that ocean's whaling resources.

In that same year, the Spanish viceroy of Mexico sent two warships, under the command of Estéban José Martínez, to found a Spanish settlement at Nootka (Mills 1925, 111). By the time Martínez arrived, there was no longer any sign of the house Meares had built (Cook 1973, 143; Mills 1925, 111; see also Manning 1905, 312–14). The Spaniards arrived on May 5, 1789, and within two months formally claimed possession (Manning 1905, 326–27; Mills 1925, 111). A British ship, the *Ifigenia Nubiana,* was already present at their arrival, while the aforementioned *Northwest America* arrived from a voyage a short time later. The *Ifigenia's* Portuguese papers authorized it to capture any Spanish, Russian, or English vessel that attacked it and to bring the ship and its crew to Macao, where the ship would be claimed as prize and its crew treated as pirates (Cook 1973, 146–52, 160). Despite the Portuguese pretense, Martínez was aware that the *Ifigenia* was in truth a British ship (151). Martínez arrested the *Ifigenia* on the basis of its "having anchored in Spanish domain without a license from the king and . . . possessing instructions violating Spanish sovereignty" (152). Authority for his claim was based in two treaties to which England and Spain were parties. The 1670 Treaty of Madrid required that each side recognize the other's claims over New World territory they occupied. The 1763 Treaty of Paris forbade British ships from visiting or trading in Spain's New World territories (152). Eventually, for lack of Spanish manpower, the *Ifigenia* was released and ordered to leave Nootka to return to Macao (155–58). The *Northwest America* was arrested a short time later, its crew sent to China aboard an American ship (160; Manning 1905, 324–25).

A third ship, Captain Colnett's *Argonaut,* arrived on July 2. Martínez's subsequent meeting with Colnett was "the real genesis of the Nootka controversy" (Manning 1905, 331). Colnett argued that he had a license from the South Sea Company, which he claimed was a "grant and license from the king of England for a project on the northwest coast" (Cook 1973, 171). Martínez was offended by Colnett's claim of being an English ambassador, as it was clear to Martínez that Colnett was simply an employee of a private firm (171). Further, Martínez saw in Colnett "a dangerous threat to Spanish control over Nootka Sound" and ordered seizure of the *Argonaut* and its crew (173–75). When the final ship, the *Princess Royal,* returned to Nootka ten days after the arrival of the *Argonaut*, it, too, was seized by the Spanish (177–79).

When news of these events reached London, there were serious diplomatic consequences. Britain took the view that "Spain was asserting a claim 'to the exclusive Right of Sovereignty, Navigation and Commerce in the Territories, Coasts and Seas' of the Pacific" (Clayton 2000a, 330, citing correspondence of the British Foreign Secretary, the Duke of Leeds). In Parliament, Prime Minister William Pitt identified the Spanish claim as "indefinite in its extent, and which originated in no treaty, nor formal establishment of a colony, nor rested on any one of those grounds on which claims of sovereignty, navigation and commerce usually rested" (*Parliamentary History* [1816] 1966, 770). One threat to wider British interests was clear to Pitt: "If that claim were given way to, it must deprive this country of the means of extending its navigation and fishery in the southern ocean, and would go towards excluding his majesty's subjects from an infant trade, the future extension of which could not but be essentially beneficial to the commercial interests of Great Britain" (*Parliamentary History* [1816] 1966, 770; see also Jackson 2005, 93–94). The importance of the South Seas whale fishery in justifying Britain's actions was proclaimed by an anonymous pamphleteer supporting Spain and ridiculing the British government: "The Southern whale-fishery, that source of inexhaustible prosperity to the commerce and navigation of Great Britain, is now affirmed to be the material point in the dispute, and the true justification for our immense and profitless exertions" (*Errors of the British Minister* 1790, 31; see also Cook 1973, 221).

The British Opposition Leader considered that Britain's objective should include Spain's "renunciation of the claim set up with so little ground of reason" concerning the Americas and the Southern Ocean (*Parliamentary History* [1816] 1966, 776; Mills 1925, 115). In his instructions to Alleyne Fitzherbert, who would be negotiating with the Spanish on Britain's behalf, Pitt's Foreign Secretary wrote that "the claim of exclusive navigation or commerce in the American or Pacific Seas is equally inadmissible . . . the court of Spain can have no ground for asserting a right to obstruct the general freedom of navigation and fisheries in the American or Pacific Seas" (cited in Mills 1925, 116).

Details of the legal debate about who had the better claim are, for my purposes, less important than its outcome (see Clayton 2000b, 183–89; Cook 1973, 206; Mills 1925, 113–14). While the British Parliament had been readying for war (see *Parliamentary History* [1816] 1966, 770–76), negotiations proved successful. In October 1790 Britain signed a convention with Spain, known as the Anglo-Spanish Convention or the Nootka Convention. The agreement gave British and Spanish actors rights of navigation and fishing—including whaling—in the Pacific Ocean and the South Seas so long as the British remained outside ten sea leagues from coastal sites already settled by Spain and ensured rights to both Britain and Spain to settle the northwestern coast of North America, and its islands, farther north than the northernmost Spanish settlement as at April 1789. In South America, Britain was prohibited from creating any new settlements south of the southernmost Spanish settlement, though it would have the right to access the coast and islands for the purposes of its fisheries and to erect temporary buildings there also for those purposes (Clayton 2000a, 331; *Parliamentary History* [1816] 1966, 916–17). Britain agreed to prevent its subjects from using whaling and fishing expeditions in the South Atlantic and Pacific as a way of conducting illicit trade with Spanish colonies (Cook 1973, 236–37). Although the Committee of South Whalers was not directly involved in these events, this outcome gave its members what they had requested a year earlier in response to Spanish aggressions against sealers on the Atlantic Coast of South America (Harlow 1964, 316–17).

Pitt faced criticism in Parliament over how the treaty negotiations had been carried out on the ground that Great Britain had yielded, among other things, "formerly unrestricted rights of navigation and fishing in the Pacific . . . in return for a partial recognition of them" (Mills 1925, 119; *Parliamentary History* [1816] 1966, 990–91). Pitt responded that "though what this country had gained consisted not of new rights, it certainly did of new advantages. We had before a right to the Southern whale fishery, and a right to navigate and carry on fisheries in the Pacific Ocean, and to trade on the coasts of any part of it north-west of America; but that right not only had not been acknowledged but disputed and resisted; whereas, by the convention, it was secured to us—a circumstance which, though no new right, was a new advantage" (*Parliamentary History* [1816] 1966, 1002; see also Jackson 2005, 94).

Exploring the events at Nootka Sound is important not only for the links those events expose between Britain's desire to exploit southern whaling grounds, its negotiation of a broader set of access rights in the Pacific Ocean, and the intersection of public and private interests in its doing so, but also for what it can tell us about the practical mechanisms by which states demarcated zones of legal authority in ocean space. I next explore two such mechanisms: maps and private agents representing sovereign authorities.

Maps and the Agents of Empire

As tools for disseminating colonial legal authority, maps unite represented understandings of geographical space with the abstracted forms of legal structures that purport to govern that space. Their depiction of the boundaries of legal authority can be contrasted with the indicia of physical authority, such as settlements, border markers, fortresses and ships at sea.

Maps have both an imaginative and a legal, or law-generating, aspect. As to the imaginative dimension, geographer and cartographic historian Brian Harley, examining early British cartography in New England, identifies how maps represented that territory as empty and uninhabited by Indigenous peoples or marked by the boundaries of Indigenous nations. This played into narratives of the space as ripe for conquest and settlement (Harley 2001, 188–89). Similarly, Thongchai Winichakul on Siam and Matthew Edney on the British colonization of India have emphasized how maps generated new realities by inventing congruent national territories out of places whose boundaries had never been defined by their inhabitants in the ways to which the map gave form (Edney 1997, 15; Thongchai 1994, 129–30; see also Anderson 1991, 170–78; Harvey 1990, 228; Hau'ofa 1994, 153; Steinberg 2001, 35).

Harley also explores mapping as a way of enabling distant observers to access territory without being physically present there. He writes that it was mapping, a "visual rhetoric," that introduced the Americas to European consciousness and that this visual introduction affected how that territory was later colonized (Harley 1992, 523–24, 528; see also Dorsett and McVeigh 2012, 63; MacMillan 2006, 151–52). Harley analyzes European powers' use of maps to sketch the borders of territories well before the arrival of Europeans to those places. Through maps, "an anticipatory geography served to frame colonial territories in the minds of statesmen and territorial speculators back in Europe. Maps were the first step in the appropriation of territory. Such visualizations from a distance became critical in choreographing the Colonial expansion of early modern Europe" (Harley 1992, 532).

This imaginative dimension, allowing both seen and unseen spaces to be conceived as congruent wholes within defined boundaries, overlaps with mapping's legal dimension: maps as an enactment or representation of sovereign legal authority over territorial space (see Dorsett and McVeigh 2012, 58; Steinberg 2009, 472). Examples abound of the ways in which this has occurred on terrestrial territory. Historian Ken MacMillan argues that in the English explorations of the New World, "cartographers made a claim to sovereignty that was much stronger than could be made through mundane or ceremonial acts of possession, or in English-language descriptions of the territory," and that the publication of these maps contributed to other nations recognizing English sovereign claims (MacMillan 2006, 150, 159–60, 177). Cartographers could use imagery within maps to demonstrate effective English control of territory (165–68). In this process, maps both represent legal claims made through other means (for instance, through physical settlement) and embody in themselves those legal claims by, as MacMillan writes, the map constituting the "claim to sovereignty."

This process repeated at the domestic level, with maps used by states claiming sovereignty as against other states over distant territory to divide that territory between domestic sovereign subjects. Even in situations where a sovereign power such as England did not have physical experience or control of a region, by marking a map or by describing in words the cartographic features that a map embodied, it nonetheless transferred legal control of space to various of its subjects. This occurred in the granting of charters for the establishment of colonies in places like Virginia and Maine (Harley 2001, 192–95) and of trading and navigation rights in the Pacific to the EIC. In these instances, maps and cartographical language did not simply reflect a preexisting set of legal relations; they also played a definitive role in creating those relations.

These examples largely relate to demarcation of legal authority over terrestrial territory. Oceans differ from land in the general impossibility of demarcating zones of control by physical means. Thus, while even on land borders are infrequently marked in their entirety by artificial physical means, static signs of occupation abound there in a way they do not in the ocean—a space that moves and fluctuates (Jones 2016, 320; Steinberg 2013, 160). To a European imagination, boundaries in the open sea are also not identifiable by geophysical referents in the way that, say, a river or a mountain range might delineate the reach of a state. Thus, "lines in the ocean speak not with the authority of a geophysicality that cannot be fully grasped but with the authority of a juridical system that conceivably can" (Steinberg 2013, 162).

These features do not make the categories—imaginative and legal—apply any less to the mapping of ocean space than to the mapping of terrestrial territory. Cartographic representations of the ocean throughout history have shaped understandings of its nature (Steinberg 2009, 480–87). A significant example is the 1494 Treaty of Tordesillas between Portugal and Spain, modifying the effect of four papal bulls of the previous year. This treaty established a line across the globe, dividing it into an Eastern and a Western hemisphere for, respectively, Portuguese and Spanish exploration and colonizing missions. The line (initially described rather than visually depicted) did not mark sovereign ownership of the ocean, but rather established rights to each nation over trade and navigation on either side of it as well as to travel in its nominated direction in order to explore and colonize the lands it found there (Jones 2016, 326–27; Steinberg 2001, 75–86). The treaty allocated to Spain and Portugal the right to claim dominion over lands that had not yet been discovered by those powers, let alone occupied by them (see Elden 2013, 243). The line was, then, both an enactment that defined legal relations between Spain and Portugal and a means for each nation to conceptualize as theirs for the taking the space—as yet unexplored—on either side.

The effect of maps cannot be divorced from the actions of states and agents in creating and deploying them. In an important monograph explaining the uneven ways in which empires transmitted sovereignty through space, historian Lauren Benton critiques scholarship linking mapping and the spread of empire as, among other things, representing the processes of imperial consolidation as being unrealistically linear and homogeneous. A map representing a territory as under the control of one sovereign authority elides the ways that sovereignty in that space could be fragmented, layered, and concentrated within particular corridors and enclaves (Benton 2010, 10–23). Benton's larger account of the spread of sovereignty is valuable here for its emphasis on the role of agents of empire in spreading sovereign claims, particularly across oceans. Benton points to European "understandings of oceans as variegated spaces transected by law" and explains the various channels through which these transections occurred: trade routes that took shape as sea lanes; jurisdictional claims to marine corridors; and "claims to specific rights over limited ranges within the sea"—these rights involving "control of commerce and navigation along vaguely defined ocean corridors" (105–6). Benton emphasizes that the mariners who made use of these sea lanes considered themselves as continuing to be bound by the legal order of home, which they carried with them along the passages they navigated (108–10). This was part of a larger pattern in which legal cultures traveled with various agents of empire, including sailors and merchants, who conceived of themselves as subjects and representatives of their sovereigns. The administration of empire necessitated the delegation of legal authority to various officials, including these agents (3).

Maps, Agents, and the Nootka Convention

Maps and agents were important in the conflict between Britain and Spain over Nootka Sound. Cartography allowed Britain to imagine regions of the Pacific as coherent, knowable zones that could be made susceptible to British imperial aspirations. Geographer Daniel Clayton has argued, for instance, that the "British Cabinet viewed the Pacific through the cartographic field of vision developed, especially, by James Cook" (2000a, 331–32). This refers to Cook's charting of the Pacific Northwest region, drawing the contours of the coastlines against a cartographic grid, assigning place-names, and his officers' description of "this region as a space awaiting commercial development" (332). Elsewhere, Clayton further explains how Britain used both the map and the commercial ledger to construct and order the Pacific and assert its power within that territory (2000b, 178–83).

Notable in these descriptions of the process by which Nootka became the subject of colonial ambitions is the extent to which the British government's imagination of how that territory could be claimed and exploited depended on the accounts and maps of a small coterie of agents. These accounts were powerful enough to lead the government to contemplate war with Spain in order to protect its asserted dominions. Mapping and accompanying voyage descriptions were influential tools, not necessarily to demarcate lines of sovereign authority from the outset, but simply to imagine the possibilities of extending such authority over a scarcely known territory.

Cartography also had a more directly legal aspect in the resolution of the Nootka controversy. First, as part of its unsuccessful claim to the territory, Spain argued that the papal bulls of 1493 (precursors to the Treaty of Tordesillas, described above) gave it legal rights over the space (Clayton 2000a, 333; Mills 1925, 113–14). Second, Britain looked to existing Spanish mapping that proclaimed territory north of California as being "unknown to Europeans" (Clayton 2000a, 333). On this basis, the British referred to measures of latitude to argue that, contrary to Spain's assertions, Spanish sovereignty claims could not extend beyond 40° north and 45° south, thereby preserving, among other things, the British whale fishery (333).

In themselves, these two contrasting outcomes cannot generate firm conclusions about the role of mapping in disseminating sovereign control, since ultimately the British prevailed in their claim over Nootka not because of their greater legal claim, but because of their greater military power (Clayton 2000a, 335). Perhaps more instrumental than maps in the staking of Britain's claims were its commercial agents, such as Captain Colnett. As Clayton (Clayton 2000a, 335) notes, "British traders were viewed as public agents—as bearers of Britain's commercial soul"(see also Clayton 2000b, 174–76). Thus, Benton's insights about the role agents played in spreading sovereign claims are borne out by the events at Nootka. Setting out in pursuit of a private commercial interest, albeit one consonant with wider state interest, the actions of such merchants as Meares and Colnett, and the events that befell them, almost led to war between Britain and Spain over rights to control territory. The events they catalyzed secured for Britain a valuable victory in that, among other things, they negated Spanish claims to control over the Pacific and maintained whaling grounds for British exploitation.

The East India Company

Britain's success in the Nootka Sound conflict did not, however, secure British merchants unrestricted access to the Pacific Ocean. To the contrary, merchants such as the Enderbys had to contend with the preexisting monopoly of the EIC (Jackson 2005, 95). As noted above, the EIC enjoyed monopoly trading rights in the Pacific and Indian Oceans as against other British merchants. In Asia, the EIC could seize goods and ships from merchants trading illegally and had authority to try these merchants. By 1685 "the Company had virtually sovereign powers east of the Cape of Good Hope, and enormous rights over the lives and property of Englishmen who lived or traded east of the Cape of Good Hope to the Straits of Magellan" (Sherman 1976, 347). Challenging this monopoly in the eighteenth century, private entrepreneurs' quests for whales became "a prime incentive in forcing open the *mare clausum* of the Pacific" (Harlow 1964, 293).

When Enderby and other entrepreneurs proposed to search for whales east of the Cape of Good Hope, the company, convinced there were few whales to be found there, assumed the whalers' true intention was to engage in illegal trade in breach of its monopoly (Harlow 1964, 304; Jackson 2005, 91–92). The whalers petitioned key government figures to be allowed access to this region. The government petitioned the EIC's directors. After protracted negotiations involving the whalers, EIC directors, and such government notables as Prime Minister Pitt, the company was persuaded to sell to the whalers licenses allowing them to access company waters. These licenses were subject to strict conditions intended to protect the company's trading interests, including tight geographical limits (Harlow 1964, 304–5; Jackson 2005, 92). The company had reason to be wary: Captain Cook's Pacific explorations had established a "back door to the Indian Ocean and the China Seas," and the Enderbys and their associated lobbyists held influence with government and an "ambition . . . to range the Pacific without hindrance" (Harlow 1964, 305).

In 1786 Parliament enacted legislation (An Act for the Encouragement of the Southern Whale Fishery) financially incentivizing South Seas whaling. The Act bowed to company demands by excluding whalers from the Indian Ocean and a sizable portion of the Pacific: ships entering the Pacific by doubling Cape

Horn could not go farther north than the equator or farther west than five hundred leagues from the American coastline, and ships were prohibited from sailing east of the Cape of Good Hope (Harlow 1964, 305–7). Further pressure from the whalers and their government allies continued to erode the monopoly over the following two decades (307, 319–26). The Committee of South Whalers was useful to British state interests in this regard—its members formed a powerful group likely to be more effective at developing Pacific commerce than smaller merchants involved in the industry, while the government realized that exploiting the gains of the Nootka Convention would require radical changes to the EIC's monopoly (321).

The whalers' success in obtaining these rights was thus the culmination of a fruitful collaboration with the state, which saw in them an opportunity to extend its commercial whaling policy and, in the process, to curtail EIC power. The dual roles of cartography are evident in the ways these arrangements were negotiated. The imaginative dimension of mapping is implicated when we recall that monopoly rights were granted to the EIC in 1600, at a time when vanishingly little was known to England about the Pacific. Before that ocean was explored, before any part of it was settled by the English, before European shipping channels were established across it, the state was able to apportion rights to its control. These rights were granted through cartographic language referencing the Cape of Good Hope and the Straits of Magellan. That language could only be understood if one had in mind what was known about the region from the maps that were available at the time (see Harley 2001, 192). Mapping as a technology was gaining in prominence in England in this era. Maps such as Mercator's and Sir Francis Drake's world maps were available in the closing decades of the sixteenth century (MacMillan 2006, 151–61). That the state was able to grant rights over territories unknown and unexplored is, at least in part, a testament to the power of maps in allowing those spaces to be imagined as exploitable territories.

In the negotiation of whaling and trading rights over the Pacific Ocean, cartography also had a legal dimension. Lines of latitude and longitude, along with measures of distance from known coasts, took on legal form in telling both whalers and the EIC what rights they could exercise in particular territories. That cartographic language, and the underlying mapping it referenced, was in itself the expression of the legal relationship. Expressing the relationship cartographically was simultaneously expressing it in law.

Agents of empire—their sovereign ties and delegated legal authority—also were involved. Competing commercial agents continued to operate within the sphere of British law. The EIC exercised delegated legal authority to punish those British actors who interfered with its monopoly, even far from British territory. The whalers recognized the advisability of taking on the EIC in the halls of the government, whose sovereign authority bound them no matter where they roamed. The government, meanwhile, harnessed private commercial actors in order to carry out its policy objectives in establishing a southern whale fishery. In breaking down the monopoly of the EIC, the whalers changed the forms of British commercial activity and claims to legal authority in the Pacific Ocean.

Conclusion

Britain's exploration of the Pacific Ocean and its negotiation of legal control in that space was closely intertwined with the quest for whales. This chapter has outlined the ways that cartography facilitated both that exploration and the legal claims to which it gave rise and how, as agents of empire, whalers and other mariners were instrumental in staking those claims. By approaching questions of legal control in the ocean through narrow filters of time (the late eighteenth century); space (the Pacific Ocean); actors (Britain and its agents); and resources (whales), this chapter has aimed to deepen and contextualize understandings of the ways in which legal regimes are motivated, enacted, and reinforced in ocean space. Technologies and national preoccupations have changed over the past two hundred years, but the complex relationships between resource claims in the oceans, the sketching of legal boundaries, and the political contestations that accompany them, persist.

Acknowledgments
I am grateful to Bronwen Morgan, Fleur Johns, Irus Braverman, Elizabeth R. Johnson, Brendan Lim, Lauren Butterly, Harry Hobbs, Andrew Byrnes, Astrida Neimanis, Susan Reid, and participants at the UNSW Law HDR work-in-progress seminar and at the Baldy Center Ocean Legalities Workshop for their helpful comments on earlier drafts of this chapter. I am grateful also to Fruzsina Korosy for assistance with image formatting.

References
Anderson, Benedict. 1991. *Imagined Communities: Reflections on the Origin and Spread of Nationalism*. Rev. ed. London: Verso.
Benton, Lauren. 2010. *A Search for Sovereignty: Law and Geography in European Empires, 1400–1900*. New York: Cambridge University Press.
Burroughs, Walter. 2010. "The Adventures of Captain James Colnett RN." *Journal of Australian Naval History* 7 (1): 53–64.

Clayton, Daniel. 2000a. "The Creation of Imperial Space in the Pacific Northwest." *Journal of Historical Geography* 26 (3): 327–50.

Clayton, Daniel W. 2000b. *Islands of Truth: The Imperial Fashioning of Vancouver Island.* Vancouver: UBC Press.

Colnett, James. (1798) 1968. *A Voyage to the South Atlantic and Round Cape Horn into the Pacific Ocean.* Reprint. Amsterdam: N. Israel.

Cook, Warren L. 1973. *Flood Tide of Empire: Spain and the Pacific Northwest, 1543–1819.* New Haven, CT: Yale University Press.

Dorsett, Shaunnagh, and Shaun McVeigh. 2012. *Jurisdiction.* London: Routledge.

Edney, Matthew H. 1997. *Mapping an Empire: The Geographical Construction of British India, 1765–1843.* Chicago: University of Chicago Press.

Elden, Stuart. 2013. *The Birth of Territory.* Chicago: University of Chicago Press.

Ellickson, Robert C. 1989. "A Hypothesis of Wealth-Maximizing Norms: Evidence from the Whaling Industry." *Journal of Law, Economics and Organization* 5 (1): 83–97.

Errors of the British Minister, in the Negotiation with the Court of Spain. 1790. London: J. Debrett. https://babel.hathitrust.org/cgi/pt?id=aeu.ark:/13960/t9m33c646;view =1up;seq=6.

Frost, Alan. 1993. "Nootka Sound and the Beginnings of Britain's Imperialism of Free Trade." In *From Maps to Metaphors: The Pacific World of George Vancouver*, edited by Robin Fisher and Hugh Johnston, 104–26. Vancouver: UBC Press.

Great Britain. 1786. An Act for the Encouragement of the Southern Whale Fishery (26 Geo III, c. 50).

Grotius, Hugo. 1950. *Commentary on the Law of Prize and Booty.* Translated from the original manuscript of 1604 by Gwladys L. Williams, with the collaboration of Walter H. Zeydel. Oxford: Clarendon.

Harley, J. B. 1992. "Rereading the Maps of the Columbian Encounter." *Annals of the Association of American Geographers* 82 (3): 522–36.

Harley, J. B. (1994) 2001. "New England Cartography and the Native Americans." In *The New Nature of Maps: Essays in the History of Cartography*, edited by Paul Laxton, 169–95. Baltimore: Johns Hopkins University Press.

Harlow, Vincent T. 1964. *The Founding of the Second British Empire, 1763–1793.* Vol 2. London: Longmans, Green.

Harvey, David. 1990. *The Condition of Postmodernity: An Enquiry into the Origins of Cultural Change.* Oxford: Blackwell.

Hau'ofa, Epeli. 1994. "Our Sea of Islands." *Contemporary Pacific* 6 (1): 148–61.

Jackson, Gordon. 2005. *The British Whaling Trade.* St. John's, Newfoundland: International Maritime Economic History Association.

Jones, A. G. E. 1981. "The British Southern Whale and Seal Fisheries, Part 2: The Principal Operators." *The Great Circle* 3 (2): 90–102.

Jones, Henry. 2016. "Lines in the Ocean: Thinking with the Sea about Territory and International Law." *London Review of International Law* 4 (2): 307–43.

Lawson, Philip. 1993. *The East India Company: A History.* London: Longman Group.

MacMillan, Ken. 2006. *Sovereignty and Possession in the English New World: The Legal Foundations of Empire, 1576–1640.* Cambridge: Cambridge University Press.

Manning, William Ray. 1905. "The Nootka Sound Controversy." PhD diss., University of Chicago, 1904, reprinted in *Annual Report for the American Historical Association for the Year 1904*, 279–476. Washington, DC: Government Printing Office.

Meares, John. 1791. *Voyages Made in the Years 1788 and 1789, from China to the N. W. Coast of America: with an Introductory Narrative of a Voyage Performed in 1786, from Bengal, in the Ship Nootka*. Vol. 2. London: Logographic Press. http://www.cap.amdigital.co.uk/Documents/Details/UCSD_F879_M468_1791_v2.

Melville, Herman. (1851) 1985. *Moby-Dick*. London: Chancellor.

Mills, Lennox. 1925. "The Real Significance of the Nootka Sound Incident." *Canadian Historical Review* 6 (2): 110–22.

Parliamentary History of England, from the Earliest Period to the Year 1803 (*Parliamentary History*). (1816) 1966. Vol. 28. Reprint. New York: AMS.

Sanger, Chesley W. 2003. "'Oil Is an Indispensable Necessity of Life:' The Impact of Oscillating Oil and Baleen (Bone) Prices on Cyclical Variations in the Scale and Scope of Northern Commercial Whaling, 1600–1900." *International Journal of Maritime History* 15 (2): 147–57.

Sherman, Arnold A. 1976. "Pressure from Leadenhall: The East India Company Lobby, 1660–1678." *Business History Review* 50 (3): 329–55.

Stackpole, Edouard A. 1972. *Whales and Destiny: The Rivalry between America, France and Britain for Control of the Southern Whale Fishery, 1785–1825*. Amherst: University of Massachusetts Press.

Steinberg, Philip E. 2001. *The Social Construction of the Ocean*. Cambridge: Cambridge University Press.

Steinberg, Philip E. 2009. "Sovereignty, Territory, and the Mapping of Mobility: A View from the Outside." *Annals of the Association of American Geographers* 99 (3): 467–95.

Steinberg, Philip E. 2013. "Of Other Seas: Metaphors and Materialities in Maritime Regions." *Atlantic Studies* 10 (2): 156–69.

Thongchai Winichakul. 1994. *Siam Mapped: A History of the Geo-Body of a Nation*. Honolulu: University of Hawai'i Press.

12. THE SEA WOLF AND THE SOVEREIGN

STEPHANIE JONES

It is important to be wary of thinking about oceans only as metaphors. Suspicion of imagined-seas is producing significant new insights into the ocean as a varying materiality: as a site of real human (particularly labor) relations and as a messy or elegant "assemblage" of the nonhuman (animal and mechanistic) and the more-than-human (natural and technological) (Anderson 2012; Blum 2010; Peters 2010; Steinberg 2013). That agenda-setting work in this field is framed by a criticism of metaphor tells us how powerful abstraction can be. Assailing metaphor affirms the historical power of the unreal: it acknowledges the sometimes conservative and sometimes revolutionary force of abstracted oceans within artistic, legal, and political cultures. I am interested in the ocean as an ongoing source of symbols, metaphors, and similes that can variously curtail or enlarge how we imagine the world. This chapter considers how one maritime metaphor—the sea wolf—expresses material authority and power.

Metaphors can deplete or illuminate a feeling, slow down or speed up the formation of an idea, deaden or enliven experimental thought (Derrida 1974). They can configure "a new pertinence, a new congruence" (Ricoeur 1978, 146). Attending to metaphors is important to understanding the constitution of authority in both public life and philosophy; and negotiating animal metaphors continues to be a central part of theoretical debates over sovereign power. Most persistently, a long tradition of theorizing sovereignty has produced what Jacques Derrida names a "genelycology": a genealogy of wolf (*lukos*) metaphors, metonyms, and tropes. Across the opening session of *The Beast and the Sovereign*, Derrida explains that we will be following,

FIGURE 12.1. Vancouver Island grey wolf (*Canis lupus crassodon*) alpha female swimming across estuary. A nonmetaphorical sea wolf. ©Bertie Gregory/naturepl.com. Reproduced with permission.

> stealthy as wolves, the trace of the wolf... the path of a track that...
> leads to the alliance (from north, south, east or west) between all these
> claimants to sovereignty who thus assemble and so resemble each other:
> the wolf, man, God. The one *for* the other... the sovereign, the wolf,
> man, God, the wolf-man, God-man, God-wolf, God-the-father-the-wolf
> or grandmother-wolf. (Derrida 2009, 57–58)

With the wolf as his central character, Derrida reads political and legal philosophy both in relation to animal fables and as an animal fable (Derrida 2009;
de Ville 2012). This method (prowling and fabular) allows him to track how
beasts and sovereigns are continually paired and to notice how all forms of this
pairing—from opposition to synecdoche—draw out ever-deeper similarities:
most importantly, their sameness in being "outside-the-law" (Derrida 2009,
17). At many points in the seminars, this is an amplification of Carl Schmitt's
influential perception that "Sovereign is he who decides on the exception"
(Schmitt 2005, 5). Derrida wolfishly circumscribes sovereignty as locatable,
determinable, and most manifest in the figure—individual and institutional—
who has the power to suspend the law (declare exception) and to reinstitute a
norm with extrajudicial force (and so is outside the law). More unstoppably,
where an animal or beast occurs in order to lend affectivity to sovereignty as
an imagined indivisibility (as a foundational violence, as an initiating contract,
as a first and last source of authority, et cetera), Derrida demonstrates how
these animals really tell us about sovereignty as always conditional, variable,
and unstable. For Derrida, where animals and beasts are cited to consolidate

sovereignty as an essential relation, they can be shown to reveal contingencies, surprises, deferrals. In his terms, demonstrating this is both to deconstruct the "classical concept of nation-state sovereignty" and to provide a way of thinking about how this deconstruction is "happening in the world today" (Derrida 2009, 75–76).

In this chapter I take license and inspiration from Derrida's animal perceptions and wolfish method: but I do so offshore. I explore how a consideration of a "genelycology" of sea wolves might inflect ideas about authority, and so I ask what the figure of the sea wolf might mean for sovereignty. This exploration and questioning is also a pursuit. Part I locates the sea wolf as a fable; part II tracks the sea wolf as a metaphor of the pirate; and in conclusion, the sea wolf is captured as a potential paradigm. In these ways, I hope to apprehend how symbols and tropes, metaphors and similes inspired by the ocean can be critical material for changing how we conceive of and address sovereign power.

Part I: Fables

Homo homini lupus. Who in the face of all his experience of life and of history, will have the courage to dispute this assertion?
—SIGMUND FREUD, *Civilization and Its Discontents*

NATURE (the Art whereby God hath made and governes the World) is by the Art of man, as in many other things, so in this also imitated, that it can make an Artificial Animal.
—THOMAS HOBBES, *Leviathan*

Colloquially, *sea wolves* as a term for wolf-fish takes us into animal waters; to deep-sea, shelf-dwelling, bottom-feeding, clam-crunching perciforms. Surfacing, we might swim toward sea wolves as wolves-of-the-sea: to the orca as a definitive maritime predator, as a superb articulation of oceanic violence, and a superlative figure of complex animal otherness. This animal seems to materialize and distill "wolf" as a rhetoric of predation: an effect compounded by the interchangeability of wolf, tiger, and lion when it comes to the naming of creatures at sea. Recently, *lobo marino* (sea wolf in Spanish/sea lion in English/ scientific name *Pinnipedia*) has been tracked back forty-two million years through the fossil record to a common ancestry with a land wolf, *Canidae*. This ancestor is the *Miacas cognate* of the Eocene era, who became the land-dwelling, flipper-bearing *Puijila darwini*, who sometime after twenty-three million years ago, moved to sea (Rybczynski, Dawson, and Tedford 2009). Here is the sea wolf, in fact. And here, beyond fables and names, we strain to comprehend different meters of time and nonhuman geographies; other measures of onshore/offshore, land and sea. We encounter an entirely unknowable idea of what might constitute—so far beyond the concerns of political theology or state theory—being-sovereign and the notion of a sovereign decision. The great effort and achievement of many of the chapters in this book is to strive to do just that, to generate a vigilance around the unknowability of how algae, vent-communities, ice-ecologies, and whales *must* be stories of life that confound the regulatory narratives of science and law (Amy Braun; Susan Reid; Katherine G. Sammler; Philip E. Steinberg, Berit Kristoffersen, and Kristen L. Shake, all this volume).

Closer to home, in the Anglo-Saxon sources, watery wolves are also both more and less fabulous than they seem. Etymologically, sea wolf might take us to Anglo-Saxon poetry and to *brimwylf* (lake or water or sea wolf) and, more particularly, to "the ocean-wolf, the hateful sea-woman" (Ebbutt 1910, 39). This is Grendel's magical mermaid mother of the tenth-/eleventh-century verse epic *Beowulf*. The "misbegotten" progeny of Cain and a primal "outlaw," she is foul and only briefly mentioned but vivid in battle and capable of towering grief (Fairman 2000, 151; Heaney and Donoghue 2002, lines 1263, 1266). The poem describes a watery she-wolf marking a beastly disorder, ascendency over generations of which proves, if only briefly, man's (*the* man's) sovereignty. The affinities between Brimwylf (the mother of the beast) and Beowulf (the sovereign)—their mutual rage, their mutual myth making, their inescapably mutual destruction—lend a prophetic and doomed imagery of mutual attentiveness to "zoopoetics" (Derrida 2002, 6). Myth here is an expression of stranger-intimacies. This is also the suggestion of work on Scandinavian pirate cultures of the ninth century, which indicates that contemporary Anglo-Saxon poetry might record the fear felt by the English, but also how the Vikings chose to portray themselves. Described generally as predatory beasts, and specifically as moving like wolves; referred to as "wave-men" and as "slaughter-wolves," the Vikings conceivably politicized their activities as a beastly becoming that is reflected back to them by the English (Price 2014, 63). While ideas of political communities and international relations in the early medieval period might make little sense in modern terms, this zoopoetics expresses a recognizably sovereign ambition. The imagery of the sea wolf expresses a threat to (English) coastal sovereignties and presents sovereignty as an ambition for dominion. But as a shared *poesis* of sea wolves, mutually created, it might also testify to the ways in which histories of dominion are also histories of integration.

Poetic, colloquial, scientific references to sea wolves can, then, be gathered into a fable of premodernity that is too vast (in time, in territory, in species, in variety of tone) to adduce to a testimony of *homo homini lupus*. Although as a modernization of this fable, Jack London's *The Sea Wolf* (1904) seems to provide belated proof. This adventure novel tells the story of Humphrey van Weyden, an urban intellectual rescued from a wreck by the charismatic Captain Wolf Larson and put to work on his ship. It is packed with tales of kidnap, failed mutiny, vengeance, and thwarted love, offering long scenes of shipboard violence as representations of man's wolfish capacity for inhumanity to man. (The word *wolf* occurs hundreds of times—obsessively, even—across the narrative, as in London's writing and life more generally.) In London's own terms, his Sea Wolf is the *Übermensch* (superhuman, overman) of "Thus Spake Zarathustra," and the novel is a denouncement of Nietzsche's triumphant allegory (London 2002, 159). The immensely strong, amoral Larson is a parabolic fascist and sociopath, natively intelligent but inexhaustibly depraved, murderous, and nihilistic. However, *The Sea Wolf* is not only a wolf fable or an anti-*Übermensch* allegory: it is a realist novel. While the ship is sometimes a synecdoche for a state of nature (an arcane scene), and sometimes an analogue of state (a technology), it is most insistently a materially oceanic site. It is a place of brutal physical and psychological exposure. In this register, the novel does not map out as an opposition to Nietszche's tale.

If Larson is the *Übermensch*, then van Weyden is *der letzte Mensch* (the last man), the allegorical other of the *Übermensch* in Nietzsche's terms. In "Thus Spake Zarathustra," this is a desultory figure, enthralled and denatured by God. If London's novel were a simple refutation of Nietzsche's parable, this figure should be recuperated in his own spiritual and moral terms. But this is only partially how the narrative unfolds. Van Weyden is both unmade and made by Larson. The narrative lingers on his physical development and broadening skills under the sovereignty of the Sea Wolf: and so his attachment to Larson is too ambiguous to meet the demands of allegorical argument. As a character of psychological realism and relation, the Sea Wolf of London's novel is perhaps closer kin to the wolves of Freud's Wolf Mann and his compulsive/delicious fairy tale fear of being devoured (Freud 1999).

Freud's case study informs psychoanalytic approaches to the wolf as a literary character across cultures (Bettelheim 1976; Zipes 1993). In this tradition, Hélène Cixous's iconic essay "Love of the Wolf" (2005) captures the wolf as our animal self and as an erotics of love as consumption, ferocity, and fear. It moves between the child's delight at the prospect of being "eaten up" and our perverse desire to be "wolfed down" to yield a metaphysics of the wolf as "the guide" to our self-destructive instincts and impulses toward sacrifice. By the end of the essay, the insistent love of the wolf has tamed the wolf; the predator has become the prey: "The Wolf is the Lamb." So Cixous understands the wolf as a way of almost-knowing the perversities of being human. This is played out in London's novel, as van Weyden is repelled and attracted, destroyed and remade, by the consuming ferocity of Larson. Via Cixous, we find in London's novel a story of sovereignty as an inchoate relation of violence and abjection, desire and fear. But the fate of Larson—the hunter turned prey, who eventually is at the mercy of van Weyden, who cannot bear to kill him—helps us to suspect that when Cixous cryptically concludes that "The Wolf is the Lamb" she is not suggesting that the wolf has become the lamb, only that the wolf will be in the place of the lamb. Unrepentant to the end, Larson is only ever a wolfish lamb. For—as all the old fables tell us—the wolf is always wolfish. As a sustained portrait of inhumanity, London's early twentieth-century novel invites us to think about modern sovereignty as, finally, an archaic and always potentially cruel prerogative.

In contrast to London's novel, film director Andrew McLaglen's *The Sea Wolves* (1980) seems to present a triumphant measure of man's humanity. His film dramatizes Operation Creek, a 1943 covert attack on a German merchant ship aimed at interrupting the relay of information to U-boats. Early scenes of the film explain that the operation of British forces in neutral Goa's territorial waters would be illegal under the laws of war, necessitating the use of unofficial (not just secret) agents. The affectionately humorous portrayal of the group of aging Allied protagonists affirms the moral necessity of the illegal operation, and the drama and tension of the film are primarily logistical, not ethical. However, the briefly portrayed U-boats (sleek and secret predators) are the most wolfish figures in the film. The title, then, is potentially descriptive of both predatory protagonists and predatory antagonists—of both the goodies and the baddies—and so brings them closer together, discomfiting the clear moral and ethical exactitudes of the film. This point becomes more resonant if we notice a century-old and continuing tradition of naming UK and US guided missiles and classes of submarine *Seawolf* (Military Analysis Network n.d.; Military Factory n.d.; Military Today n.d.; US Navy Fact File n.d.).

Attached to these technologies, the term *Seawolf* becomes Hobbes's Leviathan: sovereignty expressed as an artificial animal, a mimesis of God's killer whale. Alongside the unmanned underwater vehicles, deep-sea robotic lives, and fleets of ocean floor chemical weapons discussed by other contributors to this volume (see chapters by Irus Braverman, Jessica Lehman, Elizabeth R. Johnson, and Astrida Neimanis), this *Seawolf* materializes Hobbes's Leviathan. These weapons tell us that the state is more-than-secular in its arrogance but all-too bleakly human in its defensiveness. Further, moving from London's Sea

Wolf as the *Übermensch* to the *Seawolf* as an *Unterseeboot* (undersea boat) takes us to the rackety relationship between discourses of sovereignty and discourses of humanitarianism that emerged from the second world war.

In 1937, Schmitt complained about the Allies' attempt to define the U-boat as a form of piracy. He argued that doing so was not authorized by international law because it involved a sly declination from an established, critically sparse, nonpartisan, internationally established definition of a human activity to a definition of piracy as an unbounded, morally loaded, generally normative conception of any inhumane action or technology (Schmitt 2011, 27–31). In other words, he refutes the characterization of the submarine as piratical because this partakes in a rhetoric of humanitarianism that he refuses to acknowledge as legally legitimate. This short essay reads alongside Schmitt's monumental books of the early 1930s through to the 1940s, in which he articulates his rejection of humanity as a political-legal category and of the humanitarian as a language of law and community. In broad summary, Schmitt deplores this discourse for two reasons. He rejects it because it attempts to surpass the friend/enemy and citizen/stranger distinctions that he sees as energizing political community, giving meaning to political life, and to life as political. He also rejects it because he sees it as a trick, a deceitful pursuit of old-style sovereignty: in Derrida's summary, "the ruse of a wolf, a werewolf . . . a lying rhetoric, an ideological disguise" (Derrida 2009, 71; see also Schmitt 2002, 2005, 2006). For Schmitt, the humanitarian agenda is a denaturing liberal strategy and a betrayal of the energies of the *ius publicum Europaeum*. But it is also a farce. The attempted characterization of the U-boat as piratical (as categorically illegitimate within the laws of war), considered alongside *Seawolf* as a technology of war (where the naming carries the trace of haughty lawlessness without the legal force of "pirate"), seems to provide proof of this hypocrisy.

To name a weapon *Seawolf* is to make a boast. As a boast of post–World War II democracies, it seems to reveal a crude sovereign will for hegemony, for which the nuance of the humanitarian agenda is barely a cover. The wolf is only ever pretending to be a lamb. However, the rhetorical flourish of *Seawolf* does not necessarily lend its fullest force to Schmitt's implacable, past-century arguments about the falsities of liberalism. Rather, interpreting the *Seawolf* as a symbol of the sly fearsomeness, dubious ethics, and marginal legalities of modern liberal democracies might rather lead us to recent work on the precariousness of the world order and to the possibilities of praxis in the coming century. In part II, I track through some of this recent work in pursuit of wolfish pirates and piratical sovereigns.

Part II: Metaphors

When Hobbes founds sovereignty by reference to the state in which "man is a wolf to men",
homo hominis lupus, in the word "wolf" (lupus) we ought to hear an echo of the wargus and
caput lupinem . . . : at issue is not simply fera bestia and natural life, but rather a zone of in-
distinction between the human and the animal, a werewolf, a man who is transformed into
a wolf and a wolf who is transformed into a man—in other words, a bandit, a homo sacer.
—GIORGIO AGAMBEN, *Homo Sacer*

Where did you sail from, over the running sea-lanes? Out on a trading spree or roving the
waves like pirates, sea-wolves raiding at will, who risk their lives to plunder other men?
—HOMER (TRANS. FAGLES), *The Odyssey*

The Odyssey twice poses these questions. In book 3, Nestor politely queries
Telemachus, and in book 9 Polyphemus aggressively interrogates Odysseus
(Homer 1996, 3.81–83, 9.285–88). Robert Fagles's scholarly edition of the ancient text is more a fidelitous translation and less a creative transposition, and
this makes his decision to invoke "sea-wolves" interesting. The syntax of the
Homeric Greek suggests only one turn of phrase, and many centuries of English translators have managed their poetic decisions around an unelaborated
"pirates," though William Morris prefers "strong thieves over water" and, taken
alone, λῃϊστῆρες translates as "raider" or "robber" (Homer 1887, 3.73, 9.255). So
Fagles's mediation of pirates into sea-wolves might seem to take liberties with
the original. Although within a story that portrays a world of animals (as food,
as wealth, as sacrifice), and in the context of a plot that is driven by human/non-
human relations (men and women/gods, beasts, and ghosts), the invocation of
sea-wolves feels broadly authentic. It is of a piece with Homer's images and style.
It is evocative of an intimate political theology of gods and men as hunters and
prey. And it enlivens an arcane coastal order of half-enclosed/part-exposed seas
and islands in which man's violence is not strictly codified into legitimate and
illegitimate, but appears more fluidly as a law of nature (da Souza 1999, 2014).

Fagles's choice of metaphor tells us that Polyphemus's question is answered
at the opening of book 9 and in the middle of book 14: the two points at which
Odysseus sanguinely describes sailing to raid coastal towns—communities of
strangers, *not* declared enemies—before and after his decade fighting in Troy
(Homer 1996, 9.45–48, 14.261–66). These descriptions of his piracy are both
part of the epic order of events and continuous with the characterization of
Odysseus as a shrewd and opportunistic military leader, sea captain, and island
king. In light of all this, the reference to sea wolves makes sense as part of
Fagles's effort to translate *The Odyssey* as a Late Geometric/pre-Archaic historiography of political community; or, of a pre-Classical or pre-Hellenistic

narrative about the nature of sovereign violence. His metaphoric sea wolves are in pursuit of poetic and historical accuracy. Nonetheless, we might choose to read this poetic metaphor as an invitation to a more excessive (less metrical) engagement with pirates and their metaphors and, indeed, with pirates as metaphors.

Classically, Cicero turns to the pirate only in order to expound his definition of the legitimate enemy under the laws of war. *De Officius* gives us the pirate forcefully but merely as he to whom no obligation is owed: he appears in the text to foreground the legitimate enemy, to whom one is bound by complex duties (Cicero 1991, 141). This idea is perversely captured in Edward Coke's most famous and much-quoted summary of Cicero's pirate as *hostis humani generis*: in other words, as the "enemy of all" he is still most fully and precisely— as a modern term of international legal art—not "an enemy," not "the enemy" (Coke 2003, 200; Harding 2006). As the global imagination attests, this tradition of liminal definition has lent the pirate sharp metaphoric potential. The pirate is used to categorize the state's foundational relationship to violence, the sovereign's fundamental embattlement and imperial will, and both positive and natural law theories of state (Benton 2010; Thomson 1994; Tilly 1985). Almost as persistently, the pirate categorizes the unending energy, resourcefulness, individualism, and innovations of capitalism (Leeson 2011). More rousingly, the pirate categorizes the freedom fighter and ever-becoming socialist revolutionary (Rediker 1987, 2004, 2014). However, more recently—post-9/11—there has been a ratcheting up in the use of piratical rhetoric as an expression, warning, or promotion of world (dis)order. Piracy has become a notably high rhetorical register in which to express a vast new iteration of what was once a sporadic delimitation. Like the wave, the whale, and the remote sensor in other chapters within this book, piracy begins to appear as a form of life that has been deterritorializing and reterritorializing the ocean in wildly surreptitious ways (Stefan Helmreich; Zsofia Korosy; and Jessica Lehman, all this volume).

Analyzing international relations, it is arguable that the characterization of resistance as piracy, and the use of piracy to delimit the definition of terrorism, is enabling the hegemonic eradication of legitimate political communities (Chomsky 2003). Analyzing political history, it is arguable that eighteenth- and nineteenth-century deployments of piracy as a term of savage international art against working-class and colonial peoples has established a legal model that is fast replacing the old rules of international warfare (Policante 2014). And in a dramatic legal-poetic register, it is arguable that piracy is not coherently defined by a material space of action ("the high seas"), but gains cogency (in law, in poetry, in politics) only as a deterritorialized act of risk. In this view, centuries of definitions of piracy become proof and prophesy of a state's right to wage perpetual war, regardless of territory: indeed, of a state's right to define itself as a relation of "infinitely intense, preparatory, and provisional" violence against "unjust" enemies (Heller-Roazen 2009, 180, 186).

Together, these investigations of the vast metaphorical reach of piracy gather into a sense of the world as a legal situation defined by immanence *itself*: that is, by a looming and alarming sense that international law is ever-less categorical and that states are increasingly unbinding themselves from terms of combat and categories of combatant that traditionally have limited violence, and so we are facing a colossally hegemonic future. We might say this is a vision of a wolfish world. We might imagine sea wolves as a coming image of a prowling in-distinction between sea and land, where this blurring is an analogue for the erasure of international relations as a careful negotiation of sovereign territory. As a metaphor of the piratical, sea wolves might be a coming-symbol of a rising, howling political theology of internecine war. On the other hand, reminding ourselves of this animal might return us from piracy to pirates: from the synecdoche to a form of biological life. That is, wolves appear not as hunters, but as the hunted, within work that is concerned with twenty-first-century hegemony.

Giorgio Agamben argues that the modern state unrelentingly attests itself through the suspension of law and that this permanent "state of exception" renders the life of subjects categorically bound and "bare." In Agamben's insistent similes, the modern citizen is politically sparse and legally vulnerable like the werewolf of fable, the bandit of lore, the exiled/sacred/cursed man of Roman culture (Agamben 1998, 2005). This thesis is, in part, invigorating because it works through a set of compelling figures and analogies. Derrida points out that Agamben relies on mistranslations of his key terms and contends that his account is not cogent because sometimes Agamben seems to be describing a relation that is immemorial and at other times a relation that is definitively modern. (Agamben's reliance on classical sources requires the first, but as a completion of Michel Foucault's biopolitical insights, it must only be the second). Most sharply, however, Derrida points out that wolves are "being forgotten" (Derrida 2009, 92): they appear more often and more ambivalently in the history of European thought than it suits Agamben's purpose to recognize (Agamben 1998). This criticism of Agamben's selective use of metaphor joins to Derrida's argument that noticing the animals (*all* the animals) tells us about the importance of biopower: but it also, importantly, tells us that sovereignty cannot be accounted as a singular and inexorable relation, as Agamben argues.

What happens if we add the sea wolf to the list of wolves Agamben misses or ignores? Taking us offshore, the missing sea wolf might (to start) symbolize Agamben's startling silence on non-European situations. This silence is perhaps filled by work that understands the colony as the "location *par excellence*" of the state of exception (Mbembe 2003, 24). And this silence is critically addressed by work on colonial "states of emergency" and postcolonial sovereignties and by the argument that these are the situations and locations that define modern sovereignty as an essential relation (Hussain 2003). More critically, recognizing the "lumpy juridical order" of imperial and colonial states has led to a refusal of Agamben's thesis on the inexorable naturalization of "the exception" and insists that sovereignty is more accurately understood as processes of layering, imperfection, eccentricity, and delegation (Benton 2010, 290). Within these critical contexts, the sea wolf could symbolize the need for more complex accounts of historical geographies within debates about sovereignty. In other words, the sea wolf might—at last—become a metaphor of materiality itself, growling at the abstracted wolves within a circumscribed European history of ideas. However, as I explore, by way of conclusion, the sea wolf might have more vivid and specific paradigmatic potential than is synthesized by this metaphor of materiality.

Conclusion

Here the Negroes faced about, and though scorning peace or truce, yet fain would have had a respite. But, without pause, overleaping the barrier, the unflagging sailors again closed. Exhausted, the blacks now fought in despair. Their red tongues lolled, wolf-like, from their black mouths. But the pale sailors' teeth were set; not a word was spoken; and, in five minutes more, the ship was won.
—HERMAN MELVILLE, "Benito Cereno"

This passage describes the end of the fight for control of the *San Dominick* in Herman Melville's famous novella "Benito Cereno" (1856). Amasa Delano, captain of the American ship *Bachelor's Delight*, narrates the scene. The plot begins when Delano notices the Spanish ship is badly rigged and oddly anchored and rows out to offer help. Tensely welcomed aboard, Delano becomes increasingly confused by the oddly attentive relationships between the crew and their cargo of slaves, and particularly between the captain, Don Cereno, and his personal slave, Babo. Trying to make sense of the friable atmosphere on the ship, Delano begins to suspect Cereno has piratical designs on the *Bachelor's Delight*. But as he is leaving the *San Dominick*, it becomes clear the ship is under the control of Babo, and—threatened with death if they don't comply—Cereno and the crew have been pretending to Delano that the cargo of slaves are still under their command. Delano decides to seize the ship, rallying his crew with the promises of their share of the cargo (slaves and gold) and giving them confidence by nominating his chief mate (once a privateer, possibly a pirate) to lead the venture. The final part of the novella—in which the initial uprising by the slaves is told—is composed of the documents and depositions presented to the vice-regal courts in Lima, to which the *Bachelor's Delight* has escorted the captured *San Dominick*. Babo is sentenced to death, his body burned, his head displayed in the Plaza. Cereno, broken by the ordeal, haunted by Babo, dies soon thereafter.

Debate continues over the political entailments of this story: is it complicit with the racist tones of Delano's first-person narrative, or does it condemn racism and slavery, imperial Europe, and antebellum America? In this critical context, much is made of Melville's transposition of his source story (taken from the memoirs of the real Amaso Delano) from 1805 to 1799, inviting interpretations in the context of Toussaint Louverture's successful revolt, revolution, and establishment of the state of Haiti. These analyses sometimes indict, and sometimes redeem, the story (Beecher 2007). Alternatively—bypassing the ambiguities of voice and ignoring the weight of realist detail through which Melville builds suspense and generates moral ambivalence—it is possible to read the novella as a parable. In *Ex Captivitate Salus: Experiences from the Period 1945–47*, Schmitt writes: "I am the last conscious representative of the *jus publicum Europaeum*, its last teacher and student in an existential sense, and I am experiencing its demise just as Benito Cereno experienced the journey of the pirate ship" (quoted in Scheuerman 1999, 177; see also Beebee 2006). In the most persuasive interpretation of this startling statement, the American ship carrying the defeated Spanish captain describes "Schmitt's experience as a prisoner (both literally and metaphorically) of an ethnically and racially mixed American demos, now in control of the 'ship' of European history." In Schmitt's hands, the story is an allegory and "nightmare" about "liberal assimilationism" (Scheueman 1999, 177). Further, the emphasis on the "pirate" ship connects to Schmitt's declaration that the "Jew as Citizen of the World" is "like the pirate, who does not have the protection of any state and is not authorised by any state" (Policante 2015, 181). Through the metaphor of the pirate, then, Schmitt assembles American liberals and Jews as illegitimate within the *jus publicum Europaeum*: they are beyond the line.

There are many ways of announcing Schmitt's racism. Here, it is revealed in his reduction of Melville's story to a self-serving parable; his crude extraction of ship of state and pirate ship metaphors; his consequent failure to acknowledge the ship-bound slave as a freedom fighter. It is perhaps even more troubling when metaphors cover/reveal inadvertent repudiations. Agamben's choice to revive *homo sacer* as his limit category and central metaphor has caused perplexity in these terms. Arguably, misreading his sources allows him to define a powerful archetype for the modern citizen/subject: but returning to a more fulsome material history of *homo sacer* yields a less parabolic idea of (nonstate) excommunication, and recognizing this compromises the force of his thesis. In particular, lifting *homo sacer* from its initial formulation within histories (both classical and modern) in which slaves are "ubiquitous"—and slave revolts are far more common than historiography usually conveys—verges on disavowal (Fiskesjö 2012). That is, Agamben's metaphors—bound so heavily to expanding on Schmitt's insights—inadvertently continue Schmitt's racist ignorance/dismissal of the slave as freedom fighter and revolutionary. However, if we look at Agamben's broader textual strategies, a very different idea of his relation to material histories of lived oppression might emerge. To explicate his idea of bare life, Agamben constantly fidgets between the figure of the werewolf, the bandit, and *homo sacer*. He endlessly invokes, repeats, circles, repeats. Each figure is a version of the other; each is inadequate in itself; each takes meaning only in the process of shifting back and forth: wolf, bandit, *homo sacer*, wolf. Recognizing this, it is arguable that his metaphors do not entail a failure of recognition: rather, they perform the entrapping and deadly power of metaphor itself.

Agamben says that "the bloody mystifications of a new planetary order" prompted him to write *Homo Sacer* and that this led him to understand that "the theory of the state is the reef on which the revolutions of our century have been shipwrecked." He diagnoses sovereignty so that a new kind of political life can be made: a "coming community" (Agamben 1998, 12; 1993). This justifies his ahistorical method of working with paradigms but is also an exhortation to find new paradigms (Agamben 2002). So imagining sea wolves might—as I have explored across this chapter—vivify sovereignty as essential and indivisible, or, as disparate and divisible: but imagining sea wolves might also remind us that we need to find new (or perhaps renew old) paradigms so that we can reimagine—find new categories and limits—for relationships of authority and power.

The intrigue of a metaphor is sometimes located in the traces of previous usage or in a congestion of references (sea wolves/pirates/sovereigns). Metaphors can be strong and provocative because they gather complexity into a sleek image or smooth rhetorical turn. Equally, a rhetorical figure (a literary character or poetic trope) may be strong and provocative because it is *almost* but not quite a metaphor: because it approaches but finally refuses to partake in a lineage of metaphors. This is the sea wolf as almost but not quite a pirate or a sovereign; the pirate as like a wolf but never quite as a sovereign. Or maybe it is the ship-bound slave of "Benito Cereno": not a wolf, but wolf-like. This simile for the prey turned hunter turned prey is too bound to Melville's realist aesthetic to read allegorically and so cannot be drawn into a genelycology of conceptual wolves. On the other hand, it is hard to unbind the wolf from fable, myth, allegory, philosophy. So the wolfish-slave as a (re)new paradigm of resistance, freedom-fighting, revolution is intriguing because it is poised between abstraction and materiality. Further, in considering nonhuman forms of life at sea, this book offers huge potential for imagining new forms of human life as a juridical and political relation to sovereignty. These may not all be hopeful, and some join to warnings of an illimitably violent future world order. Yet others may surface new symbols, tropes, paradigms that grip and energize the imagination and that enjoin us to think up a different future.

Acknowledgments

This chapter has greatly benefited from the wise and detailed advice of Elizabeth R. Johnson and Irus Braverman. Many thanks are due also to Ben Jones (for directing me to *Puijila darwini*) and to Emilios Christodoulidis (for help with the Greek). I am also grateful to the participants of the Ocean Legalities workshop: the rigorous and nuanced discussions of that meeting were critical to the development of this chapter.

Note

Epigraphs: Freud 1961, 58; Hobbes (1651) 1909, 8; Agamben 1995, 105–6; Homer 1996, 3.80–83; Melville 1856, 245.

References

Agamben, Giorgio. 1993. *The Coming Community*. Translated by Michael Hardt. Minneapolis: University of Minnesota Press.

Agamben, Giorgio. 1998. *Homo Sacer: Sovereign Power and Bare Life*. Translated by Daniel Heller-Roazen. Stanford, CA: Stanford University Press.

Agamben, Giorgio. 2002. *The Signature of All Things: On Method*. Translated by Luca di Santo. New York: Zone Books.

Agamben, Giorgio. 2005. *State of Exception*. Translated by Kevin Attell. Chicago: University of Chicago Press.

Anderson, Jon. 2012. "Relational Places: The Surfed Wave as Assemblage and Convergence." *Environment and Planning D: Society and Space* 30 (4): 570–87.

Beebee, Thomas O. 2006. "Carl Schmitt's Myth of Benito Cereno." *Seminar: A Journal of Germanic Studies* 42 (3): 114–34.

Beecher, Jonathan. 2007. "Echoes of Toussaint Louverture and the Haitian Revolution in Melville's 'Benito Cereno.'" *Leviathan* 9 (2): 43–58.

Benton, Lauren. 2010. *A Search for Sovereignty: Law and Geography in European Empires, 1400–1900*. Cambridge: Cambridge University Press.

Bettelheim, Bruno. 1976. *The Uses of Enchantment: The Meaning and Importance of Fairy Tales*. New York: Knopf.

Blum, Hester. 2010. "The Prospect of Ocean Studies." *Proceedings of the Modern Language Association* 125 (3): 670–77.

Chomsky, Noam. 2003. *Pirates and Emperors, Old and New*. New York: South End.

Cicero, Marcus Tullius. 1991. *On Duties*. Translated and edited by M. T. Griffin and E. M. Atkins. Cambridge: Cambridge University Press.

Cixous, Hélène. 2005. "Love of the Wolf." Translated by Keith Cohen. In *Stigmata: Escaping Texts*, 70–82. London: Routledge Classics.

Coke, Edward. 2003. "The Third Part of the Institute of the Lawes of England: Of High Treason." In *The Selected Writings and Speeches of Sir Edward Coke*, 3 vols., edited by Steve Shepherd. Indianapolis, IN: Liberty Fund. https://oll.libertyfund.org/titles/coke-selected-writings-of-sir-edward-coke-3-vols people/sir-edward-coke.

Derrida, Jacques. 1974. "White Mythology: Metaphor in the Text of Philosophy." Translated by F. C. T. Moore. *New Literary History* 6 (1): 5–74.

Derrida, Jacques. 2002. "The Animal That Therefore I Am." *Critical Inquiry* 28 (2): 369–418.

Derrida, Jacques. 2009. *The Beast and the Sovereign: Volume 1*. Edited by Michel Lisse, Marie-Louise Mallet, and Ginette Michaud. Translated by Geoffrey Bennington. Chicago: University of Chicago Press.

de Souza, Philip. 1999. *Piracy in the Graeco-Roman World*. Cambridge: Cambridge University Press.

de Souza, Philip. 2014. "Piracy in Classical Antiquity: The Origins and Evolution of the Concept." In *Persistent Piracy: Maritime Violence and State Formation in Global Historical Perspective*, edited by Stefan Eklöf Amirell and Leos Müller, 24–50. London: Palgrave.

de Ville, Jacques. 2012. "Deconstructing the Leviathan: Derrida's *The Beast and the Sovereign*." *Societies* 2 (4): 357–71.

Ebbutt, Maud Isabel. 1910. *Hero-Myths and Legends of the British Race*. London: George G. Harrap and Company.

Fairman, Patricia Shaw. 2000. "Monster-Mothers and Minster-Mothers: The Role of the Older Woman in Anglo-Saxon Writing." *STARTI-Estudios Medievales/Medieval Studies* 1: 149–62.

Fiskesjö, Magnus. 2012. "Outlaws, Barbarians, Slaves: Critical Reflections on Agamben's *Homo Sacer*." *Journal of Ethnographic Theory* 2 (1): 161–80.

Freud, Sigmund. 1961. *Civilization and Its Discontents*. Translated by James Strachey. New York: W. W. Norton.

Freud, Sigmund. 1999. "From the History of an Infantile Neurosis." *The Standard Edition of the Complete Psychological Works of Freud: Volume 17*. Edited by James Strachey. London: Vintage.

Harding, Christopher. 2006. "*Hostis humani generis*: The Pirate as Outlaw in the Early Modern Law of the Sea." In *Pirates? The Politics of Plunder, 1550–1650*, edited by Claire Jowett, 20–38. Basingstoke, UK: Palgrave.

Heaney, Seamus, and Daniel Donoghue. 2002. *Beowulf: A Verse Translation*. New York: Norton Critical Editions.

Heller-Roazen, Daniel. 2009. *The Enemy of All: Piracy and the Law of Nations*. New York: Zone Books.

Hobbes, Thomas. (1651) 1909. *Leviathan*. Oxford: Oxford University Press.

Homer. 1887. *The Odyssey*. Translated by William Morris. London: Reeves and Turner.

Homer. 1996. *The Odyssey*. Translated by Robert Fagles. London: Penguin Books.

Hussain, Nasser. 2003. *Jurisprudence of Emergency: Colonialism and the Rule of Law*. Ann Arbor: University of Michigan Press.

Leeson, Peter T. 2011. *The Invisible Hook: The Hidden Economics of Pirates*. Princeton, NJ: Princeton University Press.

London, Jack. 2002. *No Mentor but Myself: Jack London on Writers and Writing*, edited by Dale Walker and Jeanne Campbell Reesman. Stanford, CA: Stanford University Press.

London, Jack. 2015. *The Sea Wolf*. London: Wordsworth Classics.

Mbembe, Achille. 2003. "Necropolitics." *Public Culture* 15 (1): 11–40.

McLaglen, Andrew V., dir. 1980. *The Sea Wolves*. Los Angeles: Lorimar.

Melville, Herman. 1856. "Benito Cereno." In *The Piazza Tales*, 110–271. New York: Dix and Edwards.

Military Analysis Network. n.d. "SSN-21 Seawolf-class." Accessed May 30, 2017. https://fas.org/man/dod-101/sys/ship/ssn-21.htm.

Military Factory. n.d. "USS Seawolf-SSN-21." Accessed May 30, 2017. https://www.militaryfactory.com/ships/detail.asp?ship_id=USS-Seawolf-SSN21.

Military Today. n.d. "Seawolf Class." Accessed May 30, 2017. http://www.military-today.com/navy/seawolf_class.htm.

Peters, Kimberley. 2010. "Future Promises for Contemporary Social and Cultural Geographies of the Sea." *Geography Compass* 4 (9): 1260–72.

Policante, Amadeo. 2014. "The Return of the Pirate: Postcolonial Trajectories in the History of International Law." *Política Común* 5. https://quod.lib.umich.edu/p/pc/12322227.0005.005?view=text;rgn=main.

Policante, Amadeo. 2015. *The Pirate Myth: Genealogies of an Imperial Concept*. London: Routledge.

Price, Neil. 2014. "Ship-Men and Slaughter-Wolves: Pirate Polities in the Viking Age." In *Persistent Piracy: Maritime Violence and State Formation in Global Historical Perspective*, edited by Stefan Eklöf Amirell and Leos Müller, 51–68. London: Palgrave.

Rediker, Marcus. 1987. *Between the Devil and the Deep Blue Sea: Merchant Seamen, Pirates, and the Anglo-American Maritime World, 1700–1750*. London: Verso.

Rediker, Marcus. 2004. *Villains of All Nations: Atlantic Pirates in the Golden Age*. London: Verso.

Rediker, Marcus. 2014. *Outlaws of the Atlantic: Sailors, Pirates and Motley Crews in the Age of Sail*. Boston: Beacon.

Ricoeur, Paul. 1978. "The Metaphorical Process as Cognition, Imagination, and Feeling." *Critical Inquiry* 5 (1): 143–59.

Rybczynski, Natalia, Mary R. Dawson, and Richard H. Tedford. 2009. "A Semi-aquatic Arctic Mammalian Carnivore from the Miocene Epoch and Origin of *Pinnipedia*." *Nature* 458 (April 23): 1021–24.

Scheuerman, William E. 1999. *Carl Schmitt: The End of Law*. Lanham, MD: Rowman & Littlefield.

Schmitt, Carl. 2002. *Ex Captivitate Salus: Erfahrungen der Zeit 1945/47*. Berlin: Duncker and Humblot.

Schmitt, Carl. 2005. *Political Theology: Four Chapters on the Concept of Sovereignty*. Translated by George Schwab. Chicago: University of Chicago Press.

Schmitt, Carl. 2006. *The Nomos of the Earth in the International Law of the Jus Publicum Europaeum*. Translated by G. L. Ulmen. Candor, NY: Telos.

Schmitt, Carl. 2011. "The Concept of Piracy (1937)." Translated by Daniel Heller-Roazen. *Humanity: An International Journal of Human Rights, Humanitarianism, and Development* 2 (1): 27–29.

Steinberg. Philip E. 2013. "Of Other Seas: Metaphors and Materialities in Maritime Regions." *Atlantic Studies* 10 (2): 156–69.

Thomson, Janice. 1994. *Mercenaries, Pirates, and Sovereigns: State-Building and Extraterritorial Violence in Early Modern Europe*. Princeton, NJ: Princeton University Press.

Tilly, Charles. 1985. "War-Making and State-Making as Organised Crime." In *Bringing the State Back In*, edited by Peter Evans, Dietrich Rueschemeyer, and Theda Skocpol, 169–87. Cambridge: Cambridge University Press.

US Navy Fact File. n.d. "Attack Submarines–SSN." Accessed May 30, 2017. https://www.navy.mil/navydata/fact_display.asp?cid=4100&tid=100&ct=4.

Zipes, Jack. 1993. *The Trials and Tribulations of Little Red Riding Hood*. New York: Routledge.

13. MARINE MICROBIOPOLITICS

Haunted Microbes before the Law

ASTRID SCHRADER

Did you know that microbes get jet lagged? I am not talking about the microbes that live in our guts, synchronizing their rhythms to our circadian rhythms (Thaiss et al. 2016), but free-living marine microbes, such as bioluminescent dinoflagellates or photosynthesizing cyanobacteria. Well, I did not know that until I had some flown over from San Diego, California, to Exeter in the United Kingdom for a dance performance. They were bioluminescent dinoflagellates (*Pyrocystis fusiformis*), who glow in the dark when agitated (scientists believe it is in order to attract predators of predators; they call it the burglar-alarm hypothesis) (see figure 13.1).

However, *Pyrocystis* cannot be agitated to glow at any odd time; they only glow at night. As they live on sunlight and follow a circadian rhythm, they remember when it is supposed to be nighttime. They are some of the largest of the dinoflagellates (up to one millimeter in size) and are among the easiest microbes to care for, so international travel is not beyond them. With some luck, they will survive for forty-eight hours without sunlight—that is, the time it takes to ship them halfway around the globe while taking into account the eight-hour time difference between California and the UK. With a little care and attention we adjusted their rhythm to BST (British Summer Time) so that they would glow during the British night, just in time for their stage debut. With a life span of eight to ten days, it is not surprising that *Pyrocystis* can synchronize their glow to a twenty-four-hour light and dark cycle (see figure 13.2). Photosynthesizing cyanobacteria (blue-green algae), however, can divide as rapidly as every five to six hours, and yet they, too, regulate their life-sustaining functions according to a daily light and dark cycle (Kondo et al. 1997). But how is it possible for microbes with a life span shorter than one day to maintain

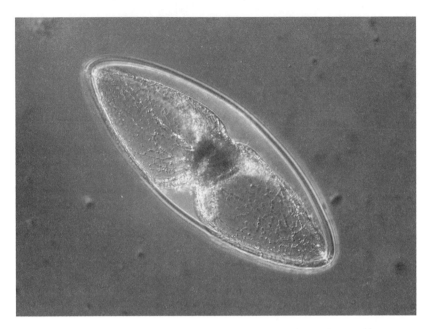

FIGURE 13.1. Dinoflagellate *Pyrocystis fusiformis*. Source: ExploringtheInvisible.com. Reproduced with permission.

a circadian rhythm?[1] More to the point, why would anyone have an internal timer set by a cycle longer than one's lifetime?

The circadian rhythms of cyanobacteria are best understood in terms of haunting, as their twenty-four-hour metabolic period exceeds their life span, manifesting a memory, a transgenerational communication, or an inheritance (in Derrida's terms, see below) that is not locatable within a present individual. In fact, I argue that all marine microbes are permanently out of sync with themselves and exist predominately hauntologically; their presence is permanently deferred and their life-sustaining doings cannot be captured at any moment in time. In *Specters of Marx*, Jacques Derrida introduces the notion of hauntology to replace an ontology that grasps "being" in only one mode of time, the present. Deconstructing the link between being and presence, being becomes a mode of inheritance for Derrida, but "inheritance is never a *given,* it is always a task. It remains before us" (1994, 54). The "logic of haunting" transcends "the opposition between presence and non-presence, actuality and inactuality, life and non-life" (12). "To haunt does not mean to be present," he writes, "and it is necessary to introduce haunting into the very construction of a concept. Of every concept, beginning with the concepts of being and time" (161). The

FIGURE 13.2. Dancer/choreographer Jane Mason with glowing dinoflagellates (*Pyrocystis fusiformis*). Photo by Benjamin J. Borley. Reproduced with permission.

hauntological existence of marine microbes not only deconstructs the opposition between life and death; it also, I will argue, makes explicit the scientific practices that contribute to the microbes' mode of existence.

Until recently it was believed that (primordial) life in the ocean began out of time and without the necessity of death. As single-celled creatures evolved into ever more complex forms, the capacities to keep time and to die were supposedly acquired. The reigning evolutionary paradigm (in which the arrow of time points from simplicity to ever greater complexity) considered the cellular organization of bacteria too simple to manifest an internal biological clock. Unicellular marine algae also were believed incapable of self-destruction (apoptosis), as death only made sense in the service of life; temporal phenomena, biological timekeeping (circadian rhythms), and death (or self-destruction) were all supposed to have a beginning in evolutionary time. These prejudices relied on a model of life that considered bounded individual multicellular, sexually reproducing organisms the norm or the only relevant forms of life. However, in the oceans, marine algae produce most of the earth's organic matter and generate at least half of the oxygen humans breathe. As concerns about global warming increase, ecologists are paying closer attention to marine phytoplankton (photosynthesizing unicellular algae) and their role in the carbon cycle. Jet-lagged marine microbes suggest we consider different ways of doing life and time. The reconfiguration of microbial existences has consequences for conceptions of justice and what counts as a subject before the law, as I explain below.

In addition to exploring the significance of haunting for human-animal relations, this chapter seeks to contribute to scholarship that is rethinking Foucauldian biopolitics in less anthropocentric terms. As the current environmental crisis demands we reconsider our overwhelmingly anthropocentric conceptions of life, the decentering of the human and the formulation of a more-than-human biopolitics have become important concerns in posthumanist scholarship (Asdal, Druglitro, and Hinchliffe 2017; Braverman 2015, 2016, this volume; Lemke 2014; Wolfe 2013). While biopolitics (Foucault 1990) highlights technologies of government that work on individual bodies and populations by exploiting the biological feature of a species, it has often been critiqued as focusing exclusively on features of the human species (see, e.g., Asdal, Druglitro, and Hinchliffe 2017; see also Haraway 1989 for an early intervention into an all-too-humanist biopolitics).[2] Roberto Esposito (2008) also highlights Foucault's apparent indecision about biopolitics as "power over life" and "power of life" or the insufficient theorization of the relationship between a (deadly) thanatopolitics and an affirmative biopolitics.

Why consider marine microbes *before the law* if, according to Derrida, beasts "have no relation to the law" because "they cannot be cruel and responsible, i.e. free and sovereign" (2009, 178)? The point is not, as Cary Wolfe reads Esposito, to grant all forms of life equal value and to "allow anthrax or cholera microbes to attain self-realization in wiping out sheep herds or human kindergartens" (Wolfe 2013, 64). Rather a more-than-human biopolitics requires a reconceptualization of political subjectivity that builds on neither freedom nor autonomy but reconfigures the relation between selfhood and the living. Doing this from within microbiology also reconfigures the relation between science and politics.

Microbiopolitics, a term coined by anthropologist Heather Paxson, is an expansion of Foucault's notion of biopolitics to include the agency of microbes in modes of social management. Building on Paxson's microbiopolitics (2008) and Wolfe's rethinking of the relationship between life and norm (2013), I seek to outline a *marine microbiopolitics* as an alternative microbiopolitics that considers the hauntological (rather than ontological) existence of microbial collectives in the ocean. The formulation of a *marine microbiopolitics* is an attempt to reconfigure the notion of politics not in order to extend it to microbes, but to reformulate it in such a way as to release it from reliance on the agency of the autonomous liberal humanist subject.

Marine microbes differ from other microbes in several ways. Unlike those agents of disease, free-living populations of microbes in the sea are increasingly comprehended as communities rather than as individuals or strains (Paxson and Helmreich 2014). And, unlike those microbes that form part of the human (or other animals') microbiome, they do not matter only as part of a multi-species ecosystem. Marine microbes do not necessarily need a host or agent to assert their particular ways of doing life and death. An important feature of a marine microbiopolitics that considers multigenerational populations of unicellular microbes in the ocean (there are freshwater ones, too) is that the biology of those microbes matters (both discursively and materially) for the realm of the (bio)politics itself rather than just for the cultural appropriation of microbial potentiality for human cultural projects. In other words, marine microbiology renders biology differently political. In the case of marine microbes, it is not a simple matter of their presence or absence that serves as a political resource, it is their performances that matter.

Marine microbes disrupt the individual/population dichotomy and the opposition between life and death that have been central to an anthropocentric notion of biopolitics. In doing so, I argue, they challenge the notion of sacrifice that has been central for the conceptualization of both the evolutionary continuation of life and the foundation of law. In the interview titled "Eating Well," Derrida asks:

> Is friendship possible for the animal or between animals? Like Aristotle, Heidegger would say: no. Do we not have a responsibility toward the living in general? The answer is still "no," and this may be because the question is formed, asked in such a way that the answer must necessarily be "no" according to the whole canonized or hegemonic discourse of Western metaphysics or religions, including the most original forms that this discourse might assume today. (1995, 278)

Derrida underscores the "sacrificial structure" of the discourses of Western metaphysics; in spite of attempts to the contrary, discourses like Martin Heidegger's remain profoundly humanistic "to the extent that they do not sacrifice sacrifice" (Derrida 1995, 279). For Heidegger only humans are worthy of moral consideration, as only they can question their being and thus know that they die.

Law in its institutional form must be distinguished from the ethical question of justice. According to Derrida, "law is always an authorized force, a force that justifies itself" (1992, 5). Law is associated with an originary violence and an unjustifiable sacrifice of those who are not protected as subjects "before the law," who do not have "right to have rights" (citing from Wolfe 2013, 8–9). Law is founded upon and institutes a limit that defines who receives legal protection and who doesn't. Justice, on the other hand, is a promise that can never be fulfilled. A promise has a spectral structure: it is always already here now (in the moment you utter it) but never arrives (as its arrival necessarily contradicts its status as a promise). Hauntological existences then "undermine the very possibility that Justice can ever be effectively limited to the 'positive' value within the binary code" that seems to be the very basis for a modern legal system (Cornell 1992, 1580). In other words, as Drucilla Cornell affirms, the deconstruction of conceptions of time that privilege the present makes clear that "justice is irreducible to the pregiven norms of any established legal system" (Cornell 1992, 1579). What is at stake here, in addition to Cornell's important point about the role of time in Derrida's "philosophy of the limit" and systems theory,[3] is not justice for microbes, but the possibility that science may make metaphysical contributions to modes of existence that challenge the notion of the "limit" on which law is founded. Haunted microbes render it necessary to sacrifice sacrifice (Derrida 1995, 279).[4]

The affirmation of haunting as a biological phenomenon changes the role of science in relation to biopolitics. Rather than assuming scientific complicity in the reductionist project of rendering life calculable, the science of marine microbiology may actually contribute to an affirmative biopolitics, establishing a new way of articulating "life" that allows for a new kind of relationship between "law" and "norm" (citing from Wolfe 2016, xvi). As Wolfe points out, under contemporary regimes of biopolitics, "the law's primary function shifts from a relationship anchored to sovereignty to one that is oriented mainly toward the constitution and perpetuation of norms" (xvii). Following Lazzarato's reading of Foucault, with the introduction of "life into history," Wolfe argues that a shift takes place of the political subject from a juridical subject to an ethical one. The ethical question for Wolfe is "to whom value matters" that he then associates with the capacity to respond. For him, the task is to think the "norm" in relation to the "form of life" in all its particularity. Haunted microbes shift the question from the relation between norms and "forms of life" to the relation between the possibility of a unified self and the living, deconstructing the "subject" of politics from within (micro)biology, allowing for modes of existences beyond present individuals or populations (or species).

For science to be able to make a conceptual contribution to the meaning of life and being—that is, to contribute to the rendering of new ontologies and the normativity of the living—the strict separation of the biological and phenomenological aspects of "life" found in Wolfe's account (Broglio 2013) must be given up.[5] I argue that Wolfe's "subject" *before the law* is constructed *after science*. Haunted microbes exist only with the help of science.

Bio-hauntings: The Circadian Rhythm of Cyanobacteria

Cyanobacteria or blue-green algae are arguably the most successful organisms on earth. Their fossilized remains were laid down over 3.5 billion years ago, they are thought to have converted our atmosphere 2.5 billion years ago, and they still fix nitrogen and produce oxygen. The chloroplast in today's plants is a symbiotic cyanobacterium. They maintain a circadian rhythm even though individual cells may not survive a single day. Within a cell, circadian rhythms are associated with molecular oscillators, usually thought of as an internal program that lets a cell anticipate environmental changes. The rhythm is maintained irrespective of the changing of environmental conditions, such as exposure to changing patterns of light and dark.

While many scientists consider bacteria too simple to evolve internal clocks, chronobiologist Susan Golden, who studies circadian rhythms in cyanobacteria at the University of California, San Diego, disagrees: cyanobacteria integrate the ability to tell time with their photosynthetic apparatus. If you live on sunlight (photosynthesis), it makes sense to be able to predict when the sun will be up. In fact, "'The great-grandchildren know what time great-grandma thought it was,' and daily cycles emerge when observing populations of bacteria" (quoted in Siegel 2016). Haunting appears here not only between generations, but also between the life of individuals and the population, as life-sustaining functions are shared by the "community" but never experienced by the "individual." A rhythm whose period extends beyond the lifetime of individual microbes requires multigenerational populations to be observed.

Cyanobacteria evolved such odd behavior because oxygen production and nitrogen fixation, their fundamental processes, cannot be accomplished simultaneously. Or so the story goes. Rather than speak of haunting, scientists suggest that the bacteria do not behave like individual reproducing cells but more like a mass of protoplasm that grows larger and larger and incidentally subdivides. Most interesting perhaps is Golden's remark that the phenomenon of daily rhythms is one that emerges in scientific observations. In other words, the circadian rhythm is not a property of the cell, but a phenomenon that includes scientific practice. As Irina Mihalcescu, Hsing Weihong, and Stanislas Leibler (2004) have shown, when the molecular mechanisms that stabilize the clock are internal to a cell and cannot be associated with interactions between the cells (as in eukaryotes), the distinction between an individual cell and a population becomes utterly undecidable. Just like the death program discussed below, circardian rhythms get associated with a molecular machinery inside a cell but are observable only in multigenerational populations (Cohen and Golden 2015).

In addition to the haunting within the photosynthesis of cyanobacteria, I consider the synchronized, collective death of marine microbes (microbial suicide) that occurs with the termination of algal blooms as an example of the collective haunting the individual form (Schrader 2017). In both cases, phenomena observed at a population level are retroactively associated with a program within an individual cell. In both cases, the notion of haunting undoes the opposition of genetic determinism (associated with an internal program) and random (external) changes, breaking down the population/individual dichotomy. It also challenges the view that survival or life in general depends on a division of labor that organizes populations into subpopulations in which one part must sacrifice itself for the survival of the other. As already pointed out, the notion of sacrifice has been foundational to conceptions of life and law and depends on a conception of time that privileges the present. For life to be ongoing in evolutionary terms, death has to be assumed a sacrifice in the service of life. The sacrifice of the nonhuman animals—the "non-criminal putting to death," as Derrida puts it—secures the human and the law, as both depend on a limit drawn in the presence. A posthumanist affirmative biopolitics would have to sacrifice the notion of sacrifice. I have argued elsewhere (Schrader 2017) that research into the death of marine microbes supports Derrida's claim that "one must . . . inscribe death in the concept of life" (Derrida 2009, 110), which may also constitute a move toward a less "anthropocentric ontology of life-death" (Calarco 2008, 90). Similarly, deconstructible law must be inscribed into justice; without the law, or any limit, deconstruction and justice would come to an end.

It is not only that marine microbiology supports Derrida's moves in suggesting alternative relationships between life and death, but in doing so it changes the role of science in the nature-cultural business of meaning-makings, as scientists modify their role from within the science. In other words, a microbiological re-rendering of life/death has epistemological, ontological, and ethical consequences. In Karen Barad's terms, the observation of haunting implies that our knowledge making practices are part of the phenomena we describe (2007). There is no way out of the loop or entanglement; the very undecidability between agencies of observation and the object of study and the necessity to provoke a cut or decision in Derrida's terms ensures the continuation of deconstruction and the possibility of justice within the scientific endeavor.

Haunting and Ethics

Heidegger has suggested that haunting—that is, being (dis)possessed by a past (and a future) or being marked by an out-of-sync-ness of the self with itself—is a quality of the human subject; it requires a historical being with a mind capable of bringing itself back to itself. In contrast, nonhuman animals would be trapped in an indefinite presence, unable to anticipate their future and thus respond rather than merely react to environmental triggers (Heidegger 1962, 2001).

Importantly, for Derrida a certain "non-contemporaneity of the living present with itself" is the condition for responsibility and justice (1994, xix). Justice is never present, as it is either not yet there or is there no longer; it never is reducible to laws or rights. Life must be open to death, good must be open to evil, peace must be open to violence, and so on (see Hägglund 2008, 43). According to Derrida, "Absolute life, fully present life, the one that does not know death," would be "absolute evil" (1994, 175). As Martin Hägglund puts it, "If life were fully present to itself, if it were not haunted by what has been lost in the past and what may be lost in the future, there would be nothing that could cause the concern for justice. . . . The struggle for justice is rather a struggle for survival that commits the struggle for justice to the spectral experience of time" (2008, 140). Such a disjointedness of the living presence also implies that there is neither a determinate origin of time nor a determinate endpoint. Thus, haunting also suggests the absence of origins.

Microbial bio-hauntings demonstrate that an out of sync-ness of the self with itself is not only a human quality or the condition for human historicity, as Heidegger would have it, but also essential for collective microbial ways of life in the ocean. Haunted marine microbes clearly anticipate and respond to environmental conditions without however requiring autonomy or individuality; they rather draw attention to the politics within biology. Science may no longer have to presuppose (metaphysical) concepts of life and death before beginning its investigations. Rather, it may become creative and make a conceptual contribution; empirical examples may intervene in transcendental figurations. Thinking of life and death (without origin) in hauntological rather than ontological terms may suggest an alternative to the notion of sacrifice as the foundation of life and law.

Microbiopolitics

In Paxson's articulation of microbiopolitics, microbes seem to become agents only insofar as they participate in the biotechnological controls of human lives, therefore calling "attention to the fact that dissent over how to live with microorganisms reflects disagreement about how humans ought to live with one another" (Paxson 2008, 16): our relations to microbes model normative relations among humans. Moreover, Paxson and Stefan Helmreich (2014) argue that since Pasteur's discovery of the germ theory, the reputation of microbes has changed from peril to promise, from dangerous germ to collaborative symbiont, but this change happened along with technological changes. Both of the labels *pathogens* and *symbionts* have been enabled by specific apparatuses of their time. While the definition of a pathogen relied upon the ability of the laboratory to isolate and grow a particular strain of microbes, much of the evidence in support of the importance and ubiquity of animal/microbial symbioses is due to advances in genome sequencing technology. The existence of haunted microbes is reliant upon the technical ability to identify molecular oscillators within a cell, their important role in many life-sustaining oceanic cycles, and the imagination of a spatiotemporal collective that challenges the individual/population dichotomy.

In the hands of Paxson and Helmreich's interlocutors, human-microbe relationships become "moral examplars," as microbes become part of model ecosystems that are no longer simply descriptive but prescriptive, "with explicitly normative aims" (2014, 171). Whether we regard microbial populations as (spatial) parts of ecosystems or as (spatiotemporal) hauntological communities matters, however. How might the temporality of haunted microbes challenge the normative demands of ecosystemic thinking?

Haunted microbiology redraws biology as underdetermined and a "yet-to-be explored possibility" (Paxson and Helmreich 2014, 167), affirming a fundamental indeterminacy in science; quite ordinary marine microbiology appears to make metaphysical innovations and reinvent its ontological politics by suggesting new relationships between generations and life and death.

Sacrifice: The Foundational Violence of the Law

In his book *Before the Law: Human and Other Animals in a Biopolitical Frame* (2013), Wolfe demonstrates how the Foucauldian notion of biopolitics can be radicalized—with Derrida's help—in order to include some animals into the community of the living that deserve our concerns. As I read it, part of Wolfe's project is to bring animal studies, which according to him has focused predominantly on ethics, together with biopolitics in order to think about animals politically and to bring ethical consideration into biopolitics.

Wolfe is particularly concerned with the billions of animals raised and killed every year under horrific conditions in the United States, simply for food (11).

Current factory farming practices, he argues, "must be seen not just as political but as in fact constitutively political for biopolitics in its modern form" (46). Genetically controlled breeding practices not only establish new norms, they also presuppose the animal as a commodity for capitalist food production. Speciesism is at the heart of modern biopolitics.

While Wolfe does not argue that we should limit our concerns to factory farm animals, he nevertheless insists on a limit to our concerns and care about nonhuman animals. It would be untenable to "unconditionally embrace all forms of life" (Wolfe 2013, 103). "We *must* choose," he insists, "and by definition we *cannot* choose everyone and everything at once" (103). Wolfe then seeks to articulate "a third way," one that can think life and norm together without falling back onto either the lexicon of "the person" or, at the other extreme, the declaration of a radical equality of all forms of life, which, he believes, "is unworkable both philosophically and pragmatically" (58). According to Wolfe, "we" must decide to whom the question of existence matters. He writes, "Is there not a qualitative difference between the chimpanzee used in biomedical research, the flea on her skin, and the cage she lives in—and a difference that matters more . . . to the chimpanzees than to the fleas or the cage? I think there is" (83). Wolfe is certainly right to take the differences between different forms of life seriously, but why should that imply to decide in advance "who" deserves to become a subject of concern or protection? And, who would constitute the "we" that would have the power to choose?

Moreover, Wolfe wants to base such a decision on a given life-form's capacity to "respond," precisely the capacity that, according to Derrida, has divided the human from the nonhuman animal throughout the history of philosophy. In his rearticulation of the relationship between forms of life and norms, Wolfe disarticulates the capacity to respond from juridical subjectivity, that is, the properties of freedom and autonomy and instead associates it with "a constitutively prosthetic relation to technicity" (Wolfe 2013, 103). In order words, "whos" are distinguished from "whats" by nature of their prostheticity (Wolfe here follows Bernard Stiegler [1998] rather than Derrida). His new limit is not structural, but functional, meaning that Wolfe leaves it to current and future ethologists to decide to whom value matters and whom to include into an expanded biopolitical collective. While he doesn't want to draw the new boundary around "classes of creatures who look like 'us'" (71), Wolfe decides that some creatures with sufficient neural tissue and plasticity have a constitutive prosthetic relationship to technicity and an exteriority (beyond their organic bodies) and can therefore anticipate and respond (Broglio 2013). In other words, Wolfe does not sacrifice sacrifice, he simply renders the limit functional so that it is no longer determinable along species lines but remains determinable in principle. The point here is not to affirm "microbial rights," even though haunted microbes (constitutively) breach this new divide, but rather the role that Wolfe ascribes to science in determining this new limit and its implication for justice. Science may move or multiply the limit but cannot change its shape or structure.

While Wolfe is concerned with the role of science in determining the limit, he assumes a progressive improvement of scientific knowledge, asserting that "in the future, we will have been wrong" (2013, 103). In other words, better understandings of animal behaviors will revise (and improve) our determination of justice that is never quite just. Here justice is a telos, a horizon or Kantian Idea progressively approached. While science and law would be able to determine its contingent content, they seem unable to reshape or re-form that limit, its temporality (its presence) and sacrificial foundation.

Thus, Wolfe would agree with Heidegger that science cannot make conceptual contributions to the meanings of life/death and being: ontologies and conceptions of time are the business of philosophers and cultural theorists. Sacrificing sacrifice requires a different logic and temporal imaginary of the limit, not just an affirmation of its historical contingency. Is there a way to move beyond Wolfe's biopolitical re-rendering of the human/animal divide as a "who"/"what" divide no longer before the law (even if without autonomy) that eschews species boundaries?

Derrida, instead, urges us to think of "a responsibility that does not stop at this determination of the neighbor, at the dominant schema of this determination" (1995, 284). Wolfe departs from the Derridean text precisely in the moment it becomes clear (within Derrida's work) that responsibilities to the living without objectifying particular relations between kinds of species requires a reconceptualization of time, that is, a notion of time that deconstructs the very opposition between metaphysical discontinuities (differences) and biological continuities (similarities) (Schrader 2012).

Abyssal Logics: A New Logic of the Limit

As environmental philosopher Ted Toadvine (2010) notes, perhaps one of Derrida's most provocative claims in *The Animal That Therefore I Am*, is his affirmation of an "abyss" between the human and the animal, a claim that some commentators have chosen to play down or simply ignore (see, e.g., Calarco 2008). I propose that what Derrida calls an *abyssal logic* enables a link between the figuration of the limit or abyss between the human and the animal and modes of knowledge production. In other words, the new logic of the limit enables a connection between the ethical "question of the animal" and modes of engagement in scientific knowledge production (Schrader 2015).

Derrida asks us to think what "a limit becomes once it is abyssal" (2008, 30–31). It is important to note that Derrida does not only suggest the multiplication of differences between humans and other animals or between kinds of animals, but by moving the limit into the animal kingdom and multiplying its edges (as some readers assume), he does not simply speak of a multiplicity of relations between humans and animals but of "a multiplicity of organizations of relations between living and dead, relations of organizations or lack of organization" (31). It not just the multiplication of differences within the animal kingdom or between human and nonhuman animal that is the central concern, but rather the thinking of difference differently (in nonoppositional terms), that is, interrogating the framework of the organization of relations, the configurations of the relationships between space and time.

Rather than disavow a radical discontinuity between humans and other animals, Derrida adopts Heidegger's notion of the "abyss" and deconstructs its meaning. For Derrida, there's no single dividing line between humans and other animals based on the ability to know death "as such," to question the meaning of Being or on any other human capacity, as Heidegger would have it, but the abyss rather becomes an opening within the subject or Being: "the moment of death within life." Death, or as Mark Hansen puts it, "something nonlived in us that remains nonliveable by us" (2004, 622), becomes the impossible possibility for a subject to be itself. "We are subjects," Hansen continues, "precisely because we are 'out-of-phase' with ourselves" (622). The abyss then can be understood as a spatial figure that resembles a structure of temporality, a haunting: "an instantaneous dissociation from the present, a différance in being-with-itself of the present" (Derrida 1993, 17).

Death as Sacrifice for the Greater Good of the Community

When marine ecologist Kay Bidle speaks of a recent "sea change of our acknowledgement of death in the sea," he does not mean the extinction of species (2015, 342). Rather, he considers the recent acknowledgment that unicellular marine microbes once regarded as immortal unless eaten by predators are, in fact, mortal. The observation of "programmed cell death in marine microbes," I have argued (Schrader 2017), challenges assumptions not only about the relationship between life and death, but also between science and politics.

The notion of death as sacrifice has been central to the neo-Darwinian understanding of evolution and human development. As biologist Douglas Green affirms, "One million cells in our bodies die every second... they die for a purpose" (2011). The purpose is to keep the organism they are part of alive: cell death is therefore necessary for life, the assumption being that some somatic cells sacrifice themselves for the continued reproduction of the germ line.

The discovery of apoptosis in human bodies may have challenged the immortality of the cell but not an original immortality (Landecker 2001); it did nothing to challenge the view that reproduction, not death, is essential to the definition of life, first established by evolutionary biologist August Weismann: "Unlike reproduction, death is not an essential attribute of the living substance" (quoted in Klarsfeld and Revah 2003, 13). Death has been acquired by adaptation, as there would be no advantage to the unlimited existence of the individual—all that matters for the succession of generations is the immortality of the germ cells. For Weismann, the body of a multicellular organism is nothing but "a secondary appendage of the real bearer of life—the reproductive cell" (quoted in Klarsfeld and Revah 2003, 16).

Weismann's theory of the division of labor between soma and germ line that renders the body obsolete in the name of reproduction might be considered analogous to Foucault's analysis of racism that differentiates a population in such a way that a power that improves life is still able to kill in the name of the health (and purity) of the population. This story changes completely for free-living, unicellular marine microbes who are not considered part of a larger system that would provide them with a purpose. These microbes have acquired mortality only very recently.

While scientific research presents overwhelming evidence for programmed cell death in various marine microbes (including cyanobacteria) (Bidle 2015, 343), it does not seem to make sense when considered within the confines of dominant evolutionary paradigms: an individual might sacrifice itself for the good of the community, but why would individual cells kill themselves for no apparent benefit? Death, to this way of thinking, was not something essential to life, but an evolutionary adaptation that allowed for greater complexity and internal differentiation: a sacrifice for the greater good of the community. Just as sovereign power over death became subordinated to the management of life in the age of biopolitics (as Foucault argued), death "is supposed to serve the interest of life" (Lemke 2011, 39).

Sacrificing Sacrifice and Synchronizing Death

In the light of recent research on the termination of algae blooms (Vardi et al 2007), in which large numbers of microbes manage to synchronize their deaths to no apparent evolutionary end, the idea that death is a sacrifice made for the greater good of the community seems to make little sense. It has been shown that intercellular communications among the microbial cells bring them into being in relation to each other while simultaneously establishing differences between them. In this scenario, individual cells can be said to be haunted by the social form (see Schrader 2017 for a more detailed description).

Immunologist Jean Claude Ameisen instead proposes "that the origin of the capacity to self-destruct may be as ancient as the origin of the very first cell" (2002, 384), suggesting that self-destruction is an unavoidable consequence of self-organization. Death becomes a certain indeterminacy that enables vulnerability and affectivity within the biopolitical calculations of life. In this reading, there is no beginning of time and no beginning or origin of death in evolutionary time. Perhaps one can say that the very idea of beginnings and ends, the beginning of time, an originary sense, or the fall into time that marks "our" human time, the beginning of norms as a binary code that oscillates between good and evil or right and wrong are anachronistic anthropocentric concepts.

Conclusion

In 2018, Florida's annual red tide (an algal bloom aggravated by nutrient runoff from industrial animal farming) reached unprecedented levels, killing Florida's sea life and populating tourist beaches with dead fish, dolphins, turtles, and manatees. Florida's toxic algae even became an important midterm election issue (Knowles 2018). Is that a case of the "power of life" or the "power over life"?

In spite of great scientific uncertainties about the pathways to death in marine microbes and fundamental indeterminacies in microbial intra-activities within an algal bloom (among microbes of the same kind and with others, e.g., marine viruses), some marine microbiologists at the University of South Florida nevertheless attempted to gain "control of harmful algal bloom by induction of programmed cell death." A patent to develop a technology that would induce the collapse of an algal bloom via assisted microbial suicide (US 2011/0021357) was granted in 2011. While this could be considered an attempt at a thanatopolitical biosocial intervention on an ecosystem scale, it is wrongheaded from an Derridean ethical point of view, not because it aims to kill large populations of microbes (who ought to have a right to live), but rather because it aims to remove the indeterminacy of death; it tries to render death calculable and to define it as a specific "limit." It is in these terms that Derrida (2009) takes issue with the death penalty. From another, perhaps affirmative biopolitical perspective, this constitutes a desire for human control that the hauntological existence of marine microbes renders utterly illusionary.

For Drucilla Cornell (1992), deconstruction is a "philosophy of the limit" and Derrida is the philosopher of the limit. Others have called Derrida a philosopher of radical finitude. Conceptions of the limit between human and nonhuman animals and conceptions of death (as limit to life) and finitude are tightly intertwined. Both are related to conceptions of time that inform ideas of justice. Autopoietic living and legal systems depend on the privileging of the present. While both systems theory and hauntology suggest the absence of origin and telos, the former replaces origin and telos with the logic of recursivity in which history has no normative implication and justice can only be the positive value of the law, as description and prescription become collapsed. Such a reflexive view of time erases the possibility of an open-ended future, the yet-to-come possibilities of microbiology. Stuck in the present, microbial systems would be like genetic programs that cannot learn from experience (Jacob 1993). Understanding microbial collectives in hauntological terms suggests a move away from the normative closures of recursively defined systems, in which a spatial limit demarcates a system from its environment as absolute exteriority. For Derrida, the movement of signification, and the movement of life in general, are possible only if the present element relates to something other than itself. Guided by différance, microbial collectives are temporized without ever achieving closure. Such a spectrality—the gap and nonclosure—at work in the logic of the promise of microbes is essential for affective science. In this way, norms and politics become part of microbiology rather than a contingent outcome; there is no subject *before the law* that is not also *after science*.

Notes

1   The term "circadian" comes from the Latin *circa*, meaning "around" or "about" (in the sense of approximately), and *diem*, meaning "day."
2   Thomas Lemke (2011, 2014) offers an alternative reading of Foucault.
3   In her essay "The Relevance of Time to the Relationship between the Philosophy of the Limit and Systems Theory," Drucilla Cornell establishes why Derridean deconstruction cannot be aligned with Niklas Luhmann's systems theory when it comes to the relationship between law and justice. Luhmann's autopoeisis of the legal system relies on a traditional conception of time that "defines the past and the future as modifications or horizons of the present" (Cornell 1992, 1580). It is this critical difference (between

spectrality or hauntology and a telos of a presence) in the conceptualization of time that Cary Wolfe neglects in his attempt to align Derrida and Luhmann in formulating a new kind of "limit" for an expanded biopolitical collective beyond the human.

4   It is important to note, as Wolfe also does in a footnote (2013, 110n34), that the notion of "sacrifice" assumes different and seemingly opposed values in Giorgio Agamben's biopolitics than in Derrida's theorization of a "sacrificial economy" in which beings can be killed without that counting as murder. When Agamben asserts that *homo sacer* "is a human victim who may be killed but not sacrificed" (1998, 83), he is referring to a different religious notion of sacrifice. It also means, however, that there are beings that can be killed without punishment before the law. Throughout this chapter I use "sacrifice" in Derrida's sense.

5   In what could be called a Stieglerian (and rather anti-Derridean) move, Wolfe sets out to distinguish "the biological wetware of specific types of life forms" from "the exteriority of technicity that rewires that wetware" (in Broglio 2013). Such a separation effectively ignores the "trace structure of time" (Wolfe 2013, 82).

References

Agamben, Giorgio. 1998. *Homo Sacer: Sovereign Power and Bare Life*. Translated by Daniel Heller-Roazen. Stanford, CA: Stanford University Press.

Ameisen, Jean Claude. 2002. "On the Origin, Evolution, and Nature of Programmed Cell Death: A Timeline of Four Billion Years." *Cell Death and Differentiation* 9 (4): 367–93.

Asdal, Kristin, Tone Druglitro, and Steve Hinchliffe, eds. 2017. *Humans, Animals and Biopolitics: The More Than Human Condition*. Abingdon, UK: Routledge.

Barad, Karen. 2007. *Meeting the Universe Halfway: Quantum Physics and the Entanglement of Matter and Meaning*. Durham, NC: Duke University Press.

Bidle, Kay D. 2015. "The Molecular Ecophysiology of Programmed Cell Death in Marine Phytoplankton." *Annual Review of Marine Science* 7: 341–75.

Braverman, Irus. 2015. "More-Than-Human Legalities." In *The Wiley Handbook of Law and Society*, edited by Patricia Ewick and Austin Sarat, 307–21. London: Wiley.

Braverman, Irus. 2016. *Animals, Biopolitics, Law: Lively Legalities*. London: Routledge.

Broglio, Ron. 2013. "After Animality, before the Law: Interview with Cary Wolfe." *Angelaki* 18 (1): 181–89.

Calarco, Matthew. 2008. *Zoographies: The Question of the Animal from Heidegger to Derrida*. New York: Columbia University Press.

Cohen, Susan E., and Susan S. Golden. 2015. "Circadian Rhythms in Cyanobacteria." *Microbiology and Molecular Biology Reviews* 79 (4): 373–85.

Cornell, Drucilla. 1992. "The Relevance of Time to the Relationship between Philosophy of the Limit and System Theory." *Cardozo Law Review* 13: 1579–1603.

Derrida, Jacques. 1992. "Force of Law: The 'Mystical Foundations of Authority.'" In *Deconstruction and the Possibility of Justice*, edited by Drucilla Cornell, Michel Rosenfeld, and David Gray Carlson, 3–67. London: Routledge.

Derrida, Jacques. 1993. *Aporias : Dying—Awaiting (One Another at) the "Limits of Truth."* Translated by Thomas Dutoit. Stanford, CA: Stanford University Press.

Derrida, Jacques. 1994. *Specters of Marx: The State of the Debt, the Work of Mourning, and the New International.* Translated by Peggy Kamuf. New York: Routledge.

Derrida, Jacques. 1995. "'Eating Well,' or The Calculation of the Subject." In *Points . . . : Interviews, 1974–1994,* edited by Elisabeth Weber. Translated by Peggy Kamuf et al., 255–87. Stanford, CA: Stanford University Press.

Derrida, Jacques. 2008. *The Animal That Therefore I Am.* New York: Fordham University Press.

Derrida, Jacques. 2009. *The Beast and the Sovereign, Volume 1.* Chicago: University of Chicago Press.

Esposito, Roberto. 2008. *Bíos: Biopolitics and Philosophy.* Translated by Timothy Campbell. Minneapolis: University of Minnesota Press.

Foucault, Michel. 1990. *The History of Sexuality.* Vol. 1, *An Introduction.* New York: Vintage.

Green, Douglas R. 2011. *Means to an End: Apoptosis and Other Cell Death Mechanisms.* Cold Spring Harbor, NY: Cold Spring Harbor Laboratory Press.

Hägglund, Martin. 2008. *Radical Atheism: Derrida and the Time of Life.* Stanford, CA: Stanford University Press.

Hansen, Mark. 2004. "The Time of Affect, or Bearing Witness to Life." *Critical Inquiry* 30 (3): 584–626.

Haraway, Donna. 1989. "The Biopolitics of Postmodern Bodies: Determinations of Self in Immune System Discourse." *differences: A Journal of Feminist Cultural Studies* 1 (1): 3–43.

Heidegger, Martin. 1962. *Being and Time.* Translated by J. Macquarrie. New York: Harper and Row.

Heidegger, Martin. 2001. *The Fundamental Concepts of Metaphysics: World, Finitude, Solitude.* Bloomington: Indiana University Press.

Jacob, François. 1993. *The Logic of Life.* Translated by Betty E. Spillmann. Princeton, NJ: Princeton University Press.

Klarsfeld, Andre, and Frederic Revah. 2003. *The Biology of Death: Origins of Mortality.* Translated by Lydia Brady. Ithaca, NY: Cornell University Press.

Knowles, David. 2018. "Red-Tide Awakening: How Florida's Environmental Woes Could Hurt GOP's Scott in Senate Race." Yahoo News, October 19. https://www.yahoo.com/news/red-tide-awakening-floridas-environmental-woes-hurt-gops-scott-senate-race-090044270.html?guccounter=1.

Kondo, Takao, Tetsuya Mori, Nadya V. Lebedeva, Setsuyuki Aoki, Masahiro Ishiura, and Susan S. Golden. 1997. "Circadian Rhythms in Rapidly Dividing Cyanobacteria." *Science* 275 (5297): 224–27.

Landecker, Hannah. 2001. "On Beginning and Ending with Apoptosis: Celldeath and Biomedicine." In *Remaking Life and Death: Towards an Anthropology of the Life Sciences,* edited by Sarah Franklin and Margaret Lock, 23–60. Santa Fe, NM: School of American Research Press.

Lemke, Thomas. 2011. *Biopolitics: An Advanced Introduction.* New York: New York University Press.

Lemke, Thomas. 2014. "New Materialism: Foucault and the 'Government of Things.'" *Theory, Culture and Society* 32 (4): 3–25.

Mihalcescu, Irina, Weihong Hsing, and Stanislas Leibler. 2004. "Resilient Circadian Oscillator Revealed in Individual Cyanobacteria." *Nature* 430 (6695): 81–85.

Paxson, Heather. 2008. "Post-Pasteurian Cultures: The Microbiopolitics of Raw-Milk Cheese in the United States." *Cultural Anthropology* 23 (1): 15–47.

Paxson, Heather, and Stefan Helmreich. 2014. "The Perils and Promises of Microbial Abundance: Novel Natures and Model Ecosystems, from Artisanal Cheese to Alien Seas." *Social Studies of Science* 44 (2): 165–93.

Schrader, Astrid. 2012. "The Time of Slime." *Environmental Philosophy* 9 (1): 71–93.

Schrader, Astrid. 2015. "Abyssal Intimacies and Temporalities of Care: How (Not) to Care about Deformed Leaf Bugs in the Aftermath of Chernobyl." *Social Studies of Science* 45 (5): 665–90.

Schrader, Astrid. 2017. "Microbial Suicide: Towards a Less Anthropocentric Ontology of Life and Death." *Body and Society* 23 (3): 48–74.

Siegel, Jerome. 2016. "Who Sleeps?" *The Scientist*, March 1. http://www.the-scientist.com/?articles.view/articleNo/45395/title/Who-Sleeps-.

Stiegler, Bernard. 1998. *Technics and Time, 1: The Fault of Epimetheus*. Translated by R. B. A. G. Collins. Stanford, CA: Stanford University Press.

Thaiss, Christoph A., Maayan Levy, Tal Korem, Lenka Dohnalová, Hagit Shapiro, Diego A. Jaitin, Eyal David, et al. 2016. "Microbiota Diurnal Rhythmicity Programs Host Transcriptome Oscillations." *Cell* 167 (6): 1495–1510.E12.

Toadvine, Ted. 2010. "Life beyond Biologism." *Research in Phenomenology* 40: 243–66.

Vardi, Assaf, Doron Eisenstadt, Omer Murik, Ilana Berman-Frank, Tamar Zohary, Alex Levine, and Aaron Kaplan. 2007. "Synchronization of Cell Death in a Dinoflagellate Population Is Mediated by an Excreted Thiol Protease." *Environmental Microbiology* 9 (2): 360–69.

Wolfe, Cary. 2013. *Before the Law: Humans and Other Animals in a Biopolitical Frame*. Chicago: University of Chicago Press.

Wolfe, Cary. 2016. "'Life' and 'the Living,' Law and Norm: A Foreword." In *Animals, Biopolitics, Law: Lively Legalities*, edited by Irus Braverman, xiii–xxi. London: Routledge.

14. "GOT ALGAE?"

Putting Marine Life to Work for Sustainability

AMY BRAUN

"Got algae?" Riffing off the successful "Got milk?" advertising campaign, a T-shirt for sale at the National Center for Marine Algae and Microbiota situates algae as part of a healthy national bioeconomy in which marine biotechnologies play an increasingly prominent role (National Bioeconomy Blueprint 2012). A growing algal biotechnology industry enrolls tiny microalgae in efforts to engineer ecologically sustainable futures, harnessing the productive and reproductive capacities of algae for a range of products that include biofuels, nutritional foods and supplements for human and nonhuman animals, cosmetic ingredients, pigments, and such applications as wastewater remediation.

Algal substitutes for existing goods may appeal to consumers concerned about both personal and environmental health, leveraging market value by responding to a range of sustainability concerns. The development and regulation of these algal products raise questions about how marine organisms are harvested, transformed, and regulated as they enter the environment, the economy, and the body in new ways. For example, products fortified with omega-3 fatty acids derived from algae are attractive to health-conscious consumers wary of the heavy metal contaminants in omega-3 supplements extracted from large pelagic fishes. Horizon, an organic dairy foods company, sells six varieties of organic milk fortified with the polyunsaturated omega-3 fatty acid DHA, advertising that it "may help support brain, heart and eye health" (Horizon n.d.).[1] Some of this DHA was derived from Schizochytrium, a rapidly multiplying species of algae that produces enhanced amounts of DHA under controlled conditions (Whoriskey 2017). If you've "got milk" fortified with DHA, you've likely "got algae" as well.

Consumer advocates objected to the addition of DHA algal oils—produced in industrial facilities by algae fed with corn syrup—to an organic food product (Whoriskey 2017). Under the US Department of Agriculture's (USDA) National Organic Program[2] regulations, organic products may be fortified with synthetic additives that are classified as "essential nutrients" by the US Food and Drug Administration (FDA). Omega-3 fatty acids like DHA are excluded from this group of approved essential nutrients but are still permitted by the USDA as additives to organic milk due to an interpretive error or an "inaccurate cross reference" to these FDA regulations (Federal Register 2012). At the time of this writing, the USDA had yet to revise the regulation after a period of public comment, recommending that the additives in question—DHA algal oil, among others—remain permitted as organic in order to avoid negatively impacting the organic industries, predicting that the delisting of DHA algal oil and other additives would harm sales of organic products (Federal Register 2012; Whoriskey 2017). Marketed as a healthy and sustainable alternative to fish oils, this industrially produced algal oil slips between agencies and regulatory regimes, simultaneously enhancing milk and contaminating it.

This chapter examines the development and regulation of the US algal biotechnology sector and, in particular, how biocapitalist relations have mediated a shift in the sector from the development of biofuels to that of high-value, commercializable products, such as omega-3-rich human and animal food supplements. Through an examination of government and scientific documents and participant observation at industry conferences, I argue that the regulation of algal commodities produced through biotechnologies renders algae an accessible and malleable resource, engineered to meet human health, environmental sustainability, and security priorities. This malleability allows for the selection and cultivation of algae's optimal biological characteristics, like Schizochytrium's rapid reproduction rate and high lipid content, channeled into the development of products designed to promote sustainable consumption. I show how algae's components become useful "bits of life" (Smelik and Lykke 2008) that circulate through economies and within human and nonhuman bodies, blurring such distinctions as organic/synthetic. The classification of these bits of life—both what they are and what they do—is crucial to assigning legal responsibility for ensuring their safety within a regulatory regime concerned with both safety and accommodating speculation.

Algae's biological potentials are often first isolated and harnessed in the lab, where biotechnologies allow scientists to manipulate the algae in order to maximize the expression of their desired traits. Biotechnologies have altered the speed, quality, and precision of manipulating organisms for human use; this allows scientists to bypass time-consuming breeding cycles and yield desired results with greater speed and specificity, processes well documented in terrestrial agricultural biotechnology (Kloppenburg 2004). Laboratory and field experiments, some including genetic modification, allow scientists to select for and enhance algae's most valuable biological components, including omega-3s like DHA, lipids for biofuel production, or proteins to supplement animal feed. Bits of algal life are "decompose[d] down to [their] molecular structures, which can be reassembled in new and unexpected ways and remediated in endlessly changing shapes" (Smelik and Lykke 2008, x), moving through laboratories, bodies, and ecosystems through a variety of sustainability initiatives. "Bits of life" describes these fragmentations and recombinations at finer and finer scales and serves as a tool for thinking through how such developments complicate the distinction between organisms and their components (Smelik and Lykke 2008, x). As a means of exploring the significance of blurred boundaries between life-forms, machines, and environments, the bits of life figure is a legacy of Donna Haraway's cyborg: as with DHA algal oil added to organic milk, circulating bits of life create new and sometimes anxious intimacies between bodies and environments (Lykke 2008, 13–14).

Understanding these components as bits of life also captures their material and semiotic valences: moving from laboratory to algae farm and then to product shelves, algal bits of life prompt a reexamination of our relationship to marine environments, energy sources, animals, and food as they seek to ameliorate (or not) ecological and population anxieties framed around sustainability and climate crisis (Smelik and Lykke 2008). Rendering nonhuman life valuable involves harnessing "both the meaning and matter of life" (Shukin 2009, 20).

Products made from marine algae also call attention to oceans and marine life as a field of extractive possibilities. Investments in marine biotechnologies are both reconfiguring global oceans as spaces for sustainable development and enrolling algae as actants in what has been termed the blue economy, a set of global environmental governance discourses that often frame oceans as sites of natural capital and business opportunity, clearly emphasizing the economic dimensions of marine sustainable development (Silver et al. 2015). Recent government and private sector interests in algal biotech aim to realize algae's potential economic value while appealing to sustainability ambitions— development that balances environmental protection, economic growth, and social benefit—now becoming central to oceans governance (Campbell et al. 2016; UN-DESA n.d.).

The material and discursive productions of potentially valuable algal bits of life provide an entry point into the regulatory regimes in which these bits are embedded. The extraction, cultivation, and optimization of algae into specialized bits of life are coupled with a complex and sometimes fragmented regulatory context that promotes speculation and technological innovation. Regulating algal biotech developments requires attention to health and safety and encouraging economic investments in future possibilities. These regulatory regimes, which are organizing around bits of life themselves, structure the conditions of possibility for remaking ocean life and enrolling it in forms of sustainability work that constantly negotiate these economic, ecological, and social imperatives. The very processes of transformation that create algal bits of life and facilitate their circulation and consumption also generate uncertainties about which bodies are responsible for their regulation and governance.

Algae Enters the Bioeconomy

The development of molecular genetics, genomics, and other biotechnologies has ushered in a new era of scientific research on processes of translation between genetic information and biological functions as well as the inventive possibilities therein (Keller 2000). The promotion of such activities aligns with US priorities to grow the national bioeconomy by supporting capitalization and commercialization of life sciences research and development. According to former US president Barack Obama's National Bioeconomy Blueprint, a set of "strategic objectives that will help realize the full potential" of the bioeconomy, agricultural and industrial biotechnologies generated an estimated $76 billion and $100 billion in revenues, respectively, in 2010 (National Bioeconomy Blueprint 2012). Some bioeconomy initiatives are consciously positioned to support environmental sustainability objectives, either through reducing the negative environmental impacts of industrial processes or generating renewable replacements for diminishing resources (OECD 2009).

Algal biofuels and algal DHA supplements fit into this category of sustainably minded biotech developments, as they are designed as replacements for petrofuels and dwindling fish stocks. Biotechnologies also create the conditions of possibility for producing, sorting, and ending life, beginning at the molecular level, drawing attention to the relationship between populations, individual bodies, and cellular components and capacities (Rose 2007). The technologically mediated ability to produce, sort, and end life increasingly extends to the oceans, as regimes of value influence decisions over the perceived importance of marine life (Irus Braverman, this volume; Susan Reid, this volume).

New life science technologies developed in tandem with forms of contemporary capitalism, such as venture capitalism, to produce *biocapital* or specific combinations of social relations that reorganize materialities and facilitate the generation of capital from biological research and technologies (Sunder Rajan 2006, 11). While many of these relations are novel due to evolving forms of both science and capitalism, biocapitalist relations themselves do not mark a new phase of capitalism per se, but are symptomatic of a global capitalist system seeking new terrains for accumulation (Harvey 2010; Moore 2015; Sunder Rajan 2006). In the United States, for example, the rise of neoliberalism as a hegemonic economic program would not have occurred without the concurrent growth of investment in biosciences and technologies (Cooper 2008).

Biotechnology is inseparable from its legislative and regulatory contexts, in which investment in economic production shifted from declining industrial sectors to the more promising field of biotech (Cooper 2008). Neoliberal economic discourse and policy were coconstitutive of the biotechnology boom of the 1980s and beyond, with both enterprises concerned with overcoming limits in the face of crises: the oil crisis of the 1970s resulted in a petroleum price spike and increasing fears of energy insecurity in the country; the divestment from and decline of large swaths of the US manufacturing sector ushered in a post-Fordist era of rising economic insecurity and poverty; and mounting evidence of environmental degradation brought into question the long-term viability of the country's post–World War II industrial growth strategy. Here biotechnologies proliferated amid new lines of research on the limits to growth (Meadows et al. 1972). As neoliberal policies reduced regulatory limits, biotechnologies offered the possibility of overcoming ecological limits by turning to living cells and tissues as new sources of generativity (Cooper 2008).

Developments in the algal biotechnology sector seek to harness the capacities of algae, transforming it into productive biocapital through technical processes, labor, and institutional frameworks that enable algal commodity production. In the following sections, I trace some of the significant relations in the making of algal biocapital in the United States, first by elaborating the characteristics of algal biomaterials, tracing the early stages of algal biofuels commodity production, and then turning attention to a scientific and industrial shift that facilitated a fuller realization of algal biocapital's promised value.[3]

Characterizing Algae's Capacities

Early federal funding for algal biofuels research came from the US Department of Energy's (DOE's) Aquatic Species Program (ASP), a relatively small component of a set of energy research and development initiatives launched by the Carter administration in the wake of the energy crisis of the 1970s. The newly created National Renewable Energy Lab housed a biofuels program dedicated to developing plant-based petroleum substitutes, including ethanol, biogas, and biodiesel (Sheehan et al. 1998). The bulk of government funding and research for biofuels focused on terrestrial crops, especially corn ethanol. Biofuels derived from aquatic species sidestepped controversial debates over the use of arable croplands for fuels rather than food, criticized for driving up food prices; algal biotechnology need not compete for space with food crop production. Areas of the arid American Southwest were identified as prime targets for large-scale algal products development, where algae could utilize the abundant sunlight without displacing other crops (Sheehan et al. 1998). Over its lifetime, from 1978 to 1996, the ASP cost approximately $25 million, just over 5 percent of the $458 million total biofuels program budget (Sheehan et al. 1998).

The ASP attempted to address these concerns by focusing on fuels derived from high-lipid algal species. Algae are a particularly attractive organism for such speculative developments because of their simple structure and their reproductive and energetic potentials. Of the many varieties of algae, this research focuses on diatoms and green algae, two types of microalgae that generate energy through photosynthesis and are found in both marine and freshwater environments. It excludes other forms of algae less suited to biofuel production, such as cyanobacteria (blue-green algae) and macroalgae (kelps and seaweeds). John Sheehan and colleagues attribute microalgae's industrial potential to its biological properties:

> Microalgae are the most primitive form of plants. While the mechanism of photosynthesis in microalgae is similar to that of higher plants, they are generally more efficient converters of solar energy because of their simple cellular structure. In addition, because the cells grow in aqueous suspension, they have more efficient access to water, CO_2, and other nutrients. For these reasons, microalgae are capable of producing 30 times the amount oil per unit area of land, compared to terrestrial oilseed crops. Put quite simply, microalgae are remarkable and efficient biological factories capable of taking a waste (zero-energy) form of carbon (CO_2) and converting it into a high-density liquid form of energy (natural oil). (Sheehan et al. 1998, 3)

Government funding provided a solid foundation for this phase of research that sought to harness such "efficient biological factories" in the context of certain physical and economic limits.

Optimizing Algae in the Face of Limits

Processes of biofuel production transform algae and its habitats. The promise of scientific innovation in this context lies in its perceived potential to improve sustainability outcomes, both in terms of efficiency (economic or energetic) and socio-environmental benefit. Biofuel research in the ASP focused on the optimization of algae in three areas: the available algal population, algal metabolism, and the algal production system.[4] First, the program gathered and categorized thousands of species from around the United States and its coastal waters, culling the collection down to about three hundred species that exhibited the most energetic potential. Desirable species had, in addition to high-lipid content, potentially high growth rates and resilience under severe ambient conditions. These last two attributes are important for the ability to produce algal biofuels at a profitable scale and to colocate algae in polluted areas so that they may draw carbon dioxide for photosynthesis from heavier polluting industries, such as coal.

Altering algae's metabolism is designed to increase its lipid content, leading to a more productive organism. Part of this research involved the search for a lipid trigger that would shift algal energy from reproductive to productive activities. Removing nutrients places algae under metabolic stress; the organisms cease cell division and channel their energetic resources into lipid production, potentially increasing their biodiesel productivity. This process proved difficult to scale up, as the loss in reproductive biomass triggered by the stress event drastically reduced overall lipid production (US DOE 2016b).

Optimization of the production system involved situating both marine and freshwater algae in large open ponds. Siting of these initial projects was designed to help alleviate various economic and environmental concerns troubling the biofuels industry: the installation of above-ground algal ponds in desert climates sequesters feedstock production in areas unsuitable for other crops; some algal species consume the nutrients found in human and animal waste, such as nitrogen, and are being cultivated for wastewater cleanup; and some species have the ability to sequester CO_2 to reduce greenhouse gas emissions (Menetrez 2012). Yet these potential benefits also present their own challenges. Many of the algal species carefully cultivated for fuel production in the lab did poorly in the field, and pond populations were quickly overtaken by local species. Relocating algal species to land otherwise unsuited to agriculture may require costly inputs with their own financial and environmental costs (US DOE 2016b).

The Aquatic Species Program attempted to respond to concerns over national energy security, with acknowledgment that the US confronted potential limits to economic growth in the face of the economy's overwhelming dependence on petroleum and its reliance on petroleum-exporting countries for those sources. Energy security concerns intersected with environmental limits to growing levels of petroleum consumption. The ASP acknowledged climate change and sought to design algal products and terrestrial algal production sites that could mitigate the pollution of coal-fired power plants while providing a cleaner source of diesel. The results of the ASP suggested that developing biofuels from algae might become a technologically feasible option, though not without significant challenges (US DOE Biomass Program 2010). When the program closed in 1996, the science was years away from an economically viable, scalable fuel that could be integrated into existing fuel infrastructures. While the ASP occupied a small niche within a small energy program, it has inspired a subsequent generation of biofuels research, prompting the resumption of an influx of federal funds toward algal biofuels.

Algal Bits of Life in Fuel, Food, and Feed

A second wave of interest in algal biofuels and associated products began in the mid-2000s. The amount of private investment in algal biofuel labs has far surpassed federal funding, even with substantial contributions from the Departments of Energy, Defense, and Agriculture and the National Science Foundation (US DOE 2016b). Much of this research has emphasized overcoming technical barriers to algal biofuel productivity (Ghasemi et al. 2012). In addition to the challenges of optimizing algal yields, algal biofuel developers aim to utilize existing petroleum and energy-delivery infrastructures to maximize cost-efficiency. Biocapitalist relations have mediated a shift in the sector's emphasis from the development of biofuels to that of high-value, commercializable coproducts. This second generation of algal biotechnology initially employed a refineries model after the petroleum industry, in which oil refinement was coupled with the manufacture of related chemicals and plastics. Coproducts refer to these nonfuel products, such as foods, nutritional supplements, and pigments that are developed from algal biomass within and through the biofuels production process. The commercialization and sale of coproducts helps make biofuels research and development more economically viable.

Algal biofuels development has since attracted significant interest from the private sector, first through single product development and later through an adapted biorefineries model pairing fuel research and coproducts (US DOE 2015). Ongoing research is buoyed by a series of public-private partnerships. Between 2009 and 2014 the DOE supported several Algae Program Research

Consortia with the goal to further the research objectives of both the public and private sectors through shared investments and information (Brown 2001; US DOE 2016b). Funded by the American Recovery and Reinvestment Act after the 2008 financial crisis, four such consortia were tasked with overcoming specific scientific and technological barriers to algal biofuel production. The largest of these, the National Alliance for Advanced Biofuels and Bioproducts (NAABB), produced innovations that project a price of algal biofuels as low as $7.50 per gallon of gasoline equivalent, down from a starting price of around $240 (US DOE 2016b). These public-private partnerships mark a reorganization of biocapitalist relations in algal products development and channel algal bits of life into other uses as well.

Private investments may increase the feasibility of producing algal biofuel products to scale, as well as disperse the different forms of intellectual property in the refinement process to different companies and sites. Lower fuel prices have made alternative biofuels less attractive to investors, with less likelihood of a shorter-term return on investments. To accommodate this, production strategies have shifted, channeling larger investments of time and resources into non-fuel coproducts that can be manufactured as part of the biofuels production and refining process. According to the US Bioenergy Technologies Office, the overall goal of the industry remains the development of scalable, sustainable algal biofuels, but developers hope to generate sufficient market demand for coproducts that may offset both economic and technical barriers to fuel production (US DOE 2016b, 124).

Algal fuel has a dual potential: as energy for capitalist industry (biofuels) and as fuel for animal and human bodies. In the manufacture of omega-3 supplements for human and animal consumption, the technological and economic barriers that prevent the large-scale integration of algal biofuels into existing energy systems lead to a rechanneling of efforts to other high-value products (ABO 2015). In *Fuel: A Speculative Dictionary*, Karen Pinkus deconstructs and destabilizes the myth of "future fuels," including the social imaginaries of greener fuels that will purportedly contribute to constructing ecologically livable futures. Fuel is a material substance, a yet-to-be-consumed source of potentiality; Pinkus attempts to decouple this potentiality from energy systems that have solidified around specific power, capital, and labor relations in the hopes of making the potential of fuel available for different uses in other imaginaries (Pinkus 2016, 3). Here, the potentiality of algae as a future machinic fuel is rechanneled into another technoscientific initiative focused on other facets of sustainability: meeting protein needs of a rapidly growing population and inserting healthful omega-3 fatty acids into different points of the food system.

The flexibility of algae to serve as different forms of fuel speaks to sustainability aspirations while reinforcing the biocapitalist relations that enable them.

Fueling with Omega-3s

Omega-3 production exemplifies algae's capacity to become different types of fuel in response to shifting political and economic conditions. Algal products contribute to a growing global market for functional foods and nutraceuticals, or foods and supplements containing compounds that may provide additional health benefits, such as fighting inflammation (Wells et al. 2017). Diets high in omega-3 fatty acids, in particular, are linked to lower risks of cardiovascular and other diseases, while omega-6 fatty acids are labeled "pro-inflammatory" because they have lower oxidative stability and are therefore more likely to release inflammatory free radicals into the body (Gatrell et al. 2015; Yaakob et al. 2014). Many Western diets contain an unfavorable balance of omega-3 to omega-6 fatty acids (Gatrell et al. 2015), providing a market opportunity for nutraceutical development of healthful omega-3s in a market expected to reach $13 billion in value in 2017 (Yaakob et al. 2014).

The most common natural source of omega-3s is fish or fish oil, though there are concerns about heavy metals toxicity in fish oils extracted from large pelagic species (Yaakob et al. 2014). Notwithstanding, its use among American adults increased from 4.8 percent to 7.8 percent between 2007 and 2012 (Clarke et al. 2015). Globally, the aquaculture industry captures the largest share of fish oil consumption at about 70 percent, but direct human consumption of fish oil is expected to increase by almost 80 percent between 2015 and 2025 (Finco et al. 2017). Projected increases in global demand have raised concerns about the sustainability of already-depleted fish stocks and the potential exposure to consumers of bioaccumulative toxins. Such concerns have spurred investments in the industrial development of omega-3s from alternative sources like micro-algae (Finco et al. 2017).

Some algal bits of life intended for human consumption as omega-3s began as by-products of biofuels manufacturing and are, in part, connected to the bio-fuels research process. The scientific development of coproducts is organized around maximizing economic productivity by using all the elements of the bio-mass raw material, including carbohydrates, fats, proteins, and other organic and inorganic molecules derived from the algal biomass (US DOE 2016b, 123). The near-term development of coproducts must increase the value of the bio-mass to make the entire biofuels production process more economically viable (US DOE 2016b, 123). These leftover bits of life derived from algal biomass are engineered to produce high volumes of coproducts, making substantial contributions to biofuels investment and development by promoting efficient and profitable uses of algal biomass.

TerraVia Holdings, Inc. provides an illustrative example of this shift from fuel to feed; its AlgaPrime DHA product has been incorporated into commercial fish feed. Contracts for the feed were purchased in 2017 by Norway's Lerøy Seafood Group, the world's second largest producer of Atlantic salmon. Citing drops in farmed salmon's omega-3 levels due to changes in fish-farming practices (Sprague, Dick, and Tocher 2016), Lerøy positioned the use of algal feed as a sustainability initiative to protect smaller fish stocks and increase the quality and health benefits of its own farmed fish (Undercurrent News 2017). In the Pacific, AlgaPrime DHA has also contributed to feeding Chilean firm Ventisqueros's Silverside Premium Pacific salmon (FIS 2017). AlgaPrime DHA varieties also feed shrimp, terrestrial livestock, and pets and were one of several of TerraVia's algae-based coproduct initiatives. Originally founded as the biofuels company Solazyme in 2003, the firm shifted away from fuels production to food and consumer products, rebranding itself TerraVia and reassigning algal biofuel production to a subsidiary firm (Fehrenbacher 2016).[5] Instead of future fuels, TerraVia produced future food in the form of cooking oils and protein and lipid powders, as well as a line of cosmetic oils. These products point toward ways of eating heavily mediated by technoscience, facilitated by the infrastructures that support a terrestrial food system and industry already transformed by biotechnology. Organisms put to work through biotechnologies are "commodities that facilitate our own daily reproduction" (Johnson 2017, 282) and also contribute to reproducing desires for health, wealth, and sustainable futures.

In becoming part of our daily reproduction, algal bits of life circulate between oceans, industries, and economies, and into human and animal bodies. Elspeth Probyn explores the role of algae in aquaculture in her multispecies ethnography of fish-human entanglements, *Eating the Ocean* (2016). In developing an ethics of eating *with* the ocean, Probyn challenges sustainability discourses that occlude other ways of knowing marine life and the complexities of the relations between humans and nonhumans. Decisions on how to eat with the ocean are "about scalar intricacy and metabolic intimacies, not moral positioning" (Probyn 2016, 130). Her exposition of omega-3s as vibrant matter that can affect mood and cognitive functions (Bennett 2010) requires also understanding these bits of life embedded in and in relations with the organisms in their life and production cycles. Knowing where omega-3s come from is just as important as knowing what they might or might not do in the body

FIGURE 14.1. Indoor inoculum production clean room at Arizona State University's Center for Algae Technology and Innovation (AzCATI) in Mesa. Photo by author.

(Abrahamsson et al. 2015; Probyn 2016, 136). Since most omega-3 supplements intended for human stomachs come from fish oil, and dietary supplements are more available to populations with higher incomes, demand for fish and fish oil supplements in wealthier markets puts pressures on already depleted fish stocks in global South countries, affecting the food security and daily protein supplies in communities where many of the small fishes are caught (Abrahamsson et al. 2015; Brunner et al. 2009; Probyn 2016). Probyn offers one suggestion for a more hopeful way of eating with the ocean, involving a promising initiative to substitute algae for smaller fish in aquaculture feed, noting the importance of smaller fishes to ocean health (2016, 154–56). However, the geographies of this reconfigured algae-fish-human entanglement, and products like AlgaPrime DHA, suggest that its "metabolic intimacies" cast a wide net that gathers a range of biotechnical, institutional, and regulatory processes that echo some of the terrestrial plant biotechnologies of the green revolution.

As algal bits of life are transformed into coproducts for sustainable living, they traverse multiscalar geographies of production and consumption (see figures 14.1 and 14.2). In a rough sketch of one such geography, algae are gathered from marine, brackish, and freshwater habitats and cultivated in labs located at

FIGURE 14.2. An Algae Raceway Integrated Design (ARID) Raceway (around thirty thousand liters) on AzCATI's precommercialization testbed facility. Photo by author.

dedicated marine centers or industrial start-up companies. As bits of life, algae are modified and optimized in the lab to maximize their most valuable components, then moved outdoors for larger scale cultivation. Moving "from flask to farm," or relocating and scaling up successful laboratory processes, poses a significant challenge to developing marketable products at a scale that attracts investors (US DOE 2016a). While TerraVia processed its algae in enclosed fermentation tanks, much of the algae farmed for industrial production are grown in open ponds, bringing its associated techno-infrastructure. Harvested algae are dewatered and industrially processed and packaged before returning to the seas as meal and fed to farmed fish. As both bits of life and realized biocapital, the circulation of algal omega-3s connects future fuels premised on speculative financial investments with value realized through coproducts, enmeshing multiple narratives of sustainability: sustaining declining fish stocks, protecting ocean health, providing nutrients for (relatively privileged) humans, and contributing to the development of climate change–mitigating fuels. The enrollment of algae in these biocapitalist relations both requires and contributes to the ongoing development of a regulatory regime flexible enough to facilitate the reproduction of these relations.

Regulating Bits of Life in the Bioeconomy

How do we regulate these "bits of life" that are being, or will be, transformed into fuels, food, feed, and other chemicals? With many parts of the algae industrial sector in their nascent stages, industry actors have been actively involved in driving an anticipatory regulatory process and determining what regulations will be needed when applied algal biotechnologies can finally scale up to profitable levels. In examining the ethics of technological innovation, Sheila Jasanoff (2016) poses the question of how society determines and assigns responsibility for risks involving new technologies. Of course, a common method is to legislate this responsibility and assign its enforcement to various governance institutions, even if, at times, this approach appears as "organized irresponsibility" (Beck 1992, quoted in Jasanoff 2016, 35). The means and ends of technologies are no longer clearly linked in linear fashion (Beck 1992, 32); in the biorefinery model of algal production, the technological means to produce algal biofuel have been diverted to new ends (coproducts) that carry a whole other host of regulatory issues beyond basic environmental protections, such as those found in the US Clean Air Act and Clean Water Act.

What the DOE (2015) acknowledges as a "complicated regulatory landscape" confronting algal bioproducts is first and foremost an exercise of classification—what is this product, and what is its intended use? However, this is less straightforward than it might appear at first glance. For example, an algal replacement product could be regulated through a different mechanism from that of the product it replaces, even though they have the same function.

In the mid-1980s, when the DOE's Aquatic Species Program was in full swing and biotechnologies began occupying a more prominent place in the US national economy (Cooper 2008), the White House Office of Science and Technology Policy (OSTP) issued federal regulations of biotech products. The Coordinated Framework for the Regulation of Biotechnology (1986) established laws to regulate products based on their intended use but not their production processes. These regulations were designed in anticipation of future biotechnical innovation, articulating a desire to balance health and safety protections with enough leeway to facilitate ongoing innovation and, subsequently, economic dividends (EPA, FDA, and USDA 2017, 4). The Coordinated Framework was updated in 1992 and again in 2017, after it became evident that biotech advancements and new products exceeded the bounds of the existing framework. However, the number and complexity of regulatory agencies and statutes have led to impediments in the sector, particularly questions of agency jurisdiction and public access to information about product safety (EPA, FDA, and USDA 2017, 5). For example, an algal biofuel coproduct produced under the biorefineries model might be regulated through either the chemical or food industries, with different laws and regulations in force (US DOE 2015, 14). Modernizing the regulations would, according to the OSTP, improve "economic growth, innovation, and competitiveness" by removing some of these perceived innovation barriers.

This regulatory modernization process is meant to define responsibilities, even if few concrete legal changes were made (EPA, FDA, and USDA 2017). The document provides case studies of hypothetical scenarios so that biotech firms can view a sample regulatory road map. Take the following case: "A unicellular alga is genetically engineered with a plant pest component to produce industrial oils for conversion into biofuels with the extracted algal biomass used for fish food" (EPA, FDA, and USDA 2017). Because the algae are genetically engineered, they are regulated under the Environmental Protection Agency's Toxic Substances Control Act (TSCA). Because they include genes from a plant pest component, they are regulated by the US Department of Agriculture, while Food and Drug Administration regulations govern the animal feed coproducts. Moving genetically modified material from the laboratory to open pond cultivation involves its own set of regulations to keep modified organisms properly contained (EPA, FDA, and USDA 2017, 50–51). The EPA is also developing the separate Biotechnology Algae Project for genetically engineered microalgae and associated products under TSCA, designed to serve as a tool to clarify confusion around submissions in anticipation of "technology ramp[ing] up to its expected level" (EPA 2015). Rendering algae as bits of life enables its circulation through bioeconomies of fuel, food, and feed while complicating the regulatory processes that govern it.

Toward Sustainable Techno-Futures?

Algal biofuels are being prepared to serve as a stand-in for depleting petroleum stocks, another impending limit to capitalist growth, especially for societies with infrastructures and ways of life organized around oil consumption. While it is too early to tell if algal biofuels will fulfill this promise, a primary objective for sustainment is the capacity for accumulation through existing (and new) energy infrastructures and regulatory frameworks by overcoming these particular limits. Algal biotechnology, and marine biotech more generally, is located on an emerging commodity frontier (Moore 2010a, 2010b) in which science and technology provide unprecedented human access to marine resources. Life science technologies facilitate access to a previously hidden store of marine genetic resources and productive possibilities for different bits of life, extending relations of biocapital into the oceans. Extracting marine resources now includes harvesting not only life itself, as with seafood, but also life's productive potentials.

Sustainability, in this particular sociotechnical imaginary, is tied to the production of biocapital. Technological developments aspire to fix algae in ways designed to make human systems more secure and more resilient to potential crisis. Such technofixes hold in tension both desired possibilities and disaster risks (Jasanoff and Kim 2015). These bits of life contain both valued socio-natural components and the promise of scientifically mediated and ecologically sustainable consumption. With biotechnologies both exploring and exploiting new development frontiers and shoring up the short-term futures of energy security through economic growth, it is tempting to view business as usual as among the most resilient of systems. Regulation is a central part of the trajectory that enrolls bits of life into sustainable techno-futures, in which legal regimes can struggle to keep pace with biotech developments that challenge existing classification systems.

As Pinkus reminds us, "That 'future fuels' are perpetually deferred only strengthens the links between hydrocarbons and the present economy" (2016, 5). Indeed, the development of future fuel and marine life necessarily relies on the carbon economy infrastructures and mimics refinery models used in petrochemical production. The development and regulation of novel bits of life, enrolled in the production of biocapital while simultaneously attempting to support ecological sustainability efforts, speaks to the promissory and even salvific tone of discourse around environmental biotechnologies (Sunder Rajan 2006). Remaking marine life on land, consuming it as fuel for machines and bodies, on land and at sea, entangles algae in a bioeconomy regulated both by present production and speculative possibility, linking biocapital, efficiency, and energy production with more intimate encounters between food, sea life, and the human body.

Notes

1   Docosahexaenoic acid, or DHA, is one of the two polyunsaturated fatty acids most commonly manufactured for human consumption. The other is eicosapentaenoic acid (EPA). See Yaakob et al. 2014.

2   The US Department of Agriculture's National Organic Program develops national standards for and regulates classification of organically produced agricultural products and their components (USDA n.d.).

3   This section draws from a theory worksheet developed by Stefan Helmreich (2008) using the framework B-C-B′, an extension to biocapital of Marx's well-known

equation M-C-M'. Here, B indicates biomaterial or algae that are full of reproductive and productive potential. The technical processes, labor, and institutional frameworks that enable algal commodity production take place between B and C. Finally, B' is the biocapital produced through this process, with value added when this biomaterial is made useful in new ways (472). I heed Helmreich's caution against assuming such organismal labor is a natural or latent part of organisms or ecosystems; instead, biotechnical life becomes productive in certain ways within and through certain relations (474). Kasdogan (2017) also refers to this framework in relation to algal biofuels and provides an in-depth analysis of the potentialities of the algal biofuels industry and its relationship to biocapitals.

4 Rose (2007) describes molecularization and optimization as two of five significant pathways through which biotechnical changes are occurring.

5 TerraVia filed for Chapter 11 bankruptcy and in September 2017 was acquired by Corbion, a biotechnology company that develops ingredients for foods and biochemicals (Corbion 2017).

References

ABO (Algae Biomass Organization). 2015. "Industrial Algae Measurements, Version 7.0." September. http://algaebiomass.org/resource-center/technical-standards/IAM7.pdf.

Abrahamsson, Sebastian, Filippo Bertoni, Annemarie Mol, and Rebeca Ibáñez Martín. 2015. "Living with Omega-3: New Materialism and Enduring Concerns." *Environment and Planning D: Society and Space* 33 (1): 4–19.

Beck, Ulrich. 1992. *Risk Society: Towards a New Modernity*. Thousand Oaks, CA: Sage.

Bennett, Jane. 2010. *Vibrant Matter: A Political Ecology of Things*. Durham, NC: Duke University Press.

Brown, Marilyn A. 2001. "Market Failure and Barriers as a Basis for Clean Energy Policies." *Energy Policy* 29 (14): 1197–1207.

Brunner, Eric J., Peter J. S. Jones, Sharon Friel, and Mel Bartley. 2009. "Fish, Human Health and Marine Ecosystem Health: Policies in Collision." *International Journal of Epidemiology* 38 (1): 93–100.

Campbell, Lisa M., Noella J. Gray, Luke Fairbanks, Jennifer J. Silver, Rebecca L. Gruby, Bradford A. Dubik, and Xavier Basurto. 2016. "Global Oceans Governance: New and Emerging Issues." *Annual Review of Environment and Resources* 41: 517–43.

Clarke, Tainya C., Lindsey I. Black, Barbara J. Stussman, Patricia M. Barnes, and Richard L. Nahin. 2015. "Trends in the Use of Complementary Health Approaches among Adults: United States, 2002–2012." *National Health Statistics Reports*, no. 79. Hyattsville, MD: National Center for Health Statistics.

Cooper, Melinda. 2008. *Life as Surplus: Biotechnology and Capitalism in the Neoliberal Era*. Seattle: University of Washington Press.

Corbion. 2017. "Innovative Microalgae Specialist TerraVia Acquired by Corbion." Press release, September 29. https://www.corbion.com/media/press-releases?newsId=2137800.

EPA (US Environmental Protection Agency). 2015. *Biotechnology Algae Project*, August 5. https://www.epa.gov/sites/production/files/2015-09/documents/biotechnology_algae_project.pdf.

EPA (US Environmental Protection Agency), FDA (US Food and Drug Administration), and USDA (US Department of Agriculture). 2017. "Update to the Coordinated Framework for the Regulation of Biotechnology." https://www.epa.gov/sites/production/files/2017-01/documents/2017_coordinated_framework_update.pdf.

Federal Register. 2012. "National Organic Program (NOP); Sunset Review (2012) for Nutrient Vitamins and Minerals." Interim rule. 77 FR 59287–91.

Fehrenbacher, Katie. 2016. "Solazyme Ditches Biofuels (and Name) in a World of Cheap Oil." *Fortune*, March 16. http://fortune.com/2016/03/16/solazyme-terravia-ditches-biofuels/.

Finco, Ana Maria de Oliveira, Luis Daniel Goyzueta Mamani, Júlio Cesar de Carvalho, Gilberto Vinícius de Melo Pereira, Vanete Thomaz-Soccol, and Carlos Ricardo Soccol. 2017. "Technological Trends and Market Perspectives for Production of Microbial Oils Rich in Omega-3." *Critical Reviews in Biotechnology* 37 (5): 656–71.

FIS (Fish Information and Services). 2017. "Chilean Salmon Sustainability Focus." *Fish Information and Services*, April 27. https://fis.com/fis/techno/newtechno.asp?l=e&id=91368&ndb=1

Gatrell, Stephanie K., Jong Gun Kim, Theodore J. Derksen, Eleanore V. O'Neil, and Xin Gen Lei. 2015. "Creating ω-3 Fatty-Acid-Enriched Chicken Using Defatted Green Microalgal Biomass." *Journal of Agricultural and Food Chemistry* 63: 9315–22.

Ghasemi, Y., S. Rasoul-Amini, A. T. Naseri, N. Montazeri-Najafabady, M. A. Mobasher, and F. Dabbagh. 2012. "Microalgae Biofuel Potentials (Review)." *Applied Biochemistry and Microbiology* 48 (2): 126–44.

Harvey, David. 2010. *The Enigma of Capital and the Crises of Capitalism*. Oxford: Oxford University Press.

Helmreich, Stefan. 2008. "Species of Biocapital." *Science as Culture* 17 (4): 463–78.

Horizon. n.d. Accessed March 28, 2019. https://horizon.com/products/milk/organic-milk-dha-omega-3.

Jasanoff, Sheila. 2016. *The Ethics of Invention: Technology and the Human Future*. New York: W. W. Norton.

Jasanoff, Sheila, and Sanh-Hyun Kim, eds. 2015. *Dreamscapes of Modernity: Sociotechnical Imaginaries and the Fabrication of Power*. Chicago: University of Chicago Press.

Johnson, Elizabeth R. 2017. "At the Limits of Species Being: Sensing the Anthropocene." *South Atlantic Quarterly* 116 (2): 275–92.

Kasdogan, Duygu. 2017. "Potentiating Algae, Modernizing Bioeconomies: Algal Biofuels, Bioenergy Economies, and Built Ecologies in the United States and Turkey." PhD diss., York University.

Keller, Evelyn Fox. 2000. *The Century of the Gene*. Cambridge, MA: Harvard University Press.

Kloppenburg, Jack. 2004. *First the Seed: The Political Economy of Plant Biotechnology, 1492–2000*. 2nd ed. Madison: University of Wisconsin Press.

Lykke, Nina. 2008. "Feminist Cultural Studies of Technoscience." In *Bits of Life: Feminism at the Intersections of Media, Bioscience, and Technology*, edited by Anneke Smelik and Nina Lykke, 3–15. Seattle: University of Washington Press.

Marx, Karl. 1976. *Capital, Volume 1*. London: Penguin Classics.

Meadows, Donella H., Jorgen Randers, Dennis L. Meadows, and William W. Behrens. 1972. *The Limits to Growth: A Report for the Club of Rome's Project on the Predicament of Mankind*. New York: Signet.

Menetrez, Marc Y. 2012. "An Overview of Algae Biofuel Production and Potential Environmental Impact." *Environmental Science and Technology* 46 (13): 7073–85.

Moore, Jason W. 2010a. "'Amsterdam Is Standing on Norway' Part I: The Alchemy of Capital, Empire and Nature in the Diaspora of Silver, 1545–1648." *Journal of Agrarian Change* 10 (1): 33–68.

Moore, Jason W. 2010b. "'Amsterdam Is Standing on Norway' Part II: The Global North Atlantic in the Ecological Revolution of the Long Seventeenth Century." *Journal of Agrarian Change* 10 (2): 188–227.

Moore, Jason W. 2015. *Capitalism in the Web of Life: Ecology and the Accumulation of Capital*. London: Verso.

"National Bioeconomy Blueprint." 2012. The White House. https://obamawhitehouse .archives.gov/sites/default/files/microsites/ostp/national_bioeconomy_blueprint _april_2012.pdf.

OECD (Organisation for Economic Co-operation and Development). 2009. "The Bioeconomy to 2030: Designing a Policy Agenda." Paris: OECD.

Pinkus, Karen. 2016. *Fuel: A Speculative Dictionary*. Minneapolis: University of Minnesota Press.

Probyn, Elspeth. 2016. *Eating the Ocean*. Durham, NC: Duke University Press.

Rose, Nikolas. 2007. *The Politics of Life Itself: Biomedicine, Power, and Subjectivity in the Twenty-First Century*. Princeton, NJ: Princeton University Press.

Sheehan, John, Terri Dunahay, John Benemann, and Paul Roessler. 1998. "A Look Back at the US Department of Energy's Aquatic Species Program: Biodiesel from Algae." National Renewable Energy Laboratory (NREL) close-out report NREL/TP-580-24190, July. https://www.nrel.gov/docs/legosti/fy98/24190.pdf.

Shukin, Nicole. 2009. *Animal Capital: Rendering Life in Biopolitical Times*. Minneapolis: University of Minnesota Press.

Silver, Jennifer J., Noella J. Gray, Lisa M. Campbell, Luke W. Fairbanks, and Rebecca L. Gruby. 2015. "Blue Economy and Competing Discourses in International Oceans Governance." *Journal of Environment and Development* 24 (2): 135–60.

Smelik, Anneke, and Nina Lykke. 2008. "Bits of Life: An Introduction." In *Bits of Life: Feminism at the Intersections of Media, Bioscience, and Technology*, edited by Anneke Smelik and Nina Lykke, ix–xix. Seattle: University of Washington Press.

Sprague, M., J. R. Dick, and D. R. Tocher. 2016. "Impact of Sustainable Feeds on Omega-3 Long Chain Fatty Acid Levels in Farmed Atlantic Salmon, 2006–2015." *Scientific Reports* 6: 21892.

Sunder Rajan, Kaushik. 2006. *Biocapital: The Constitution of Postgenomic Life*. Durham, NC: Duke University Press.

Undercurrent News. 2017. "Norwegian Salmon to Be Raised on Feed Made with Algae." *Undercurrent News*, 25 April. https://www.undercurrentnews.com/2017/04/25 /norwegian-salmon-to-be-raised-on-feed-made-with-algae/.

un-desa (un Department of Economic and Social Affairs). n.d. "Blue Economy Concept Paper." Accessed July 24, 2016. https://sustainabledevelopment.un.org/content /documents/2978BEconcept.pdf.

usda (US Department of Agriculture). n.d. "National Organic Program." Accessed March 11, 2019. https://www.ams.usda.gov/about-ams/programs-offices/national -organic-program.

US doe (US Department of Energy). 2015. "Bioproducts to Enable Biofuels Workshop Summary Report." December. https://www.energy.gov/sites/prod/files/2015/12/f27 /bioproducts_to_enable_biofuels_workshop_report.pdf.

US doe (US Department of Energy). 2016a. "Algal Biology Toolbox Workshop Summary Report." May. https://energy.gov/sites/prod/files/2016/09/f33/algal_biology _toolbox_workshop_summary_report.pdf.

US doe (US Department of Energy). 2016b. "National Algal Biofuels Technology Review." June. https://www.energy.gov/sites/prod/files/2016/06/f33/national_algal _biofuels_technology_review.pdf.

US doe (US Department of Energy) Biomass Program. 2010. "National Algal Biofuels Technology Roadmap." May. https://www1.eere.energy.gov/bioenergy/pdfs/algal _biofuels_roadmap.pdf.

Wells, Mark L., Philippe Potin, James S. Craigie, John A. Raven, Sabeeha S. Merchant, Katherine E. Helliwell, Alison G. Smith, Mary Ellen Camire, and Susan H. Brawley. 2017. "Algae as Nutritional and Functional Food Sources: Revisiting Our Understanding." *Journal of Applied Phycology* 29 (9): 949–82.

Whoriskey, Peter. 2017. "How Millions of Cartons of 'Organic' Milk Contain an Oil Brewed in Industrial Vats of Algae." *Washington Post*, June 5. https://www .washingtonpost.com/news/wonk/wp/2017/06/05/how-millions-of-cartons-of -organic-milk-contain-an-oil-brewed-in-industrial-vats-of-algae.

Yaakob, Zahira, Ehsan Ali, Afifi Zainal, Masita Mohammad, and Mohd Sobri Takriff. 2014. "An Overview: Biomolecules from Microalgae for Animal Feed and Aquaculture." *Journal of Biological Research-Thessaloniki* 21 (1): 6.

15. "CLIMATE ENGINEERING DOESN'T STOP OCEAN ACIDIFICATION"

Addressing Harms to Ocean Life in Geoengineering Imaginaries

HOLLY JEAN BUCK

Climate Engineering: So Far, a Terra-Centric Proposition

For land-based dwellers, climate change impacts are often measured and modeled in terms of temperature and precipitation—and then sea-level rise or how the ocean encroaches upon us. If we were ocean dwellers, our working groups and panels might be studying a different triple threat: ocean acidification, ocean warming, and deoxygenization. Ocean acidification in particular has been called the "other CO_2 problem" or climate change's "evil twin." These three processes work together to make an Anthropocene ocean uncharted waters.

Numbers are often used to signal how radically different the ocean is becoming: the oceans have absorbed 90 percent of the warming from human emissions; oxygen concentrations are expected to decrease 3 to 6 percent in the twenty-first century (IPCC 2014); and the ocean has absorbed a third of the CO_2 that humans have emitted since the industrial revolution. This absorption of CO_2 is what causes ocean acidification. In brief, CO_2 does not simply dissolve into water; it reacts with water to change seawater chemistry. In preindustrial times, surface ocean water was weakly alkaline, with a pH of 8.2. It has now fallen to 8.1 (Doney et al. 2009). This drop sounds deceivingly minimal. But pH is measured on a logarithmic scale; this drop corresponds to an increase in surface ocean acidity by 26 percent. By 2100, pH could be 7.8 or 7.9, representing a doubling of acidity (Fennel and VanderZwaag 2016). These numbers are hard to absorb; they represent drastic changes in the medium of life for countless species (not to mention changes in weather). Acidification often is visualized in terms of marine organisms who struggle to build their calcium carbonate shells and skeletons in an increasingly corrosive environment, expending greater energy to have protection and form. More broadly, an acidifying ocean affects fundamental biogeochemical processes in marine ecosystems and could have far-reaching consequences (Doney et al. 2009).[1]

But we live on land. As climate change continues to be more apparent, more research and hope may be put into practices and technologies to improve climatic conditions on land. Climate engineering interventions have been grouped into approaches that remove carbon dioxide from the atmosphere (carbon dioxide removal or negative emissions technologies) and those that reflect incoming sunlight (albedo modification or solar geoengineering). When researching solar geoengineering approaches on a global scale, scientists most often measure their impacts on atmospheric temperature and precipitation. In general—and in line with temperature targets set by the United Nations Framework Convention on Climate Change (UNFCCC)—the assumed objective of these interventions is to reduce temperatures. As research progresses, however, specific studies are emerging on how to design climate interventions for other objectives, such as maintaining Arctic temperature without disrupting tropical precipitation (Kravitz et al. 2016), or reducing sea-level rise (Jackson et al. 2015), as well as studies on aspects like vegetation response and crop yields (reviewed in Irvine et al. 2016).

Can climate engineering help the triple threat faced by ocean life? Is ocean restoration a possible design objective, and if so, how would it be reconciled with more strictly anthropocentric or terra-centric goals? The science thus far is limited and not very encouraging. Carbon removal methods sound like they would have potential to help ocean acidification, but, unfortunately, they do not seem to work at the time scales relevant to many living things, including humans. In a study of the long-term response of oceans to carbon removal from the atmosphere, climate scientist Sabine Mathesius and colleagues (2015) found that even a "probably unfeasible" CO_2 extraction rate of twenty-five gigatons carbon (GtC) per year could not bring ocean conditions back to preindustrial times, nor even a low-carbon mitigation scenario, within the period they simulated—up to the year 2700. In part, this has to do with how the ocean mixes: surface acidity levels recover very quickly when atmospheric carbon concentrations are geoengineered back to preindustrial levels, but "the vast deep ocean remembers past human interference for several centuries, at least" (Mathesius et al. 2015, 1111). Or, as Astrida Neimanis reminds us in this volume, the sea is "a repository of deep pasts—a well of remembrance." Moreover, for many ecosystems, it is not just the acidity at a point in time that is relevant, but the *rate* at which preceding changes occurred. Slow ocean turnover means that the ocean's interior pH can only be restored to a preindustrial state over millennia (Mathesius et al. 2015).

Solar geoengineering also does not help ocean acidification. Generally speaking, since this "sunshade" technology does not reduce carbon emissions but simply blocks incoming light, the oceans would continue to acidify.[2] Paul Crutzen, who popularized both the terms Anthropocene and geoengineering, saw this as not a flaw, but a strength of the idea: because solar geoengineering would not do anything about ocean acidification, political action to control emissions would still be necessary (Morton 2015, 153). Here, Crutzen's assumption that the oceans would motivate any kind of action seems tragically flawed. The climate regime has virtually ignored ocean acidification, compared to the magnitude of the changes involved, focusing instead on global mean temperatures. In both climate engineering and climate politics more broadly, the oceans are pushed to the margins.

Generally, ocean acidification with regard to climate engineering is considered a "powerpoint sentiment": required to acknowledge but not developed. Simple reasons may account for this: First, the oceans do not have a singular voice speaking for them, and the governance of climate engineering is often speculated upon using the nation-state model. Second, understanding the science of ocean warming, deoxygenization, and acidification is complex, with poorly communicable metrics like pH. Third, the time-scale of this problem can feel even more distant than that of climate change itself. Fourth, climate engineering is posited as a solution to a problem framed by humans and their biases. Looking through an oceanic lens underscores the inadequacy of solar geoengineering and other climate engineering approaches; it highlights their limitations for solving the complete problem.

Climate engineering as a sociotechnical imaginary is contingent upon a series of absences: the absence of political will and social pressure for mitigation, the absence of information on the seriousness of the climate problem, the relative absence of the oceans in constituting what climate change is really about. Without these absences, climate engineering makes no sense. Mark Fisher, writing on hauntology ("the agency of the virtual" or "that which acts without fully existing"), explains that "everything that exists is possible only on the basis of a whole series of absences, which precede and surround it, allowing it to possess such consistency and intelligibility that it does" (2014, 18). If geoengineering could become a stronger specter, perhaps it could haunt us into focusing on these absences, into questioning them. That is, the efficacy of geoengineering in changing the course of events may well turn out to be discursive or virtual rather than biophysical. The mere idea of it in policy discussions may clarify how important immediate mitigation action is.

Attempts to fill in the absences around climate engineering—for example, pointing out that the potential benefits of many climate engineering ideas are not extended to the oceans—may not impact the contours of discussions about climate engineering because no one is currently saying that climate engineering is optimal or even adequate. Climate engineering is posited as an emergency measure, a worst-case stab at ameliorating a little bit of the pain. Giving voice, valuation, and legal status to the oceans and their life-forms would make it clear that climate geoengineering options are not enough: but as no one believes they *are* enough, no debate has been shifted by articulating this point alone. In the future, it may be necessary to continually assert that a world enacting stratospheric aerosol geoengineering is in essence a world with a significant failure: a world where the rich have maintained an iron grip hold on institutions, and facts, and chosen to sacrifice entire realms of life and experience. Stratospheric aerosol geoengineering must be continually recognized for what it is. It must always be an emergency measure, not an option that rational consumers can pick off the shelf and put into their shopping carts. As long as scientists continue to maintain control of discourse about it, this understanding seems likely to hold.

Although no one is currently framing climate engineering as a sufficient solution, bringing these questions about oceanic and nonhuman life to the forefront allows for an honest discussion of climate engineering's purpose, prospects, and limitations. Hence, this chapter uses oceanic experience as a spur to think about the following: What could a climate intervention strategy that accounts for nonhumans look and feel like? What kinds of institutions, cultural norms, and legal actions would be needed to realize a climate designed for the flourishing of those beyond land-based humans? In the following section, the chapter discusses the current state of governance of ocean acidification and climate engineering as a means of understanding how our systems of governance/legal infrastructures seem to privilege strategies like geoengineering over these others. Then, in the third and fourth sections, the chapter turns to a more speculative discussion of how future-oriented legalities could encourage alternative futures of ecosystem design and care.

Governance of Ocean Acidification and Climate Engineering: Overlapping Patchworks

Let us turn back to the present and past and cover some background on the existing legalities of ocean acidification and climate intervention. If climate change is in effect a problem in several domains—terrestrial, atmospheric, and oceanic—how is it that one of these domains has been virtually ignored in the eyes of the law? Ocean acidification has not been included in the mandate of any international treaty (Herr et al. 2014). Because international environmental law has developed in an issue-specific way, legislation on ocean acidification would have to reference and coordinate existing overlapping regimes, such as the climate, marine pollution, and atmospheric pollution regimes (Baird, Simons, and Stephens 2010).

The obvious place for legislation on ocean acidification would be the UNFCCC. However, the current climate regime focuses on temperatures, and governments have set aspirational targets based on temperature rather than greenhouse gas concentrations, such as the Paris Agreement's aspirational target of limiting warming to well below 2°C, and pursue efforts to curb it to 1.5°C, above preindustrial temperatures. The UNFCCC actually promotes enhancing sinks and reservoirs of carbon, including forests, oceans, and coastal ecosystems (Fennel and VanderZwaag 2016). Moreover, as put in a Global Ocean Commission report, the UNFCCC is "already creaking under a very heavy load of 'special interests,' including forests, agriculture, cities and water" (GOC 2013).

The United Nations Convention on the Law of the Sea (UNCLOS) encourages states to control marine pollution but cannot do much to regulate the emissions causing the problem. A third convention separate from the UNFCCC and UNCLOS, the biodiversity-focused UN Convention on Biological Diversity (CBD), has spent time improving scientific research into ocean acidification and has highlighted the need to adapt to it. It has also emphasized the need for climate mitigation measures and encouraged a precautionary approach to ocean fertilization geoengineering (Fennel and VanderZwaag 2016). However, like other international treaties, the language of the CBD tends to be nonbinding. The UN General Assembly addressed ocean acidification in a 2013 resolution (Resolution 68/70 on Oceans and Law of the Sea), which encouraged states to research the issue and increase efforts to address it on national, regional, and international levels. These efforts, however, largely are fragmented and follow a voluntary, soft-law approach of codes and suggestions—not legally binding. Most analysts do not see bright prospects for an international agreement specifically aimed at ocean acidification (Fennel and VanderZwaag 2016).

Part of the reason for the lack of attention to ocean acidification is because ocean governance has traditionally been approached within various sectors—waste dumping, overfishing issues within regional fisheries management organizations, Antarctic ecosystem protection, and so on. Ocean acidification, being a global issue, faces the same challenges to climate change in this respect. The ocean, being in many cases beyond national jurisdiction, is governed apart. Furthermore, negotiating a pH target for the oceans could be difficult in terms of both spatial and temporal scales: ocean acidity can vary greatly from place to place, and inertia in the climate system means that even when emissions are curbed, pH will continue to fall for decades (Fennel and VanderZwaag 2016).

Just as ocean acidification is relatively absent from climate policy and ocean governance discussions, the emerging literature on legalities of climate engineering and stratospheric aerosol injection is relatively silent on ocean acidification with only minor exceptions. For example, at the tenth conference of the parties of the CBD held in 2010 in Nagoya, Japan, decision X/33 on biodiversity and climate change was adopted. X/33 invites parties to consider the guidance that no climate-related geoengineering activities that may affect biodiversity take place pending scientific review (Bodle et al. 2012). This nonbinding guidance is the only legal language to address climate engineering generally, though several other regimes would apply to specific strategies or uses. Other international instruments pertain to geoengineering and the oceans in specific contexts: UNCLOS sets a legal framework for all ocean geoengineering activities, and the London Convention / London Protocol regulates dumping at sea, making it relevant to some ocean geoengineering techniques, such as iron fertilization or even deep seabed CO_2 storage (Bodle et al. 2012). In general, however, the relevant conventions are focused on preventing pollution in the oceans rather than dealing with activity that is intentionally modifying climatic or oceanic conditions. They are preventative and precautionary, not forward-looking.

Legalities of Scientific Research: Actions for the Now

What could a forward-looking climate intervention strategy that accounts for nonhumans look and feel like? At present, there is no advocacy in this direction, as many see climate engineering for other species as a contradictory or impossible proposition; that is, climate engineering is necessarily a human intervention that disrupts ecologies. Three prior understandings shape whether the prospect of multispecies-oriented climate engineering is possible and worth considering: how quickly one believes society can transform, whether the moral hazard is real, and what the counterfactual scenario is. For example, Naomi Klein writes that these technologies "respond to the lack of balance our pollution has created by taking our ecosystems even further away from self-regulation . . . if we sign on to this plan and call it stewardship, we effectively give up on the prospect of ever being healthy again"; she also writes compellingly that "nothing on earth would be outside the reach of humanity's fallible machines, or even fully outside at all. We would have a roof, not a sky—a milky, geoengineered ceiling gazing down on a dying, acidified sea" (2014,

260). On the other hand, given the planetary transformation already committed, as Oliver Morton writes, "if your only concern was preserving biodiversity, the choice of an Engineered Planet where temperatures stay stable over a Greenhouse Planet where they climb seems a pretty obvious one" (2015, 257). So much depends upon the counterfactual scenario—and whether climate engineering is considered a substitute for mitigation. The term *moral hazard*, borrowed from economics, refers to whether or not solar geoengineering reduces the incentives and energy for mitigation or has "mitigation deterrence" effects (McLaren 2016). Some have suggested that learning about geoengineering causes people to be more energized about mitigation, while others suggest that it distracts from it—the ways the specter of geoengineering haunts the discussion are still unresolved (see Corner and Pidgeon 2014; Merk, Pönitzsch, and Rehdanz 2016).

We do not yet know if various climate intervention ideas and practices could be beneficial for nonhumans—and beneficial is highly relative to the counterfactual climate change scenario. But we should continue in the tradition of law encouraging scientific research, as the CBD does, and write the law that helps us find out. If law can help make explicit what we need to know for responsible interventions, then we need to think about how consideration and care are written into both the research questions and the process and how they would be explicitly mandated in the research mission. An overarching legal framework for climate engineering based on the UN Sustainable Development Goals could be a good start, as Goal 14 on oceans has a target of minimizing and addressing the impacts of ocean acidification: this at least places it in the conversation. Ongoing thinking about humanitarian and human rights approaches to climate engineering governance regime could be expanded (Suarez and van Aalst 2016), as the underlying logic behind these approaches is recognizing those who do not currently have a voice. All of these steps for near-term climate engineering governance are imaginable from where we are now.

A key arena of near-term legalities toward multispecies geoengineering is generating science with other species in mind. Globally, a first baseline step is to look at climate interventions in terms of improving ocean health and removing other stressors. Ecosystems are more resilient to manage acidification and warming if other stressors are removed via such measures as marine-protected areas and clearance of invasive species (GOC 2013). Providing for these measures could be part of any international compromise on climate intervention. A lot of fundamental data must first be gathered to begin to understand how climate change is changing the oceans. A second baseline step is emphasizing that scientific research can also be shifted to emphasize nonhuman life, including looking at both (1) what types of climate interventions can help ocean life relative to damaging climate change scenarios, and (2) the related question of what types of interventions can help ocean acidification.

On the first question, for example, reef scientist Elena Couce and colleagues (2013) found that while unmitigated climate change leads to a collapse in suitable shallow reef habitat driven by sea-surface temperatures, there are solar geoengineering scenarios that could perhaps avert this collapse and provide slightly improved environmental conditions farther north. While solar geoengineering "fails to tackle the causes or consequences of ocean acidification," these researchers conclude that these shallow reef ecosystems could see some benefit from solar geoengineering interventions even if they do not tackle ocean acidification because higher sea surface temperatures are so detrimental to coral (Couce et al. 2013, 1804). Regional modifications, such as marine cloud brightening, have shown some promise in simulations for curbing surface sea temperature rise and aiding reefs (Latham et al. 2013). But beyond studies of specific ecosystems like reefs, there needs to be scientific research into more fundamental processes, for example, how large-scale aerosol-based solar geoengineering would affect fundamental processes like nutrient cycling, or marine photosynthesis, as primary production is linked to the depth of light penetration (Williamson et al. 2012).

On the second question of whether solar geoengineering interventions can help ocean acidification, Philip Williamson and Ralph Bodle observe in a Convention on Biological Diversity technical report that "the often-made statement that 'ocean acidification is unaffected by SRM' is technically incorrect, since SRM cooling reduces biogeochemical feedbacks that would otherwise release additional CO_2 from terrestrial sources," such as soil carbon, tundra methane and forests (Williamson and Bodle 2016, 75). On the other hand, simulations show that stratospheric aerosols will not alter surface ocean acidification, but they would create negative acidification effects on the seabed (Tjiputra, Grini, and Lee 2016).

What about carbon removal approaches to climate engineering, such as the concept of ocean alkalinization—of adding lime to the oceans? The mathematics of this on a global scale do not seem to work out: as Oliver Morton (2015, 250) points out, pulling a billion tons of carbon out would require putting two billion tons of lime into the ocean, and that is even before adding in the energy costs from all the mining and transport. Globally, ocean alkalinization has been found to be relatively ineffective as a carbon-removal and sequestration strategy, even when applied at an "optimistically large" level of deployment, against a high business-as-usual climate change scenario (representative concentration pathway of 8.5) (Keller, Feng, and Oschiles 2014). Ocean liming is less effective than solar geoengineering at countering ocean pH changes (Williamson and Bodle 2016). However, it is possible that there may be some local applications of ocean liming for particular sites, though with a steep price tag (Feng et al. 2016). On the other hand, the annual economic damages of ocean acidification have been estimated to be between $528 and $870 billion (Herr et al. 2014). These damages will largely be borne by small island states that rely on coral reefs. Better calculations and projections of impacts are necessary for assessing climate interventions, but this is only one part of what is needed; legalities for multispecies-focused geoengineering go far beyond scientific research. Here I simply suggest that it matters how the studies are done, how the research questions are framed, and for whom we seek answers—for humans or for others—and that legal regimes can help broaden scientific inquiry beyond geoengineering.

Legislating New Forms of Responsibility: Speculations for the Long Future

In this final section, I will describe the responsibility dilemma faced by multispecies-oriented climate engineering and suggest some alternative approaches to climate engineering that may be the best hope for outcomes favorable to nonhumans. Climate change is already fraught with unresolved questions of liability, harm, recompense, and justice; the idea of *intentionally* modifying the climate expands these. In the Anthropocene-as-*bildungsroman*, this is the moment of our growth into more responsible beings. This responsibility can be interpreted either in terms of taking responsibility for our past messes/crimes (an arena for which there are legal precedents in terms of reparations or recompense) or in terms of taking responsibility for the continuing functioning of earth systems (which some analysts believe is necessary because we have intervened so much and for which there is much less legal precedent) (Arora 2017; Haraway 2016; Pálsson et al. 2013; Steffen et al. 2011). The dilemma is *how* to take responsibility, since there can be a tension between taking responsibility and depriving a being of agency. How do we care for and support the existence of a force or collective with which we can't communicate? Andreas Philippopoulos-Mihalopoulos articulates the dilemma when he writes,

> The only position left to assume is that of responsibility. No longer able to hide behind a benevolent anthropocentrism or a well-wishing eco-centrism, the human is de facto placed in the center of the wound. But how to redescribe things in a way that neither absolves a body from the

responsibility of situating itself, nor inebriates this body with the illusion of control over the assemblage, or indeed the whole world if we are talking about human-centered bodies?" (2016, 204)

Many scholars venturing down this line of inquiry have mentioned how simply giving rights or voice to nonhumans doesn't suffice, in terms of lively or transhuman legalities—the well-wishing ecocentrism is strewn with traps. For legal scholars Richard Janda and Richard Lehun, the Anthropocene illustrates a conflict between human and nonhuman law that "cannot be overcome by substituting for human law an embrace of the nonhuman or trans-human" (2016, 177). Dealing with this conflict of laws involves not only recognizing it, but also producing a capacity within human law to respond to its signals (Janda and Lehun 2016, 181). Eben Kirksey, Craig Schuetze, and Stefan Helmreich also write about the issues of representation and interpretation—about the limits of "ventriloquism" that claims to speak for others and the limits of Latour's thinking that nonhumans have "speech impedimenta" (2014, 3), which human spokespeople can help to fill in.

In light of these limitations, what does a responsibility that doesn't involve stopping at recognizing or embracing, or "speaking for," look like? Philippopoulos-Mihalopoulos says that responsibility becomes situational, the "juridical responsibility of situating one's body within an assemblage" and extended, unrestricted by the immediate context (2016, 204); he writes also of the responsibility of withdrawal—which is how to learn to situate one's self.

Climate engineering complicates the picture because, first, it implies intervention (typically placed in opposition with withdrawal as a course of action) and, second, it implies design—design for a client, as in engineering, and presumably a client with particular needs and specifications. The design is in response to their needs and objectives. But when it comes to nonhumans, their design goals cannot be articulated, and so there cannot be equal participation because of this communication challenge. Legal scholar Jedediah Purdy explains this dilemma:

> A political community can create rights in those who can't participate—
> you might think of the Endangered Species Act and animal-welfare
> legislation as doing this—and of course people's interactions with non-
> human animals will feed into human politics, and quite appropriately.
> But there is a limit. The idea of something like multi-species democracy
> shows a failure to understand what is at stake in democracy: joint partici-
> pation in creating a common world, culminating in an authoritative de-
> cision about its shape (which of course can be revisited and contested).

I wonder whether the idea that we could share a democracy with animals doesn't show the depth of our confusion—and despair—about democracy itself. (Quoted in Andersen 2015)

So, at best, climate engineering could be inclusive but nonparticipatory—which is what global-scale climate engineering is most likely to be anyway. One could impose a new set of specifications and goals—for example, creating a climate that allows the most creatures to thrive—but then there's the question of whether some species, ecologically speaking, are more important to the functioning of ecosystems than others, and this leads to great complexity. There are also broader concerns about designer ecosystems voiced by ecologists: that restoring ecosystems with human-centered thinking can amount to "incrementally cobbling together a function-specific, poorly understood nature" (Mansfield and Doyle 2017, 24).

On the other hand, the time frame of our thinking should perhaps be longer than what comes easily to mind: beyond midcentury or 2100. Astrobiologist David Grinspoon believes that attempting geoengineering anytime soon would be "completely insane," stating that "given how much we have yet to learn, we really should not be let anywhere near the controls of planet Earth," even though we are already engineering Earth in various ways ("perhaps engineering Earth only in the way that your infant is 'engineering' your home media system when she sticks cookies in the DVD slot") (2016, 188, 190, 197). Grinspoon, who thinks in terms of millennia, does not consider radical geoengineering to be an option for the current climate crisis. Yet he believes such research should not be prohibited because "if we can ensure our own survival over (or even muddle through) the next few centuries, then we will eventually want to employ more obtrusive planetary engineering and learn to engineer our planet's climate, intentionally pulling it toward stability," for which we will need both planetary science and self-knowledge (Grinspoon 2016, 197).

In the remainder of this chapter, then, I will consider a different version of climate engineering in the long term and the legal and other social institutions that might enable taking responsibility for some dimensions of the climate system. The responsibility here is not just the response-ability (Haraway 2016) of sensing what stressors are coming to which species and altering rates of what substances go into the atmosphere or oceans, but something forward-looking, a responsibility for design, care, and maintenance. Rather than climate engineering or intervention, I will use the term "design," which I find more aspirational than engineering, more personal than intervention, and more adaptive than planning. Care is design taken through time, tending to our designs.

Barbara Adam and Chris Groves write that "responsibility requires that we involve ourselves in *tending* to a relationship by providing what is needed by another person or persons" (2011, 22). This form of nonreciprocal responsibility is associated with care: "Care is therefore both future directed and, in the first instance, always attached to specific individuals. It is thereby specifically directed toward their futures, and is therefore tied to futures which are embedded in distinct contexts of concern. Consequently, it constructs lived and living futures" (Adam and Groves 2011, 22). Care, in their vision, is a constructive force; it fills in embedded futures rather than abstract and decontextualized futures.

The present disciplined approaches to climate design, which are in their infancy, largely absent ocean life from their calculations (and many other things as well). To be clear, this is not necessarily the fault of the scientists, but of the system in which they operate, which siloes disciplines and treats the future as an unknown and emptied arena. If the coming centuries might entail taking responsibility for ecosystems in order to repair them, from designing them to caring for them, we will need to correct for these absences, but this system will entail different institutions. For this future care–oriented version of designing ecosystems or ecological processes to emerge, we would have to imagine an entirely different set of customs, rituals, and practices. Imagine: a primary education where students spend time learning to relate and think with other species, learning from traditional ecological knowledge as well as other forms of science. Multispecies experience is also a part of university curricula. Elizabeth R. Johnson suggests that sea organisms can be science fictions powerful enough to transform "our understanding of ourselves, expand our own embodied capacities, [and] reconfigure who and what constitute 'us' through an engagement with the sea out of which we emerged" (2018, 142). This engagement with other forms of being can be embedded into education. Students could learn to be responsive to the needs of other species and to successfully care for a whole ecosystem for a period of time in order to graduate in ecological care and design. The licensing of the profession requires hours of apprenticeship; then they specialize, coming to know specific organisms or niches in detail, becoming experts in connection with a whole. Research proposals are assessed on how well they express care for others, reviewed on broader multispecies impacts and responsibility-merit. Caretakers spend time with nonhumans, meditate with them, perhaps say prayers or repeat their intentions before engineering: a reverent set of practices. The various occupations that involve earth-shaping, from farming to aquaculture to materials production, have similar training and practices. Clearly this is science fiction, or beyond science fiction. Yet to say that this is beyond human nature or capacity ignores the ways in which our species takes care: privileging the nature, or psychopathy, of those in our species who have been in power for far too long as the norm or standard or essence of what we are.

At what point in this process does law step in? Law can codify responsibilities of repair when harm has been done. But legally, does the "responsibility to fix" harmed environments carry into a "responsibility to make" new ones? One can imagine a scenario in which climate polluters agree to pay the costs of local ocean liming and restorative programs. Climate engineering could be made contingent on mitigation and adaptation, as suggested by Albert Lin (2013): a nation might pledge to finance twenty dollars of adaptation for every dollar committed to climate engineering research and deployment, or nations could condition use of climate engineering on the adoption of climate mitigation measures. One could extend this logic into the marine sphere and fund marine ecosystem restoration in this way. But, at present, the responsibility for repair does not generally carry into a responsibility to make new ecosystems.

This could change: law is made and continually remade, as legal scholar David Delaney (2016) writes; its strength is in being explicit. On the one hand, it seems like the cultural shift toward responsibility and care must come first; we reorient our thinking, and then the law makes it explicit, spells out what can and cannot be done. On the other hand, perhaps law's function is to initiate and encourage the cultural shift: it certainly has done so in the past, in terms of environmental legislation and cradle-to-grave practices for waste, for example—forward-thinking law pushes the culture forward. At a minimum, and in the near term, law can provoke us to ask the questions that will give us some indication of the lives and deaths of other species, of the stressors we create for them. In the long term, perhaps law can evolve to be more forward-looking and push us toward careful design.

Notes

1 The closest geological analogue to the current acidification was during the Paleocene-Eocene Thermal Maximum (PETM), some fifty-five million years ago, which presents some challenges for studying changes in ocean pH.

2 This was one of Alan Robock's "20 Reasons Why Geoenginering Is a Bad Idea" (2008), and more nuance can be added to it: as Damon Mathews, Long Cao, and Ken Caldeira put it, there would be "second-order interactions between climate engineering, the global carbon budget and ocean chemistry, which may either slightly decrease or slightly increase the rate of ocean acidification, depending on uncertain future changes in terrestrial carbon sinks" (2009). While it is also possible that solar geoengineering would have a slightly beneficial net effect on the oceans, lessening the CO_2 rise in the atmosphere by causing enhanced terrestrial CO_2 uptake and avoiding positive feedbacks, modeling has shown that it may worsen ocean acidification in the deeper

ocean (Tjiputra, Grini, and Lee 2016). At this point, the science of solar geoengineering's effect on oceans (1) is limited and (2) indicates that it will not substantially help ocean acidification (Keller, Feng, and Oschiles 2014; Mathews, Cao, and Caldeira 2009). There are possibilities that some solar geoengineering scenarios could help ocean ecosystems in other ways, for example, by limiting sea surface temperature rise (Couce et al. 2013).

References

Adam, Barbara, and Christopher Groves. 2011. "Futures Tended: Care and Future-Oriented Responsibility." *Bulletin of Science, Technology and Society* 31 (1): 17–27.

Andersen, Ross. 2015. "Nature Has Lost Its Meaning." *The Atlantic*, November 30. http://www.theatlantic.com/science/archive/2015/11/nature-has-lost-its-meaning/417918.

Arora, Saurabh. 2017. *Defying Control: Aspects of Caring Engagement between Divergent Knowledge Practices.* STEPS Working Paper 90. March 20. Brighton, UK: STEPS Centre.

Baird, Rachel, Meredith Simons, and Tim Stephens. 2010. *Ocean Acidification: A Litmus Test for International Law.* Sydney: Sydney Law School Legal Studies Research Paper No. 10/139.

Bodle, Ralph, with Gesa Homan, Simone Schiele, and Elizabeth Tedsen. 2012. "The Regulatory Framework for Climate-Related Geoengineering Relevant to the Convention on Biological Diversity." Part II of *Geoengineering in Relation to the Convention on Biological Diversity: Technical and Regulatory Matters.* Technical Series No. 66. Montreal: Secretariat of the Convention on Biological Diversity.

Corner, Adam, and Nick Pidgeon. 2014. "Geoengineering, Climate Change Skepticism and the 'Moral Hazard' Argument: An Experimental Study of UK Public Perceptions." *Philosophical Transactions of the Royal Society A: Mathematical, Physical and Engineering Sciences* 372 (2031).

Couce, Elena, Peter Irvine, L. J. Gregoire, Andy Ridgwell, and E. J. Hendy. 2013. "Tropical Coral Reef Habitat in a Geoengineered, High-CO_2 World." *Geophysical Research Letters* 40 (9): 1799–1804.

Delaney, David. 2016. "Lively Ever After: Beyond the Cult of Immateriality." In *Animals, Biopolitics, Law: Lively Legalities*, edited by Irus Braverman, 211–17. New York: Routledge.

Doney, Scott C., Victoria J. Fabry, Richard A. Feely, and Joan A. Kleypas. 2009. "Ocean Acidification: The Other CO_2 Problem." *Annual Review of Marine Science* 1: 169–92.

Feng, Elias Yuming, David P. Keller, Wolfgang Koeve, and Andreas Oschlies. 2016. "Could Artificial Ocean Alkalinization Protect Tropical Coral Ecosystems from Ocean Acidification?" *Environmental Research Letters* 11 (7): 074008.

Fennel, Katja, and David L. VanderZwaag. 2016. "Ocean Acidification: Surging Science and Lagging Law and Policy Responses." In *Routledge Handbook on Maritime Regulation and Enforcement*, edited by Robin Warner and Stuart Kaye, 342–62. New York: Routledge.

Fisher, Mark. 2014. *Ghosts of My Life: Writings on Depression, Hauntology and Lost Futures.* Washington, DC: Zero Books.

GOC (Global Ocean Commission). 2013. "Climate Change, Ocean Acidification and Geo-Engineering. " Policy Options Paper No. 2. Oxford, UK: Global Ocean Commission.

Grinspoon, David. 2016. *Earth in Human Hands: Shaping Our Planet's Future.* New York: Grand Central.

Haraway, Donna. 2016. *Staying with the Trouble: Making Kin in the Chthulucene.* Durham, NC: Duke University Press.

Herr, Dorothee, Kirsten Isensee, E. Harrould-Kolieb, and C. Turley. 2014. *Ocean Acidification: International Policy and Governance Options.* Gland, Switzerland: IUCN.

IPCC (Intergovernmental Panel on Climate Change). 2014. "Climate Change 2014: Synthesis Report. Contribution of Working Groups I, II, and III to the Fifth Assessment Report of the Intergovernmental Panel on Climate Change." Geneva: IPCC.

Irvine, Peter J., Ben Kravitz, Mark G. Lawrence, and Helene Muri. 2016. "An Overview of the Earth System Science of Solar Geoengineering." *WIREs Climate Change* 7 (6): 815–33.

Jackson, Lawrence S., J. A. Crook, Andrew Jarvis, D. Leedal, Andrew Ridgwell, Naomi Vaughan, and Piers M. Forster. 2015. "Assessing the Controllability of Arctic Sea Ice Extent by Sulfate Aerosol Geoengineering." *Geophysical Research Letters* 42 (4): 1223–31.

Janda, Richard, and Richard Lehun. 2016. "The Conflict of Human and Nonhuman Laws." In *Animals, Biopolitics, Law: Lively Legalities,* edited by Irus Braverman, 175–92. New York: Routledge.

Johnson, Elizabeth R. 2018. "Beneath the Skin of the Earth: Stories of Life and Warfare." In *Unreachable Empires*, edited by Sigismond de Vijay, 135–77. Zurich: JRP Editions.

Keller, David P., Ellias Y. Feng, and Andreas Oschiles. 2014. "Potential Climate Engineering Effectiveness and Side Effects during a High Carbon Dioxide–Emission Scenario." February 25. *Nature Communications* 5: 3304.

Kirksey, Eben, Craig Schuetze, and Stefan Helmreich. 2014. "Introduction: Tactics of Multispecies Ethnography." In *The Multispecies Salon*, edited by Eben Kirksey, 1–28. Durham, NC: Duke University Press.

Klein, Naomi. 2014. *This Changes Everything: Capitalism vs. the Climate.* New York: Simon & Schuster.

Kravitz, Ben, Douglas MacMartin, Hailong Wang, and Philip J. Rasch. 2016. "Geoengineering as a Design Problem." *Earth System Dynamics* 7 (2): 469–97.

Latham, John, Joan Kleypas, Rachel Hauser, Ben Parkes, and Alan Gadian. 2013. "Can Marine Cloud Brightening Reduce Coral Bleaching?" *Atmospheric Science Letters* 14 (4): 214–19.

Lin, Albert. 2013. "Does Geoengineering Present a Moral Hazard?" *Ecology Law Quarterly* 40 (3): 673–712.

Mansfield, Becky, and Martin Doyle. 2017. "Nature: A Conversation in Three Parts." *Annals of the American Association of Geographers* 107 (1): 22–27.

Mathesius, Sabine, Matthias Hofmann, Ken Caldeira, and Hans Joachim Schellnhuber. 2015. "Long-Term Response of Oceans to CO_2 Removal from the Atmosphere." *Nature Climate Change* 5 (12): 1107–13.

Mathews, H. Damon, Long Cao, and Ken Caldeira. 2009. "Sensitivity of Ocean Acidification to Geoengineered Climate Stabilization." *Geophysical Research Letters* 36 (10): L10706.

McLaren, Duncan. 2016. "Mitigation Deterrence and the 'Moral Hazard' of Solar Radiation Management." *Earth's Future* 4: 596–602.

Merk, Christine, Gert Pönitzsch, and Katrin Rehdanz. 2016. "Knowledge about Aerosol Injection Does Not Reduce Individual Mitigation Efforts." *Environmental Research Letters* 11 (5): 054009.

Morton, Oliver. 2015. *The Planet Remade: How Geoengineering Could Change the World.* Princeton, NJ: Princeton University Press.

Pálsson, Gísli, Bronislaw Szerszynski, Sverker Sörlin, John Marks, Bernard Avril, Carole Crumley, Heide Hackmann, et al. 2013. "Reconceptualizing the 'Anthropos' in the Anthropocene: Integrating the Social Sciences and Humanities in Global Environmental Change Research." *Environmental Science and Policy* 28 (April): 3–13.

Philippopoulos-Mihalopoulos, Andreas. 2016. "Lively Agency: Life and Law in the Anthropocene." In *Animals, Biopolitics, Law: Lively Legalities*, edited by Irus Braverman, 193–210. New York: Routledge.

Robock, Alan. 2008. "Twenty Reasons Why Geoengineering May Be a Bad Idea." *Bulletin of the Atomic Scientists* 64 (2): 14–18.

Steffen, Will, Åsa Persson, Lisa Michele Deutsch, Jan Zalasiewicz, Mark Williams, Katherine Richardson, Carole Crumley, et al. 2011. "The Anthropocene: From Global Change to Planetary Stewardship." *Ambio* 40 (7): 739–61.

Suarez, Pablo, and Maarten K. van Aalst. 2016. "Geoengineering: A Humanitarian Concern." *Earth's Future* 5 (2): 183–95.

Tjiputra, Jerry, A. Grini, and H. Lee. 2016. "Impact of Idealized Future Stratospheric Aerosol Injection on the Large-Scale Ocean and Land Carbon Cycles." *JGR Biogeosciences* 121 (1): 2–27.

Williamson, Philip, and Ralph Bodle. 2016. "Update on Climate." *Geoengineering in Relation to the Convention on Biological Diversity: Potential Impacts and Regulatory Framework.* CBD Technical Series No. 84. Montreal: Secretariat of the Convention on Biological Diversity.

Williamson, Philip, Robert T. Watson, Georgina Mace, Paulo Artaxo, Ralph Bodle, Victor Galaz, Andy Parker, et al. 2012. "Impacts of Climate-Related Geoengineering on Biological Diversity." Part I of *Geoengineering in Relation to the Convention on Biological Diversity: Technical and Regulatory Matters.* CBD Technical Series No. 66. September. Montreal: Secretariat of the Convention on Biological Diversity (SCBD).

Afterword

ADEQUATE IMAGINARIES FOR
ANTHROPOCENE SEAS

STACY ALAIMO

As popular books and films such as Richard Ellis's *The Empty Ocean,* Charles Clover's *The End of the Line,* and Sylvia Earle's *The World Is Blue: How Our Fate and the Ocean's Are One* sound their warnings, a new era in marine conservation is underway, an era in which prevailing imaginaries of oceanic abundance are countered by revelations of scarcity, devastation, and impending collapse. The conception of the ocean as inexhaustible, as an open space to be freely plundered, has long held sway. Even Rachel Carson believed, at least until 1950 when *The Sea around Us* was first published, that the immense seas were immune from anthropogenic harms. The fantasy of inexhaustibility continues to underwrite capitalist and neocolonialist exploits of areas conveniently considered outside the terrains of nation-state, law, or concern. For environmental thinkers and posthumanists, Hugo Grotius's 1609 concept of the *Mare Liberum* offers a cautionary tale, as freedom in this formulation interpellates economic and political subjects into untrammeled extractivism[1] made possible by the supposedly unalterable abundance of the sea.

Alison Rieser, in her chapter, *"Clupea liberum*: Hugo Grotius, Free Seas, and the Political Biology of Herring,*"* tells how *Mare Liberum* was countered by John Selden's *Mare Clausum,* revised in 1635 with assistance from the British king. The Mare Clausum defended the enclosure of seas around the British Isles, claiming sovereignty. The way in which the global ocean is carved up into national territories, fishing and mining zones, and marine protected areas, even as warming waters, acidification, pollution, and countless living creatures cross these boundaries, raises questions about the tensions between legal conceptions of sovereignty, scientific accounts of ocean ecologies, and the possibility of global marine conservation in Anthropocene seas. Many of the essays in this collection analyze the legal, historical, and theoretical conceptions of sovereignty (Jennifer L. Gaynor; Stefan Helmreich; Elizabeth R. Johnson; Stephanie Jones; Zsofia Korosy; Katherine G. Sammler; Philip E. Steinberg, Berit Kristoffersen, and Kristen L. Shake). But the oscillation between conceptions of the seas as open or closed continues to be a means of economic, political, and legal contestation. Published as a pair, the *Mare Liberum* and the *Mare Clausum* were dubbed the "battle of the books." Rieser concludes that the herring "co-produced" the early modern legal doctrines of the seas or, more provocatively, that the "battle of the books was won by *Clupea liberum*," free herring. That the herring could swim in uninvited and win the battle of the books leads us to ponder larger questions about the relation of human conceptions of the ocean to the material realities of the oceans themselves as well as the way in which discursive, including legal, skirmishes may have rather extensive effects that ripple across space and time.

Moreover, the importance of one type of fish to coproducing enduring legal doctrines suggests broader questions about the liveliness of other ocean creatures, ecologies, and materialities. While posthumanists and new materialists may delight in the herring's actions, as an instance of nonhuman agency, a natural history of the seas would actually register very few victories for nonhuman species and far too many losses. The introduction to this collection demonstrates, for example, how ill equipped existing legal regimes that focus on endangerment have been in accounting for and measuring coral decline. As research and scholarship on the oceans develop, it may be helpful to consider, with Grotius in mind, how human ideologies, discourses, and paradigms can have tremendous power and yet, conversely, how the species, ecologies, materialities, and physical forces of the seas have their own agencies and interrelations. More importantly, however, we need theories and methodologies that can contend with the interactions or even "intra-actions" (Barad) between what we used to divide into "nature" and "culture," as the Anthropocene calls us to contend with a world in which there is no "nature" untouched by human activity, not even at the bottom of the sea. In "Wave Law," for example, Stefan Helmreich reveals how even something as formidable and seemingly invincible as ocean waves may be affected by anthropogenic forces, to the extent that legal struggles to "save the waves" have sprung up.

Tracing entanglements between human and more-than-human forces is especially difficult given that still so very little is known about the seas, especially the deep seas, and especially about ecological interrelations in these spaces. This volume, and the blue humanities and oceanic science studies more broadly, may contribute to the urgent project of tracing, assembling, critiquing, and conceptualizing ways of knowing aquatic multispecies environments. That this volume is so capacious, including topics based in different geographical regions, historical periods, and governmental modalities spanning various disciplinary frames and methods, suggests the many challenges with which oceanic studies must contend in order to contribute to the imaginaries that seas require in the twenty-first century.

Whatever the specific topic, it may be useful to consider whether turning from the terrestrial to the aquatic shifts methodologies, epistemologies, ontologies, and ethics.[2] To what extent does fathoming the seas require disciplinary crossings and the creation of new concepts, theories, and frameworks? Science and technology studies (STS) may be well positioned to traverse disciplines in ways that are particularly generative for oceanic studies, since so many topics require engaging with scientific research about the geophysical, chemical, and biological aspects of the seas. Elizabeth R. Johnson and Irus Braverman put forth a provocative starting point for *Blue Legalities*: "Rather than start with an assumption of law as a prediscursive entity," this volume begins with "the seas themselves," and then investigates "various laws as socio-scientific, heterogeneous, and material phenomena." Susan Reid's intrepid and poetic essay, "Solwara 1 and the Sessile Ones," epitomizes the merits of this approach, as it submerges inchoate, potentially legal, questions into abyssal and benthic realms, disclosed by marine biology and encountered through posthumanist theories. She asks, "How might an ecologically tilted imaginary guide ocean legalities and generative practices that respect and respond to conditions for livability?"

Constructing adequate imaginaries is a formidable task, as the oceans, with their volume as well as their breadth, remain not only difficult to fathom, but also resistant to solid legal apportionments. The scale of the seas presents challenges that are (often simultaneously) technological, scientific, political, conceptual, philosophical, and legal. While a multitude of relations and occurrences within ocean ecologies and Anthropocene seas elude narrative structures, they may be captured by other means. Several of the essays included here discuss modes of data collection and visualization, from mapping as a mode of claiming sovereignty for Britain in the eighteenth century in the Nootka Sound (Korosy) to the thirty-five hundred drifting floats of Argo's sensing networks which measure temperature and salinity (Lehman). These Argo drifters are especially intriguing when they provoke anxious questions about sovereignty, territoriality, and militarism even as the data they are capturing seem modest and benign. Asking whom contemporary marine science serves, Jessica Lehman echoes critiques of Anthropocene discourses: "arguments that marine scientific research benefits all humankind assume that there is a unitary notion of the human, which should override the inevitable fact that not all humans will benefit equally, and, in some cases, may even be harmed."

Understanding that there is not a unitary "human" that marine science would benefit is invaluable for social and economic justice. These inquiries need be complemented, however, with multispecies analyses that consider the unequal distribution of benefits and harms not only between different groups of humans, but also across different nonhuman groups and ecological zones. Would it be possible to compare the extent to which marine science has resulted, across different times and places, in benefits or harms to various marine creatures? Do the standard practices and the funding mechanisms of marine science end up benefiting corporations and privileged peoples while harming particular ocean species and ecologies along with Indigenous and other less privileged peoples? Are there international legal frameworks in place that could even begin to address such questions? In other words, how much of marine science has been yoked to large-scale, industrial, resource extraction and how much has been dedicated to conservation and to the cultural and subsistence practices of small communities? And, relatedly, how has conservation been propelled by entirely utilitarian and anthropocentric motives rather than by more biocentric, ecocentric, or kincentric[3] aims? To what extent have the funding streams for marine sciences affected what we know and what we don't know? As scholars sort through the entanglements of science, law, and politics, multispecies perspectives are crucial for warding off futures in which a diminished number of species struggle to inhabit largely empty or monocultural seas, teeming with resilient jellyfish and little else.[4]

Scientific, technological, political, and legal factors also intertwine when it comes to the possibilities for ocean conservation. Even though the *Mare Clausum*, which defended the enclosure of seas around the British Isles, aimed to benefit one polity exclusively, enclosure could nonetheless be a mechanism for warding off full-scale plunder of the seas by various entities. The tragedy of the commons cannot be prevented without some sense of the commons as such, nor without a conception of limited resources. Johnson and Braverman cite legal scholar Surabhi Ranganathan, explaining that "conservation efforts that vilified common resource management in the seas have ended up sparking legislation that dispossessed both Indigenous and settler communities alike from critical resources" (2016). For centuries, people in Oceania and Micronesia have protected specific marine areas and species for conservation purposes. Kenneth Ruddle explains that in establishing the international law of the sea, Westerners assumed the "universal validity" of their laws and disparaged the laws of Indigenous peoples as "primitive" (2008, 14). In the 1970s, however, tropical marine biologist R. E. Johannes charged that it was Western laws that were "primitive," in contrast to the traditional laws of the Pacific Islanders with whom he worked. The Pacific Islanders, Johannes contended, "knew their resources were finite and their traditional laws reflect this knowledge" (Ruddle 2008, 14).

Whereas traditional laws and other localized practices may be based on a recognition of finitude, large-scale industrialized fishing operates without a sense of limits or a respect for specific ocean habitats and ecosystems as actual places, despite their fluidity. The development of Marine Protected Areas (MPAS), as recommended by the International Union for the Conservation of Nature and Natural Resources (later, the IUCN) at their 1975 Tokyo conference, is a potentially crucial means for curbing the destruction of ocean ecologies. Also, much less directly, the very demarcation of marine zones worth protecting may offer alternatives to the industrialized imaginary of the seas as a void. Philip E. Steinberg's formative work, *The Social Construction of the Ocean*, argues that both industrialized and postmodern capitalism construct ocean space as a "great void" rather than as a "distinct place or environment" (2001, 164–65). The very process of designating particular sites as MPAs that are important to preserve may provoke a wider consideration of how various human activities affect marine ecologies, bringing specific realms of the ocean within the domain of human concern.

When it comes to the fluid seas, however, boundaries can be fantastically elusive. Even something as seemingly solid as ice turns out to be an ontologically slippery site—or, to put it more appropriately, to be a dynamic interaction, or zone of probability, as Steinberg, Berit Kristoffersen, and Kristen L. Shake's chapter on the Barents Sea in the Norwegian petrostate, "Edges and Flows: Exploring Legal Materialities and Biophysical Politics at the Sea Ice Edge," keenly demonstrates. In order to regulate extraction and conservation in the warming Arctic, the ice edge must be mapped. But how to do so, when it is "not simply a geophysical boundary; it is also a zone of interaction and interchange that forms a vital link between physical, chemical, biological, and legal systems in the polar regions and beyond." Their account of the ice is not unlike a new materialist sense of material agency and intra-action in which "relata" (what we would ordinarily consider to be stable entities, objects, or things) do not "preexist relations" (Barad 2007, 140). Rather, as Karen Barad explains, drawing on Niels Bohr, "relata-within phenomena emerge through specific intra-actions" (2007, 140). All is process, dynamism, and emergence.

What is crucial here, however, is that Steinberg, Kristoffersen, and Shake move from an onto-epistemological analysis toward a recommendation for a "a legal geography of the ice edge" that would "account not only for sea ice's dynamism in both space and time and its ontological indeterminacy, but also for the way it draws connections among physical, chemical, and biological processes that scientific scholars all too often perceive to be in isolation." Essentially, they propose a sea ice management system informed by the precautionary approach: "New forms of mapping and legislating would be required for a politics of probability and processes." Their essay demonstrates how innovative theoretical scholarship can be relevant for real-world problems, as it offers workable paradigms and lucid policy recommendations.

Indeterminacy and category confusion surface from another locale, this time in Jennifer L. Gaynor's chapter, "Liquid Territory, Shifting Sands: Property, Sovereignty, and Space in Southeast Asia's Tristate Maritime Boundary Zone," which discusses the industrial production of land. She explains: "Taking sand from the marine world and reconstituting it to create terrestrial places, land reclamation changes the shape of both land and sea and alters coastal ecologies." What will the environmental effects of these vast land reclamation projects be? Are there any national or international environmental legal frameworks or governing bodies adequate to the task of attending to the nonhuman species and ecologies that could be harmed by the production of land from the sea? Broadly speaking, how can national and international legal frameworks be conceptualized in ways that would be adequate for differing ecological zones within a world in which land can be produced and seascapes can be altered at this vertiginous scale?

While Gaynor and several other essays in the volume use sovereignty in a conventional legal sense—namely, to establish territorial boundaries—for Indigenous peoples sovereignty can also be an intellectual and cultural matter. Indeed, traditional ecological knowledges, multispecies ontologies, and cosmopolitical visions may challenge the dominant modes of being and knowing that undergird international law. To take an example that seems extraordinarily counterintuitive to many of us, consider that the Māori whakapapa does not divide the land from the sea. Moreover, Māori intellectual sovereignty[5] entails discarding something so integral to Western culture—the belief in human sovereignty over nature. Katherine G. Sammler, in "Kauri and the Whale: Oceanic Matter and Meaning in New Zealand," explains that when New Zealand granted personhood to a national park in 2014, Pita Sharples, minister of Māori affairs, stated that this legislation provides "a profound alternative to the human presumption of sovereignty over the natural world" (quoted in Sammler). Indigenous philosophies that do not declare sovereignty over something Western settler-colonialists have cordoned off as a separate realm of nature, severed into land and sea, may be more adept at understanding the complex interactions and interrelations that swirl through specific sites where ocean species and ecologies are threatened. Thus, Indigenous knowledges and activism offer alternative paths for conceptualizing and countering colonialist and capitalist practices of extraction and the legal regimes that accompany and govern such practices. Moreover, they may afford more potent modes of concern for oceans that are not presumed to be disconnected from terrestrial human lives. Karin Amimoto Ingersoll, for example, describes a "seascape epistemology" of the Kanaka Maoli (Native Hawaiians) that "provides a decolonizing methodology for Kanaka by revealing hidden linkages between water and land that speak to Indigenous ways of knowing and being, to historical means of political, social and cultural survival" (2016, 20).

The Māori and Kanaka sense of the sea and the land as intimately interconnected contrasts with settler-colonial visions of the ocean as an alien space. The metaphor of the oceans as another planet, filled with alien creatures, has been extremely common in European and North American literature, film, popular culture, and popular science. Two of James Cameron's films, one a documentary about deep-sea science (*Aliens of the Deep*, 2005) and one a science fiction film (*The Abyss*, 1989), for example, subordinate the exploration of the deep seas to space travel and cinematically transform ocean creatures into space aliens. I've argued elsewhere that this popular figuration may be harmful for ocean conservation, as it configures the seas, especially the deep seas, as a realm untouched by human incursions (Alaimo 2012, 2014). It entices with an anachronistic sense of innocent discovery, in a space ostensibly free of guilt from histories of colonialist oppression and ecological harm. The alien seas are imagined to be the final frontier, where the excitement of discovery need not be dampened by messy ethical and political encumbrances—a *Mare Liberum* for the twenty-first century, circulating through film, digital media, and other modes of popular culture. This vision is quite different, it should be noted, from the alien oceans that Stefan Helmreich analyzes in his magnificent book *Alien Ocean: Anthropological Voyages in Microbial Seas*, where the human is saturated with microbial oceanic natures: "This is not human nature reflecting ocean nature. It is an entanglement of natures, an intimacy with the alien" (2009, 284).

This sense of intimacy with the alien rarely surfaces, however, in theoretical, popular, and visual accounts of the Anthropocene, in which the *anthropos* seems to stand apart, as a force upon the planet, who escapes entanglement with other agencies, assemblages, materialities, and beings.[6] The oceans are ignored in many popular accounts of the Anthropocene, which seize upon the geological origins of the concept to stress the palpability, or even the solidity, of "Man's" impact on the world.[7] The species arrogance that seeps through some of these accounts—that of having left one's permanent mark on the world—may be difficult to extend to fluid seas, which provoke more complicated ontologies and epistemologies. Seen from another perspective, the concept of the Anthropocene swirls together biological and chemical, as well as geological, processes that involve the seas and the atmosphere as well as terrestrial geographies. While the popular versions of alien seas pose the pelagic and abyssal zones as outside the reach of human incursions, the Anthropocene seas are already saturated with the intended and unintended consequences of human activity. The very temperature and chemical composition of the seawater has been altered by the massive release of CO_2 since the beginning of the industrial era, not to mention the enormity of the effects of the extractive industries, be they biological or mineral, as well as the dumping of radioactive, plastic, and other waste.

Several of the essays included here consider the Anthropocene seas as sites of chemical dumping, capitalist plunder, technological mediation, the translation of matter and energy into data, biotechnology, and numerous modes of militarism. The seas that have been considered utterly alien to terrestrial humans are now the site for countless alterations, infiltrations, technologies, and mediations, many of which determine, intentionally or inadvertently, what lives and what dies. Several of the essays herein offer vital provocations for considering what the human role will or should be in future seas, even as they focus on the human as part of technological and other assemblages or on the prosthetic extensions of the human bodies, minds, knowledges, and intentions. In "Robotic Life in the Deep Sea," Irus Braverman, calling for "a more comprehensive scholarly consideration of the biopolitical enlisting of robots both to make die and to make live," asks "whether it matters, physically, socially, and legally, if the acts of making live and making die are carried out by machines rather than by humans and, also, whether it matters that they target nonhuman animals." Braverman analyzes the autonomous robots designed to kill crown-of-thorns starfish that have been invading coral reefs, citing one scientist who sees the avatar-driven robots as "essentially an extension of the human."

Elizabeth R. Johnson, in "The Hydra and the Leviathan: Unmanned Maritime Vehicles and the Militarized Seaspace" describes the US military's designs for an army of machines that mimic marine life, populating the sea with futuristic, militaristic, "electric sheep": "Robotic lobsters, clams, tuna, and crabs have all marched (or swum) forth from DARPA's coffers to demonstrate the potentials of robotics in military security." Johnson writes that DARPA (Defense Advanced Research Projects Agency), an explicitly futuristic US enterprise, aims to keep humans (with their troublesome bodily needs) away from the site of naval battles. Chillingly, "the seas appear in the DoD's strategic visioning to be evacuated of human and other life-forms. Machinery and physical matter take over as the primary elements of concern in the operational environment."

We could ask, with Braverman and Johnson, whether it would matter if the acts of making live and making die are carried out by genetically engineered creatures rather than robots or humans. Australian artist Patricia Piccinini, in her "Nature's Little Helpers" series of works, creates, for example, lifelike sculptures of creatures she conceptualizes as genetically engineered in order to protect and save other, endangered, species. The fierce "Bodyguard" with menacing teeth was ostensibly created to protect a small, endangered bird, the "Golden Helmeted Honeyeater," from encroachment. Piccinini writes that along with ethical and environmental issues she is interested in the "possibility of the unpredictable relationship between the [bird] and its bodyguard, and between them and us" (2004, n.p.). Less visually charismatic perhaps, marine algal biotechnologies are also the site for unpredictable relations, as Amy Braun argues in "'Got Algae?': Putting Marine Life to Work for Sustainability," explaining that not only are the algae themselves being remade by biotechnology, but so are the scientific, economic, and legal dimensions of the growing blue economy that is driven by the vexed notions of sustainable development and resilience. Both terms, I would note, tend to pose nonhuman life as a resource for human use; they greenwash capitalism while actually paying scant attention to the needs of nonhuman species, even in the midst of the Sixth Great Extinction (Alaimo 2013, 2016).

Discourses of sustainability that reduce nature to a resource for human use and futuristic seas populated by robots and machines fail to account for nonhuman lives and agencies. Predominant visual depictions of the Anthropocene also erase nonhuman creatures, as they scale up and away. Even at this grand scale, however, the Anthropocene could, to some degree, be visualized as an epoch in which species other than the human still exist. We can imagine scenes that depict the deadly overlaps between shipping channels, military routes, and cruise ship traffic and the migration routes of whales. Or we could consider an aquatic, sonic Anthropocene that charts collisions between shipping noise, military sonar blasts, and cetacean soundings. The now-iconic scaling up of Anthropocene visualizations, epitomizes the "God's-eye view," the "conquering gaze from nowhere," the "view of infinite vision," of an unmarked, disembodied perspective, which Donna Haraway critiqued decades ago, offering a feminist and environmentalist epistemology of "situated knowledges" (1991, 188–89) as an alternative. To speculate about the Anthropocene and, especially, the Anthropocene seas, requires scale shifting as a practice of situated, transcorporeal epistemologies (Alaimo 2016). The predominant versions of the Anthropocene that scale up and away serve to reinstate a universal human objective observer who is actually merely particular. As Sylvia Wynter explains, "Human and Humanity were created as the enunciated *that projects and propels to universality the local image* of the enunciator" (quoted in McKittrick 2015, 109; italics in original). How to reconcile multiple human sites of enunciation and multiple cultures, sciences, and epistemologies when reckoning with the global seas remains a problem for environmentalism, Indigenous sovereignty, legal pluralism, and social justice.

Given that it may be difficult to imagine how we could map, experience, or conceptualize the unfathomable seas from anything other than a God-like human position far above and outside the planet, it may be helpful to consider some robotic technologies that offer intriguing possibilities. Braverman, interviewing marine scientist Christian Voolstra, describes the OceanOne technology as a glove. This "haptic technology," enables "a sense of touch [to be] communicated through the robot to the human controller—the connection between the two described as 'direct and instantaneous.'" This technology, in my view, offers the potential for immersive onto-epistemologies that can foster less distant and arrogant modes of knowing the deep seas. While the predominant scientific vision objectifies and removes the human from the scene, this technology enables a sense of human knowledge making practices as immersed rather than transcendent. While we could jettison the dualism between reality and representation by thinking with Bruno Latour about how truth is to be found in chains of mediations—"*continuing* the flow," "elongating the cascade of mediations" (2010, 123)—we could also linger with the sense of immediacy, which collapses distance even across vast scales. Speculative fictions have conjured up this sort of knowledge practice—the haptic, the immediate, the felt— as more posthuman and potentially more environmentally ethical.

Take Octavia Butler's *Xenogenesis* trilogy,[8] in which the alien oankali species *taste* as a mode of detecting the genetics of other creatures, enjoying the knowledge practice as a pleasurable, sensual encounter. Consider Melody Jue's concept of "intimate objectivity," developed from feminist science studies and Nnedi Okorafor's 2016 Afrofuturist novel *Lagoon,* a science fiction text that merges marine biology and Indigenous cosmology (Jue 2017). Or ponder Vilém Flusser and Louis Bec's *Vampyroteuthis infernalis,* which critiques the scientific "spirit of objectivity," imagining instead, scientific practices that would be less unlike the vampire squid's onto-epistemologies, practices in which the sciences would "serve as luminescent organs, adorning fabulous tentacles with which the vampyroteuthis—one hopes—can be felt" (2012, 73). That this mode of science would mimic the creature it is investigating may return us back to the robotic lobsters and other military-designed creatures Johnson discusses, leading us to ponder how difficult it is to disentangle the ethical and political dimensions of onto-epistemologies. New materialisms, as they have been deeply informed by poststructuralism and science studies theories of perpetual emergence and intra-activity (Barad 2007), proffer no solid foundations, which means that our imaginaries, desires, ontologies, epistemologies, politics, and practices may not always align.

For example, if the citizen science initiative whereby nonscientists could participate in surveilling the ocean floor comes about, how would it affect the participants? Braverman explains that "an easily accessible control system (for example, using a smartphone)" would enable laypersons "to deploy the robots across oceans." She states: "If this vision materializes, a fleet of robots will soon roam the oceans, mapping the ocean floor, collecting images, and monitoring a variety of environmental 'pests.'" Will participants be interpellated as subjects within particular ideological structures of big science? Will they take their atomistic, consumerist presumptions about the extermination of household pests and extend them across the seas? Or will their participation be experienced as an immersed transcorporeal praxis, which would entail scale-shifting reflections on their own entanglements as consumers, citizens, and potential ocean conservation activists? As the scientists and nonscientists extend their own bodies and selves into these technological manners, could they find themselves pondering vital questions about what it means to be human within the Anthropocene? In this volume, Astrida Neimanis elucidates how complicated ethics and politics become within radically uncertain epistemologies: "how do we account for ourselves and our actions when that self, and the bodies and environments it effects, refuse full knowability, certainty, and boundedness in time and space?"

If we now inhabit a world in which even the waves need saving, a world in which the recognition of the Anthropocene both bolsters human arrogance and demands human responsibility, there is no chance that, when it comes to ocean ecologies, we will not have been wrong. As Cary Wolfe writes in *Before the Law: Humans and Other Animals in a Biopolitical Frame*, "We *must* choose and by definition we *cannot* choose everything and everyone at once. But this is precisely what ensures that *in* the future we *will have been wrong*" (2013, 103; emphasis in original). The implications of this statement are too numerous and sobering to be adequately addressed here. However, when it comes to the hauntological existence of marine microbes, the protagonists of Astrid Schrader's chapter, it is no longer clear whether the notion of choice is the best strategy for developing an affirmative biopolitics. Schrader claims that "haunted marine microbes" remodel our understanding of "politics within biology." Drawing on

Wolfe, Heather Paxson and Stefan Helmreich, and Jacques Derrida, she develops a marine microbiopolitics that is hauntological rather than ontological in order to "suggest an alternative to the notion of sacrifice as the foundation of life and law."

One of the many ways in which "we" will have been wrong is discussed by Holly Jean Buck in her essay, "'Climate Engineering Doesn't Stop Ocean Acidification': Addressing Harms to Ocean Life in Geoengineering Imaginaries." As the title suggests, Buck analyzes how climate geoengineering plans ignore the oceans, posing questions that are crucial for imagining what sorts of interventions would be required to foster multispecies futures. "What could a climate intervention strategy that accounts for nonhumans look and feel like? What kinds of institutions, cultural norms, and legal actions would be needed to realize a climate designed for the flourishing of those beyond land-based humans?"

In my own recent work, I have been grappling with the question of what it would mean to extend human concern to the bottom of the seas and what it would take to cultivate an ethics that would include creatures who are not only not human, but fabulously different from the sort of species—usually terrestrial or mammalian—that manage to gain some sort of human recognition, legal or otherwise. Susan Reid's chapter, "Solwara 1 and the Sessile Ones," describes how deep-sea mining would disrupt the ocean depths. The benthic and abyssal species and ecologies, which are not at all well understood, are soon to be devastated by legally sanctioned seabed mining. Reid writes: "In the juridical imaginary, the ocean is valued as mineral stockpile, oil reserve, fish tank and food pantry, cabinet of potential pharmaceuticals, and endless supplier of materials in the service of the human project. It is an imaginary underpinned by cornerstone neo-liberal values: cheap nature converted for capitalism's gain." Capitalism's quick gains are terribly out of sync with the temporalities of deep-sea ecologies. As Reid explains, "Mining is a violence of immediacy to which creaturely communities can barely adapt in time, if at all." Legal temporalities also are violently out of sync with the pace of sessile lives, which suggests the need to develop legal imaginaries in tune with biodiverse temporalities and the precautionary approach. As Reid argues, "There is a compelling place in law to better recognize the different registers of temporality. Legal apparatuses must be put in place that acknowledge life stages and associated vulnerabilities of creatures on the same plane as the commercial claims of corporations."

Neimanis's chapter, "Held in Suspense: Mustard Gas Legalities in the Gotland Deep," also grapples with temporal disjunctions, such as how the 1993 Convention on the Prohibition of the Development, Production, Stockpiling and Use of Chemical Weapons and on their Destruction does not address the weapons already at the bottom of the sea: "these benthic wartime souvenirs are out of time with the legal regimes that want to call us to account." As she analyzes the perplexing environmental threat that discarded weapons pose, she asks us to pause and consider specific moments within multispecies seascapes, such as how past military conflicts are "reanimated by the chemical burn on the snout of a seal." Neimanis argues that "although we might imagine the law as primarily concerned with fixity, the ocean legalities of the Gotland Deep illuminate how suspension's refusal to ever fully arrive also frames the legal regimes that might address these caches." Rather than criticize the "incapacity of legal regimes to contain the ineffability of these weapons dumps," Neimanis challenges us to rethink "how ocean legalities could better live with suspension in the Anthropocene." Her provocative essay, which advocates "an ethics of curiosity and care" and calls us "to do politics even if we know they are always incomplete," complements or circumvents Wolfe's haunting presentiment that we will have been wrong. This essay, and the volume as a whole, may help us develop adequate imaginaries for Anthropocene seas, imaginaries that can inspire and sustain us through what will surely be an era of unsettling suspense.

Notes

1 There are many recent definitions of "extractivism," but Macarena Gómez-Barris offers one potent explanation of her concept of the extractive zone: "The 'extractive zone' names the violence that capitalism does to reduce, constrain, and convert life into commodities, as well as to the epistemological violence of training our academic vision to reduce life to systems" (2017, xix).

2 An interrelated question would be to what extent thinking with water shifts onto-epistemologies (see MacLeod, Chen, and Neimanis 2013; Neimanis 2017).

3 "Kincentric" is Enrique Sálmon's term (2000).

4 For scientific visions of gelatinous futures, where the oceans to come resemble those of the distant past, before many marine species had evolved, see, for instance, Richardson et al. 2009.

5 For an excellent analysis of the ways in which the term "sovereignty" is used in Indigenous studies see "Sovereignty" by Kirby Brown, who explains that "Native and allied scholars over the past two decades have put sovereignty to work for a variety of political, intellectual, and methodological projects" (2018, 83). He adds: "We now speak of intellectual sovereignty (Warrior), representational sovereignty (Weaver), visual sovereignty (Raheja), cultural sovereignty (Singer), rhetorical sovereignty (Lyons "Rhetorical"), sitcom sovereignty (Tahmahkera), sovereign selves (Carlson), sovereign erotics (Driskill et al.; Rifkin Erotics), sovereign bodies (L. Simpson), temporal sovereignty (Rifkin, Beyond), and a host of other conceptual framings" (83).

6 See my critique of Dipesh Chakrabarty's important appraisal of the Anthropocene in *Exposed* (2016, 148–56).

7   One of many examples would be "Rock Solid Evidence of Anthropocene Seen in 2018 Minerals We Made" (Whyte 2017).

8   Octavia Butler's *Xenogenesis* trilogy was originally published individually as *Dawn* (1987), *Adulthood Rites* (1988), and *Imago* (1989) and later republished together as *Lilith's Brood* (2000).

References

Alaimo, Stacy. 2012. "Dispersing Disaster: The Deepwater Horizon, Ocean Conservation, and the Immateriality of Aliens." In *Disasters, Environmentalism, and Knowledge*, edited by Sylvia Mayer and Christof Mauch, 175–92. Heidelberg: Bavarian American Academy, Universitätsverlag.

Alaimo, Stacy. 2013. "Bring Your Shovel." Manifesto for inaugural issue of *Resilience: A Journal of the Environmental Humanities* 1 (1). http://muse.jhu.edu/article/565555.

Alaimo, Stacy. 2014. "Feminist Science Studies: Aesthetics and Entanglement in the Deep Sea." In *Oxford Handbook of Ecocriticism*, edited by Greg Garrard, 188–204. New York: Oxford University Press.

Alaimo, Stacy. 2016. *Exposed: Environmental Politics and Pleasures in Posthuman Times.* Minneapolis: University of Minnesota Press.

Barad, Karen. 2007. *Meeting the Universe Halfway.* Durham, NC: Duke University Press.

Brown, Kirby. 2018. "Sovereignty." *Western American Literature* 53 (1): 81–89.

Butler, Octavia. 2000. *Lilith's Brood.* New York: Grand Central Publishing.

Earle, Sylvia A. 2009. *The World Is Blue: How Our Fate and the Ocean's Are One.* Washington, DC: National Geographic Society.

Flusser, Vilém, and Louis Bec. 2012. *Vampyroteuthis infernalis.* Minneapolis: University of Minnesota Press.

Gómez-Barris, Macarena. 2017. *The Extractive Zone: Social Ecologies and Decolonial Perspectives.* Durham, NC: Duke University Press.

Haraway, Donna J. 1991. "Situated Knowledges: The Science Question in Feminism and the Privilege of Partial Perspective." In *Simians, Cyborgs, Women: The Reinvention of Nature,* 183–202. New York: Routledge.

Helmreich, Stefan. 2009. *Alien Ocean: Anthropological Voyages in Microbial Seas.* Berkeley: University of California Press.

Ingersoll, Karin Amimoto. 2016. *Waves of Knowing: A Seascape Epistemology.* Durham, NC: Duke University Press.

Jue, Melody. 2017. "Intimate Objectivity: On Nnedi Okorafor's Oceanic Afrofuturism." *Women's Studies Quarterly* 45 (1 and 2): 171–88.

Latour, Bruno. 2010. *On the Modern Cult of the Factish Gods.* Durham, NC: Duke University Press.

MacLeod, Janine, Cecilia Chen, and Astrida Neimanis. 2013. *Thinking with Water.* Montreal: McGill-Queens University Press.

McKittrick, Katherine, ed. 2015. *Sylvia Wynter: On Being Human as Praxis.* Durham, NC: Duke University Press.

Neimanis, Astrida. 2017. *Bodies of Water: Posthuman Feminist Phenomenology*. London: Bloomsbury.

Okorafor, Nnedi. 2016. *Lagoon*. New York. Saga.

Piccinini, Patricia. 2004. "Bodyguard." Artist Statement for Robert Miller Gallery, New York. http://www.patriciapiccinini.net/writing/26/240/113.

Ranganathan, Surabhi. 2016. "Global Commons." *European Journal of International Law* 27 (3): 693–717.

Richardson, Anthony J., Andrew Bakun, Graeme C. Hays, and Mark J. Gibbons. 2009. "The Jellyfish Joyride: Causes, Consequences, and Management Responses to a More Gelatinous Future." *Trends in Ecology and Evolution* 24 (6): 312–22.

Ruddle, Kenneth. 2008. "Introduction to the Collected Works of R. E. Johannes, Publications on Marine Traditional Knowledge and Management." Publication of Marine Resource Management and Knowledge Information Bulletin No. 23: 13–24.

Sálmon, Enrique. 2000. "Kincentric Ecology: Indigenous Perceptions of the Human-Nature Relationship." *Ecological Applications* 10 (5): 1327–32.

Steinberg, Philip, E. 2001. *The Social Construction of the Ocean*. Cambridge: Cambridge University Press.

Whyte, Chelsea. 2017. "Rock Solid Evidence of Anthropocene Seen in 2018 Minerals We Made." *New Scientist*, March 1. https://www.newscientist.com/article/2122874-rock-solid-evidence-of-anthropocene-seen-in-208-minerals-we-made.

Wolfe, Cary. 2013. *Before the Law: Humans and Other Animals in a Biopolitical Frame*. Chicago: University of Chicago Press.

Contributors

STACY ALAIMO is professor of English at the University of Oregon. Alaimo's books include *Undomesticated Ground: Recasting Nature as Feminist Space* (2000), *Bodily Natures: Science, Environment, and the Material Self* (2010), which won the Association for the Study of Literature and Environment (ASLE) book award for ecocriticism, and *Exposed: Environmental Politics and Pleasures in Posthuman Times* (2016). She also coedited *Material Feminisms* (2008) and edited the volume *Matter* (2016) in the Gender series of Macmillan Interdisciplinary Handbooks. Alaimo is currently writing the monograph *Composing Blue Ecologies: Science, Aesthetics, and the Creatures of the Abyss* and is coediting a book series, Elements, for Duke University Press.

AMY BRAUN is a PhD candidate in geography at the University of North Carolina at Chapel Hill, with research interests in political ecology, technoscience studies, and development studies. Her current work explores the role of marine biotechnology in sustainable development discourse and practice, focusing on the development of algal products and the enrollment of oceans and marine life in sustainability projects.

IRUS BRAVERMAN is professor of law and adjunct professor of geography at the University at Buffalo, SUNY. Her books include *Zooland: The Institution of Captivity* (2012) and *Wild Life: The Institution of Nature* (2015). Her latest book, *Coral Whisperers: Scientists on the Brink* (2018), gleans insights from more than one hundred interviews with leading coral scientists to document a community caught in an existential crisis and alternating between despair and hope. Her essays have been published in *Critical Inquiry*, *Public Culture*, *Geoforum*, *Antipode*, *BioSocieties*, and the *Annual Review of Law and Social Science*.

HOLLY JEAN BUCK is a NatureNet Science Fellow at UCLA's Institute of the Environment and Sustainability. Her research interests include agroecology and climate-smart agriculture, energy landscapes, land use change, new media, and science and technology studies. She has written on several aspects of climate engineering, including humanitarian and development approaches to geoengineering, gender considerations, and the social implications of scaling up negative emissions. She is the author of *After Geoengineering: Climate Tragedy, Repair, and Restoration* (2019).

JENNIFER L. GAYNOR, a scholar of Southeast Asia and its surrounding seas from the early modern period to the present, earned her PhD in history and anthropology at the University of Michigan, Ann Arbor, and is currently a research fellow at the University at Buffalo's Baldy Center for Law & Social Policy. Her first book, *Intertidal History in Island Southeast Asia: Submerged Genealogy and the Legacy of Coastal Capture* (2016), received honorable mention for the Benda Prize, and she has published articles in *Radical History Review*, the *Journal of World History*, and *Anthropological Quarterly*. She co-leads an endeavor under the auspices of the Association for Asian Studies, with funding from the Henry Luce Foundation, to support the field of law, society, and justice in the Asian Studies context.

STEFAN HELMREICH is professor of anthropology at MIT. He is the author of *Alien Ocean: Anthropological Voyages in Microbial Seas* (2009) and of *Sounding the Limits of Life: Essays in the Anthropology of Biology and Beyond* (2016). His essays have appeared in *Critical Inquiry*, *Representations*, *American Anthropologist*, and *The Wire*.

ELIZABETH R. JOHNSON is an assistant professor of human geography at Durham University, UK. She writes on emerging ties between the biosciences and technological innovation and how they are changing understandings of human and nonhuman life. Her writing has appeared in journals including *South Atlantic Quarterly*, *Annals of the Association of American Geography*, *Society and Space*, *Theory, Culture and Society*, and *Ephemera: Theory and Politics in Organization*. She is currently working on a monograph titled *Life's Work: The Politics of Biological Productivity*.

STEPHANIE JONES is an associate professor of English at the University of Southampton. She researches the Indian Ocean and writes within the intersection of law and literature. Specifically, she has written about the poetics of maritime law, fictional and historical piracy and privateering, literary and legal belonging, and East African and South Asian literatures. She is currently writing a book about pirates.

ZSOFIA KOROSY is a doctoral candidate in law at the University of New South Wales (UNSW). She holds undergraduate degrees in arts (politics and international relations) and law from UNSW and a master's degree in law from Yale Law School. Korosy's research examines the development of international law as it regulates the fishing and whaling resources of the Pacific Ocean. Her work is supported by an Australian Government Research Training Program Scholarship.

BERIT KRISTOFFERSEN is an associate professor in political geography and political science at the University of Tromsø, Norway. Her research explores how present and future challenges are negotiated in the Arctic, climate change strategies, changing environmentalism, resource networks and politics relating to natural resources, and how this can be analyzed across scales.

JESSICA LEHMAN is an assistant professor in human geography (environment and society) at Durham University, UK. Her essays on global ocean politics and science have been published in *Geoforum*, *Environment and Planning D*, *Political Geography*, *Social Studies of Science*, *International Social Science Journal*, *Multitudes*, and *The New Inquiry*.

ASTRIDA NEIMANIS is a senior lecturer in the Department of Gender and Cultural Studies of the University of Sydney, on Gadigal Land, in Australia. Her writings include *Bodies of Water: Feminist Posthuman Phenomenology* (2017) and the coedited volume

Thinking with Water (2013), as well as numerous other scholarly and artistic texts on water, weather, and bodies. Other projects include the *Hacking the Anthropocene!* event series and the COMPOSTING *Feminisms and Environmental Humanities* research group, which she coordinates with Jennifer Mae Hamilton. Neimanis is also an associate editor of the journal *Environmental Humanities* and a key researcher with the Sydney Environment Institute.

SUSAN REID is a PhD candidate in the Department of Gender and Cultural Studies at the University of Sydney, where she is researching ocean and juridical imaginaries, relationalities, and justice. She is a writer, artist, curator, and lawyer admitted to the Supreme Court of the Australian Capital Territory. She also has a master's degree in design and a master's of international law and is actively involved with national environmental and climate action advocacy.

ALISON RIESER is professor of geography at the University of Hawai'i at Mānoa and professor emerita at the University of Maine Law School. She has broad experience as a fisheries policy advisor to governments and NGOs. Her book on the classification of endangered marine species, *The Case of the Green Turtle: An Uncensored History of a Conservation Icon,* was published in 2012. She is the author of numerous journal articles on the history of fisheries and ocean governance. Her current book project is a historical geography of herring.

KATHERINE G. SAMMLER is an assistant professor of global studies and maritime affairs at California State University Maritime. She conducts research at the intersection of science and politics in the realm of oceans, atmospheres, and outer space. Her work considers the role of knowledge, law, and power in defining global commons, access, and environmental justice. She is currently conducting research on the earthly politics of outer space infrastructure. She has also been investigating colonial temporalities, cosmic simulacrum, and Native sovereignty movements atop two mountains on the Big Island of Hawai'i.

ASTRID SCHRADER is a lecturer in the Department of Sociology, Philosophy, and Anthropology at the University of Exeter, UK. She works at the intersections of feminist science studies, human-animal studies, new materialisms, and posthumanist theories. Schrader is particularly interested in scientific research on marine microbes. Her work has been published in *Social Studies of Science, Environmental Philosophy, differences, Body and Society, Catalysts: Feminism, Theory, Technoscience, and Postmodern Culture* (PMC). She co-edited a special issue of *differences* titled "Feminist Theory out of Science."

KRISTEN L. SHAKE is a PhD candidate in geography at Clark University, where her dissertation explores the connections that persist between changing sea ice conditions and law in the Bering and Beaufort Seas. She earned a bachelor of science in geography and a master of science in oceanography from the University of Alaska, Fairbanks. Her research interests include Arctic marine policy, polar climate change, legal geography, and science communication.

PHILIP E. STEINBERG is professor of political geography and director of IBRU: The Centre for Borders Research at Durham University, UK. His research focuses on the projection of social power to spaces whose geophysical and geographic characteristics make them resistant to state territorialization, including the ocean (*The Social Construction of the Ocean* [2001]), the Arctic (*Contesting the Arctic* [2015]), the universe of electronic communication (*Managing the Infosphere* [2008]), and the delta city (*What Is a City?* [2008]). He presently directs the Leverhulme Trust–funded ICE LAW Project and is editor-in-chief of *Political Geography*.

Index

ice albedo feedback cycle, 89
ice edge: characteristics of, 86–87; confusion about term, 93, 101n2; management of, 96–99; mapping, 89–96, 315–16; zone versus edge, 93, 100
Ifigenia Nubiana, 224
ignorance, 5–7
imaginaries: aqueous, 45, 47; deep sea mining and, 31–36; difficulties of constructing, 313; industrialized, 315; judicial, 27, 32; matter distinguished from, 7; militarization and, 7, 187, 190, 192, 196; ocean mapping and, 227, 232; oceans as unfathomable, 45–46, 311; planetary, 157; technological, 290, 297; time and, 41, 266
immortality, 268
IMO (International Maritime Organization), 73
indeterminacy, 13, 77, 85–86, 264, 269–70, 316
Indigenous peoples, 63–70, 227, 314–17, 323n5. *See also* Māori people
individual/population dichotomy, 17, 132, 168, 258–59, 261–66
Indonesia, 117–19, 120, 122
Ingersoll, Karin Amimoto, 317
Inter caetera (Among Other Laws), 209
Intergovernmental Oceanographic Commission (IOC), 168
International Convention for the Safety of Life at Sea, 131
International Maritime Organization (IMO), 73
International Regulations for Preventing Collisions at Sea (COLREG), 161
International Seabed Authority (ISA), 29–31, 35
International Tribunal for the Law of the Sea (ITLOS), 115–16
In the Wake (Sharpe), 10
IOC (Intergovernmental Oceanographic Commission), 168
ironsand mining, 77–79
island building. *See* land reclamation
iwi, 70. *See also* Māori people

Jakarta Bay, 120–22
James I, King, 210, 212
Janda, Richard, 304
Japan, 79, 112
Japanese whalers, 75–76
Jasanoff, Sheila, 6, 132–33
Johannes, R. E., 314

Johnson, Elizabeth R., 156, 306, 313, 318
Jones, Stephanie, 7
joystick mining, 33–34
justice versus law, 259–60, 263. *See also* Derrida, Jacques

Kanaka Maoli, 317
KASM (Kiwis Against Seabed Mining), 77
Kauri and the Sperm Whale (Kauri Rāua Ko Parāoa), 65–66
kauri trees, 65–67
kayaktivism, 79–80
Khatib, Oussama, 158–59
ki uta ki tai, 66
Kiwis Against Seabed Mining (KASM), 77
Klein, Naomi, 300
knowledge production: colonial expansion and, 232–33; fantasy blurring with, 7; immersion in, 320; law and, 5–6; limits of, 29, 59; militarization and, 194, 196, 197; science and technology and, 153, 156, 169, 193, 248; traditional ecological knowledge and, 306, 316–17; waves and, 131–32, 139–40. *See also* epistemology
Kohno, Nadao, 135
Korosy, Zsofia, 13
Kristoffersen, Berit, 13, 315–16

land, theories about, 113
land reclamation: by China, 107–12; domestic politics and, 119–22; importance of, 122–23; industrial production and, 112–14; international disputes about, 114–19; in South China Sea, 109–12; strategy issues, 122
landscape ecology, 113
land-sea binary. *See* ice edge; New Zealand
latency of chemical weapons, 54
Latour, Bruno, 10, 304, 320
law: coral reefs as not fitting with, 18; ecologies on same plane as, 32; justice versus, 259–60, 263; knowledge and ignorance and, 5–7; limits of, 58; macro and micro scales of, 5; plurality of, 4–5; time and, 56–57, 322; turbulence and, 1–5, 19–20; unblackboxing the, 3; wicked problems and, 19. *See also* Derrida, Jacques; waves and wave law; *specific conventions, entities, and treaties*
Law of the Seas. *See* UN Convention on the Law of the Seas (UNCLOS)

Morton, Oliver, 301, 302
Mt. Taranaki, 77–78
MPAs (Marine Protected Areas), 12, 301, 315
Munk, Walter, 132
Murphy, Michelle, 54–55, 58, 59
mustard gas, 45–46, 50–52, 60n1

National Alliance for Advanced Biofuels and
    Bioproducts (NAABB), 283
National Bioeconomy Blueprint, 278
National Data Buoy Center, 135, 140n2, 141n8
National Oceanic and Atmospheric Adminis-
    tration (NOAA, US), 1, 16, 178–79
National Renewable Energy Lab, 280
National Weather Service, 133, 141n8
natural prolongation principal, 36
Nautilus Minerals' Solwara 1, 30, 33–34, 313.
    See also deep sea mining
navigation: in EEZ, 71, 73; robots and, 160–61;
    in territorial seas, 190; UNCLOS and, 79–80;
    weather reports for, 131–35
Neimanis, Astrida, 6–7, 11, 296, 322–23
Nekton Foundation, 156–57
Nereus, 155
Netherlands, 121–22, 136, 206–7
New Zealand: activism in, 64–65, 69–71, 77–80;
    baselines and, 68–69; deep sea mining and,
    70–71, 77–79; Foreshore and Seabed Act,
    69–71; materiality and, 71–73; nuclear test-
    ing and, 74–75; overview of, 63–65, 80–81;
    Western versus Indigenous views of ocean,
    63–70; whaling vessels and, 75–76
Nietzsche, Friedrich, 241
Nipa Island, 118–19
NOAA (National Oceanic and Atmospheric
    Administration, US), 1, 16, 178–79
nonhuman lives. See more-than-human; specific
    creatures
nonreciprocal responsibility, 306
Nootka Convention (Anglo-Spanish Conven-
    tion), 226, 229–31
Nootka Sound, 219–20, 223–26, 229–31
Northwest America, 223, 224
Norway. See sea ice
Norwegian Polar Institute (NPI), 90, 93–94, 97
Nuclear Free Zone, Disarmament, and Arms
    Control Act (1987), 74
Nuclear Free Zone Extension Bill, 74–75
nuclear testing, 74–75

ocean acidification: governance and, 298–302;
    impacts of, 8–9; measurement of, 295; reme-
    diation difficulties with, 159, 296–97, 302–3.
    See also climate engineering
ocean alkalinization, 302–3
ocean boundaries: materiality and, 63–64; tur-
    bulence and, 14, 64–65, 69; UNCLOS and,
    11–15, 34–36, 63, 68–69, 71–73, 190; Western
    versus indigenous views of, 63–68
ocean justice, 32
ocean literacy, 162
oceanography, 167
OceanOne, 157–59, 320
oceans: demystification attempts, 1, 5–6; erasure
    and, 45–46; governance of as wicked prob-
    lem, 19; tensions surrounding, 2; turbulence
    and, 5, 76, 186, 188, 193; viewed as blank
    spaces, 1, 311, 317; warming of, 8; wave energy
    spectra, 132
ocean sensing: Argo for, 165–67, 170–71,
    174–79, 313; geopolitical dimensions of,
    176–79; international organizations involved
    in, 168–69; new methods for, 169–72; over-
    view of, 165–66, 179–80; territory issues, 174,
    177–78, 313; UNCLOS and, 172–73
Octopus: Physiology and Behavior of an Ad-
    vanced Invertebrate (Wells), 16
Odyssey, The (Homer), 244–45
Office of Naval Research (ONR), 187
Office of Science and Technology Policy
    (OSTP), 288–89
"Of Other Spaces" (Foucault), 183–84
oil and gas exploration, in Barents Sea, 89–90,
    93, 95–100
oil drilling, 79–80
Oil Free Seas, 79
Oldenbarnevelt, Johan, 213, 214
omega-3 fatty acids, 275–76, 283–87
ONR (Office of Naval Research), 187
On the Law of War and Peace (Grotius), 213, 214
ontology: colonialism and, 80; hauntology and,
    256; Indigenous versus Western, 66, 81; life
    and death and, 262; suspension and, 49, 59;
    wet ontology, 15, 17, 76
organic food, 275–76
Organisation for the Prohibition of Chemical
    Weapons (OPCW), 57
OSPAR Code of Conduct for the North East
    Atlantic, 160

vno-ncw (Confederation of Netherlands Industry and Employers), 121
Voolstra, Christian, 148, 157, 159, 320
Voorendt, Mark, 136

Wachenfeld, David, 149–50
war, 51–52, 57. *See also* militarization of the sea
waste management, 11, 47, 53–55, 322–23
water as universal solvent, 47
Water Will Come: Rising Seas, Sinking Cities, and the Remaking of the Civilized World, The (Goodell), 8
Watson-Wright, Wendy, 175
wave commerce, 134
wave height, 131–32
waveob, 132
waves and wave law: Canute and the Waves story about, 129–30; overview of, 130–31; scientific and legal codes about, 131–35; shore protections and, 135–36; wave protections and, 136–41
Weaver, Philip, 156
Weismann, August, 268
Wells, Martin, 16
Welwood, William, 210, 211
wet ontology, 15, 17, 76

whakapapa, 66, 68, 77, 81, 316
whaling, 221–22, 231–33
whaling vessels, 75–76
Whanganui River, 81
white-herring bounties, 215. *See also* herring
Williamson, Philip, 302
Winichakul, Thongchai, 227
wmo (World Meteorological Organization), 132–33, 135, 175
Wolfe, Cary, 258, 259, 264–66, 271n5, 321–22
wolf-fish. *See* sea wolves
"Wolf is the Lamb, The" (Cixous), 241–42
Wolf Mann, 241
wolves, 237–39. *See also* sea wolves
"workable Arctic," 88–89
World Climate Research Program, 168
World Meteorological Organization (wmo), 132–33, 135, 175
World War I, chemical weapons and, 45
Wynter, Sylvia, 320

X/33 (decision), 300

zone of transition, 99
zones of probabilities, 100